BTEC NATIONAL SPORT

Sports Development and Fitness options

Ray Barker, Graham Saffery, Rob Saipe, Louise Sutton, Andy Miles

www.heinemann.co.uk
✓ Free online support
✓ Useful weblinks
✓ 24 hour online ordering

01865 888058

withdrawn

ACCESSION No. T062382

CLASS No. 796·077

Inspiring generations

KT-428-923

Heinemann Educational Publishers
Halley Court, Jordan Hill, Oxford OX2 8EJ
Part of Harcourt Education

Heinemann is the registered trademark of
Harcourt Education Limited

© Ray Barker, Andrew Miles, Graham Saffery, Rob Saipe, Louise Sutton 2004
First published 2004

09 08 07 06 05 04
10 9 8 7 6 5 4 3 2 1

British Library Cataloguing in Publication Data is available
from the British Library on request.
ISBN 0 435 45509 5

Copyright notice
All rights reserved. No part of this publication may be reproduced in any form or by any means (including
photocopying or storing it in any medium by electronic means and whether or not transiently or incidentally
to some other use of this publication) without the written permission of the copyright owner, except in
accordance with the provisions of the Copyright, Designs and Patents Act 1988 or under the terms of a licence
issued by the Copyright Licensing Agency, 90 Tottenham Court Road, London W1T 4LP. Applications for the
copyright owner's written permission should be addressed to the publisher.

Edited by Jan Doorly
Designed by Artistix
Typeset and illustrated by Tek-Art, Croydon, Surrey
Original illustrations © Harcourt Education Limited, 2004
Cover design by Tony Richardson at the Wooden Ark Ltd
Printed in the UK by The Bath Press Ltd
Cover photo: © Getty/Digital Vision

Tel: 01865 888058 www.heinemann.co.uk

Contents

Acknowledgements

The authors and publisher would like to thank the following for permission to reproduce copyright material.

Human Kinetics for lifestyle evaluation form (page 99) and medical history questionnaire (page 100) from *Advanced Fitness Assessment and Exercise Prescription*, © 1998 by Vivian Heyward – Human Kinetics, Champaign, IL USA. The book is available in local bookshops or by telephoning 0113 2555665

Human Kinetics for consent form (page 113) from *Health Fitness Instructors Handbook*, © 1997 by E. Howley and B. Franks – Human Kinetics, Champaign, IL USA. The book is available in local bookshops or by telephoning 0113 2555665

News International for interview with Paula Radcliffe, *Sunday Times*, 13 April 2003 (page 187)

The International Organisation for Standardisation for use of their logo (page 256)

The English Federation of Disability Sport for use of their logo (page 291)

UK Sport for use of their logo (page 295)

British Gymnastics for permission to reproduce material from their website (page 299)

Sport England (pages 300 and 304)

Basketball Camps (page 302)

Humber Sports Partnership (page 306)

Leisure Opportunities magazine for the article on page 334, ©Cybertrek 2003 tel +44 (0)1462 431385 www.leisuremedia.com

The Lawn Tennis Association for permission to reproduce *Club Vision* leaflet (page 335)

Crown copyright material is reproduced under Class License No. C01W0000141 with the permission of the Controller of HMSO and the Queen's Printer for Scotland

We are grateful to the following for permission to reproduce photographs:

Action Plus, page 190
Action Plus/Adam Bailey, page 312
Action Plus/Steve Bardens, pages 43, 84
Action Plus/Chris Brown, page 187
Action Plus/Matthew Clarke, page 205
Action Plus/Richard Francis, pages 191, 218
Action Plus/Jim Gund/Icon, page 182
Action Plus/Mike Hewitt, page 196
Action Plus/Glyn Kirk, pages 109, 194, 212, 215, 242, 326
Action Plus/Leo Mason, page 183
Action Plus/Neil Tingle, pages 49, 203, 207, 232, 288, 316
Alamy/Scott Hortop, page 241
Alamy/Mark Dyball, page 261
Alamy/Photofusion Picture Library, page 275
Alamy/Ian Thraves, page 134
Alamy/View Stock, page 268
Gareth Boden, pages 12, 15, 19, 21
Trevor Clifford, page 4
Corbis/Harcourt Index, pages 44, 46, 60, 73, 83, 85, 91, 98, 133, 136 (left), 147, 150, 231, 238, 250, 296
Getty Images/Daniel Berehulak, page 149
Getty Images/Shaun Botterill/Allsport, page 141
Getty Images/Darren England, page 118
Getty Images/Spencer Platt, page 37
Peter Gould, page 8
KPT Power Photos, page 330
Photodisc, pages 2, 31, 74, 89, 146, 163, 248, 264, 290, 324
Rex Features/Action Press, page 293
Rex Features/Nicholas Bailey, page 285
Rex Features/D.P.P.I., page 294
Rex Features/Robert Judges, page 229
Rex Features/Mykel Nicolaou, page 308
Rex Features/SHOUT, page 321
Rex Features/Sipa Press, page 136 (right)
sports coach UK, page 213

Every effort has been made to contact copyright holders of material reproduced in this book. Any omissions will be rectified in subsequent printings if notice is given to the publishers.

Foreword by Warwick Andrews, sports coach UK

This *BTEC National Diploma in Sport* options book is designed to support students' learning and adds great value to the core book for the BTEC National Diploma. Using these two essential resources, students can have a better appreciation of the diverse aspects of the world of sport.

For many young people, the sports industry offers a variety of opportunities for employment and to enjoy life-long involvement, whether it is at the recreational or elite end of the performance ladder. The BTEC National Diploma is a well-recognised qualification and can lead on to other types of qualifications, such as NVQs, as well as providing a solid foundation for those students wishing to study at a higher level. We at **sports coach UK** support the principles of life-long learning and positively encourage students to continue to further their knowledge and skills through qualifications such as the BTEC National Diploma.

Success in sport requires partnership and co-operation between organisations, employers, sports clubs and participants. All at **sports coach UK** strongly believe that by creating effective partnerships with those involved in sport, we can help the UK become a healthy and active nation and also one that competes at the highest level. This book demonstrates how coaching and sports development can work closely together to produce a valuable sports environment.

Through the range of subjects, tasks and activities in this book, students can start to appreciate the work of **sports coach UK** and how it can interact with a variety of people and organisations within the sports industry. For more information on the products and services of **sports coach UK**, please visit our website at www.sportscoachuk.org.

sports coach UK wishes you every success with your studies and in the opportunities open to you in the sporting world.

About this book

The BTEC National Diploma is a practical, work-related course. You will learn by undertaking projects, tasks and assignments drawing on industry practice, activities and experience.

This options text contains a bank of knowledge that you can use to complete the optional units in the qualification, which count for both the certificate and diploma stages of the award. It has been written as an exact match to the specifications for the BTEC National in Sport, and also provides case studies to broaden your knowledge and scenarios to discuss in class or with your tutor, to deepen your understanding.

The optional units included are:

- Unit 8 Nutrition for Weight Management
- Unit 10 Fitness Testing
- Unit 11 Training and Fitness
- Unit 13 Principles of Coaching
- Unit 14 Enterprise in Sport
- Unit 16 Sports Development.

Course structure

The structure of the BTEC National Diploma is based on the study of the four core units with a further 14 specialist units enabling you to study particular areas in more depth. You can follow one of three pathways:

- Performance and Excellence
- Sports Development and Fitness
- Outdoor Education.

This text supports units taken in the Sports Development and Fitness pathway. The accompanying core textbook, *BTEC National Sport*, provides comprehensive coverage of the core units plus Unit 5, The Body in Action.

Features of the book

Throughout the text a number of features are designed to encourage reflection and discussion and to help relate theory to practice.

- **What you need to learn:** key knowledge points that you will have learnt by the end of the unit.
- **Think it over:** thought-provoking questions that can be used for individual reflection or group discussion.
- **Theory into practice:** practical activities that require you to apply theoretical knowledge to work and play in sport.
- **Key concepts:** issues and facts that you should be aware of.
- **Case studies:** examples of real situations to help you link theory to practice.
- **Assessment activities:** activities that address the assessment requirements of the course.

As with the core book, a wide range of experienced professionals have contributed their expertise, in the hope that it will support you in your chosen studies and provide you with a firm foundation for extending and developing your interests.

We do hope that you enjoy your course, and wish you good luck and every success in achieving your qualification and in your future work.

NUTRITION FOR WEIGHT MANAGEMENT

Introduction to Unit 8

This unit introduces you to the links between nutrition, health and exercise. You will learn about the fundamentals of a healthy diet and consider the links between diet and disease, exploring aspects such as obesity, coronary heart disease, diabetes and eating disorders. You will delve into the important role that nutrition has to play in weight management, and examine nutritional strategies for both weight loss and weight gain.

The unit will also provide you with an understanding of the influence of nutrition on exercise performance, along with a solid foundation of knowledge on which to develop good eating practices for yourself and the case studies you use in the assessment for this unit. You will also consider factors that affect food intake and choice, and methods of collecting and analysing dietary information.

By the end of this unit you should be able to demonstrate the application of nutrition and weight management principles through examination of the diets of a range of sports and fitness clients.

Assessment

This unit is internally assessed by your tutor. A variety of activities are included here to help you understand and appreciate good nutrition and sensible weight management. Through analysing case studies, considering thought-provoking questions, undertaking practical activities and researching the subject through further reading and exploring the Internet, you will develop a sound understanding of healthy eating strategies, recommended nutrient intakes, dietary assessment techniques and menu planning.

Throughout the unit there are tasks for you to complete that will introduce you to the key themes and concepts you need to understand when undertaking your assessment activities. These tasks range from individual investigations, to working in pairs to practise interviewing techniques, and working as part of a small group. You will find it useful to invest in a notebook to record the findings of your research and investigations for later discussion with your tutor.

For the assessment of this unit you will be asked to produce nutritional strategies for:

- two selected sports
- someone wanting to lose weight
- someone wanting to gain weight.

Real-life case studies are preferable as these allow you to develop your skills in communicating and working with fitness and sportspeople. However, where this is not possible your tutor should be able to provide you with a suitable case scenario.

After completing this unit you should be able to achieve the following outcomes.

Outcomes

1 Examine the components of a healthy diet

2 Investigate and plan nutrition strategies for a range of clients

3 Explore the factors that might influence weight management

4 Investigate weight management programmes for two selected clients.

What you need to learn

- The components of a healthy diet
- Factors influencing weight management
- Safe and effective weight management strategies and programmes
- Nutritional strategies to support physical activity, sport and exercise.

Introduction to nutrition for weight management

Nutrition is fundamental to life and essential throughout the life cycle. The right balance of nutrition is essential to both physical and mental growth and development, performance and productivity in daily living, and our general health and well being, particularly our ability to defend against and recover from disease.

All activity stimulates the body's need for fuel and fluid, and good nutrition is seen as important to performance in sport and exercise. Knowledge of the nutrients that the body requires, along with their different functions, provides the basis for the science of nutrition. The study of nutrition is a relatively new area of scientific study and one in which new discoveries are constantly being made.

Good nutrition, and in particular healthy eating, sounds simple in theory, but is often difficult to achieve in practice, particularly for those with busy lifestyles or intense training programmes. Nutritional topics now appear regularly in our media and in advertising, often presenting us with contradictory information on what is good for our health. This is particularly true in relation to sensible weight management.

The pursuit of sound nutritional practices to support health and fitness came to prominence in the 1980s with the introduction of the first set of healthy eating guidelines published by the National Advisory Council on Nutritional Education. The continued and increasing awareness of the role of good nutrition in health and exercise performance makes it essential that accurate advice and information are available. Frequently, misinterpretation of scientific information serves to confuse rather than enlighten the public in their attempt to implement sound nutritional practices.

It is also important to remember at the outset of this unit that where sport is concerned there should be no conflict between eating for health and eating for performance. The sound foundations of the sports performer's diet lie in the pursuit of healthy eating through a balanced and varied diet.

Key concept

There should be no conflict between eating for health and eating for performance.

Shops and supermarkets offer a wide variety of fresh foods

Get-set introductory activity

In your notebook, write down everything you had to eat and drink yesterday. Ensure you record sufficient information on the different types of food, their portion size and the cooking methods used, being sure to include all snack items as well as meals. You will use this information in future exercises throughout this unit. This will be known as your '24-hour diet recall'.

Theory into practice

It is essential at the start of your study into nutrition and weight management to become familiar with the terms and definitions used. Before you read on any further take a minute to jot down in your notebook what you understand by the following terms:

- nutrition
- diet
- healthy eating
- balanced diet
- sports nutrition.

You'll find definitions for these terms, and many others that you'll come across in this unit, in the glossary at the end of the unit (page 65). Each time you come across a new term, look it up so that you are sure you understand what it means.

Now take five minutes to think about all the factors that might influence food intake and choice. Jot down these ideas in your notebook. A list of 10 factors is good going, but a list in excess of 20 factors is excellent.

The list you have devised may include simple factors such as likes and dislikes, time, money, taste, accessibility, culture and convenience, but also others such as fashions and trends promoted by celebrities and sports personalities in the media, and food packaging and advertising, which can have a huge influence on our choice of food. Awareness of these factors will assist you in formulating realistic and achievable dietary goals when undertaking the case studies for the assessment in this unit.

Theory into practice

1 How many nutrition-related topics have featured in the news in the past two weeks?

2 Pick up a copy of a daily newspaper. Scan it for nutrition-related features and advertisements. How many are there? In particular, how many have you found relating to weight loss or obesity?

The components of a healthy diet

The foods we consume contain the nutrients carbohydrate, protein, fat, vitamins, minerals, fibre and water. The amounts of these nutrients vary from food to food.

Most foods we eat are categorised based on their carbohydrate, protein and fat content, but they usually consist of more than one of these nutrients. For example, bread is categorised as a carbohydrate food because it contains more carbohydrate than protein or fat, but it is also a source of these nutrients and others such as vitamins, minerals and fibre.

The nutrients found in our food are also categorised according to the relative amounts required by the body. Carbohydrate, protein and fat are termed **macronutrients**, as they are required in relatively large amounts on a daily basis. These nutrients are also the energy-providing nutrients of our diet. Vitamins and minerals, on the other hand, are termed **micronutrients** as they are required in much smaller, and in some cases minute, amounts. Despite our relatively small requirements for these nutrients, many play a critical role in regulating chemical reactions in the body.

The aim of this section is to provide you with an introduction to the macro- and micronutrients needed in a healthy diet and investigate their sources, functions and requirements. We will also look at the effects of good and poor nutrition on health and performance.

What you need to learn

- The components of a healthy diet
- Recommended nutrient intakes for a healthy diet
- Healthy eating guidelines and the UK National Food Guide Principles
- The concept of energy balance.

Carbohydrates

All the carbohydrates consumed in our diet are composed of the elements carbon, hydrogen and oxygen. The main role of carbohydrates is energy production. They form the body's most readily available source of energy, and can be accessed rapidly. One gram of carbohydrate, whether this is derived from sugar or starch, will provide approximately 4 kilocalories of energy. The carbohydrate foods we eat are typically divided into two basic types, and are generally referred to as either simple or complex.

Key concept

The main role of carbohydrate in the diet is energy production.

Simple carbohydrates

These are essentially sugars and are formed from single and double sugar units. They are easily digested and absorbed to provide the body with a quick energy source. The simplest unit of carbohydrates is the **monosaccharide**, the most common of which in our diet is glucose. Saccharide means sugar, mono means one; therefore a monosaccharide is a single sugar unit. Glucose is vital for the optimal functioning of our nervous system, and is often referred to as blood sugar. Glucose is also used to produce adenosine triphosphate (ATP), the compound required for muscle contraction.

Other monosaccharides in our diet include fructose, also known as fruit sugar as it is found in fruits and vegetables, and galactose found in milk. Monosaccharides mostly occur combined together in carbohydrate foods. When two monosaccharides are found together they form a **disaccharide**, or what is known as a double sugar. The most common disaccharide in our diet is sucrose or table sugar, of which most of the population is thought to consume too much. Other disaccharides include lactose, found in milk, and maltose found in beer and cereals.

Carbohydrate foods include bread, rice, pasta, potatoes and cereals

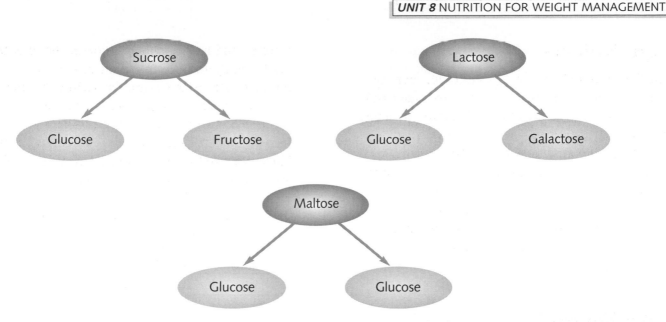

Double sugars or disaccharides and their monosaccharides

Longer chains of these simple sugar units are known as **polysaccharides** or complex carbohydrates. These allow large quantities of glucose to be stored in the cells of plants as starch, or in animals as glycogen in the muscles and liver. Ultimately all carbohydrate consumed in our diet will end up as glucose, to provide energy.

Complex carbohydrates

These are commonly known as starches and constitute an important source of energy in most diets. As previously mentioned, they are composed of many sugar units so are also termed **polysaccharides.** These are broken down more slowly within the body and provide a sustained release of energy over longer periods. Complex carbohydrates should form the largest percentage of our total carbohydrate intake. Unrefined sources such as wholemeal bread and wholegrain rice and pasta are preferable, as they also contain a higher nutritional value by way of micronutrients and fibre.

High carbohydrate foods	
Simple	**Complex**
sugar, syrup, jam, honey, marmalade, sugary fizzy drinks, boiled sweets, fudge, fruit juice, sports drinks	bread, bagels, crispbread, crackers, rice, pasta, noodles, couscous, potatoes, breakfast cereals, pulses, root vegetables

After we eat foods containing carbohydrate our blood sugar level rises, which stimulates the pancreas to secrete the hormone insulin. The role of insulin is to normalise blood sugar levels and aid the transport of glucose from the blood into the cells. Glucose will then be used directly by the cells for energy or stored as glycogen, a long-chained carbohydrate, in the liver and muscles if it is not required immediately to provide energy. Glycogen is a crucial source of glucose for fuelling daily activity.

Key concept

Any excess carbohydrate not required to replenish the body's glycogen stores will be converted to fat and stored in the body's adipose tissue.

The majority of carbohydrate stored in the body, around 80%, is stored in the muscles. The remainder is stored in the liver, with a small amount of circulating blood glucose. Carbohydrate that is stored in the liver as glycogen is essentially used to keep a constant supply of glucose to fuel the brain by maintaining appropriate levels of blood glucose, while muscle glycogen is principally used to fuel activity, particularly of a high intensity.

Carbohydrate can only be stored in the body as glycogen in limited amounts, approximately 375-475 grams in the average adult – equivalent to approximately 1500-2000 kilocalories. Our day-to-day stores of glycogen are influenced by dietary carbohydrate intake and levels of physical activity or training. Regular exercise can encourage our muscles to adapt to store more glycogen. This is an important training adaptation for the serious sportsperson, particularly those involved in endurance-type sports. During sport and exercise glycogen is broken down to glucose to supply the muscles with energy.

The intensity and duration of the activity will influence the rate and amount of glycogen usage. The harder the activity and the longer it is under-taken, the more glycogen is used. When these stores become depleted less energy is available to continue exercising hard, fatigue occurs, and the activity will slow or stop. The more depleted glycogen stores become following a bout of exercise, the longer it takes to restore them to pre-exercise levels.

Average adult glycogen stores	
Muscle	325 g
Liver	100 g
Blood glucose	15-20 g

Key concept

The intensity and duration of exercise influence the rate and amount of glycogen usage. The harder the exercise and the longer its duration, the greater the depletion of glycogen.

Carbohydrate requirements

To support health and performance it is recommended that around 50-60% of our total daily calorie intake is derived from carbohydrates. Greater intakes may be required by sportspeople engaged in regular intense training; for example, a marathon runner or a triathlete may require up to 65-70% of total energy to be provided by carbohydrates.

However, the sedentary individual eating for health will require around 50% of total daily calorie intake

to be supplied by carbohydrate, of which the majority should be from starchy sources. This would equate to around 250 g per day for the average female, and 300 g per day for the average male. For the type of sportsperson described earlier this may increase to 400-600 g per day or more. As a simple guide, the following carbohydrate requirements can be prescribed based on activity levels.

Level of daily activity	Grams of carbohydrate per kilogram of body weight
< 1 hour	4-5 g
1 hour	5-6 g
1-2 hours	6-7 g
2-3 hours	7-8 g
4 hours plus	8-10 g

Theory into practice

Based on your current body weight and levels of physical activity, estimate your carbohydrate requirements in grams per day. Record your answer in your notebook. Do you think your carbohydrate requirements are constant, or do they vary from day to day?

Whether eating for health or performance, the best approach to achieving an adequate carbohydrate intake is to eat at regular intervals and ensure that all meals and snacks are centred around starchy carbohydrate foods. People with high carbohydrate requirements may need to eat more frequent meals and snacks or rely on a greater intake of simple carbohydrates to achieve their requirements. Where greater intakes of simple carbohydrates are necessary to assist in meeting energy and carbohydrate requirements, care should be taken that the over-consumption of sweet foods, often referred to as 'empty calories' because they provide few other nutrients, does not displace more nutrient-dense sources of carbohydrate in the diet.

In the past carbohydrates suffered from a poor reputation with those trying to lose weight, as it was thought that they contributed to obesity. This might be true if they are consumed in excess of overall energy requirements, but carbohydrates contribute fewer calories per gram than fat. Dietitians and scientists promote the consumption of high carbohydrate intakes and deem this to be an essential component of a healthy diet.

Key concept

The best way to achieve an adequate carbohydrate intake is to ensure that all meals and snacks are based around starchy carbohydrate foods.

Carbohydrate content of common foods in the diet	
Food	Approximate carbohydrate content per serving
2 large slices of bread	30 g
1 pitta bread	45 g
1 large naan bread	80 g
1 bagel	50 g
1 tortilla	20 g
1 chapatti	30 g
3 crispbreads	30 g
1 large jacket potato	45 g
1 medium portion of chips	55 g
1 medium portion of new potatoes	35 g
1 medium portion of boiled potatoes	35 g
1 large serving of rice	60 g
1 large serving of spaghetti	90 g
1 medium serving of couscous	35 g
1 slice pizza	35 g
2 Shredded Wheat	30 g
2 Weetabix	30 g
1 medium serving of muesli	50 g
1 large tin of baked beans	60 g
3 tablespoons of sweetcorn	10 g
3 tablespoons of peas	10 g
3 tablespoons of carrots	10 g
1 digestive biscuit	10 g
1 Jaffa cake	10 g
1 currant bun	30 g
1 wholemeal scone	20 g
1 cereal bar	20 g
1 bag of crisps	10 g

Food	Approximate carbohydrate content per serving
1 pint of milk	30 g
1 small pot of yogurt	25 g
1 small can of rice pudding	30 g
1 medium banana	30 g
1 apple	10 g
1 orange	10 g
2 satsumas	10 g
1 handful of raisins	15 g
5 dried apricots	15 g
1 small carton of fruit juice	20 g
1 can of Lucozade drink	60 g
1 can of lemonade	20 g
1 can of cola	35 g
1 standard Mars Bar	40 g
1 small bar of milk chocolate	30 g
2 teaspoons of honey	15 g
2 teaspoons of jam or marmalade	10 g
1 tube of fruit gums	20 g
2 teaspoons of sugar	10 g

Theory into practice

Take a look at your 24-hour diet recall and, using the list of approximate carbohydrate content of common foods, estimate your carbohydrate intake for the day. If you have eaten foods not in this list you will need to refer to food composition tables to find out the carbohydrate content. In the UK the principal source of information on the nutritional composition of common foods in our diet is McCance and Widdowson's tables on the composition of foods (see the list of Resources for this unit, on page 64). These display the nutrient content of foods per 100 g, so when using these tables you need to be sure how much you have eaten to estimate the nutrient content correctly.

1 Did you meet your estimated carbohydrate requirements?
2 If you did not meet your estimated requirements, devise a day's menu to meet your carbohydrate needs. A template to assist you with this activity can be found in Menu Plan 1 on page 68 at the end of this unit.

Fibre

Fibre is a complex carbohydrate. **Non-starch polysaccharide** (NSP) is the new scientific term for dietary fibre. NSP forms the main component of plant cell walls and these are the principal component of dietary fibre. They resist digestion by the stomach and small intestine and provide bulk in the diet, which aids the transit of food through the digestive system.

Fibre is obtained from wholegrain cereals, nuts, pulses, fruits and vegetables. It is thought to have a role in both preventing and treating certain diseases including cancer of the colon, diabetes, heart disease and irritable bowel syndrome. A high fibre intake accompanied with a high fluid intake also helps to keep the bowel functioning efficiently. Adequate amounts may also play a role in weight control by helping to achieve satiety – the feeling of being full.

Two types of fibre are found in the foods listed above, classified according to their solubility in water as either soluble or insoluble. Soluble fibre can be found in oats, rye, barley, peas, beans, lentils, fruits and vegetables. This type of fibre is important in the control of blood glucose and cholesterol. Insoluble fibre is found in whole-wheat bread, rice and pasta, wholegrain breakfast cereals and fruits and vegetables too. It is thought to be important in the prevention of bowel disorders. A healthy diet requires a good mix of both types of fibre, with adults requiring around 18 g per day. As a population we have a long way to go to achieving adequate intakes of this nutrient, as current average intakes are around 12 g per day.

Fibre intakes can be increased by eating a wide variety of unrefined carbohydrate foods, such as wholemeal bread, whole-wheat pasta or wholegrain rice, choosing wholegrain breakfast cereals, eating potatoes in their skins, and by adding beans, lentils and peas to dishes such as soups, casseroles, pasta, rice and salads, as well as eating at least five servings of fruit and vegetables each day.

Key concept

Non-starch polysaccharide is the new scientific term for dietary fibre.

A healthy diet should be high in fibre-rich foods

Fats

It is very important to note that fat is an essential nutrient for the body. Fats, or lipids as they are also termed, are, like carbohydrate, composed of the chemical elements carbon, hydrogen and oxygen, but in different ratios. The ratio of hydrogen to oxygen is much higher; this explains why fat is a more concentrated source of energy than carbohydrate.

Triglycerides form the basic component of fats. Each triglyceride is made up of a glycerol molecule with three fatty acids attached. It is to these two substances that triglycerides are broken down when digested and absorbed by the body. Fats consumed in our diet are obtained from both animal and vegetable sources and are of two main types, **saturated** or **unsaturated**.

Fatty acids contain chains of carbon atoms to which hydrogen atoms attach themselves. The number of hydrogen atoms relative to the number of carbon atoms determines if a fatty acid is classified as saturated or unsaturated. If all the carbons are associated with two hydrogens, the fat is saturated, but if one or more of the carbons is without hydrogen then the fat is unsaturated. Unsaturated fatty acids can be of two kinds: **monounsaturated** or **polyunsaturated**.

All fats consumed in our diet are in fact a mixture of these three different fatty acid types. Dietary fats that contain a majority of saturated fatty acids are generally solid at room temperature, like butter and ordinary margarine, and are generally found in foods of animal origin such as meat, eggs and dairy foods; the two exceptions are palm and coconut oil, which are plant sources. Fats that are composed of mainly unsaturated fatty acids are usually liquid at room temperature, such as olive or sunflower oils.

Research suggests that there is a strong link between the development of coronary heart disease and high levels of saturated fat in the diet, while consumption of monounsaturated fats is thought to have health benefits by helping to reduce cholesterol levels. Most dietary experts recommend that we should cut back on our fat intake for health. However, this is also sound advice for the sportsperson as it will allow him or her to consume a greater proportion of energy intake from carbohydrates to maintain glycogen stores, to support training and competition.

Fats have many and varied functions within the body, but the primary function is to provide a concentrated source of energy, forming the body's largest potential energy store. Even the leanest of individuals will have large amounts of energy stored as fat. Fat is more than twice as energy dense as the other macronutrients, yielding 9 kilocalories per gram.

Fats also have many other functions. They protect and cushion the vital organs, provide a structural material for cells and act as an insulator preventing heat loss. Animal fats are a source of the fat-soluble vitamins A, D, E and K. Fats also provide flavour and texture to foods, features that often lead to over-consumption. In some foods fat content may be high but not obvious, and these fats are known as hidden fats. Examples are those found in cakes, biscuits and pastries.

There are two essential unsaturated fatty acids that the body requires to maintain good health, and these must be provided by the diet: **linolenic** and **linoleic acid**. These essential fatty acids assist in the production of hormones and the regulation of the immune function and blood pressure. In addition, these essential fatty acids appear to offer protection from cardiovascular disease.

Sources and types of fat in the UK diet		
Saturated	**Monounsaturated**	**Polyunsaturated**
full fat dairy products, butter, hard margarine, lard, dripping, suet, fatty meat, meat pies, paté, cream, cakes, biscuits, chocolate, coconut, coconut oil	olive oil, olive oil spreads, rapeseed oil, corn oil, peanuts, peanut butter, peanut oil	soft margarine, low-fat spreads labelled high in polyunsaturated fats, sunflower oil, safflower oil, soya oil, oily fish, nuts

BISHOP BURTON COLLEGE

Key concept

There are two essential unsaturated fatty acids that must be provided by the diet, **linolenic** and **linoleic acid**.

Theory into practice

Take another look at your 24-hour diet recall. What types of fat do you eat? Are there many sources of hidden fat in your diet? Do you think you eat too much fat? What might you need to do to reduce your intake of fat?

Fat requirements

National diet and nutrition surveys have shown that the average diet in the UK contains around 40% of calories from fat, a level deemed by experts to be too high. To promote good health and to fall in line with healthy eating principles it is recommended that fat intakes are reduced to 30-35% of total calorie intake. This equates to around 70 g per day for the average female and 90 g per day for the average male. Of this only 6-10% should be derived from saturated fats. Sportspeople involved in regular intense activity may need to reduce their overall fat intake further to around 25-30% of total energy consumed to achieve adequate carbohydrate intakes, but in absolute terms this may equate to the same quantity of intake as that of the sedentary individual, as sportspeople will be eating more calories to meet their increased energy requirements.

Key concept

Government guidelines recommend 70 g of fat per day for the average female and 90 g per day for the average male.

Cholesterol

Cholesterol is a fat-like substance essential for the structure of cell membranes. The body is able to make cholesterol whether or not it is consumed in the diet. Dietary cholesterol is found in animal foods, such as egg yolks, offal and shellfish.

Fat content of common foods in the UK diet	
Food	Approximate fat content per serving
1 medium portion of thin cut chips	20 g
1 medium portion of thick cut chips	10 g
1 medium portion of roast potatoes	10 g
1 medium baked potato	0.2 g
1 medium portion of new potatoes	0.2 g
1 medium portion of boiled potatoes	0.2 g
1 medium portion of cheddar cheese	15 g
$\frac{1}{2}$ pt of whole milk	5 g
$\frac{1}{2}$ pt of semi-skimmed milk	2.5 g
$\frac{1}{2}$ pt of skimmed milk	0.3 g
1 small lean steak grilled	5.0 g
1 small chicken fillet grilled	3.0 g
1 small cod fillet grilled	1.0 g
2 large thin sausages grilled	20 g
Butter spread average on 1 slice of bread	10 g
Margarine spread average on 1 slice of bread	10 g
Low fat spread average on 1 slice of bread	5 g
1 small chocolate bar	15 g
1 small packet of crisps	10 g

Cholesterol has been implicated in the development of atherosclerosis, which is associated with coronary heart disease. However, it is generally thought by nutrition experts that dietary cholesterol has little effect on blood cholesterol. Blood cholesterol levels appear to be affected to a much greater extent by the level of saturated fat in the diet. High dietary intakes of saturated fat can encourage the body to produce greater quantities of cholesterol in the liver.

Trans fatty acids (TFAs)

Trans fatty acids are formed when polyunsaturated oils are hydrogenated in order to harden them to be used in food manufacturing. This alters the chemical structure of the fat. TFAs are believed to behave in the body in a similar way to saturated fats, in that high intakes of TFAs are thought to increase the risk of heart disease. Current Department of Health guidelines recommend an intake of TFAs of no more than 2% of total energy intake, or 5 g per day. The main sources of TFAs in the UK diet are margarines, pastries, biscuits and cakes.

Key concept

Blood cholesterol levels are thought to be affected to a much greater extent by the level of saturated fat in the diet than the level of dietary cholesterol intake.

A certain level of cholesterol is required to maintain health, as it is an important component of cells and some hormones. Regular exercise and a reduction in fat intake, particularly that derived from saturated sources, is thought to reduce the risks associated with elevated blood cholesterol levels. Cholesterol is found bound to lipoproteins, complex fats combining lipids and protein. These are the main form of transport for fat in the blood, transporting fats from the digestive system to storage sites. Although lipoproteins exist in several different forms, the two primary types are:

- high-density lipoproteins (HDL) – often referred to as good cholesterol
- low-density lipoproteins (LDL) – often referred to as bad cholesterol, as it is associated with promoting the fatty plaque build-up in the arteries of the heart.

Proteins

Proteins have a variety of functions that are essential to maintaining optimal health and physical performance. They also contain the chemical elements carbon, hydrogen and oxygen, but are more complex in structure and also contain nitrogen; some proteins may also contain other elements such as sulphur or iron.

Proteins are relatively large molecules of which amino acids are the simplest units, often referred to as the building blocks of proteins. There are 20 known amino acids which are required by the body. Different proteins contain different numbers and combinations of these amino acids. Of the 20 there are eight amino acids which the body is unable to make for itself, and as a result these are termed **essential amino acids** (EAAs) – they are a necessary part of our diet. The remaining amino acids are termed non-essential: the body is able to synthesise these if all the EAAs are present.

At this point in your study into nutrition it is not necessary for you to be familiar with the names and functions of the individual amino acids as this is quite a complex subject, but you should note that the body needs all 20 amino acids to be present simultaneously for protein synthesis to occur, to sustain optimal growth and functioning.

Key concept

There are eight amino acids which the body is unable to make for itself, and as a result these are termed essential amino acids (EAAs).

The chief role of protein in the body is to build and repair tissue, but proteins may also be used as a secondary source of energy when carbohydrate and fat are limited, such as towards the end of prolonged endurance events or during the severe energy restriction that may accompany dieting.

Proteins, like carbohydrates, have an energy value of approximately 4 kilocalories per gram. Unlike carbohydrate and fat, the body is unable to store excess protein. All proteins carry out functional roles in the body, therefore daily protein ingestion is required. When protein intake exceeds requirements to support growth and repair, the excess amino acids are broken down, the nitrogen component is excreted and the rest of the molecule is used to provide energy immediately or is converted to fat or carbohydrate and stored for later use.

Protein foods in the diet, like carbohydrates, are classified into two groups. The value of foods for meeting the body's protein needs is determined by their composition of amino acids. Foods that contain all of the eight essential amino acids are termed **first-class** or **complete** proteins. These are mainly foods of animal origin such as eggs, meat, fish, milk and other dairy products, but also soya.

Foods that are lacking in one or more of the essential amino acids are termed **second-class** or **incomplete** proteins. These are foods from plant

The typical UK diet includes adequate protein

sources such as cereals, bread, rice, pasta, pulses, nuts and seeds. Vegetarians and, in particular, vegans must make sure that they eat a wide variety of these foods in careful combinations to ensure that adequate intakes of all essential amino acids are achieved – for example beans and wheat complement each other well.

Protein foods	
Complete	**Incomplete**
meat, poultry, offal, fish, eggs, milk, cheese, yogurt, soya	cereals, bread, rice, pasta, noodles, pulses, peas, beans, lentils, nuts, seeds

Protein requirements

Normal adult protein requirements as recommended by dietitians are in the region of one gram per kilogram of body weight per day, so a 70 kg person would require 70 g of protein. Dietary reference values suggest 0.75 g per kilogram of body weight per day are required with the average UK diet, significantly exceeding the reference nutrient intake for protein set at only 45 g per day for an adult female and 55.5 g per day for an adult

male. Active individuals require greater intakes of protein in order to promote tissue growth and repair following training and competition.

Overall, protein intake should represent between 12% and 15% of our total daily energy intake. Requirements for protein may increase in times of illness and rapid growth, and are higher during pregnancy and lactation.

Key concept

The reference nutrient intake for protein is 45 g per day for adult females and 55.5 g per day for adult males.

In sports circles the misguided belief that additional dietary protein will automatically help to build muscle has been perpetuated since the times of the ancient Greeks. Regular exercise does increase protein needs, but most people already eat enough protein in the typical diet, unless of course their diet is severely calorie restricted. The sports performer is also likely to be eating more food to meet increased calorie requirements, and therefore should automatically be eating more protein to meet any theoretical increase in requirement.

High intakes of protein foods, particularly those of animal origin, often lead to high intakes of fat at the expense of the carbohydrates that are vital to replacing energy stores after exercise. Simply eating additional protein foods will not increase muscle size and strength. Equally, spending hours in the gym lifting heavy weights will not produce gains in strength and muscle bulk without the support of an adequate diet. Eating sufficient calories to meet metabolic requirements within a healthy, balanced and varied diet should negate the need for protein supplementation. Gaining weight and muscle mass will be covered in more detail in later sections of this unit.

A simple guide to estimating daily protein requirements	
Type of activity	Grams of protein per kilogram of body weight
Predominantly sedentary	1 g
Predominantly endurance	1.2-1.4 g
Predominantly strength	1.2-1.7 g

Theory into practice

1 Using the information outlined above, estimate your daily protein requirement.

2 Now take another look at your 24-hour diet recall and, using the list of protein content of common foods opposite, estimate your protein intake for the day. If you have eaten foods not in this list you will again need to refer to food composition tables to find out their protein content. Remember the food tables display the nutrient content of foods per 100 g, so when using these tables you need to be sure how much you have eaten.

3 If you did not meet your requirement devise a day's menu to meet your protein needs. A template to assist you with this activity can be found in Menu Plan 2 on page 69 at the end of this unit.

Key concept

From the table opposite you will notice that the carbohydrate foods that should form the basis of a healthy diet also provide a source of protein.

Protein content of common foods in the diet	
Food	Approximate protein content per serving
1 small lean steak	24 g
1 small chicken fillet	24 g
1 average portion of fish	24 g
1 small portion of soya mince	10 g
1 pint of milk	18 g
1 small pot of yogurt	6 g
1 small can rice pudding	7 g
1 medium portion of cheddar cheese	10 g
2 eggs	12 g
1 large slice of pizza	12 g
2 thin slices of bread	2 g
2 Shredded Wheat or Weetabix	4 g
1 large portion of pasta	14 g
1 large portion of rice	8 g
1 large jacket potato	4 g
1 small bag of crisps	2 g
1 small bar of chocolate	2 g
1 cereal bar	3 g
1 banana	1 g
1 small bag of peanuts	12 g
1 tablespoon of sesame seeds	2 g

Vitamins

Vitamins are vital, non-caloric nutrients required in very small amounts by the body. They perform specific metabolic functions and prevent particular deficiency diseases. Unlike macronutrients, they do not have a common chemical structure.

Most vitamins required to maintain health cannot be produced by the body and must be supplied by the diet – the exceptions are vitamin D, which the body is able to synthesise by the action of sunlight on the skin, and vitamin K, which can be produced by the bacteria of the large intestine. Vitamins play essential roles in regulating many of the metabolic processes of the body, particularly those that release energy. They are also required to support growth, immune and nervous system function, and some are involved in the production of hormones.

Vitamins are obtained from a wide variety of plant and animal sources and are grouped into two broad categories based on their solubility as either fat- or water-soluble. Vitamins A, D, E and K form the fat-soluble group of vitamins, with the B vitamins and vitamin C making up the water-soluble group.

The body requires differing amounts of each vitamin, with specific vitamins having specific functions. Our individual vitamin requirements vary and are determined by age, sex, state of health and levels of physical activity. The Department of Health has set Dietary Reference Values for all nutrients for different groups of healthy people within the UK population. The reference nutrient intake (RNI) value should meet the needs of practically all individuals in the population (97%). A balanced and, more importantly, varied diet that provides an adequate energy content should supply sufficient intakes of all vitamins.

It is important to note that some vitamins, like drugs, can be harmful to health if consumed in large amounts above the body's requirements. This is particularly true for the fat-soluble vitamins as they have the potential to be stored in the body. The only situation in which large doses of any vitamin may be beneficial is when the body has a severe deficiency of a particular vitamin, or when it is unable to absorb or metabolise vitamins efficiently. Supplementation with high doses of any vitamin should always be medically supervised and not self-prescribed.

Key concept

Individual vitamin requirements vary and are determined by age, sex, state of health and physical activity level.

Fat-soluble vitamins

All fat-soluble vitamins have a number of common features. As the term suggests they are found in the fatty or oily parts of foods. Once digested they are absorbed and transported in the lymph and ultimately reach the blood. As a result of their insolubility in water, they are not excreted in the urine and can accumulate in the body, in the liver and adipose tissue.

Vitamin A (retinol or carotene)

Major sources in the UK diet: liver, dairy products, eggs, vegetables (particularly those that are brightly coloured), oily fish, fish oils and fortified margarines.

Main functions: visual processes, normal growth, healthy skin and connective tissue.

UK reference nutrient intake: men 700 µg, women 600 µg, children 400-600 µg depending on age.

Symptoms of excess: liver toxicity, dry skin and hair loss; birth defects if taken by pregnant women.

Symptoms of deficiency: nightblindness is associated with inadequate levels of intake. Anaemia can also be associated with vitamin A deficiency as there is a link between this nutrient and red blood cell formation.

Vitamin D (calciferols)

Major sources in the UK diet: dairy products, oily fish and fish oils, fortified margarines and cereals.

Main functions: increases calcium absorption and regulates bone formation.

UK reference nutrient intake: assumed not to require a dietary source as long as there is adequate exposure of the skin to sunlight.

Symptoms of excess: toxicity is rare but high intakes may cause high blood pressure, nausea, loss of appetite and thirst associated with a high urine output.

Symptoms of deficiency: brittle bones and bone deformities resulting in rickets in children and osteomalacia in adults.

Fruit and vegetables are a rich source of vitamins, particularly vitamin C

Vitamin E (tocopherols)

Major sources in the UK diet: pure vegetable oils and spreads, eggs, meat, fish, wholegrain breads and cereals, nuts and seeds.

Main functions: acts as an antioxidant protecting against tissue damage, reducing the risk of heart disease and cancer. It may also play a role in recovery after exercise.

UK reference nutrient intake: no RNI value has been set for this vitamin.

Symptoms of excess: toxicity is rare.

Symptoms of deficiency: extremely rare but may result in neurological problems and loss of muscle co-ordination.

Vitamin K

Major sources in the UK diet: green leafy vegetables, soya, seaweed, offal and dairy products.

Main functions: plays a major role in blood clotting.

UK reference nutrient intake: no RNI value has been set for this vitamin.

Symptoms of excess: toxicity is rare.

Symptoms of deficiency: extremely rare but has the potential to result in an increased risk of haemorrhages.

Water-soluble vitamins

This group is formed from the B group of vitamins and vitamin C. As you will see many of the B vitamins serve similar functions, facilitating the use of energy within the body. As a group the water-soluble vitamins have different characteristics from the fat-soluble group. Excesses are excreted via the urine and as a result the body has only limited stores, necessitating regular intakes. It should be noted that many of these vitamins are destroyed by food processing and preparation.

Vitamin B1 (thiamin)

Major sources in the UK diet: wholegrain breads and cereals, pulses, offal, red meat and yeast extracts.

Main functions: energy release from carbohydrates, and the normal functioning of the central nervous system

UK reference nutrient intake: men 1.0 mg, women 0.8 mg, children 0.5-0.7 mg depending on age.

Symptoms of excess: excess is excreted, therefore large doses are rarely toxic.

Symptoms of deficiency: a condition known as beri beri which affects the nervous system, causing excessive fatigue, heavy legs and breathlessness on exertion.

Vitamin B2 (riboflavin)

Major sources in the UK diet: offal and red meat, dairy produce, fortified cereals, green vegetables and yeast extracts.

Main functions: energy release from carbohydrates, protein and fat.

UK reference nutrient intake: men 1.3 mg, women 1.1 mg, children 0.6-1.0 mg depending on age.

Symptoms of excess: excess is excreted, therefore large doses are rarely toxic.

Symptoms of deficiency: non-specific but often found in conjunction with other B vitamin deficiencies.

Vitamin B6 (pyridoxine)

Major sources in the UK diet: meat, wholegrain breads and cereals, dairy products, pulses, nuts, bananas and green vegetables.

Main functions: protein, carbohydrate and fat metabolism, red blood cell formation and the normal functioning of the central nervous system.

UK reference nutrient intake: men 1.4 mg, women 1.2 mg, children 0.7-1.0 mg depending on age.

Symptoms of excess: excess is excreted, but very high doses may cause numbness.

Symptoms of deficiency: there is no clear deficiency syndrome associated with this vitamin, but signs may be similar to other B vitamin deficiencies such as anaemia, irritability and fatigue.

Vitamin B12 (cyanocobalamin)

Major sources in the UK diet: meat, fish, offal and dairy produce, some fortified breakfast cereals and yeast extracts.

Main functions: protein, carbohydrate and fat metabolism, red blood cell formation, normal functioning of the central nervous system, and promoting growth and cell development.

UK reference nutrient intake: men 1.5 µg, women 1.5 µg, children 0.5-1.0 µg depending on age.

Symptoms of excess: excess is excreted, therefore large doses are rarely toxic.

Symptoms of deficiency: results in a condition known as pernicious anaemia.

Biotin

Major sources in the UK diet: cereals, beer, milk and dairy produce, meat and eggs.

Main functions: energy release from carbohydrates, proteins and fats.

UK reference nutrient intake: no RNI value has been set for this vitamin.

Symptoms of excess: excess is excreted, therefore there is no danger from high doses.

Symptoms of deficiency: loss of hair and scaly skin.

Niacin

Major sources in the UK diet: red meat, poultry, fish, dairy produce, cereals and yeast extracts.

Main functions: energy release from carbohydrates, proteins and fats.

UK reference nutrient intake: men 17 mg, women 13 mg, children 8-12 mg depending on age.

Symptoms of excess: excess is excreted, but very large doses may cause hot flushes.

Symptoms of deficiency: results in a condition known as pellagra that affects the skin.

Folic acid

Major sources in the UK diet: offal, green leafy vegetables, pulses, cereals, oranges, bananas and yeast extracts.

Main functions: regulates cell growth and red blood cell formation and protects against neural tube defects pre-conceptually and during the early stages of pregnancy.

UK reference nutrient intake: men 200 µg, women 200 µg, children 70-150 µg depending on age.

Symptoms of excess: high intakes are rarely toxic, however very large doses may reduce zinc absorption.

Symptoms of deficiency: a type of anaemia in which the red blood cells are larger than normal.

Pantothenic acid

Major sources in the UK diet: offal, meat, pulses, nuts, eggs, green vegetables and yeast extracts.

Main functions: protein, carbohydrate and fat metabolism.

UK reference nutrient intake: no RNI value has been set for this vitamin.

Symptoms of excess: excess is excreted, therefore large doses are rarely toxic.

Symptoms of deficiency: has no specific symptoms.

Vitamin C (ascorbic acid)

Major sources in the UK diet: green leafy vegetables, soft or citrus fruits and fruit juices, peppers, potatoes, white bread and milk.

Main functions: healthy connective tissue and gums, iron metabolism and absorption, wound healing and antioxidant properties.

UK reference nutrient intake: men 40 mg, women 40 mg, children 25–35 mg depending on age.

Symptoms of excess: excess is excreted, but large doses may increase the likelihood of kidney stones.

Symptoms of deficiency: scurvy, a condition of progressive weakness and fatigue, delayed wound healing, poor growth and bleeding gums.

Antioxidant vitamins

Beta-carotene, a form of vitamin A, and vitamins C and E are probably the most well known of the antioxidant nutrients in our diet and are often referred to as the 'ACE' vitamins. Research suggests that antioxidants can help to prevent damage to the body from the effects of free radicals.

There has been a lot of interest in the role of antioxidants from both the health and performance perspectives. Intense training may deplete the body's stores of these vitamins. It is thought that they could have an important role to play in the protection of muscle fibres from free radical damage during exercise, and in reducing post-exercise muscle soreness, but more research is required in this area. Eating a wide range of fruits and vegetables and choosing those that are in season will ensure a good intake of these vitamins.

Those that are brightly coloured, in particular those that are orange, green or leafy, are good sources.

Prevention of cardiovascular disease and cancer appear to be the two major health benefits associated with adequate intakes of these antioxidant vitamins. Recent research has indicated that increased consumption of fruits and vegetables has a protective effect against a range of different forms of cancer, but the precise mechanism for this effect remains unclear. In relation to cardiovascular disease, antioxidant vitamins are thought to have a role to play in reducing blood clot formation.

In order to reduce the risk of these chronic diseases, health professionals recommend that we eat more fruit and vegetables, with a minimum daily target set at five portions each day, equivalent in weight to 400 g.

Minerals

Minerals are also vital, non-calorie nutrients that are essential to life, and like vitamins they are required in small or even trace amounts. Minerals are classified in terms or the relative amounts required by the body, and can be placed broadly into two categories. **Macro-minerals** are those that are required in relatively large amounts, sometimes as much as several hundred milligrams, such as calcium. Those required in smaller quantities (micrograms) are usually referred to as **trace elements**. Examples are copper and selenium.

Essential macro-minerals and trace elements in the diet	
Macro-minerals (required in milligrams)	**Trace elements (required in micrograms)**
Calcium	Chromium
Fluoride	Copper
Iron	Iodine
Magnesium	Manganese
Phosphorus	Molybdenum
Potassium	Selenium
Sodium	
Zinc	

All minerals are essential to health and form important components of the body's tissues such as bone, connective tissue, enzymes and hormones. Some have essential roles to play in nerve function and muscle contraction; others regulate fluid balance in the body.

Levels of minerals within the body are closely controlled by absorption and excretion to prevent excessive build-up. Some minerals compete with each other for absorption, especially iron, zinc and copper. The next few pages outline the sources, functions and requirements for these nutrients. As you will see, deficiency states are much more clearly defined for some minerals than others.

Calcium

Major sources in the UK diet: milk, cheese, yogurt, nuts, pulses, green leafy vegetables, dried fruit, white bread and tinned fish with bones.

Main functions: bone and tooth structure, blood clotting, transmission of nerve impulses and muscle contraction.

UK reference nutrient intake: men 700 mg, women 700 mg, children 350-1000 mg depending on age.

Symptoms of excess: toxicity is rare, but high doses may interfere with the absorption of other nutrients, particularly zinc.

Chromium

Major sources in the UK diet: meat, wholegrain cereals, pulses and nuts.

Main functions: facilitates glucose uptake.

UK reference nutrient intake: no RNI value has been set for this mineral.

Symptoms of excess: rarely toxic in high doses.

Dairy products are a rich source of minerals, particularly calcium

Copper

Major sources in the UK diet: meat, cereals, vegetables, tea and coffee.

Main functions: enzyme synthesis.

UK reference nutrient intake: men 1.2 mg, women 1.2 mg, children 0.3-0.8 mg depending on age.

Symptoms of excess: toxic in high doses.

Fluoride

Major sources in the UK diet: seafood, drinking water and tea.

Main functions: bone and tooth formation.

UK reference nutrient intake: no RNI value has been set for this mineral.

Symptoms of excess: mottled teeth.

Iodine

Major sources in the UK diet: seafood and dairy produce.

Main functions: thyroid function and production of thyroid hormones.

UK reference nutrient intake: men 140 µg, women 140 µg, children 140 µg.

Symptoms of excess: rarely toxic, but repeatedly high intakes can cause hyperthyroidism.

Iron

Major sources in the UK diet: offal and red meat, fortified breakfast cereals, pulses, green leafy vegetables, wholegrain cereals, dried fruits, nuts and seeds.

Main functions: red blood cell formation, oxygen transport and utilisation.

UK reference nutrient intake: men 8.7 mg, women 14.8 mg, children 1.7-11.3 mg depending on age.

Symptoms of excess: constipation and reduced zinc absorption.

Symptoms of deficiency: iron deficiency anaemia.

Magnesium

Major sources in the UK diet: green leafy vegetables, dairy produce, cereals, potatoes, beer and coffee.

Main functions: muscle contraction and transmission of nerve impulses, bone formation and energy metabolism.

UK reference nutrient intake: men 300 mg, women 270 mg, children 55-300 mg depending on age.

Symptoms of excess: rarely toxic in high doses.

Symptoms of deficiency: may result in muscle weakness.

Manganese

Major sources in the UK diet: nuts, dried fruit, cereals and tea.

Main functions: enzyme synthesis.

UK reference nutrient intake: no RNI value has been set for this mineral.

Symptoms of excess: rarely toxic; any excess is easily excreted by the body.

Molybdenum

Major sources in the UK diet: present in trace quantities in many foods.

Main functions: enzyme synthesis.

UK reference nutrient intake: no RNI value has been set for this mineral.

Symptoms of excess: toxicity is unlikely.

Phosphorus

Major sources in the UK diet: cereals, meat, fish, dairy produce, green vegetables, potatoes, eggs and nuts.

Main functions: bone and tooth formation.

UK reference nutrient intake: men 550 mg, women 550 mg, children 270-775 mg depending on age.

Symptoms of excess: prolonged high intakes may interfere with blood calcium levels.

Potassium

Major sources in the UK diet: fruit and vegetables, potatoes, milk, meat, cereals, nuts, fruit juices, coffee and yeast extracts.

Main functions: muscle contraction, nerve conduction and fluid balance.

UK reference nutrient intake: men 3500 mg, women 3500 mg, children 700-3500 mg depending on age.

Symptoms of excess: excess is easily excreted.

Selenium

Major sources in the UK diet: seafood, meat, wholegrain cereals, milk, eggs and Brazil nuts.

Main functions: acts as anti-oxidant mineral.

UK reference nutrient intake: men 75 µg, women 60 µg, children 10-70 µg depending on age.

Symptoms of excess: toxic in very large doses, therefore supplementation with selenium is not advised.

Sodium

Major sources in the UK diet: table salt, cheese, tinned vegetables, ready-made meals

Crisps and savoury snacks are high in sodium, and should be eaten only in moderation

and sauces, processed meats, savoury snacks and yeast extracts.

Main functions: regulation of fluid balance and blood pressure.

UK reference nutrient intake: men 1600 mg, women 1600 mg, children 210-1600 mg depending on age.

Symptoms of excess: repeatedly high intakes may cause high blood pressure.

Zinc

Major sources in the UK diet: meat, fish, eggs, dairy produce, green vegetables, wholegrain cereals and pulses.

Main functions: enzyme synthesis, wound healing and immune function.

UK reference nutrient intake: men 9.5 mg, women 7.0 mg, children 4.0-9.5 mg depending on age.

Symptoms of excess: nausea and vomiting. Prolonged high intakes may interfere with copper, iron and manganese metabolism.

Symptoms of deficiency: poor appetite, taste changes, delayed wound healing and suppressed immune function.

Vitamin and mineral requirements of sportspeople

Sportspeople often believe they have higher requirements for vitamins and minerals than the average person. There is no doubt that an adequate supply of all the vitamins and minerals outlined in the previous section is necessary for health, but whether regular exercise increases requirements is a different matter. The scientific consensus is that exercise does not particularly increase the need for micronutrients, although there may be a case for increased requirements of nutrients involved in energy metabolism.

As mentioned earlier, individual requirements are dependent on age, sex, health status and levels of physical activity. It is conceivable that those who are more active may require more than their sedentary counterparts, but generally the sportsperson will be eating greater quantities of food to meet increased energy requirements, and as a result will be automatically increasing vitamin and mineral intakes – that is, of course, as long as nutrient-dense foods are chosen.

Vitamin and mineral supplementation

The vitamin and mineral supplementation industry is worth millions of pounds and, with a vast array of products available, it is easy to see why people would be tempted to try these products in case they might improve health, and in the case of the sportsperson boost performance. In general it is thought that if an individual consumes a well-balanced and, more importantly, varied diet that adheres to the National Food Guide principles and is sufficient to meet his or her energy needs, adequate vitamin and mineral intakes will easily be achieved.

Taking large quantities of some vitamins and minerals can be harmful to health. As outlined earlier, vitamin A is particularly toxic if consumed in large doses, while large intakes of zinc can interfere with the body's balance of other micronutrients such as copper, iron and manganese.

In relation to sport, supplements will not enhance the performance of the individual who is already well nourished and consuming adequate intakes within a well-balanced and varied diet. However, supplements might be useful to those people in any of the following categories:

- dieters who consistently consume low energy intakes
- vegetarians, in particular vegans, who may eat a limited variety of foods
- females who may be planning to become pregnant: a 400 microgram daily folic acid supplement is advised to reduce the risk of neural tube defects such as spina bifida
- elderly people with a poor appetite
- the chronically ill.

VITAMINS MINERALS and DIETARY SUPPLEMENTS

In these circumstances it is important that advice on supplementation is sought from a qualified professional.

Nutrients for special consideration

Calcium and iron are two micronutrients worth special consideration in relation to health and performance.

Calcium

Calcium is essential for healthy bones and teeth. If the diet contains insufficient calcium the bones can become thin and weak, making them more susceptible to osteoporosis and fractures. Vitamin D is required to promote the absorption of calcium within the body. As previously mentioned, our main source of vitamin D is exposure of the skin to sunlight.

Those at potential risk of calcium deficiency include females who are underweight with a low percentage body fat, those with a low energy intake and those who over-train. Smoking and high intakes of caffeine and alcohol are thought to suppress vital bone-building cells in the fight against osteoporosis.

Iron

Adequate iron intakes are important to all sportspeople who are regularly engaged in intensive training. Iron is required for the formation of haemoglobin in the red blood cells which is vital for carrying oxygen around the body. Deficiencies in iron intake may leave the sportsperson lacking in energy and affect the quality of training.

Certain factors can help or hinder the absorption of iron from the diet. Absorption is aided by the inclusion of a vitamin C source at each mealtime, and hindered by excessive intakes of tea, high fibre foods, and supplementing with other minerals such as calcium and zinc.

Females are much more likely to suffer from iron deficiency than males, but individuals are at greater risk if they are vegetarian and do not eat red meat, have erratic eating patterns, frequently follow low calorie or fad diets, eat a diet lacking in variety or with an extremely high fibre content, undertake frequent bouts of heavy endurance training, or experience any heavy bleeding, such as menstrual bleeding in females.

Water

Water is often overlooked as a nutrient, but it is one of the most important. The body cannot survive more than a few days without water; it is essential to life and performs numerous functions. Water acts as the main transport mechanism in the body, carrying nutrients, waste products and internal secretions. It also plays a vital role in temperature regulation, particularly during exercise, and aids the passage of food through the digestive system.

Water is the largest component of the body mass, making up around 50-60% of total body weight. Actual amounts will vary depending on age, sex and body composition. Muscle has a higher water content than fat tissue, therefore leaner individuals will have a higher water content that fatter individuals of the same body mass.

Water is lost from the body though a number of routes including urine, faeces, evaporation from the skin and expired breath. If water loss is high the body will become dehydrated. Under normal circumstances the body maintains a balance between fluid input and output. The table below illustrates the balance between the body's sources of water intake and the routes of water loss.

Daily water balance for a sedentary 70kg adult male			
Daily water input		Daily water output	
Source	ml	Source	ml
Fluid	1200	Urine	1250
Food	1000	Faeces	100
Metabolism	350	Skin	850
		Lungs	350
Total	2550	Total	2550

Fluid requirements

To maintain water balance the sedentary individual requires around 2-2.5 litres of fluid per day, the equivalent of 6-8 cups. Around 10% of our daily fluid requirements are gained from the metabolic processes that release water within the body. The other 90% is derived from our diet. Approximately 60% of this comes directly from fluids and the other 30% from food, particularly foods with a high water content.

During exercise, fluid requirements increase according to the type, duration and intensity of the exercise and the environmental conditions under which it is taking place. The body's water losses can be very rapid when exercising in hot weather. The longer and harder the exercise, and the hotter and more humid the conditions, the greater the fluid losses that are likely to occur.

Dehydration can significantly impair performance capacity, resulting in losses of strength, power and aerobic endurance. Dehydration results in a decreased blood volume and an increase in cardiac output. This leads to a reduced delivery of oxygen and nutrients to the working muscles. Small losses, as little as 2% of body mass, can begin to affect performance adversely. Vigorous activity can result in profuse sweating, leading to greater losses of around 3-4%. Preventing dehydration and ensuring adequate fluid intakes before, during and after exercise will be discussed in later sections of this unit.

Key concept

Water is the largest component of body mass, making up around 50-60% of total body weight. For maintaining water balance, the sedentary individual requires around 2-2.5 litres of fluid per day, the equivalent of 6-8 cups.

Alcohol

Alcohol is not essentially a nutrient, but is worth a mention, particularly as reducing intakes may be crucial to effective weight management for some.

Alcohol is produced from the fermentation of carbohydrates by yeasts. Like fat it is a relatively concentrated source of energy, providing 7 kilocalories per gram. However, this energy is unavailable to working muscles during exercise. The majority of alcohol is broken down by the liver at a fixed rate, about one unit per hour. Any energy derived from alcohol in excess of energy requirements will be stored as fat.

Those trying to lose weight should attempt to limit alcohol intakes. Current safe limits recommended by the Health Education Authority are up to 3-4 units per day for men, and for women up to 2-3 units per day. It is also advisable to spread alcohol intake throughout the week, to avoid binges, and to include two or three alcohol-free days each week.

Energy needs and energy balance

Energy is essential to life. It is obtained from the food we eat and used to support our **basal metabolic rate** (the minimum amount of energy required to sustain the body's vital functions in a waking state), and all activity carried out at work and leisure. At some times in life extra energy is required, such as during pregnancy and lactation, illness and growth spurts.

Expressed simply, an individual is in energy balance when the amount of energy taken in (energy input) equals the amount of energy expended (energy output). He or she will neither be losing nor gaining weight. Energy input comes from the food and drink we eat. There are four major components to energy output: **resting metabolic rate, dietary thermogenesis**, physical activity, and **adaptive thermogenesis**. Let's take a closer look at these components of energy expenditure.

Resting metabolic rate (RMR) can account for up to 60-75% of total energy output and represents the largest component of our total daily energy expenditure. RMR is closely related to lean body mass and as a result is influenced by body composition. Muscle tissue is much more metabolically active than fat tissue. Gains in muscle mass will result in increases in RMR. RMR is also influenced by our age, sex and genetic background. In relation to weight management, repeated low energy intakes as a result of dieting may lead to a reduction in RMR, resulting in a decline of up to 30% during periods of prolonged severe energy restriction. RMR also declines with increasing age and from the age of 30 years RMR is thought to decline by about 2% per decade.

Dietary thermogenesis (DT) refers to the energy expended above that of RMR for the processes of digestion, absorption, transport and storage of food. It is influenced by the calorie content and composition of the meals consumed in our diet along with our individual nutritional status. High energy intakes and a regular eating pattern are thought to help us maintain higher rates of dietary thermogenesis, while skipping meals and restrictive dietary practices lead to a reduction in this component of total energy expenditure.

Physical activity (PA) represents the most variable component of our total energy expenditure. This is the additional energy expended above the RMR and DT, and will obviously contribute more to total daily energy expenditure in active individuals. Exactly how much will vary according to how active our general lifestyle is, how often, how energetically, and for how long we participate in sport and exercise, and what type of activity it is.

Adaptive thermogenesis (AT) is energy expenditure that occurs as a result of environmental or physiological stresses placed on the body, such as a change in temperature that may require the body to respond by shivering, or stress that causes anxiety or fidgeting.

Key concept

Energy balance is achieved when energy input equals energy output.

When energy intake exceeds expenditure, this is referred to as **positive energy balance** and weight is gained. If intake is less than requirements to meet energy expenditure, the additional energy required will be drawn from the body's fat reserves and weight will be lost. This is referred to as **negative energy balance**. Even small imbalances in energy intake and expenditure can produce profound effects on body composition and weight.

Theory into practice

Is energy balance important in sport?

Jot down your thoughts in your notebook for later discussion with your tutor.

Most sportspeople are concerned about either attaining or maintaining an optimal body weight. There are some sports in which weight restrictions apply; these are termed weight category sports and

Energy balance is achieved when energy input equals energy output

Energy input

Energy output

include body building, boxing, horse racing, martial arts and rowing. In these sports the sportsperson must compete within a given weight range.

For some other sports, an increased body size might be advantageous, such as for American football. For others it may be crucial to maintain a low body weight, which for some may be below their natural weight. These might be considered as weight-controlled sports, and include sports such as distance running, gymnastics and diving. These sports may present challenges in maintaining a nutritionally adequate diet while reducing or maintaining weight. A variety of inappropriate weight loss practices can be found in this connection, such as fasting or skipping meals, laxative abuse, binging and purging, and intentional dehydration by the use of sweatsuits or saunas.

Theory into practice

1 What are the nutritional consequences of the unhealthy weight loss practices identified above?

2 What impact might these have on performance in sport?

Recommended nutrient intakes

In the late 1980s, the government set up a panel of experts to review the Recommended Daily Amounts (RDAs) of nutrients for the UK population, and new **Dietary Reference Values** (DRVs) were established. The phrase 'dietary reference value' is an umbrella term that can be applied to any of the following measures of nutrient intakes:

- **Reference Nutrient Intake (RNI)**: this is the amount of a nutrient, not including energy, which is thought to be sufficient for almost any individual (97% of the population). The level of intake is usually set above that which most people need, and individuals meeting this value of intake for

any nutrient are unlikely to be deficient. The RNI figures for nutrient requirements are in many cases similar to the old RDA values. RNI values are those that are most often used by nutrition professionals in the nutritional assessment of dietary intake.

- **Estimated Average Requirement (EAR)**: this is an assessment of the average requirement for food energy or nutrients. Many individuals will require more than the EAR, and many will require less. The EAR is the value most used when assessing energy requirements and intakes.

- **Lower Reference Nutrient Intake (LRNI)**: this is the amount of a nutrient thought to be sufficient to meet the needs of the small numbers in the population who have low requirements. The vast majority of individuals will require much more than the LRNI. If individuals are consistently eating less than the LRNI for any particular nutrient, they may be at risk of deficiency of that nutrient, and dietary intake should be monitored more closely.

- **Safe intakes**: this term is used to indicate the intake of a nutrient where there is insufficient scientific information to estimate the distribution of requirements within a population. It represents an intake that is thought to be adequate for most people's needs but not so high as to cause undesirable effects on health.

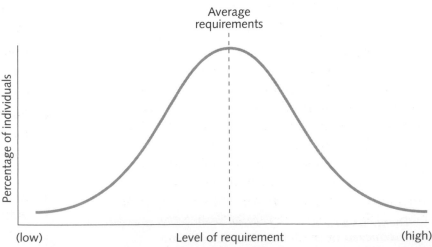

The normal distribution curve of nutrient requirements in a population

To find out more about dietary reference values you can take a look at the Department of Health's Report on Health and Social Subjects 41: *Dietary Reference Values for Food Energy and Nutrients for the United Kingdom*, HMSO, 1991.

Key concept

Dietary reference value is an umbrella term that can be applied to the other terms relating to nutrient intakes: RNI, EAR, LRNI, and safe intakes.

Healthy eating

Now that you are familiar with the requirements for and the sources and functions of nutrients, this section will evaluate the influence of nutrition and eating habits on health and performance.

What you need to learn

- Healthy eating principles and the guidelines of the UK National Food Guide
- How to keep a detailed food and activity record
- How to evaluate your own eating and activity patterns in relation to these principles and guidelines
- The importance of food labelling.

Foods that we eat in our diet are popularly classed as good or bad, healthy or unhealthy, with healthy eating often viewed by many as a hardship or a chore. But in fact we should take a different view of healthy eating: there are no good or bad foods, only good or bad uses of food, and it is better to look at the overall balance of foods eaten as either healthy or unhealthy. No foods need to be excluded from the diet completely. Doing this usually makes them seem more desirable and often leads to greater consumption in the long run – a common problem with many dieting regimes.

Healthy eating involves choosing the right foods in the right balance most of the time to provide all the essential nutrients and energy required by the body to maintain it in optimal health. The principles of healthy eating essentially aim to reduce the risk of chronic disease such as coronary heart disease, obesity, diabetes and cancer, but following these principles will also benefit sports performance. Remember, as stated at the start of this unit, there should be no conflict between eating for health and eating for performance. Healthy eating principles should form the solid foundations on which sportspeople can build more specific nutritional strategies to support training and competition.

Key concept

Healthy eating involves choosing the right foods in the right balance to provide all the essential nutrients and energy required by the body, to maintain it in optimal health and reduce the risk of chronic disease.

A simple guide to healthy eating

- Eat the correct amount to maintain a healthy body weight.
- Cut back on fat intake, particularly fat from saturated sources.
- Eat plenty of foods with a high starch and fibre content.
- Don't eat sugary foods too often.
- Use salt sparingly and reduce reliance on convenience foods.
- Ensure adequate intakes of vitamins and minerals by eating a wide variety of foods.
- If you drink alcohol, keep within sensible limits.
- Enjoy your food and don't become obsessed with your diet or dieting.

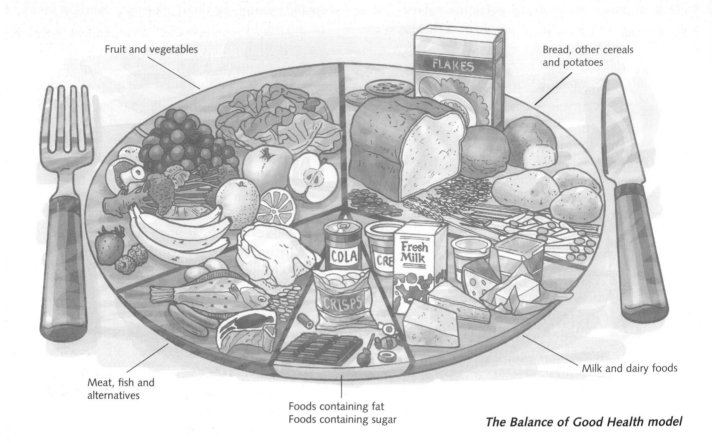

Fruit and vegetables

Bread, other cereals and potatoes

FLAKES

COLA

CRE

Fresh Milk

CRISPS

Meat, fish and alternatives

Foods containing fat
Foods containing sugar

Milk and dairy foods

The Balance of Good Health model

The National Food Guide

The Balance of Good Health model has been adopted as the UK's National Food Guide. It was devised by the Health Education Authority as a new and simplified means of helping people to understand healthy eating. The model attempts to make adopting a healthier diet easier to implement by identifying the types and proportions of foods required to achieve a healthy, balanced and varied diet, based around the five main food groups.

As you can see (above), the model depicts a plate with divisions of varying sizes representing each of these five groups. Those that have a larger proportion of the plate should feature in larger proportions in our diet, while those with the smallest share should be consumed in much smaller quantities, or used only as occasional foods in the case of those with a high fat and sugar content.

This UK guide to healthy eating applies to most people in the population, including those who engage in regular exercise and sport. It does not, however, apply to children under the age of five. One of the main aims of this guide is to allow nutrition educators to promote consistent messages about healthy eating and a balanced diet.

The key messages are that we should aim to:

- base all our meals around starchy foods
- include at least five servings of fruit and/or vegetables in our diet each day
- include milk and dairy foods, if possible three servings per day
- eat smaller portions of meat or fish, and try alternatives such as pulses
- limit our intake of foods with a high fat or sugar content.

The table on page 29 shows suggested proportions for the different foods groups within the UK National Food Guide, and identifies the key nutrients contributed by each of these groups.

Suggested proportions of different foods groups in the UK National Food Guide				
Food group	**Food types**	**Serving size**	**Amount recommended**	**Main nutrients supplied**
Bread, cereals and potatoes	Bread, rolls, muffins, bagels, crumpets, chapattis, naan bread, pitta bread, tortillas, scones, pikelets, potato cakes, breakfast cereals, rice, pasta, noodles, cous cous and potatoes	3 tbsp breakfast cereal, 1 Weetabix or Shredded Wheat, 1 slice of bread, $\frac{1}{2}$ pitta, 1 heaped tbsp boiled potato, pasta, rice, cous cous	These should form the main part of all meals and snacks About a third of total volume of food consumed each day	Carbohydrate, NSP mainly insoluble, calcium, iron and B vitamins
Fruit and vegetables	All types of fresh, frozen, canned and dried fruits and vegetables except potatoes, and fruit and vegetable juices	1 apple, orange, pear, banana, 1 small glass of fruit or vegetable juice, 1 small salad, 2 tbsp vegetables, 2 tbsp stewed or tinned fruit in juice	At least 5 portions each day About a third of total volume of food consumed each day	NSP – especially soluble, vitamin C, folate and potassium
Milk and dairy products	Milk, yoghurt, cheese and fromage frais	$\frac{1}{3}$ pint milk, $1\frac{1}{4}$ oz cheese, 1 small carton of yoghurt or cottage cheese	2-3 servings per day About a sixth of total volume of food consumed each day	Protein, calcium, vitamins A and D
Meat, fish and alternative protein sources	Meat, poultry, fish, eggs, pulses and nuts Meat and fish products such as sausages, beefburgers, fish cakes and fish fingers	2-3 oz of lean meat, chicken, or oily fish, 4-5 oz white fish, 2 eggs, 1 small tin baked beans, 2 tbsp nuts, 4 oz Quorn or soya	2 servings per day About a sixth of total volume of food consumed each day	Protein, iron, zinc, magnesium and B vitamins Pulses provide a good source of NSP
Foods containing fat and sugar	Fat-rich: butter, margarine, cooking oils, mayonnaise and salad dressings, cream, pastries, crisps, biscuits and cakes Sugar-rich: sweets, jams, honey, marmalade, soft drinks, biscuits, cakes and pastries	1 tsp butter or margarine 1 tsp vegetable or olive oil 1 tsp mayonnaise	These should be eaten sparingly and where possible lower fat options selected Extra energy provided by sugars may be useful in meeting carbohydrate requirements for active individuals	Fat-rich: fat, essential fatty acids and some vitamins Sugar-rich: carbohydrate and some vitamins and minerals

Theory into practice

Visit your local supermarket, doctor's surgery and health promotion department. Collect a selection of booklets and leaflets on health and nutritional matters.

Choose the best of these to review and consider the following questions:

- In relation to dietary advice, do they provide information compatible with healthy eating to achieve a balanced diet, as outlined in the UK National Food Guide?
- Does the advice seem unbiased, or does it promote particular brands or products?
- Does it quote scientific evidence from reputable sources?
- Has the booklet or leaflet been devised by a nutritionist or dietitian?

If you feel confident that the information these booklets and leaflets contain has been produced by a credible nutrition professional, and is balanced, sensible and independent, they are likely to be a useful source that you may wish to use when formulating the advice for your case studies.

Look again at the booklets and leaflets that you discarded because they did not meet the criteria outlined above. What might be the dangers of using biased information produced by unreliable sources?

Key concept

The Balance of Good Health model is the UK's National Food Guide, devised by the Health Education Authority as a simplified means of helping people to understand and implement healthy eating guidelines.

Putting it into practice – dietary analysis

Evaluating eating and activity habits

As discussed earlier, healthy eating should be something to be enjoyed by all, and not simply endured. Before you can safely and effectively plan and implement healthy eating programmes

and nutritional strategies to support training and competition for your case study assessments, you need to be able to critically evaluate your own eating habits and activity patterns, and consider the relationship between them.

How do you know if you are eating a well-balanced diet? To assess your own eating habits, keep a record in your notebook of all food and drink you consume for at least a three-day period, which should include one weekend day. For a more detailed evaluation, record your intake for a full week.

Write down everything you eat and drink. You must be as accurate and honest as possible, and be sure not to modify your usual intake at this stage, otherwise you will not be evaluating your typical diet. You will need to carry your notebook around with you at all times and record food and drink as it is consumed, to avoid forgetting any items. Your record should describe the following.

- The type of food and drink consumed, and how much. Either estimate the portion size using standard household measures, such as slices of bread, pints of fluid, tablespoons of vegetables, etc., or give the weight. You can weigh the food yourself or record the weight from any packaging.
- The time that the food and drink was consumed and where you were when you ate it. These points are often useful when assessing external factors that affect your dietary intake.
- Any activity or exercise you took part in, including an indication of its duration and intensity, i.e. light, moderate or hard.

Theory into practice

Look at your food and activity record and compare it to the Balance of Good Health guidelines. You may find it useful to create a simple tally chart to record the number of servings consumed from each of the five food groups.

Write a short account of your evaluation in your notebook. You may wish to write this up in more detail as part of a final report to contribute to your assessment for this unit.

As well as the types and amounts of food you eat, your record may give you an idea about how your daily life dictates what, when, where and why you eat.

Theory into practice

Take another look at your food record and ask yourself the following questions.

- In relation to healthy eating principles, is your diet better than you first thought or is there plenty of room for improvement? What healthy eating goals might you not be achieving? Are there any that you achieve with ease?

- Are your meal times structured and regular? Do you leave long gaps between your meals? Do you eat any differently at weekends? What might influence this?

- What types of foods feature frequently in your diet, and which are eaten only occasionally? Do you eat an extensive variety of foods from all the five food groups, or base your diet around only a few foods?

- What constraints do you foresee that may prevent you from making any of the necessary changes you may have identified as a result of this evaluation? Do you think you will be able to overcome them?

Jot down your ideas in your notebook and summarise the changes you might want to make. Make sure they are realistic. Try to implement these changes over the coming weeks while studying this unit. Tackle them one at a time – they don't all need to be achieved overnight! This is an important point to remember when formulating dietary recommendations and menu plans.

This dietary analysis will provide you with a useful index of the strengths and limitations of your dietary intake, and can be applied to your case studies.

Key concept

A daily food record can be a useful tool in determining what, when, where and why you eat.

Dietary assessment techniques

There are a number of methods for collecting information on what people eat and drink. These include the 24-hour diet recall, the diet history or interview technique, daily food records or diaries, weighed food intake records, and food frequency questionnaires.

Keeping a record of everything you eat and drink requires planning

BISHOP BURTON COLLEGE

Two of these methods use records of consumption made at the time of eating; one records the weight of the food eaten (weighed food intake record), the other uses estimates of weights (food record or diary). The other three methods attempt to assess diet and food consumption in the recent or distant past by asking subjects about their food intake. These methods may be used to recall usual food intake in the recent or distant past, for example the previous day (24-hour recall), over the past few weeks (diet history), or questionnaires (food frequency).

You have already had some experience of two of these techniques in the activities in this unit, but further practice in their application is required before you undertake your case studies so you can develop a better level of skill at obtaining dietary intake information.

Key concept

Any detailed or complex dietary analysis incorporating major dietary changes, particularly those relating to medical conditions, should always be referred to a qualified State Registered Dietitian, or an Accredited Sports Dietitian where it concerns an athlete or sportsperson. The usual means of referral to a State Registered Dietitian are through a general practitioner, consultant or dentist.

Theory into practice

Work with one of your classmates. Before you start, decide on an appropriate template that could be designed for the purpose of recording all necessary information relating to meal times, types of food and fluid consumed, and the cooking methods used.

1 Take it in turns to interview each other to recall all food and drink consumed in the past 24 hours. Use your template to record the details of your interview.

2 What are the main advantages and disadvantages of this method of dietary intake recording? Jot down your ideas in your notebook for later discussion with your tutor.

3 Interview the same person again, but this time ask him or her to recall everything eaten and drunk in the past seven days. Record the details using the same template.

4 What are the main advantages and disadvantages of this method of dietary intake recording? Jot down your ideas in your notebook for later discussion with your tutor.

You may choose to use this technique in gaining information on dietary intake for your case studies. It is important when interviewing people about their dietary habits to adopt a professional approach and maintain confidentially. It should always be borne in mind that an individual's food intake is a very personal issue, and this information should be handled sensitively. It is also necessary to ask if there are any medical factors that impact on food habits, such as diabetes or allergies. These cases should always be referred to a qualified professional for dietary advice.

24-hour diet recall

This method of dietary information collection is quick and easy to use. The interviewer questions the subject to collect information on what he or she usually eats and drinks. This method relies heavily on memory to recall all food and drink consumed, but is usually achievable in those without memory problems. The method is useful in assessing the quality of food intake and may reveal obvious dietary imbalances, such as a potentially high fat intake or a deficiency in calcium due to the exclusion or limited intake of dairy foods. However, it is rarely adequate to provide a quantitative estimate of nutrient intakes to allow for comparison with Dietary Reference Values. The main value of this method is as a starting point on which to base further dietary investigation.

The diet history or interview

This method is also relatively quick and easy to use. The interviewer again questions the subject to collect information on what he or she usually eats and drinks, but over a longer time period. This method, too, relies heavily on memory to recall all food and drink consumed in the period specified. It is important to note that recollections of this kind nearly always underestimate intake, and there is also the danger of fabrication to impress the interviewer. The method is, however, useful in assessing the quality of dietary intake and may be able to reveal obvious dietary imbalances in the same way as the 24-hour recall. Again, this forms a useful starting point for further dietary investigation.

Daily food record or diet dairy

This method can give a good overall guide to the types and quantities of food and drink consumed during the recording period. At least three days should be recorded and one of these should be a weekend day to take account of the often different food patterns at weekends. For a more detailed picture, a seven-day record is recommended.

When dealing with sportspeople, the record should include rest and competition days as well as training days.

Theory into practice

Refer back to your own daily food and activity record.

Consider the main advantages and disadvantages of this method of dietary intake collection. Jot down your ideas in your notebook for discussion with your tutor.

Weighed food intake

With the weighed food intake method, individual foods are weighed before consumption. This method is very time consuming and intrusive, and could lead to distortion of the overall pattern of foods consumed in order to make weighing and recording easier – foods may be chosen because they are easy to weigh, and not necessarily reflect those usually consumed.

Limitations

All the methods outlined in this section provide basic information on eating patterns, and each has limitations to be taken into account when

Weighing all your food before consumption can be time-consuming

interpreting and evaluating eating patterns. Evaluations of this kind are only as representative of normal intake as the record itself is.

Further analysis of your diet diary

Your diet diary can be analysed further for nutrient content, either manually by looking up all foods and fluids consumed in the food composition tables, recording the nutrient values and adding them up, or by using a computerised dietary analysis programme such as the one at www.dietsure.com. This will list all nutrients, do all the necessary calculations and compare your intakes to Dietary Reference Values.

Theory into practice

1   Choose a typical day from your food record to be analysed using a computer analysis programme. This should allow you to compare nutrient intakes for the day to appropriate Dietary Reference Values.

2   Using the same day, undertake an analysis using food composition tables. *McCance & Widdowson's The Composition of Foods*, 6th edition, is the most comprehensive available.

    Using this method, analyse your intake of energy, carbohydrate, protein, fat, fibre, vitamin C, calcium and iron. Record these using an appropriately designed table.

    You will need to establish portion sizes of foods and drink consumed. To do this you can refer to the Food Standards Agency's *Food Portion Sizes*, 3rd edition. This reference tool provides up-to-date information on the typical weights and portions of common foods eaten in the British diet.

3   Compare and evaluate the data obtained from these two different forms of analysis. Record your thoughts in your notebook, to be presented in a report incorporating the use of graphs, tables and charts to show your findings.

When assessing the effectiveness of dietary advice, it may be necessary to undertake progress reviews by way of interviewing or keeping a diet record to ensure the dietary recommendations have been adhered to and that short-term goals have been met. Consideration can then be given to medium- and long-term goals or targets.

For example, a short-term goal may be to make simple substitutions in the diet in order to adopt healthy eating guidelines. A medium-term goal may be to lose 6 kilos in six months. A long-term goal would be to ensure the weight loss is maintained without any negative impact on the nutritional quality of the diet.

The importance of food labelling

Most foods in our diet are categorised based on their macronutrient content, but they usually consist of more than one of these nutrients, as well as vitamins, minerals, fibre and water. Take bread as an example; it consists of a large amount of carbohydrate, a smaller amount of protein and an even smaller amount of fat, and is a useful source of many micronutrients. Wholemeal varieties will provide a good source of fibre too.

If we are to follow healthy eating guidelines it is important to know exactly what we are eating. Many of our foods are now conveniently packaged, and it has therefore become more important to be able to read and understand food labels to make informed choices about what we eat.

Food labelling regulations

Since the late 1980s all processed foods and non-alcoholic beverages sold in the UK have been required by law to display a list of their ingredients in descending order of weight. The first few ingredients listed are present in the greatest quantities, while additives and preservatives are usually found at the bottom of the list and are present in very small quantities.

Some food manufacturers provide information on the nutritional value and content of their products.

If this information is provided, it must be presented in a standard format specified by food labelling regulations to enable the consumer to compare products. Also included on food labels are any nutritional claims made by the food manufacturer.

The information given on a label allows us to determine the relative proportions of nutrients provided per serving, in particular carbohydrate, fat and protein, along with energy content, but the label may also provide information on:

- where the product comes from
- whether the product is value for money
- ingredients we might want or need to avoid
- the facts behind any nutritional claims
- a taste or flavour we might be looking for
- the preparation methods for the product
- food storage and preparation instructions, to avoid spoilage and food poisoning.

'Budget Buy Baked Beans' label		
Nutrition information		
Typical values	**per 100g**	**per serving**
ENERGY	355 kJ	735 kJ
	84 kcal	174 kcal
PROTEIN	5.2 g	10.8 g
CARBOHYDRATE	15.4 g	31.9 g
of which sugars	6.0 g	12.4 g
FAT	0.3 g	0.6 g
of which saturates	trace	0.1 g
FIBRE	3.7 g	7.6 g
SODIUM	0.4 g	0.8 g

Nutritional claims – *what do they mean?*

A vast array of modified products is now available to assist us in meeting the goal of healthy eating. These products are marketed with a range of nutritional claims that relate to the calorie, fat, sugar and fibre content of foods, but what do these actually mean?

Theory into practice

Visit your local supermarket and investigate the labels of foods with the following nutritional claims. Record your findings in your notebook for discussion with your tutor.

- low fat
- reduced fat
- virtually fat free
- 95% fat free
- low in saturates
- reduced sugar
- low sugar
- sugar free
- no added sugar
- reduced calorie
- low calorie
- high fibre
- reduced sodium.

1. What kinds of products promote these claims?
2. Would you consider these to be core or peripheral foods in our diet?
3. Do any of these claims mean the same thing?
4. What impact might this have for the consumer?

Learning to analyse food labels can reveal some alarming truths about the nutritional composition of foods. To be able to make an informed choice about the foods we eat we really need to be able to calculate the number of calories contributed by each of the macronutrients fat, carbohydrate and protein. Remember that healthy eating targets recommend a daily calorie intake composed of 50% from carbohydrate, 30-35% from fat and 15-20% from protein. The nutrition panel on a food label will usually tell you per 100 g of the product:

- the number of kilocalories
- the number of grams of fat
- the number of grams of carbohydrate
- the number of grams of protein.

What you actually need to know is the percentage of calories coming from each of the three macronutrients. To find this out, you need to remember:

- 1 g of fat provides 9 kilocalories
- 1 g of carbohydrate provides 4 kilocalories
- 1 g of protein provides 4 kilocalories.

The following formulae can be applied to calculate the percentage of energy in kilocalories contributed by the three macronutrients.

Formula for calculating the percentage of kilocalories from fat:

$$\frac{\text{Number of grams fat} / 100 \text{ g} \times 9 \times 100}{\text{Total number of kilocalories} / 100 \text{ g}}$$

Formula for calculating the percentage of kilocalories from carbohydrate and protein:

$$\frac{\text{Number of grams carbohydrate or protein} / 100 \text{ g} \times 4 \times 100}{\text{Total number of kilocalories} / 100 \text{ g}}$$

Theory into practice

Choose three different food labels and analyse them for the percentage of energy contributed by carbohydrate, protein and fat.

Do these labels make any nutritional claims? If they do, are these accurate or misleading?

Record your findings in your notebook for discussion with your tutor.

Possessing the ability to appraise food labels accurately is more important than ever because of changes that have taken place in recent years in our food choice and intake. A much greater range of foods is now available, with new foods entering the market daily – some claiming particular health benefits. Along with this, our traditional eating patterns have changed. Recent food surveys suggest there is a greater reliance on highly processed and convenience foods, while new food technologies are being developed such as genetically modified and functional foods, which further challenge consumer opinions and choice.

The influence of nutrition on health and performance

A team of global experts from the World Health Organisation (WHO) and the Food and Agriculture Organisation (FAO) have concluded that a diet consisting of less saturated fat, sugar and salt and more fruit and vegetables is key to combating the risks of chronic disease. The burden of chronic diseases is increasing worldwide. In this section we will focus on some of these diseases and consider in more detail the impact that nutrition and eating habits might have on health and the development and treatment of these disorders.

What you need to learn

- Factors or conditions that affect food intake and choice
- The influence of nutrition on health and well being
- Nutrition-related disorders
- The role of nutrition professionals.

Theory into practice

1 Before we take a closer look at the influence of nutrition on health and performance, consider ways in which you think nutrition and eating habits might influence health and list them in your notebook for later discussion with your tutor.

2 Now consider ways in which nutrition and eating habits might influence performance in sport and exercise, and list them in your notebook.

Obesity

Obesity is now clearly recognised as a disease in its own right, one which is now thought to be largely preventable through lifestyle changes particularly to our diet and activity patterns.

In spite of high incidences of dieting among particular groups of the population, obesity continues to be a growing problem and is increasingly becoming a major public health concern. Undeniable evidence suggests that fitness and fatness have a profound effect on our health, but the fitness and nutrition boom of the 1980s, in response to the emergence of healthy eating principles, appears to have had little impact on the increasing incidence of overweight and obesity that now faces our nation – it is predicted that 25% of the adult population will be obese by 2010.

In 1992 the government set out specific health targets for tackling obesity in its report on a strategy for health in England, called 'The Health of The Nation'. This called for a reduction in the percentage of men and women between the ages of 16 and 64 who were obese, classified as a body mass index (BMI) of more than 30, by at least a quarter and a third respectively by the year 2000. This means that obesity in men should have fallen from 8% to no more than 6%, and in women a fall from 12% to 8% should have been observed.

However, it is clear that the current trend is moving away from, rather than towards these targets. Currently, 38% of the UK population is classed as overweight and a further 20% obese. Another cause for concern is the rising rates of overweight and obesity now seen in children: one in four UK children are currently classified as overweight, and one in ten obese.

In terms of the health risks associated with obesity, there is strong evidence to suggest that people with a BMI of more than 29 have an increased risk of illness and death, particularly from cardiovascular risk factors. The risk of developing other conditions such as gallstones, respiratory diseases, maturity-onset diabetes and some forms of cancer is also higher in those who are overweight.

Being overweight or obese can also aggravate other health problems, such as arthritis and lower back pain, and may contribute to emotional distress and disorders in sufferers – negative thoughts and feelings towards their body may lower their self-esteem and reduce their quality of life.

Think it over

Excess body weight and obesity result when energy intake exceeds energy expenditure – but is this traditional view too simplistic to explain the problem?

As a group, consider all the possible causes for the rising rates of overweight and obesity in the UK population.

Being overweight or obese may cause health problems

Causes of obesity

The general consensus suggests there is no single cause of obesity. Both environmental and genetic factors are thought to play a role in the development of obesity. Research has suggested that genetic make-up can predispose an individual to obesity, rather than make it inevitable, while lifestyle and environmental factors may result in the development of obesity in those who are predisposed to it.

Diabetes

Diabetes is a common endocrine disorder that currently affects over a million people in the UK. It is a condition that results from either a complete lack of insulin production by the pancreas, or a reduction in insulin production so that the body is unable to use it effectively to control blood sugar levels. Normally the uptake of glucose by the cells is controlled by insulin. When there is a lack of insulin, glucose cannot enter the cells to be used for energy. This leads to raised blood glucose levels, which give rise to the common symptoms of increased thirst, passing large volumes of urine, weight loss, tiredness and blurred vision.

Types of diabetes

There are two different types of diabetes, type I and type II. With type I diabetes, until recently referred to as insulin-dependent diabetes, the pancreas stops producing insulin completely. This type of diabetes usually occurs before the age of 40-45, and is treated by insulin injections and diet.

Type II diabetes develops when the pancreas produces some but not enough insulin to meet the body's requirements. This type usually occurs over the age of 40, although with increasing numbers of people overweight or obese it is now seen in individuals below this age. It is treated by diet alone or by diet and tablets, and in some cases insulin injections may also be required to stabilise blood glucose levels. This type of diabetes is commonly associated with obesity, which causes insulin resistance. Insulin resistance may also occur during pregnancy, leading to the condition known as gestational diabetes.

Diabetes brings an increased risk of other diseases such as heart disease, kidney disease and stroke, and also an increased risk of infections. Contrary to popular opinion, excess sugar in the diet is in itself not thought to lead to diabetes – unless it is associated with obesity as a result of excess calorie intake.

The diet proposed for people with diabetes is now not a special one. The dietary guidelines for diabetes are based around the normal healthy eating diet recommended for everyone – low in fat and sugar and high in fibre. There is no need to use special diabetic foods, which are often expensive and high in calories and fat. A healthy diet will help to keep blood glucose within normal limits, and control weight and cholesterol levels. People suffering from diabetes are encouraged to:

- eat regular meals with similar amounts of starchy carbohydrate foods
- eat more high fibre starchy foods
- reduce sugar intake
- reduce fried and fatty foods
- drink alcohol only in moderation
- reduce salt intake
- achieve and maintain a healthy body weight.

Increased levels of physical activity and the achievement and maintenance of a healthy body weight have a critical role to play in both the prevention and treatment of diabetes, particularly type II diabetes.

Theory into practice

Compare the guidelines proposed above to those for the rest of the population. What similarities do you observe? Record your ideas in your notebook for later discussion with your tutor.

Diabetic sportspeople who exercise regularly may need to consume greater quantities of healthy complex carbohydrate. In addition to careful control of total calorie and carbohydrate intakes, the timing and regularity of meals and snacks is important to ensure that low blood sugar (hypoglycaemia) is avoided.

Coronary heart disease

Coronary heart disease (CHD) is a major cause of death and ill health. Rates in the UK are among the highest in the developed world.

There is no single cause of coronary heart disease. However, the underlying condition of atherosclerosis is a degenerative condition of the arteries characterised by the deposit of fatty substances in the lining of the artery walls. Over time these fatty deposits build up and impair the flow of blood. If a narrowed artery supplying blood to the heart becomes blocked, this results in a heart attack (or myocardial infarction).

A number of risk factors increase the likelihood of developing CHD. Blood cholesterol level is an important risk factor, but so are other factors such as obesity, smoking, physical inactivity and high blood pressure. The major risk factors for the development of coronary heart disease are:

- raised blood cholesterol
- raised blood pressure
- cigarette smoking
- inactivity
- obesity.

Other risk factors include:

- diabetes
- age
- gender
- family history
- previous heart attack.

These risk factors can be classified according to whether they can be modified or not to reduce overall risk.

Theory into practice

Look at the risk factors above and divide them into two categories based on whether you feel they are modifiable or unmodifiable. Record your ideas in your notebook for discussion with your tutor.

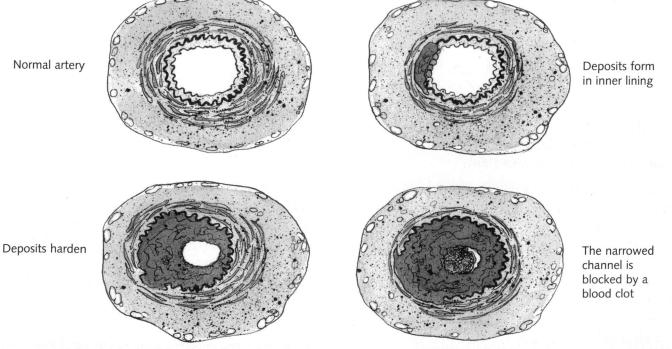

Normal artery

Deposits form in inner lining

Deposits harden

The narrowed channel is blocked by a blood clot

The development of atherosclerosis

The risk of CHD is thought to be reduced by eating less saturated fat and salt and sufficient quantities of omega fats, fruit and vegetables. The COMA Report (1994) on cardiovascular disease has proposed the following recommendations for a cardio-protective diet:

- eat more starchy foods, especially those that are high in fibre
- eat more fruit and vegetables, at least five portions per day
- eat more oily fish, up to two or three times per week
- eat less fat, particularly saturated fat
- eat less salt
- drink alcohol in moderation, only one or two units per day.

Theory into practice

Compare these guidelines to those of the UK National Food Guide. What similarities do you observe? Record your ideas in your notebook for discussion with your tutor.

Cancer

Dietary factors are believed to contribute to the development of some forms of cancer. A report by COMA in 1998 on the nutritional aspects of the development of cancer proposed the following dietary recommendations for protection against cancer:

- maintain a healthy body weight
- eat more fruits and vegetables, at least five portions each day
- increase intake of non-starch polysaccharide
- decrease intake of red and processed meat.

It is advised that these recommendations are followed in the context of the wider recommendations for a healthy balanced diet rich in cereals, fruit and vegetables. Again you will have noticed many similarities with general recommendations for healthy eating.

Eating disorders

The incidence of eating disorders has grown in recent years. In today's society there are immense pressures to be thin, and disordered eating patterns are particularly common among fitness and sports participants. Some individuals will go to great lengths to achieve a desirable body image, failing to eat a well-balanced diet as a result of their attitudes towards food intake.

Anorexia nervosa (starving oneself) and **bulimia nervosa** (binge eating) are the two extremes of disordered eating, but are not primarily about food. They are usually symptoms of underlying emotional and psychological suffering. Eating disorders can be caused and maintained by a variety of different factors, but can often start with dieting.

Women are more likely to develop eating disorders than men. Anorexia nervosa usually develops between the ages of 15 and 25, and many sufferers may go on to develop bulimia nervosa at a later stage. People who have low self-esteem and perfectionist tendencies are particularly vulnerable to developing these conditions. Those with eating disorders become over-concerned with body shape and weight. Both conditions cause physical and psychological suffering and may even result in death. The first step in the treatment process of both of these conditions is the recognition of the problem by the sufferer.

Eating disorders are common among sportspeople, particularly females. Evidence suggests that sportspeople often have a higher level of body dissatisfaction, and a greater preoccupation with their body weight and shape. These traits could result from the emphasis placed on the aesthetic qualities required for success in some sports, such as gymnastics, figure skating and diving, or the perceived requirement for a low body weight for success in other sports such as distance running.

Researchers have been able to identify common personality characteristics in those at risk of developing disordered eating patterns. These include perfectionism, compulsiveness, obsession, competitiveness and high degrees of self-motivation. These could be viewed as the essential traits required by elite sports performers!

A person with anorexia nervosa diets and often exercises excessively, reducing the body weight to a level at least 15% below the average expected weight for his or her height. In women sufferers there will be a loss of menstrual periods. They will usually display an intense fear of becoming fat but will often deny this at all costs, especially if confronted about their eating behaviour. Low self-esteem is another common feature, connected with body weight and shape. Sufferers are often extremely knowledgeable about food and particularly its calorie content, due to their preoccupation with such issues.

Individuals with bulimia nervosa will suffer episodes of binge eating, in which vast quantities of food are consumed in a short space of time, during which they will feel unable to control their behaviour. To inhibit weight gain they may self-induce vomiting, misuse laxatives, fast, or exercise excessively. Bulimia nervosa may be more difficult to detect as many sufferers are of normal body weight.

Those suffering from an eating disorder will usually attempt to keep their behaviour secret and may deny that they have a problem if confronted. Sufferers often remain ambivalent about receiving help to change their behaviour, as the disorder becomes a way of coping with life. These conditions are complex mental and physical disorders that do not usually improve without help. In serious cases, medical treatment by a team of qualified professionals including doctors, psychologists and dietitians is required.

As you will have discovered in previous sections, maintaining an optimal body weight is a key health goal, but eating-disordered behaviour is not the means to achieve this. If you or a friend or relative exhibit any of the behaviours identified here, help can be sought from your doctor or the Eating Disorders Association, whose address and telephone helpline numbers can be found in the Resources list at the end of this unit.

Warning signs for anorexia nervosa and bulimia nervosa	
Anorexia nervosa	**Bulimia nervosa**
Dramatic loss of weight	Noticeable weight loss or weight gain or frequent weight fluctuations
Preoccupation with food, calories, and body weight	Excessive concern about body weight and shape
Cessation of the menstrual cycle in females	Irregular menstrual cycle in females
Social withdrawal, preferring to eat alone	Secret eating
Irritability, depression and anxiety	Disappearing after eating
Excessive or obsessive exercising	Mood swings, irritability, depression and anxiety
	Poor dental and gum health
	Calluses on the back of the hand from self-induced vomiting

Nutrition professionals

The British Dietetic Association (BDA)

The British Dietetic Association is the professional association for qualified dietitians in the UK and was founded in 1936. To be a member of the BDA, dietitians must hold a recognised qualification that provides them with state registration. All State Registered Dietitians (SRD) are bound to work within a professional code of conduct as set out by the Council for Health Care Professions, and to provide safe and unbiased information regarding nutrition.

The work of a dietitian can be undertaken in a variety of settings, with a wide range of different people who have different nutritional needs and problems. Dietitians are qualified to translate often complex scientific information about food and nutritional issues into straightforward practical dietary advice. As well as providing impartial advice about nutrition and health issues, they also counsel on food-related problems, such as food allergy or intolerance, and treat those suffering from ill health and disease.

Most dietitians in the UK work within the National Health Service, with many working in one or more of the specialist areas of dietetics – for example diabetes, cardiac rehabilitation, children's health, cancer, HIV and Aids. Others work with people in the community in GPs' surgeries, day centres and schools or by visiting people in their own homes. Some work in the food industry, or for food supplement companies; others work in sport, while some are involved in furthering the scientific understanding of nutrition through research. With the ever-growing public interest in nutrition and health, many dietitians now work in journalism or with the media to ensure that reliable and correct messages concerning nutrition are communicated to an often confused public.

Accredited Sports Dietitians are State Registered Dietitians who have undertaken further specialist training in the area of sports nutrition and exercise physiology. They help sportspeople to understand what, when and how much they should eat and drink to support their preparation for, participation in, and recovery from sport and exercise. Their work may involve liaising with sports teams and their coaches to provide a wide range of information on topics such as sports drinks and supplements, as well as a providing practical support on issues such as monitoring fluid balance and hydration.

The Nutrition Society

Nutritionists research and apply scientific knowledge to promote understanding of the effects of diet on the health and well being of animals and humans, but do not work with individual patients or clients to prescribe specific dietary advice in the same way as State Registered Dietitians. The Nutrition Society acknowledges quality in the practice of its members by awarding the titles of Registered Nutritionist and Registered Public Health Nutritionist.

Public Health Nutritionists apply the science of nutrition for the benefit of the population as a whole, or specific groups within the population such as children or the elderly. They study the interactions between diet and diseases in the population, for example heart disease and cancer, as well as deficiency disorders such as anaemia. Public Health Nutritionists may also be involved in nutritional aspects of health promotion. The Nutrition Society sets and promotes high standards, enabling employers, the media, and of course, the general public to identify appropriately qualified individuals when seeking nutritional information. Members on the register are expected to adhere to the society's Code of Ethics.

Nutritional strategies

In this section we will focus on some of the issues you may have identified in your investigation into the influences of nutrition on health and performance for the activity on page 36. We will consider in more detail the impact that nutrition and eating habits might have on performance in sport and exercise. In particular, we will take a closer look at fuels and fluids and identify practical strategies for athletes and sportspeople to keep fuelled and hydrated.

What you need to learn

- The nutritional demands of different sports
- Nutritional strategies to support the preparation for, participation in and recovery from sport and exercise
- Nutritional strategies to support injury and illness.

Key concept

All physical activity stimulates the body's need for fuel and fluid, and good nutrition is vital to both health and performance. Achieving adequate energy and fluid intakes should be the most important nutritional considerations of all those regularly engaged in competitive sport.

Energy is measured in kilocalories (often called simply calories) and kilojoules, with 1 kcal equal to 4.2kJ. As outlined in earlier sections of this unit, the different macronutrients, along with alcohol, supply different amounts of energy per unit of weight:

1 g protein   = 4.0 kcal = 17 kJ

1 g carbohydrate = 4.0 kcal = 17 kJ

1 g alcohol   = 7.0 kcal = 29 kJ

1 g fat   = 9.0 kcal = 38 kJ

Achieving an adequate energy intake should be the most important nutritional consideration of all sportspeople. Individual energy requirements are related to age, sex and body mass, along with activity rates, taking into account factors such as intensity, frequency and duration.

The potential fuels available to our exercising muscles as an energy source are listed above. However, their relative value as fuels for activity differs. Protein may be used during prolonged periods of exercise and towards the latter stages of endurance events like the marathon, for example, particularly if fat and carbohydrate as sources of fuel within the working muscles have become limited. Alcohol, as you know, cannot be metabolised by working muscles. That leaves fat and carbohydrate, which are stored in the muscles as glycogen, as the main energy fuels for exercising muscles. Exercising muscles prefer glucose as a fuel, particularly as the intensity of the activity being undertaken increases.

When we exercise, our muscles use energy at a rate that is directly proportional to the intensity of the activity we are undertaking. If this energy is not replaced as it is used up, the muscles are unable to maintain their rate of work and the intensity of the activity will need to be reduced or even stopped as fatigue sets in.

Energy is produced within our muscles when muscle cells (resembling miniature power stations) burn up fuel, carbohydrate and fatty acids, in the presence of oxygen, to make a biochemical known as **adenosine triphosphate** (ATP). This is the substance that makes our muscles work. The process is known as **aerobic metabolism** as oxygen is required to support the process. ATP can also be formed without the presence of oxygen by **anaerobic metabolism**. In this case only

carbohydrate is used for fuel. If carbohydrate is not available the intensity of the activity has to be reduced to a level where energy requirements can be met by fat.

Theory into practice

For the following activities, consider whether it is fat or carbohydrate that contributes the majority of energy:

- sprinting 100 m
- running a marathon
- walking
- team sports such as soccer and rugby.

Maintaining glycogen stores is essential to successful sports performance, and a high carbohydrate diet is crucial to maintaining optimal stores. As mentioned earlier, 50-60% of the sportsperson's total daily energy intake should be consumed in the form of carbohydrate. Unfortunately the body is able to store only a limited supply of energy as glycogen, so stores need to be replenished regularly. In order to keep these stores optimal, sportspeople should aim to eat a high carbohydrate diet at all times, eat a carbohydrate-rich meal or snack 1-4 hours prior to training or competition to maximise glycogen stores, and try to eat a carbohydrate-rich snack within the first half hour to two hours after training or competition when the muscles' capacity to restock glycogen stores is at its greatest.

Carbohydrate loading can be used by endurance athletes

Theory into practice

Devise a five-point plan for a sports performer to maintain optimal glycogen stores. You may choose to use this plan later when formulating recommendations for your case study.

Carbohydrate loading

As previously discussed, the amount of glycogen available for storage in our muscles is related to the amount of carbohydrate consumed in our diet and the level and intensity of activity undertaken. For most sports, eating a diet that consists of 5-10 g of carbohydrate per kilogram of body weight will maintain liver and muscle glycogen stores. However, the aim of carbohydrate loading is to increase the capacity of the muscles to store glycogen above their normal level. This may be useful to sportspeople who compete in endurance events that last longer than 90 minutes, such as marathon running, triathlons and endurance swimming.

Key concept

The goal of carbohydrate loading is to increase the capacity of the muscles to store glycogen above their normal level, usually in preparation for an endurance event.

When muscle cells run out of glycogen, fatigue will occur. High pre-event glycogen stores should help to delay the onset of fatigue and improve

performance during the latter stages of an endurance event.

Exercise scientists have discovered that it is possible to encourage muscles to store more glycogen than normal by the process of glycogen supercompensation. The traditional carbohydrate-loading regime, developed in the 1960s by Scandinavian scientists working with endurance cyclists, involved completing an exhaustive bout of exercise seven days prior to the endurance event to deplete the muscles of glycogen, followed by three days of carbohydrate starvation and continued training to further deplete stores, with a switch to a three-day loading phase with a high carbohydrate diet – for most this would require a carbohydrate intake close to or in excess of 10 g per kilogram of body weight – and very light training during the latter stages of preparation. The general principle behind this approach is that the initial depletion phase causes the muscles to over-compensate during the loading phase, thereby storing more glycogen than usual. However, depletion was shown in some cases to cause feelings of extreme fatigue and irritability and was associated with a reduced resistance to injury and infection. This is not exactly the best preparation for a major endurance event.

More recent studies have been able to demonstrate that equally good results can be achieved by omitting the depletion phase. In this modified version of carbohydrate loading, the sportsperson continues to eat a normal carbohydrate intake of approximately 50-60% of total calorie intake for the first three days of preparation, and increases this up to 70% of calorie intake in the last three days accompanied by a reduction in training intensity. This modified loading technique appears to offer elevated muscle glycogen levels without the need for the depletion phase and the associated negative side effects.

Three to four pounds in weight is typically gained in the last three days of preparation. This is largely water, which is stored with glycogen. While this can make the sports performer feel heavy at the start of the event, the extra fluid will be useful to help to prevent dehydration later on.

Although carbohydrate loading as described here will not benefit all sports performers, all those regularly training and competing in sports should focus on consuming a high carbohydrate diet at all times, and will benefit from a carbohydrate-rich meal or snack before training or competition.

Modified carbohydrate loading guide		
Days before race	Training intensity and duration	Dietary carbohydrate intake
7	Intense 90 mins	Usual 50-60% carbohydrate diet
6	Moderate 45-50 mins	Usual 50-60% carbohydrate diet
5	Moderate 40-45 mins	Usual 50-60% carbohydrate diet
4	Moderate 30 mins	Usual 50-60% carbohydrate diet
3	Moderate 20 mins	70% carbohydrate diet
2	Light 20 mins	70% carbohydrate diet
1	Rest	70% carbohydrate diet
Race day		High carbohydrate pre-race meal

Fluid balance and hydration

As previously discussed, water is one of the most important nutrients required by the body. Water losses may be as high as a litre per hour during endurance-type exercise. This could be even higher if the exercise takes place in hot or humid conditions.

Fluid losses incurred by sportspeople during training and competition are linked to the body's need to maintain temperature within very narrow limits. During exercise, body temperature rises and the extra heat this produces is lost through sweating, the process of evaporation of water from the skin's surface. If fluid lost through sweating is not replaced there is a risk of dehydration and performance may suffer.

Dehydration can affect performance by reducing strength, power, and aerobic capacity, while severe dehydration can cause heat stroke and has the potential to be fatal. A loss as small as 2% of body mass can be enough to begin to affect ability to perform muscular work. For a 75 kg male this would be equivalent to fluid loss of only $1\frac{1}{2}$ litres from the body. It is therefore important to minimise the risks of dehydration, and very important to note that thirst is a poor indicator of the body's hydration status.

In an attempt to minimise the effects of fluid loss during training and competition, sportspeople should always be encouraged to begin fully hydrated and to drink plenty both during and after the activity. Establishing patterns of fluid intake should be an integral part of the training process of all those engaged in competitive sporting activities. Training should be used as the opportunity to practise well-rehearsed fluid replacement strategies that run smoothly in competitive situations.

Key concept

Dehydration can hinder performance by affecting strength, power, and aerobic capacity.

Sportspeople should drink plenty of water

Many factors can influence the effectiveness of fluid replacement strategies. Fluid replacement can be speeded by drinking still, cool drinks of a reasonable volume that are not too concentrated, and they obviously must be palatable to drink. The more intense the activity undertaken, the more the absorption of fluid is slowed. Unpleasant symptoms experienced when drinking during exercise usually mean the sportsperson has left it too late to start drinking and the body is already dehydrated.

Weight and urine colour checks can provide a very useful and simple way of monitoring fluid status during and after training. A weight reduction of 1 kg during a training session is equivalent to a 1 litre fluid loss. Frequent trips to the toilet to pass plentiful quantities of pale-coloured urine are an indicator of good hydration, whereas scant quantities of dark-coloured urine would indicate a

poor level of hydration. These simple weight and urine checks before and after exercise can provide useful tools to assist in determining fluid requirements post-training or during competition.

Fluid replacement strategies for exercise		
Before	**During**	**After**
300-500ml 20-30 minutes before activity	150-300ml every 15-20 minutes **or** 600-1200ml/h	Based on body mass lost, replace losses by 150%

Theory into practice

Devise a simple five-point plan to ensure that sportspeople maintain an adequate state of hydration. You may choose to use this plan later when formulating recommendations for your case study.

Categories of sport

The vast array of sports that exist can be categorised into the following groups:

- multi-sprint or team sports such as soccer
- strength sports such as sprinting
- endurance and ultra-endurance sports such as marathon running and the triathlon
- weight category sports such as boxing
- aesthetic sports such as diving.

Each of these categories of sport requires sound nutritional strategies to support successful performance. Winning, avoiding injury and illness, and improving fitness are what matter to most competitive sportspeople. With the intermittent nature of team sports, the intensity at which they are performed can alter at any time. These changes in intensity are irregular and can be random, and may draw significantly on the body's glycogen stores. Performance may be impaired towards the end of a match if glycogen stores are running low.

Numerous weight loss methods and restrictive dietary practices are commonly used by sportspeople within weight category and aesthetic sports, with potential dangers to both health and performance.

Theory into practice

Choose a sport which is not named in the bullet points above. Consider which category of sport it belongs to and examine the specific nutritional practices and requirements associated with the sport. Record the findings of your research in your notebook for discussion with your tutor.

Performance eating

Optimal performance in sport and exercise requires optimal nutrition. Sportspeople should pay careful attention to foods that can enhance, not hinder, their preparation for, participation in and recovery from training and competition. Most sportspeople will obtain all the energy and nutrients they need by eating to appetite and choosing a balanced and varied diet. This section will consider simple techniques for estimating energy, macronutrient and fluid requirements and suggest practical nutritional strategies to assist sportspeople in achieving an adequate diet to support health and performance.

Key concept

Good nutrition has a big part to play in aiding recovery between training sessions, allowing the sports performer to realise adaptations in response to the training programme.

Theory into practice

Sportspeople face a number of problems in achieving adequate nutritional intakes. Spend 10 minutes considering the dilemmas that may face sportspeople in achieving their nutritional requirements and record your thoughts in your notebook for discussion with your tutor.

When developing sound eating habits and nutritional strategies to support training and competition, the following issues are important:

- the types of food eaten to support training and competition
- the timing of meals and snacks around training and competition
- ensuring a balanced diet is achieved in respect of all nutrients
- maintaining a sufficient fluid intake
- encouraging an adequate calcium and iron intake, particularly for females
- promoting long-term health and reducing the risk of chronic disease
- the problems of travelling to training and competition venues
- minimising the risk of injury and illness.

The nutritional requirements for different sports and sportspeople will vary according to:

- the type of sport and training methods undertaken
- the intensity of training or competition
- the duration of training or competition
- the frequency of training or competition
- the training status and fitness level of the sportsperson.

Good nutrition can make its greatest contribution in aiding recovery between training sessions. For the regular sports performer, performance improvements are the product of the body's adaptation to the demands of training. Sound nutrition has its biggest impact in supporting the sports performer in training consistently and effectively to achieve the desired adaptations. To achieve steady improvements, all sportspeople must ensure that their diet consistently meets the demands placed on their bodies by training and competition.

The Balance of Good Health principles (see page 28) should be used to plan meals. These principles should form the foundations on which to develop more specific sports nutrition strategies. Sportspeople should be encouraged to eat sufficient carbohydrate and start refuelling as soon as possible after training, when muscle capacity to refuel is at its greatest. This may mean avoiding the restriction of traditional meals times. Eating may need to be fitted in around the training process, with smaller, more frequent meals and snacks being necessary. Snacks and fluids should be carried in the kit bag at all times.

Rest days are also important, and this time should be used to recover from the stresses of training and competition. A high fluid intake should be encouraged at all times. In many sports, post-match alcohol consumption is part of traditional practices, but it is important to rehydrate with other fluids before drinking alcohol after training and competition. Where an injury has been sustained, alcohol consumption may delay the recovery process and should be avoided for at least 48 hours.

Theory into practice

1 Devise a list of simple training and competition guidelines for sportspeople. You may choose to use this list when advising your case study.
2 To support this list of guidelines, identify a number of appropriate items for the kit bag that could be used to replenish energy stores and fluid balance after exercise.

Estimating energy and macronutrient requirements

You can use the following simple techniques to estimate energy, macronutrient and fluid requirements. To estimate energy requirements you first need to calculate basal metabolic requirements (BMR) in kilocalories per day, by using the following equation. W is weight in kilograms.

Males	10-17yrs	BMR = 17.7W + 657
	18-29yrs	BMR = 15.1W + 692
	30-59yrs	BMR = 11.5W + 873
	60-74yrs	BMR = 11.9W + 700
Females	10-17yrs	BMR = 13.4W + 692
	18-29yrs	BMR = 14.8W + 487
	30-59yrs	BMR = 8.3W + 846
	60-74yrs	BMR = 9.2W + 687

Schofield et al, 1985

Theory into practice

Calculate your BMR and record your answer in kilocalories per day in your notebook for later discussion with your tutor.

To estimate your total energy requirements you also need to consider your level of physical activity and training. The simplest method of estimating your total energy requirement is by multiplying your BMR by your PAL (physical activity level). Calculating PALs requires you to make an assumption about the energy demands of both your occupational and non-occupational activity levels. Refer to the table on the next page. M = Male and F = Female.

PALs for three levels each of occupational and non-occupational activity						
Non-occupational activity	Occupational activity					
	Light		Moderate		Heavy	
	M	F	M	F	M	F
Non-active	1.4	1.4	1.6	1.5	1.7	1.5
Moderately active	1.5	1.5	1.7	1.6	1.8	1.6
Very active	1.6	1.6	1.8	1.7	1.9	1.7

Dept of Health COMA Report 41 (1991)

Theory into practice

Calculate your total energy requirements using the PAL that corresponds to your occupational and non-occupational activity levels, and record your answer in kilocalories in your notebook for discussion with your tutor.

Once you have calculated an estimate for total energy requirements, the amount of carbohydrate, fat and protein you require can be predicted. Remember, in general sportspeople require an energy distribution of 50-60% of calories from carbohydrate, 12-15% from protein and 25-30% from fat.

Theory into practice

For this exercise, assume you are a sportsperson in regular training and calculate the calories required in your diet to be contributed by the three different macronutrients. Record your answers in kilocalories in your notebook for discussion with your tutor.

Once you know how many kilocalories are required from each of the three macronutrients, you can calculate the number of grams of each that you need, remembering that carbohydrate and protein provide 4 calories per gram and fat 9 calories per gram.

Theory into practice

Calculate the grams of carbohydrate, protein and fat required in your diet by dividing the kilocalories required by the appropriate energy value, and record your answers in your notebook for discussion with your tutor.

Theory into practice

Plan a day's diet for a female endurance athlete who has an energy requirement of 2500 kilocalories. In particular, pay attention to achieving an adequate carbohydrate intake and calculate the amount of energy to be contributed by carbohydrate, and the number of grams of carbohydrate this equates to.

A template to assist you with this activity can be found in Menu Plan 3 on page 70 at the end of this unit.

Estimating fluid requirements

Normal fluid requirements are in the region of 30-35 mls per kilogram of body weight per day, or 1 ml per calorie of energy requirement. As a rough guide, therefore, basic fluid requirements based on body weight can be estimated using the following formula:

Fluid requirement = 30-35 mls per kg body weight

Fluid requirements can also be predicted from calculations to estimate energy requirements. But remember, as discussed earlier, additional fluid will be required by sportspeople to cover sweat losses both during and after training and competition.

Theory into practice

1 Using either of the methods identified above, estimate your basic daily fluid requirements.
2 Consider how you could monitor you fluid status during exercise. Record your thoughts in your notebook for discussion with your tutor.

Food selection

Before training or competition

Essentially many of the principles of preparing for a competition mirror those of the training diet. For a competition, the pre-event meal should aim to top up muscle and liver glycogen stores and should therefore be carbohydrate rich, but also low in fat and fibre and contain a moderate amount of protein. It should be remembered that larger meals will take longer to digest and that nerves can result in delayed digestion.

Competition is not a time to experiment with new foods. The pre-event meal should therefore be composed of familiar foods, and also provide adequate fluids. Solid foods can usually be consumed with comfort up to two hours before an event, but liquid meals or carbohydrate drinks can be consumed up to 30 or 60 minutes before.

Sports performers engaging in events lasting longer than 90 minutes should be advised, where possible, to taper training in the week leading up to the event, include a rest day, and consume a higher than normal carbohydrate and fluid intake.

Theory into practice

Devise suitable pre-event meal strategies for use by sportspeople competing at the different times of day identified below.

- 9.30 am (early morning competition)
- 2.30 pm (afternoon competition)
- 6.00 pm (early evening competition).

Record your ideas in your notebook for discussion with your tutor.

During training or competition

During training and competition, fluid loss is a major consideration. During intense training or competition isotonic sports drinks – which assist with fluid replacement but also provide a source of fuel – may be beneficial especially if training or competition lasts longer than 60 minutes. During endurance or ultra-endurance events lasting longer than four hours, solid foods may be required. In these instances energy bars or gels might be useful as a more concentrated source of carbohydrate. Regular sports performers should be encouraged to practise their fluid and fuelling regimes in training to ensure that they do not run into any unexpected problems during competition.

After training or competition

What is consumed, how much and how soon after an intense workout or competition can all influence the recovery process. Refuelling should begin as soon as possible. Sensible choices in terms of food and fluids will allow the sports performer to recover more quickly for the next training session, particularly for those in intense training or those who have multiple daily workouts, or rounds of a competition.

It is important to refuel as soon as possible after each workout or competition. The longer refuelling is delayed the longer it will take to fully refuel. The sports performer may find it easier to have more small, frequent meals and snacks at regularly spaced intervals to help to maximise glycogen synthesis.

To refuel efficiently a high carbohydrate diet is required. Post-exercise carbohydrates that are easy to eat and digest are preferred. Sports performers should be advised to consume a high-carbohydrate (at least 50 g) low-fat snack as soon as possible after training or competition, preferably within the first half hour, when the muscles' capacity to refuel is at its greatest, and ensure that they eat their next meal, which should be rich in carbohydrate, within two hours.

After exercise, the replacement of fluids lost through sweating should also be a priority. Rehydration should start immediately. Drinks containing carbohydrates will also assist with energy and glycogen replacement. These may be particularly useful if the activity has been very intense and resulted in a suppression of appetite and a reluctance to eat solid foods.

After training or competition, high-carbohydrate, low-fat snacks and plenty of fluid are needed

Theory into practice

Through a variety of means, research the range of sports drinks available for discussion with your tutor. Pay particular attention to the three different types of sports drink: hypotonic, isotonic and hypertonic, and when these might best be used.

Case study

1 Jon is competing in a national badminton tournament tomorrow. Suggest a suitable pre-competition meal and provide some advice on how he might ensure that he keeps fuelled and hydrated during the tournament.

2 Sayeed has recently taken up the triathlon. His usual diet consists of a macronutrient energy distribution of 40% carbohydrate, 40% fat and 20% protein. He is about to enter his first major competition.

- What effect could this macronutrient distribution have on his performance?
- What practical advice could you offer to improve his diet?
- What could Sayeed do in his preparation for the competition to help to delay fatigue?

Sports supplements and ergogenic aids

Sportspeople are always looking for something that will provide them with a competitive advantage. Some try to achieve this through dietary manipulation, such as carbohydrate loading; others use ergogenic aids such as creatine. Fad diets and misconceptions regarding training, pre-event and weight control meals are prevalent in sport. The financial cost of these practices and nutritional supplements is often high, and misinformation is often used to support practices that are at best questionable and often harmful. Sportspeople may be better rewarded by investing their money in other credible aspects of sports science support, such as qualified nutritional advice, sports psychology and better training techniques and equipment.

Think it over

As a group, allocate dietary practices and supplements to be investigated individually or in pairs. Discuss the nature of this activity with your tutor.

Research the dietary practice or supplement you have been assigned, particularly its safety and effectiveness, and the rationale for its use in sport.

What is the cost of the practice or supplement? Is it worth the expense?

Share the findings of your research with your group, and answer any questions they may have on the dietary practice, nutrient supplement or ergogenic aid you have investigated.

Assessment activity 8.1

As you have discovered, sound nutritional practices are important to athletic performance. All physical activity stimulates the body's need for fuel and fluids.

1 Identify **two** sportspeople who participate in different sports and on whom you can undertake the process of dietary assessment. You may wish to consider your own diet if you are actively engaged in sport at a competitive level, and use the information you have gathered through the practical activities undertaken in this unit.

2 Select an appropriate method to collect dietary intake information from these sportspeople. Analyse the information you have obtained and write a report on your findings which suggests, where necessary, appropriate modifications or improvements to support the health and performance of these individuals.

To assist you in this task, use a combination of manual and computer-based methods of processing and analysing nutrient intake information. In presenting your report you may want to look back at the activities you have undertaken while working through this unit.

Weight management

We have already seen that nutrition is an integral part of health and fitness. Recent surveys suggest that around one in five men and one in three women are currently trying to lose weight. Countless people take up sport or exercise in an attempt to lose or control body weight, while being an appropriate weight, size or body shape may be important for many sports.

What you need to learn

- The difference between body type and body composition
- The advantages and disadvantages of different methods of assessing weight and body composition
- The safety and effectiveness of different weight loss techniques
- Safe and effective weight management strategies to lose or gain weight.

Key concept

Successful weight management relies on maintaining the balance between energy intake and energy expenditure.

Body image

As you have already discovered in the section on eating disorders, body image can have a significant influence on an individual's eating and exercise habits. Objective measures of body type and body composition can help in constructing and monitoring exercise and lifestyle modification programmes to manage weight.

As you will already be aware, individuals come in a variety of different shapes and sizes. However, the most commonly used method of classification of body type is known as **somatotyping**. This classification method recognises three basic body types.

- The **endomorph** is someone who has a heavy build, rounded shape, a tendency to gain weight, and generally finds weight loss difficult.
- The **mesomorph** is someone who has a muscular build and large bone structure.
- The **ectomorph** has a slim build, long limbs, and delicate bone structure, with a low body fat and muscle content, and usually finds it difficult to gain weight.

| Mesomorph | Ectomorph | Endomorph |

The three basic somatotypes

Very few individuals fit neatly into these extremes. Most of us own characteristics of each body type to a varying degree, and although it is fashionable for many women in particular to want to be slim and ectomorph-like, it is important to note that it is not possible to alter our basic body type.

Body mass index (BMI)

The body mass index is an index of body fatness. BMI is the ratio of body mass expressed in kilograms to the square of height in metres.

BMI = body mass in kg ÷ height in m²

BMI assumes that there is no single weight for a person of a specific height, but that there is a healthy weight range for any given height. BMI can be used to classify different grades of weight. A ratio between 20 and 24.9 is deemed desirable for both men and women. Values above this level are associated with increased risk of disease. Extremely muscular individuals, such as

sportspeople involved in strength sports, may have high values, but these will not reflect the same degree of risk as those of a sedentary individual with the same BMI.

BMI classifications	
< 20	underweight
20–24.9	healthy desirable weight
25–29.9	overweight
30–40	moderately obese
40+	severely obese

Theory into practice

1 Using your weight and height, calculate your BMI and determine your BMI classification.

2 Consider any limitations there may be to using BMI and its classifications. Record your thoughts in your notebook for discussion with your tutor.

Waist circumference

More recently this measure of fatness has become a common index for determining health risk, particularly of coronary heart disease. The theory behind this measure is that a high percentage of body fat particularly in the abdominal region is associated with an increase in risk of CHD. A waist circumference of more than 94 cm in men and more than 80 cm in women suggests central obesity.

Body composition

The body is composed of a perplexing number of cells, tissues, organs and systems but the components of most interest to exercise scientists and nutritionists are muscle, bone and fat. Body composition simply refers to the amount of lean body mass and body fat that makes up our total body weight. Lean body mass includes the bones, muscle, water, connective and organ tissues. Body fat includes both our essential and non-essential fat stores.

In relation to health, it is fat weight not total body weight that is most important in determining risks. Total body weight alone is of little importance, particularly with sportspeople, but too many people base their weight loss regimes on what they see on the bathroom scales. Although weight is useful in some respects, body composition has become a more important health indicator.

Sportspeople and those actively engaged in fitness regimes are often concerned about their weight, whether for performance or health reasons. Unlike your basic body type, it is possible to alter your body composition, with exercise generally having the effect of increasing lean body mass and decreasing body fat. On the whole women tend to have a greater percentage of their total body weight as fat. Average figures are around 25% of total body weight as fat for adult women, and about 15% for adult men.

Methods of assessing body composition include:

- skinfold thickness
- underwater or hydrostatic weighing

- body impedance analysis
- near infra-red interactance
- body plethysmography.

All of these methods (which are outlined below) have most merit in measuring changes in body composition over time, rather than absolute values. A number of steps can be taken to minimise potential errors in measuring changes in body composition over time:

- always use the same method
- ensure the subject is always assessed by the same person
- take repeat measurements at the same time of day.

Skinfold thickness

With this technique callipers are used to measure the thickness of skinfolds at various sites, with the biceps, triceps, sub scapula and supra iliac crest being the most common anatomical sites of measurement.

The sum of these measurements is then used to calculate percentage body fat, using a method that takes into account the age and sex of the subject using equations or tables. This is a relatively cheap and convenient method, but does require a high degree of skill. This method is thought to be generally reliable if performed correctly but has been shown to have an error margin of ± 3-4% and may not be effective for use on very fat or very thin subjects.

Underwater or hydrostatic weighing

This is considered to be one of the most accurate methods of assessment of body composition. However, it is expensive and time consuming to perform and can be potentially stressful to the subject, requiring him or her to be totally submerged in water. The technique measures body density that can be translated mathematically into percentage body fat, and relies on Archimedes' principle of water displacement to estimate body density. As a technique it is rarely used, because of its expense.

Body impedance analysis (BIA)

BIA is fast becoming the standard technique for assessment of body composition, particularly in the health and fitness sector. Bioelectrical impedance machines have an advantage over callipers in providing a quick, easy and non-invasive method of estimating percentage body fat. There is now a range of equipment that uses BIA principles to assess body composition. Some require the attachment of electrodes to the hands and feet of the subject (Bodystat), others require the subject to stand on specially designed scales (Tanita) or grip handles (Omron).

BIA measures the resistance to the flow of an electrical current through the body, using the fact that different body tissues display different impedance to the flow of the current. Tissues that contain a large amount of water, such as lean tissue, provide a lower impedance than tissues such as bone and fat.

When using BIA techniques a number of assumptions have to be made, and equations applied, to obtain a body fat percentage figure. One potential drawback to this method is that impedance measurements are related to the water content of tissues. This means that for accurate results, subjects must be fully hydrated, and they are required to abstain from exercise and substances which exert a diuretic effect – such as alcohol or caffeine – for a period of at least 24 hours prior to the test. Invalid results may also be obtained for women if they are measured immediately before or during menstruation, when the body water content may be higher than normal.

Near infra-red

In this method a wand emitting infra-red light is placed against (usually) the biceps muscle of the upper arm. The infra-red beam contains two specially selected frequencies which interact with chemical bonds found in high concentrations in fatty tissue, but which do not interact with those found in lean tissue. The fattier the tissue the less infra-red light is reflected back to the wand. An equation is then used to calculate percentage body fat taking into account weight, height, sex and a calculation called FIT: the product of exercise frequency, intensity and duration.

Body plethysmography

This is a relatively new and expensive method of assessing body composition which applies the gas law to determine body volume. It requires the subject to sit in a structure resembling a pod (hence the nickname 'Bod Pod'), comprised of two chambers, both of a known volume. Changes in pressure between the two chambers are recorded and various equations are applied to compute the percentage of body fat.

Theory into practice

Using the Internet, undertake a search using the search term 'body composition assessment'. Evaluate the range of body composition assessment products available in terms of their affordability, ease of application and suitability for use with sports performers.

Record your findings in your notebook for discussion with your tutor.

Weight loss approaches

More than half of the UK population is now fatter than considered to be ideal for health. One pound of fat is approximately equivalent to 3500 kilocalories. As previously discussed, an individual is said to be in energy balance if energy intake is equal to energy output. When energy input exceeds energy output the excess energy will be stored as fat or must be used up in activity if weight gain is to be avoided.

Since there is no magic way to lose weight, in an attempt to reduce weight one can reduce energy intake by eating less. However, one of the major problems associated with the restriction of energy intake over long periods is ensuring that the nutritional quality of the diet is maintained. Chronic calorie restriction also leads to the loss of other tissues as well as body fat. This results in a series of changes that alter energy output and slow down the rate at which the body's fat stores are reduced. When attempting to lose weight it is important not to over-restrict energy intake as this can be detrimental to health and impair performance in sport and exercise.

Instead of altering calorie intake, those trying to reduce weight can increase the amount of energy expended by taking more exercise or increasing the intensity of physical activity, but to lose a pound of weight a week this would require the equivalent of a daily six-mile run, which is hardly realistic for most of the overweight population. Therefore, the most effective way to reduce weight is thought to be a combination of a sensible reduction in energy intake with a progressive programme of increased physical activity to bring about a negative energy balance of 500-600 kilocalories per day.

Erratic attempts at dieting to cut down calories and lose weight are commonplace in today's weight-conscious society, but the long-term effectiveness of the vast range of slimming diets, dieting products and commercial weight-reduction programmes is often questionable – some even have the potential to be considered harmful to health.

Think it over

Working in a small group:

1 Consider the vast array of weight-loss methods now available to those seeking to lose weight.

2 Identify potential problems with any of these methods in terms of their safety and effectiveness. In considering their effectiveness you should particularly think about their role in weight maintenance once weight loss has been achieved.

Dieting has a high failure rate for many who seek weight loss. There may be many reasons for this, with a social, psychological or physiological basis. From a social standpoint individual lifestyles make it difficult to adhere to the strict dieting regimes prescribed by many of the 'fad' dieting practices that you may have identified, particularly those that are very restrictive in terms of choice and variety. Psychologically, binge eating can result from the 'all or nothing' syndrome, with dieters believing they are either 'on' or 'off' a diet and being unable to moderate dietary intake sensibly. Physiologically, changes resulting from substantially decreased food intake result in a reduced metabolism and a reduction in the body's ability to burn calories.

When calorie intake drops significantly below that which is required to function, below a level required to support BMR, the body will compensate by making what it has go further. Metabolic rate falls and the body's ability to store fat increases as a result of an increase in the activity of the enzymes that store fat. Any rapid weight loss achieved in the initial stages of dieting slows, and the dieter often becomes disillusioned and resumes former eating patterns, feeling a failure. Despite loss of some fat in the early stages of the diet, decreases in lean body mass will also have occurred as a result of the body's need to keep a constant supply of blood glucose available to the brain. Where there is a lack of sufficient carbohydrate in the diet, low blood glucose levels give rise to feelings of lethargy and tiredness, and the body slows down, expending less energy. To maintain a constant level of blood glucose the body has to make its own, and it is only able to do this from protein not fat.

It has been estimated that losses in lean body mass can account for up to a quarter of the total weight lost through dieting; on a typical crash diet where up to 6–8 lbs in weight may be lost in a week, as much as 2 lbs of this loss could be lean body mass. This is obviously a significant problem for the dieter, as muscle burns calories. If muscle is lost, the body's ability to burn calories declines, metabolism falls and further weight loss and weight maintenance are even more difficult. Another potential problem is that there is a high probability that if pre-dieting eating habits are resumed the muscle that is lost will be replaced by fat.

Safe and effective weight control

Popular dieting methods include the currently-in-vogue high protein/low carbohydrate diets, commercial slimming clubs, food-combining

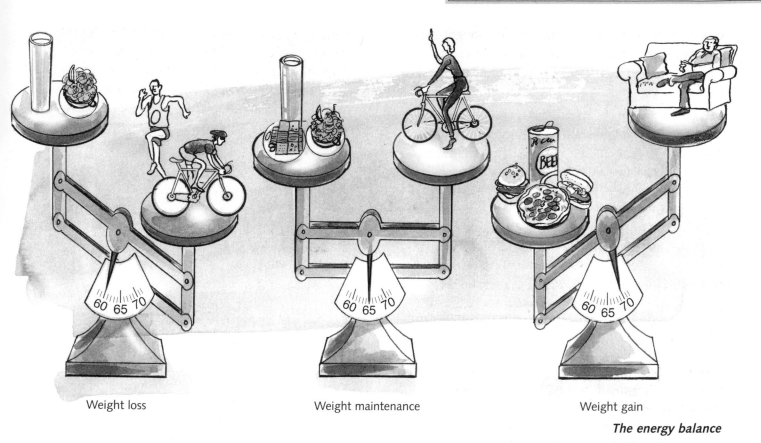

Weight loss   Weight maintenance   Weight gain

The energy balance

methods, meal-replacement products and single-food diets, to name but a few.

Research has shown, however, that a combination of lifestyle changes to diet and activity levels are more likely to result in long-term success than diet or exercise alone.

A healthy diet and exercise programme designed to encourage weight loss should:

- provide realistic and achievable goals for weight loss

- avoid vast reductions in calorie intake

- preserve lean body mass and maintain metabolic rate

- gradually lead to favourable changes in body composition

- ensure a high percentage of energy in the diet from carbohydrates

- maintain a low percentage of energy in the diet from fat

- provide optimal vitamin and minerals intakes

- promote self-monitoring of progress

- encourage physical activity.

A successful diet and exercise programme must also emphasise weight maintenance. This is often overlooked, especially with many 'fad dieting' practises. Anyone can put their mind to losing weight in the short term, but very few people manage to maintain weight loss over a prolonged period of time and they often regain more weight than they have lost once they return to pre-diet eating habits.

Key concept

Successful diet and exercise programmes focus on weight maintenance as a key component.

The role of exercise in weight loss and maintenance

The highly mechanised environment that we live in today has significantly reduced the opportunities open to us to incorporate moderate physical activity into our daily living, but exercise has a crucial role to play in weight loss and weight maintenance.

First, increased physical activity elevates total daily energy expenditure, helping to maintain a higher energy output. In the case of weight loss, it can assist in achieving a negative energy balance. Regular endurance-type exercise improves the ability of our muscles to burn fat as a fuel, while regular resistance-type exercise can help to combat the loss of lean body mass that often occurs as a result of dieting. Gains in lean body mass, contributing to an increase in resting metabolic rate, can further aid weight loss and maintenance by increasing energy requirements even at rest.

The best approach is to undertake a combined programme of progressive cardiorespiratory and resistance training in which training sessions should aim to expend at least 250 kilocalories. A lifelong commitment to regular exercise is essential to facilitate weight maintenance.

Theory into practice

Traditional weight loss programmes are rarely successful, so what do you think would be key features in an ideal weight management programme? Jot down your ideas in your notebook for discussion with your tutor.

Case study

Rachel has a problem with her weight. Over the past 15 years she has attempted to lose weight many times, through a variety of self-motivated 'fad diets' or organised commercial weight-loss programmes. Each time she has been successful in losing weight, but later regained the weight lost and usually more besides.

Her last attempt was through a popular commercial weight-loss programme that advised a negative energy balance of around 600 kilocalories per day and encouraged a programme of regular physical activity. Within 3-4 months Rachel had achieved her target weight, but in doing so she had restricted her calorie intake

further than recommended by the programme as she had found it difficult to adhere to a programme of regular physical activity. Once she had achieved her target weight she maintained the diet for another month, but after a holiday where she had been more relaxed about her diet she returned to her normal pre-diet eating habits. Her weight began to increase slowly at first, but within 3-4 months it had exceeded her pre-diet weight.

Consider what might have happened to cause this. Jot down your thoughts in your notebook for discussion with your tutor.

Gaining weight

For some people, weight management is about gaining weight, not losing it. Weight can be gained in two ways: by increasing the amount of fat or the amount of lean body mass. Both will register as increases in weight on the scales, but the results will be very different in terms of body composition.

Gains in fat weight are relatively easy to achieve – as most people wishing to lose weight would testify – but gains in lean body mass can only be achieved as a result of adaptations to a progressive strength training programme, supported by an adequate diet. The strength training provides the stimulus for muscles to grow, while adequate nutrition provides the opportunity for them to grow at an optimal rate.

Rates of weight gain are dependent on our genetics and body type. To gain strength and size it is necessary to achieve a slightly positive energy balance, somewhere in the region of an extra 500 calories per day, and a protein intake of about 1.4-1.7 grams per kilogram of body mass. Eating a high protein diet, or supplementing with amino acids (as is common practice for many sportspeople wishing to gain muscle bulk and size) will not in itself lead to great increases in muscle size or strength. What is more important is achieving an adequate energy intake.

Case study

An athlete who would like to increase his muscle mass asks you for advice regarding the use of protein supplements, having recently read about these products in a popular health and fitness magazine. The magazine strongly suggests that amino acid supplementation is an essential part of any muscle-building programme. He informs you that he already consumes large amounts of first-class protein foods at regular intervals throughout the day as meals and snacks.

1 What nutritional and training advice would you offer this athlete?

2 What additional information on the athlete's diet and exercise habits might you require to formulate appropriate diet and exercise advice?

Special groups

The aim of this section is to outline the special nutritional considerations for different groups in the population, such as children, older adults, vegetarians and the injured or ill.

Children

The transition through infancy, childhood and adolescence to adulthood involves enormous changes in body size and composition. The constituents required to support growth and development will be obtained from the diet.

During early infancy, breast or formula milk can adequately provide for all nutritional needs. Weaning occurs at around 4-6 months, to accustom the baby to new foods and provide nutrients that can no longer be supplied in sufficient quantities by milk alone. Between the ages of one and five, children consolidate their early experiences with food and learn to become more independent with regard to feeding. During this time, nutrient-dense foods should be considered due to the small capacity of the stomach.

Once children are at school the diet is much more affected by external influences, and it is at this point that the sound foundations of healthy eating should be established. Once adolescence is reached, eating habits often succumb to pressure from peers.

The nutritional requirements of children are different from those of adults. All children, whatever their age, require a balanced and varied diet to support their growth and development. Active children will obviously need more calories than their inactive friends. Eating the correct foods in the right quantities will help them to perform well in sport and recover from it more quickly. The diets of active children should encourage healthy eating habits, maintain a healthy body weight and composition, and provide an adequate energy, carbohydrate and protein content, a healthy amount of fat, sufficient vitamins and minerals and an adequate fluid content.

It is important for children of all ages to be encouraged to establish a normal eating pattern to promote good eating habits for life. Healthy eating habits during childhood will help to prevent anaemia, overweight, poor growth and tooth decay. A pattern based around three meals each day, with breakfast being very important, supported by appropriate energy-boosting snacks, should ensure all nutrient and energy needs are met.

Growth takes place rapidly during childhood and adolescence. Due to the demands of growth, children require higher energy intakes in proportion to their body weight than adults. Adolescents in particular should be encouraged to fill up on carbohydrate-rich foods such as bread, rice, pasta and potatoes, and avoid high fat and sugary foods in large quantities. Carbohydrates should provide 50-55% of total energy intake at this time. Meals should be based around healthy eating principles and the UK National Food Guide.

Protein intake must be sufficient to meet the demands of growth and development as well as training, and as for adults a regular supply is required in the diet, but relative to body mass protein requirements are higher than those of adults. However, getting enough protein is not likely to be a problem if a good quality source of protein is consumed at each meal.

Requirements for several micronutrients are at their highest during the adolescent years, but it is very common at this time for children to become preoccupied with their body weight and image, and they may experiment with fad diets which may interfere with nutrient intakes. Adequate calcium and iron intakes are particularly important; due to rapid periods of growth, the need for these nutrients is high.

In relation to participation in sport and exercise a high intake of fluid should also be encouraged as young sports performers are at high risk of dehydration. Children have a less efficient thermoregulatory system than adults and as a result are more susceptible to heat stress. Added to this, children are less likely to voluntarily replenish fluid losses during sport or exercise, and therefore need to be frequently reminded to drink during training or competition.

Older people

The needs of this group depend very much on the individual's general health and level of physical activity. A fit elderly person will require a normal, healthy balanced diet and dietary requirements will be no different from those of younger adults. However, fluid intake may require special attention in relation to sport and exercise. Older sports performers, like children, appear to be less efficient at dissipating heat through sweating. This can be compounded by an accompanying reduced sensation of thirst with advancing age, so extra care is required when training and competing in hot, dry conditions.

The majority of older people become less active with increasing age, resulting in a corresponding decrease in energy requirements. A nutrient-dense diet is important with advancing age as nutritional needs remain high but appetite decreases. Keeping active can help to maintain appetite and avoid weight gain. However, many elderly people eat poorly because they lack the motivation or ability to cook meals. This may be compounded by a low income, dental problems or poor eating habits developed in earlier years.

Injury or illness

Injury and illness are the dread of all serious sports performers. Diet can have a crucial role to play in the prevention of and recovery from both injury and illness.

Drained muscle glycogen stores are associated with fatigue, as is dehydration. The dehydrated sports performer fatigues more rapidly, both mentally and physically. Lapses in concentration can result in poor technique, which may result in injury. The injured sports performer may need to reduce overall food consumption while attempting to maintain an adequate nutrient intake to avoid unnecessary weight gain during the recovery phase. In particular, a decrease in the reliance on simple carbohydrates as compact sources of energy may be needed.

To maintain an efficient immune system, sportspeople should be encouraged to eat a wide range of foods in a balanced diet, avoid stress, get

Injury is the dread of all sports performers

plenty of sleep and maintain a healthy body weight. As mentioned on page 9, the essential fatty acids linoleic and linolenic acid are also important for maintaining a healthy immune system, so over-restriction of fat should be discouraged. Oily fish are a good source of the EFAs, along with sunflower, safflower, peanut and corn oils.

Vegetarians and vegans

Vegetarianism is becoming increasingly popular, with vegetarian diets now thought to be associated with a reduction in health risks such as those posed by cancer and coronary heart disease. A well-planned vegetarian diet that excludes meat and fish can provide all the energy, protein and other nutrients required by sportspeople in order to maintain health, and meet the demands of training and competition.

However, the term vegetarian means different things to different people. There are a range of eating patterns that may now be described as

vegetarian, ranging from the demi-vegetarian (a term used to describe someone who excludes only red meat from the diet), to the strict vegan who does not consume any foods of animal origin whatsoever. Generally, those who eat poultry or fish have little to worry about. Similarly, ovo-lacto-vegetarians who consume dairy foods and eggs should still find it relatively easy to obtain all nutrients, although low fat options may be advised to ensure the recommended intakes for saturated fat are not exceeded.

It is vegans who need to take extra care in planning meals to meet their nutrient requirements. The nutrient most difficult to obtain in the vegan diet is vitamin B12, as it is only found in foods of animal origin. Some breakfast cereals are fortified with this vitamin, as are some yeast extracts, but it is unlikely that these sources would provide sufficient intakes, and a regular supplement is generally advised by dietitians. However, always check with a pharmacist before self-prescribing supplements. An adequate calcium intake can

	Meat	Fish	Eggs	Milk	Cereals	Vegetables	Fruit	Nuts
Demi-veg	✘	✔	✔	✔	✔	✔	✔	✔
Ovo-lacto-vegetarian	✘	✘	✔	✔	✔	✔	✔	✔
Lacto-vegetarian	✘	✘	✘	✔	✔	✔	✔	✔
Vegan	✘	✘	✘	✘	✔	✔	✔	✔

✘ Foods excluded
✔ Foods included

Various types of vegetarian diets

usually be achieved by the inclusion of fortified soya milk in the diet. Vitamin D, essential for calcium absorption, is available in fortified soya margarines and can be produced by the body with adequate exposure to sunlight. Iron from vegetable sources is less well absorbed than the iron found in meat, but this can be enhanced by the inclusion of a vitamin C source at the same meal.

Theory into practice

Suggest nutritional reasons why a vegetarian diet might be considered a healthier option than an omnivorous diet.

Case study

Gita is a junior national squad cross-country athlete. She is a student and demi-vegetarian. Recently she has been feeling very run down and wonders if this is linked to not eating red meat.

From a consultation, you establish she has a very irregular meal pattern with often long gaps between meals, meaning that she fails to refuel adequately after training sessions.

Make some recommendations about Gita's diet and eating practices.

Assessment activity 8.2

The aim of the following assessment activity is to demonstrate a critical understanding of the principles of safe and effective weight management programmes.

1 Identify **two** people who require contrasting weight management advice.

2 Select an appropriate method to collect dietary intake information from these individuals. Analyse the information you have obtained and write a report on your findings which suggests, where necessary, appropriate modifications to support their different weight management needs. Be sure to describe the factors that affect weight management and the role that

different professionals might play in supporting these individuals in achieving their weight management goals.

3 Produce an effective weight management programme for these different individuals. Include dietary information and a menu plan.

To assist you in this task, use a combination of manual and computer-based methods of processing and analysing nutrient intake information. In presenting your report you may want to look back at the activities you have undertaken while working through this unit.

Check your knowledge

1 Define the term **diet**.

2 Define the term **reference nutrient intake** (RNI). What is the significance of this dietary reference value?

3 What are the major factors in the development of obesity?

4 What health risks does obesity pose?

5 What are the current guidelines on safe alcohol intakes?

6 List four routes of water loss from the body.

7 Because water losses are greater during exercise, the sportsperson needs to employ sound strategies for fluid replacement. What might be the signs and symptoms of dehydration, and how might these be avoided?

8 What are the advantages and disadvantages of high carbohydrate content in a sports drink?

9 Describe the skinfold thickness method of measuring body composition. Why is this method one of the most widely used field techniques for assessing body composition in sportspeople?

10 List two micronutrients for special attention in the diet of athletes. Why might these nutrients be of particular concern in the diets of females?

11 How soon do you need to eat after a hard training session, and why is it so important to eat afterwards?

Assessment guidance

For this unit's assessment, you are required to produce nutritional strategies for:

- a selected sport
- someone wanting to lose weight
- someone wanting to gain weight.

You are also required to evaluate the diets of two contrasting sportspeople. For one of these you may wish to consider your own diet if you are actively engaged in sport at a competitive level, and use the information you have gathered through the practical activities undertaken in this unit.

To gain a pass:

- ✔ describe the components and effects of a healthy diet
- ✔ maintain a diary or logbook for two contrasting clients over a period of two weeks commenting on their food intake and diet
- ✔ identify suitable nutrition strategies for the two selected clients
- ✔ describe the factors that affect weight management and the role of different professionals who give advice and support
- ✔ produce an effective weight management programme for two contrasting clients that includes dietary information and meal planning.

To gain a merit:

- ✔ compare the food intake and diet of two contrasting clients
- ✔ explain the nutrition strategies for the two selected clients
- ✔ explain the importance of advice and support given by professionals
- ✔ compare the needs of two contrasting clients and devise an effective weight management programme.

To gain a distinction:

- ✔ critically evaluate the food intake and diet of two contrasting clients, drawing valid conclusions and commenting on their

suitability and fitness for purpose
- ✔ critically analyse the suggested nutrition strategies, justifying the choices made
- ✔ assess the effectiveness of the advice and support given by professionals, providing further suggestions and recommendations
- ✔ critically analyse the weight management programmes, providing alternatives and further recommendations.

Merit

1 You will be expected to work more independently throughout the assessment activities, to select appropriate case studies and methods for the collection of dietary information, and produce appropriate nutritional strategies.

2 You will be expected to show more depth and breadth in your understanding of dietary assessment methods, for example the advantages and disadvantages of the different methods and their application.

3 You will be expected to demonstrate greater evaluation of the dietary information you have obtained, along with the results of your dietary analysis.

4 You will produce reports on your cases studies that are well presented and demonstrate a degree of critical analysis of the theoretical and practical elements of the dietary assessment process, and show an awareness of the role of professional nutrition advisors.

Distinction

1 You will work with a high degree of independence throughout the assessment process, select appropriate case studies and methods for the collection of dietary information, and produce appropriate nutritional strategies.

2 You will be able to demonstrate an excellent and critical understanding of the dietary assessment methods you have used, and the impact these might have on your findings.

3 You will undertake a critical and thorough evaluation of the dietary information you have obtained, along with the results of your dietary analysis.

4 You will produce reports on your case studies that are excellently presented, original, and demonstrate a high degree of critical analysis of the theoretical and practical elements of the dietary assessment process. You will demonstrate a critical awareness of the roles of professional nutrition advisors.

Resources

Department of Health: Report on Health and Social Subjects 41. *Dietary Reference Values for Food Energy and Nutrient for the United Kingdom*, 1991, Her Majesty's Stationery Office

Food Standards Agency: *Food Portion Sizes*, 3rd edition, 2002, Her Majesty's Stationery Office

Food Standards Agency: *McCance and Widdowson's The Composition of Foods*, 6th summary edition, 2002, Royal Society of Chemistry

Griffin, J: *Food for Sport, Eat Well, Perform Better*, 2001, Crowood Press

McArdle, WD, Katch FI & Katch WL: *Essentials of Exercise Physiology*, 2nd edition, 2000, Lippincott, Williams & Wilkins

Maughan, RJ & Burke, LM: *Sports Nutrition: Handbook of Sports Medicine and Science*, 2002, Blackwell Science

Schofield, WN, Schofield, C, James, WPT: 'Basal metabolic rate – review and prediction', *Human Nutrition: Clinical Nutrition (39)*, supplement, 1985

Useful contacts and websites

British Nutrition Foundation
High Holborn House
52-54 High Holborn
London WC1 6RQ
www.nutrition.org.uk

Eating Disorders Association
First Floor
Wensum House
103 Prince of Wales Road
Norwich
Norfolk NR1 1DW
Helpline   01603 621414
Youth Helpline   01603 765050
Recorded Message   0891 615466
www.edauk.com

The Health Development Agency (formally the Health Education Authority)
Trevelyan House
30 Great Peter Street
London SW1P 2HW
www.hda-online.org.uk

The Nutrition Society
10 Cambridge Court
210 Shepherds Bush Road
London W6 7NJ
www.nutsoc.org.uk

The Vegetarian Society
Parkdale
Dunham Road
Altrincham
Cheshire WA14 4QS
www.vegsoc.org

Dietitians in Sport & Exercise Nutrition
PO Box 22360
London W13 9FL

Glossary

Absorption: the movement of digested food from the stomach and small intestine into the body tissues and blood.

Adaptive thermogenesis: energy expenditure that results from the body's response to environmental and physiological stress.

Adenosine triphosphate: a high-energy phosphate compound found in the body and one of the major forms of energy available for immediate use by the body during activity.

Aerobic: energy processes that take place in the presence of oxygen.

Anaerobic: energy processes that take place in the absence of oxygen.

Anaemia: a condition of subnormal levels of red blood cells and haemoglobin.

Anorexia nervosa: a psychological disorder in which sufferers starve themselves.

Antioxidant: a compound that may offer protection from oxidative processes.

Atherosclerosis: the formation of plaque on the artery wall restricting blood flow.

Balanced diet: a term that describes a diet that provides the correct amount of all the nutrients required by the body without excess or deficiency.

Basal metabolic rate: the measurement of energy expenditure in the body in a rested and fasted state.

Bioelectrical impedance analysis: a method of body composition assessment using electrical resistance.

Body composition: the ratio of lean body mass to fat mass in an individual.

Body image: the image or impression an individual has of his or her own body.

Body mass index: an index of body fatness used as a measure of obesity.

Body plethysmography: a method of body composition assessment using air displacement.

Bulimia nervosa: a psychological condition in which sufferers have episodes of binge eating, and perhaps self-induce vomiting or misuse laxatives to avoid weight gain.

Calorie: more accurately kilocalorie, the traditional unit for measuring the energy value of food, defined as the heat required to raise one gram of water by one degree from 15-16 degrees centigrade.

Carbohydrate loading: a dietary strategy employed by endurance athletes to increase the glycogen levels of the liver and muscle prior to competition.

Cholesterol: a fat-like substance implicated in the development of heart disease.

Coronary heart disease: a degenerative disorder of the heart primarily caused by atherosclerosis.

Demi-vegetarian: an individual who refrains from eating red meat but usually includes poultry, fish and dairy foods in the diet.

Diabetes: a disorder of carbohydrate metabolism caused by a lack of or insufficient production of insulin, resulting in high blood glucose levels.

Diet: a term to describe the usual eating habits and food consumption of an individual.

Dietary reference values: standards for recommended nutrient intakes as proposed by the Department of Health COMA Report 41 (1991).

Dietary thermogenesis: the increase in metabolic rate subsequent to the ingestion of a meal.

Digestion: the process by which enzymes break down the food we consume in our diet into smaller substances to facilitate absorption by the body.

Disaccharide: sugars that are composed of two monosaccharides, the most common of which in the diet is sucrose.

Eating disorder: a serious psychological disorder involving the avoidance, excessive consumption, or purging of food as characterised by anorexia nervosa or bulimia nervosa.

Ectomorph: the body type of a person with a slim build, long limbs and delicate bone structure.

Endomorph: the body type of a person with a heavy build and rounded shape.

Ergogenic: work-enhancing.

Essential amino acids: those amino acids that must be obtained from the diet and cannot be synthesised by the body.

Essential fatty acids: those fatty acids that must be obtained from the diet and cannot be synthesised by the body.

Estimated average requirement: the dietary reference value that relates to nutrient intakes estimated to meet the requirements of 50% of individuals in a population group.

Excretion: the removal by the body of potentially toxic end-products from metabolism, normally via the urine and faeces.

Fad diet: dieting practices that are based on fashionable but unsound principles.

Fatigue: a generalised or specific feeling of tiredness.

Food: any substance derived from plants or animals containing a combination of the nutrients carbohydrates, fats, proteins, vitamins, minerals, non-starch polysaccharide, water and alcohol, the amounts of which will vary from food to food, necessitating a varied diet to achieve adequate intakes.

Free radical: an atom or compound with an unpaired electron, thought to cause cellular damage.

Functional foods: foods that contain additive substances intended to provide health benefits beyond that of basic nutrition.

Glycacmic index: an index expressing the effects of carbohydrate foods on the rate and amount of increase in blood glucose levels following ingestion.

Glycogen: the principal storage form of carbohydrate, stored in the liver and muscles.

Healthy eating: a term used to describe the pursuit of a balanced diet to support health and reduce the risks of chronic disease.

High density lipoprotein: a protein-lipid complex found in the blood that transports fats.

Insulin: the hormone produced by the pancreas, important in the control of carbohydrate metabolism.

Kilocalorie: see calorie.

Kilogram: a unit of mass from the metric system, equivalent to 2.2 pounds.

Lean body mass: body weight minus body fat, primarily muscle, bone and other non-fat tissues.

Linoleic acid: an essential fatty acid.

Linolenic acid: an essential fatty acid.

Low density lipoprotein: a protein-lipid complex found in the blood that transports fats.

Lower reference nutrient intake: the amount of a nutrient thought to be sufficient to meet the requirements of only a small number of individuals in a population group – those who have low levels of requirement.

Macro-minerals: minerals required by the body in relatively large amounts.

Macronutrients: nutrients that are required by the body in daily amounts greater than a few grams, such as carbohydrate, fat and protein.

Megadose: an excessive amount of a substance, above the normal dose – usually used to refer to vitamin or mineral intakes.

Mesomorph: the body type of a person with a muscular build and large bone structure.

Metabolism: the sum of all the chemical processes or reactions taking place within the body.

Microgram (µg): one millionth of a gram.

Micronutrients: nutrients that are required by the body in daily amounts of less than a few grams, such as vitamins and minerals.

Milligram (mg): one thousandth of a gram.

Monosaccharide: single sugar units, the most common of which is glucose.

Near infra-red interactance: a method of body composition assessment using infra-red technology.

Negative energy balance: a situation where energy output exceeds energy input and weight is lost.

Non-essential amino acids: amino acids that can be synthesised by the body and are therefore not required to be supplied by the diet on a daily basis.

Non-starch polysaccharide: the new scientific term for dietary fibre.

Nutrition: a term to describe the means by which the energy and nutrients in food are taken in by the body to sustain growth and development and keep it alive and healthy.

Polysaccharide: a complex carbohydrate made up of many sugar units.

Positive energy balance: a situation where energy input exceeds energy output and weight is gained.

Reference nutrient intake: the amount of a nutrient thought to be sufficient to meet the requirements for almost all individuals in a population group.

Resting metabolic rate: the energy required for all physiological processes at rest.

Safe intake: the term used to indicate the intake of a nutrient where there is insufficient scientific information to estimate the distribution of requirements within a population.

Skinfold thickness: a method of body composition assessment using skinfolds.

Somatotyping: a classification method that recognises three basic body types: endomorph, mesomorph and ectomorph.

Sports nutrition: a term to describe the influence of nutritional strategies on sports performance during the preparation for, participation in and recovery from training and competition.

Trace elements: minerals required by the body in very small amounts.

Trans fatty acids: fats produced by the hydrogenation of oils that closely resemble saturated fats in structure.

Underwater weighing: also referred to as hydrostatic weighing, a method of body composition assessment using water displacement.

Vegan: a vegetarian who eats no animal products whatsoever.

Waist circumference: a measure of obesity using the circumference of the waist at its narrowest point.

Menu Plan 1

Carbohydrate requirement =

Meal	Food	Carbohydrate content (grams)
Breakfast		
Lunch		
Evening meal		
Supper		
Snacks		
Milk		
	TOTAL	g

Menu Plan 2

Protein requirement =

Meal	Food	Protein content (grams)
Breakfast		
Lunch		
Evening meal		
Supper		
Snacks		
Milk		
	TOTAL	g

Menu Plan 3

A day's diet for someone who has an energy requirement of 2500 kilocalaries.

Calculate: energy from carbohydrate _____   grams of carbohydrate _____

Meal	Food	Carbohydrate (grams)	Kcals
Breakfast			
Lunch			
Evening meal			
Supper			
Snacks			
Milk			
		TOTALS	

FITNESS TESTING

Introduction to Unit 10

This optional unit introduces you to the concepts of health screening and fitness testing. You will look at the different health-related fitness components, for example aerobic fitness, and their importance to factors such as weight management and disease prevention. You will also investigate the fitness requirements of a variety of contrasting sporting activities. In addition to practical fitness testing, you will also explore health screening and how it relates to fitness testing.

Assessment

Because of the nature of fitness testing, this unit is very practical. You are encouraged to take part in a number of testing sessions, to improve your understanding, knowledge and practical skills.

In your assessment you are expected to explain the purpose and importance of health-related fitness for two contrasting sports, for example marathon running and shot putting. In addition to this, for three contrasting sports you have to describe the different fitness requirements. Then you must identify, describe and administer a number of suitable fitness tests for two clients, who should possess different individual needs – for example a

football player recovering from injury and a middle-aged person wishing to improve his or her flexibility. Prior to the testing session you are to prepare and use appropriate health screening for your clients. Finally, you will be expected to give feedback to your clients detailing their level of fitness.

After completing this unit you should be able to achieve the following outcomes.

Outcomes

1 Examine the purpose and importance of health-related fitness

2 Investigate the fitness requirements of three contrasting sports

3 Examine the practice of health screening and fitness testing

4 Prepare and conduct appropriate fitness tests.

What you need to learn

● The meaning and importance of health-related fitness

● How the fitness requirements of sports differ from one another

● How health screening and fitness testing are carried out.

Health-related fitness

Components of health-related fitness

There are many definitions and explanations of fitness – it is a complex subject. Health-related fitness relates to those components of fitness which make up our health status: strength, muscular endurance, aerobic endurance, flexibility and body composition.

Think it over

1 Think about your own fitness level. Using the scale on the next page, make a judgement about your fitness level and discuss the scores you have chosen with others in your group.

2 On your own, write down your definition of fitness and the key words which you think relate to the term fitness. As a group, discuss some of the ideas you have generated.

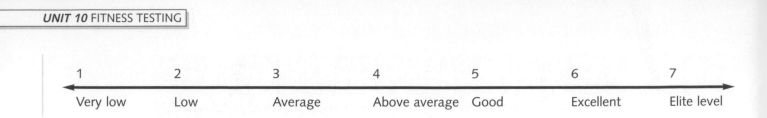

Through your discussion in the activity above, it may have become clear that different people have different ideas about what fitness is. Fitness can be further classified into the following categories:

- **total fitness:** this relates to an optimal quality of life including social, spiritual and physical well being

- **physical fitness:** a level of fitness based on fitness test scores, with good scores meaning the subject has a low chance of developing health problems (this is also known as health-related fitness)

- **motor fitness:** a level of fitness which allows the individual to perform an activity, task or sport.

Key concept

There is a clear difference between health-related and skill-related components of fitness. Skill components relate to sporting performance, and as you will learn they include agility, balance, reaction time, power, speed, and co-ordination.

Strength

Strength is also known as muscular strength. It is important for everyone, and not only athletes. Strength can be defined as the ability of a specific muscle or muscle group to exert a force in a single maximal contraction to overcome some form of resistance. In everyday life this resistance would be classed as an activity that requires a level of strength to perform, for example picking up and carrying shopping bags from the supermarket. A good level of strength allows the individual to perform daily tasks involving strength without feeling fatigue or tiredness. As well as this, a good level of strength:

- helps maintain good posture in old age
- helps maintain an independent lifestyle, for example being able to climb the stairs at home
- helps to avoid certain types of injures – for example back injuries
- helps with co-ordination while moving – for walking and running.

In relation to sport, strength is vital for a number of activities, such as:

- weightlifting – to lift a heavy weight
- boxing – to produce a powerful punch
- gymnastics – for example, upper body strength is important to maintain a handstand.

Think it over

Draw up a list of 10 other sports or exercises which require a good level of strength. Discuss your answers with other members of your group.

Muscular endurance

Unlike strength, which involves the muscle performing one action, muscular endurance involves the muscle making a number of continuous movements. Muscular endurance can be defined as a specific muscle or muscle group, such as the biceps, making repeated contractions over a significant period of time (possibly over a number of minutes). There are a number of everyday activities that require good muscular endurance, for example:

- using a vacuum cleaner
- digging the garden
- cleaning the windows
- peeling the vegetables.

All these activities would be classed as requiring a

An increase in the weight lifted requires an increase in strength

good level of muscular endurance because they require a number of muscular contractions over a number of minutes. Muscular endurance is also important for most sports. For example, a hockey midfield player would need to make numerous sprints over 10 to 20 metres during the game at high speed, which requires a good level of muscular endurance in the legs.

Think it over

It is important to be clear about the distinction between muscular endurance and muscular strength in relation to sporting activities. In small groups, with your tutor's support, draw up a list of 10 sporting activities that require muscular endurance and 10 that require strength.

Aerobic endurance

Aerobic endurance is also known as stamina or aerobic fitness. It is defined as the ability of the cardio-respiratory system to supply the exercising muscles with oxygen to maintain the aerobic exercise for a long period of time. Another common term related to the concept of aerobic endurance is Vo$_2$ **maximum**, which is the maximal amount of oxygen uptake that can be used by the athlete during aerobic exercise, such as long-distance swimming, running or cycling.

Key concept

It is important to understand that the Vo$_2$ maximum is not the amount of oxygen inhaled by the athlete, but rather the amount extracted and used by the working muscles. Vo_2 maximum can be measured using the following units:

- $L.min^{-1}$ (litres per minute) – used by the body while exercising
- $ml.kg^{-1}min^{-1}$ (millilitres per kilogram of body mass per minute) – used by the body while exercising.

Aerobic endurance is important for any sporting activity because good levels of aerobic fitness will supply the muscles with the oxygen required for exercise. As well as helping to decrease body fat, a good level of aerobic fitness can lead to improved confidence and psychological well being.

Aerobic endurance can help with daily tasks such as walking to work or doing the gardening and housework. A good level of aerobic endurance allows the individual to take part in sport, leisure and recreational activities. However, poor aerobic endurance can lead to a decrease in the mobility of an individual and consequently his or her independence, for example if he or she is unable to walk to the shops. Lack of mobility can also lead to exclusion from social events; for example, a person may be unable to join in a walk with friends.

Aerobic endurance is one of the most vital influences on our health and lifestyle. The benefits of a having good aerobic endurance through training and exercise are:

- decreased body fat
- increased oxygen to the muscles
- increased efficiency of the digestive system
- decreased stress levels
- increased removal of waste products (toxins, etc.).

Aerobic endurance forms the basis of fitness for virtually every sport. If an athlete has a reduced aerobic endurance, possibly due to a long-term injury, this will lead to a decrease in other fitness components such as muscular endurance. Therefore, poor aerobic endurance will lead inevitably to a poor sporting performance.

There are a number of events which rely almost exclusively on aerobic endurance, such as marathon running, long-distance swimming and cycling.

Think it over

On your own, draw up a list of 10 other sports which require a good level of aerobic endurance. Discuss your answers with other members of your group.

Jogging is a good way of improving aerobic endurance

Key concept

Aerobic endurance is vital for a number of daily activities, such as cycling to work, and especially for the athlete, for example the marathon runner.

Flexibility

Good flexibility allows you to pick up the shopping bags from the floor or to reach for something. Flexibility is defined as the ability of a specific joint, for example the knee, to move through a full range of movement. A flexible joint will possess a greater range of motion, which should aid the performance of skills.

Flexibility is often undervalued and under-trained. Sports performers tend to perform stretches for a couple of minutes at the start and end of their session within the warm-up and cool-down. However, flexibility is as important as aerobic endurance and should be specifically trained. The health and lifestyle benefits associated with a good level of flexibility are:

- improvement of posture
- prevention of lower back pain
- maintenance of healthy joints
- reduction in the risk of injury
- better dynamic balance (balance while moving)
- reduction in muscle soreness after exercise
- increased blood flow and nutrients to the joints.

Body composition

Body composition is the amount (normally expressed as a percentage) of body fat and lean body tissue in an individual. Lean body tissue is water, blood, skin, muscle and bone. From a health perspective, it is important to have low levels of body fat.

The health complications of excess body fat are discussed in relation to weight management later in the unit.

In a sportsperson, increased levels of fat can accumulate through inactivity caused by injury or during the off season, and can lead to a decrease in performance. You can see this when footballers return to pre-season training in July and are carrying extra weight, which has to be lost. An increase in body fat can reduce the fitness of a player by making him or her slower.

Frequency of exercise

Frequency in relation to exercise is used to mean either the number of sessions per week, or the number of exercises within the session – for example a session of 20 press ups. In terms of health-related fitness and the frequency of exercise needed for fitness, there are number of guidelines to follow. For an in-depth review of frequency, see Unit 11, Training and Fitness (page 132).

Duration of exercise

Duration is the length of the exercise in terms of time or distance covered. It will be discussed in Unit 11.

Rest, recuperation and over-training

After a period of exercise it is important to give the body time to recover through rest and recuperation. While resting the body repairs and heals itself. For example, during strength training muscle fibres break. A rest period allows the fibres to repair themselves and then eventually become stronger.

Rest periods incorporated into a training programme reduce the chance of over-training. Over-training syndrome is the dangerous result of too many workouts without an adequate rest. There are a number of symptoms associated with over-training which can affect the health of the individual:

- loss of appetite
- increased chance of developing infections, viruses, etc.
- change in sleep patterns
- change in psychological state – for example, depression

- reduction in sporting performance
- overuse injuries – for example, shin splints.

Individuality

It is important for you to understand that each individual will have different fitness levels throughout his or her life. While at school, most children tend to have a high level of fitness through involvement in sports and games. As people get older their fitness levels tend to decrease because of a reduction in physical activity.

It is also important for you to understand that individuals will have different strengths and weaknesses. For example, some individuals will have good levels of fitness in relation to flexibility but possess poor aerobic endurance. An athlete will have certain goals – he or she may have good strength but may wish to improve speed because it is important for the relevant sport.

The goals and intentions of the client

Based on the principle of individuality, the sports practitioner must understand the specific goals and intentions of the client. Some individuals who start a training programme will wish only to improve their health-related fitness so that it helps with disease prevention and allows them to have a normal lifestyle. However, from a sporting perspective an athlete's goal may be to improve just one component of fitness, for example flexibility, with an end goal of improving performance.

Case study

Brian, a college basketball player, has decided to start a new training programme after a number of poor performances recently, which have resulted in his being dropped from the team. He has decided to train for aerobic endurance, as he has been feeling fatigued in the latter stages of games. He also feels he has added extra body fat recently, which has probably detracted from his performances.

1 What in your opinion are the two main goals for Brian?

2 What are Brian's two main intentions in relation to health-related fitness?
3 Which components of health-related fitness are affected by an increase in body fat?

Reversibility

If an individual reduces training there will be a reduction in fitness; that is because fitness is **reversible**. A reduction in exercise, in terms of frequency and/or duration, will lead to a decrease in the individual's health-related fitness as well as sports performance. This means that if a person reduces the amount of exercise or training done, fitness levels will drop. This reduction may be due to a variety of factors, such as injury or lack of motivation.

Case study

Mr Baxter, the manager of Sunshine Gym, is concerned that there has been a significant drop in the numbers of people using the gym in February and March, compared to January. After conducting some research, he discovers that the main reason is people making and then breaking a New Year's resolution.

1 Make a list of other possible reasons why people may have reduced or even stopped their training at Sunshine Gym.
2 Suggest some strategies for overcoming these problems.

The process of reversibility of physical fitness takes place over a week or a number of weeks, and not during normal rest days between exercise sessions. Reversibility can take place in any part of the body or any component of fitness, such as:

- decrease in strength due to weaker muscles
- decrease in aerobic endurance due to a reduction in the capacity of the cardiovascular system.

Activity schedule

When designing a training or testing programme with a client, it is important to take into account his or her activity schedule. The training or testing programme should be based around the free time the client has. Every client will need a different testing and training schedule, as people are likely to have the following commitments:

- work
- family
- social
- home
- hobbies.

Assessment activity 10.1

As a sports practitioner it is important to identify the activity schedule of your clients, because this allows you to plan the testing and training schedule. In addition to this it helps you to understand the time constraints on your client, and helps you to develop a relationship.

1   Choose two people with contrasting lifestyles, for example a college student and a disabled athlete (you can choose a fellow class member for one of these). Interview the two people about their activity schedule by asking them about their commitments (as listed above).

2   Using the information from the interviews, complete a timetable for each like the following, showing their daily commitments.

Name:			
	Morning	Afternoon	Evening
Mon			
Tues			
Weds			
Thurs			
Fri			
Sat			
Sun			

3   After completing the timetable, discuss it with your interviewee and describe when would be the best time to schedule in three testing and training sessions of one hour each. After your discussion, add the sessions to the timetable.

4   Keep these timetables, as they will become useful when you are planning your fitness testing sessions with your two contrasting clients.

Importance of health-related fitness

Key concept

You already know that physical fitness can benefit health. Some of these benefits can be summarised as follows:

- prevention and treatment of high blood pressure
- control of body weight
- reduction in the chance of developing certain cancers, for example colon cancer
- enhancement of the immune system
- reduction in the chance of developing cardiovascular diseases
- reduction in the chance of developing depression, and increase in confidence and self-esteem.

This section will discuss in more depth the links between health-related fitness and concepts such as weight management, disease prevention and stress management.

Ability to carry out daily activities

Regardless of an individual's age, gender or sporting ability, he or she needs a good level of health-related fitness for a normal lifestyle.

Key concept

Failure to maintain good fitness levels will reduce an individual's quality of life, for example reducing the chance to take part in social activities. Poor fitness influences the ability to do daily tasks such as:

- walking/cycling to work
- shopping in the supermarket
- picking up the children from school
- climbing the stairs at home.

Once an individual reaches a low level of fitness, he or she may enter a vicious circle in which the capability for daily activities is further reduced. The flow chart below illustrates this process.

> Because of a poor level of fitness the individual is unable to perform most types of exercise, which over a period of time leads to an even lower level of health and fitness.

⬇

> The reduction in fitness and health is accompanied by a reduction in the individual's psychological well being, for example decreased confidence and motivation.

⬇

> This reduction in confidence and motivation for the individual is likely to lead to a further reduction in the desire to exercise.

⬇

> The decreased levels of health and fitness, possibly coupled with a poor diet, over a period of time are likely to lead to diseases such as hypertension and obesity.

Weight management

Key concept

Regular exercise aids the process of weight management, which has overall implications for health. The importance of weight management in relation to sport is discussed in Unit 8, Nutrition for Weight Management, and Unit 11, Training and Fitness.

There has been a rapid rise in the number of people in the UK who have been diagnosed as clinically obese (with a body mass index above 30 – see page 125). Shown below are obesity figures produced by the Department of Health in 1998, by gender and profession.

Obesity among people aged 16 and over, by social class of head of household and gender, 1998		
	Percentages	
	Women	Men
Unskilled manual	31.4	19.3
Semi-skilled manual	27.9	16.3
Skilled manual	26.4	20.4
Skilled non-manual	19.3	16.6
Managerial and technical	19.9	16.2
Professional	15.1	12.0

Source: Health Survey for England, Department of Health

Theory into practice

Research the latest figures for obesity in the UK, and particularly the trends among children. Summarise your findings.

The International Obesity Activity Force estimated in 2002 that one billion people in the world, or one in six, are overweight or obese.

A reduction in body fat percentage for an overweight or obese person can reduce the risk of developing heart diseases, strokes, diabetes, hypertension and some forms of cancer.

As a person gets older the body stores more fat, and this is mainly because of a decrease in physical activity and a reduction in the metabolic rate. The role that exercise and a good level of health-related fitness can play in weight management cannot be overstated. Specifically, the benefits of exercise are that it:

- increases calorie usage
- increases the uptake of fat
- leads to an increase in the amount of lean muscle tissue.

For weight management to be successful, exercise should be linked to a reduction in calorie intake, for example a reduction in the amount of fatty food consumed. When your calorie intake matches your energy expenditure through daily activities and exercise, your weight will stay the same.

(a) calories in food > calories used = WEIGHT GAIN

(b) calories in food < calories used = WEIGHT LOSS

(c) calories in food = calories used = WEIGHT BALANCE

Calorie intake should match energy expenditure

Disease prevention

The benefits of exercise for reducing body fat are well documented. However, there is now evidence to suggest that regular exercise can reduce the chances of developing certain diseases, such as:

- coronary heart disease (CHD)
- non–insulin-dependent diabetes mellitus
- some types of cancer
- osteoarthritis
- osteoporosis.

However, these benefits are only associated with physical activity over a long period of time (years). Long-term exercising increases the number of white blood cells, the main component of the immune system. Exercise can also help individuals who suffer from certain conditions such as asthma.

Case study

A recent study looked at the effect that exercise can have on children who suffer from asthma. The study looked at 42 children aged from eight to 16 and evaluated the effect that aerobic training had on their condition. The children cycled for 30 minutes in three sessions per week over a period of two months. The results showed that a reduction in the use of inhaled and oral steroids was associated with the exercise programme.

1 What other forms of aerobic exercise could the children have done?

2 Apart from the medical benefits, what other benefits can children gain from exercising?

3 Given the principle of reversibility, what do you think would happen to the children's condition if they stopped exercising after the two-month trial period?

Stress management

Experts have agreed for a number of years that a good level of fitness attained through regular exercise can reduce stress levels and the effects of stress, for example inability to sleep. Stress is a risk factor for developing:

- hypertension
- some forms of cancer
- ulcers
- headaches.

Key concept

Exercise has a positive effect on the individual's psychological well being, for example bringing increased self-confidence. People suffering from depression can also benefit from exercise.

During exercise the brain releases a larger amount of endorphins, which are powerful mood-elevating chemicals. Exercise often helps individuals to relieve negative emotions such as frustration and anger. The benefits of exercise on the psychological state can be summarised as:

- increased self esteem
- reduced anxiety levels
- increased confidence
- enjoyment
- better mood states.

Think it over

Work in a group. Think about the feelings you have during and after exercise. Although you probably feel physically tired, you should also experience a number of positive emotions. Discuss your thoughts to see if there are any common experiences.

For some individuals who are suffering from excessive levels of stress, in order to be beneficial exercise needs to be linked to a variety of other treatments, for example stress-management training by a trained expert in cognitive (mental) therapies.

Improved performance and effectiveness

A poor level of fitness will have a dramatically negative influence on performance and effectiveness. Imagine a football player who has a slight calf strain and plays despite the injury. The performance is likely to be poor as there will be a reduction in the speed at which the player can sprint. There are numerous examples at elite level where the performance has been poor due to a reduction in the athlete's fitness level.

Case study

While playing for Manchester United against Deportivo of Spain in the Champions League in 2002, David Beckham broke a bone in his foot because of a bad tackle. Although Beckham recovered to play in the World Cup that summer, it is widely accepted that he was not 100% fit, which led to a reduced performance level.

1 Why is it vital to be 100% fit in elite level sport?

2 Which components of fitness may have been affected by this injury?

3 What is the difference between being fit and match fitness?

Think it over

In a small group, produce a spider diagram (see the example started below) showing the factors that may influence an elite athlete's fitness level. Discuss your answers with other groups.

Current fitness guidelines

Within the health and fitness industry a great deal of information is available regarding the best way to exercise, in terms of the type, how long and when you should exercise. However, it is important for you to understand that some of this information may be misleading and incorrect. When dealing with clients it is important to use properly researched and valid guidelines. Three bodies that are widely accepted as providing sound information are the Health Development Agency, the American College of Sports Medicine, and the British Association of Sport and Exercise Sciences.

Health Development Agency

In 1999 the government produced a white paper called 'Saving Lives: Our Healthier Nation'. Subsequently the Health Development Agency (HDA) was formed in April 2000 as a special authority working with the aim of improving the health of people in England. The main focus of the HDA is to:

- gather evidence from research as to what works
- provide advice on areas of good practice
- support all those working to improve the public's health.

The HDA works in partnership with others, such as local authorities and the National Health Service. In terms of fitness guidelines and in conjunction with other health bodies, for example the American College of Sports Medicine, the HDA supports the following guidelines for healthy aerobic activity (swimming, running, cycling etc.):

- exercise 3 to 5 days each week
- warm up for 5 to 10 minutes before aerobic activity
- maintain your exercise intensity for 30 to 45 minutes
- gradually decrease the intensity of your workout, then stretch to cool down during the last 5 to 10 minutes
- for weight loss, your aerobic activity should be at least 30 minutes for 5 days per week.

Theory into practice

In pairs, produce an A3-sized poster based on the above guidelines which could be displayed in your local fitness centre. The poster should give the guidelines and highlight the health benefits of being aerobically fit, for example decreased body fat. It should be colourful and include pictures, and be informative but not too technical. Note down the key references and data which support the points you are making.

American College of Sports Medicine (ACSM)

As with the HDA, the ACSM's mission is to increase public awareness of the health benefits of regular physical activity. It does this by providing information for health and fitness practitioners. This information, for example the guidelines for healthy aerobic activity shown previously, is distributed through a number of publications, such as books, videos, journals, news conferences and electronic news magazines.

It is important to understand that although the organisation has clear links with America its research and guidelines are used throughout the world with the aim of improving individuals' health and awareness of health-related issues.

British Association of Sport and Exercise Sciences (BASES)

In this country BASES works in the field of sport and exercise science. The membership of BASES includes academics and health/fitness practitioners. Among its aims is to promote the relevance of sport and exercise to society.

Theory into practice

Research the role of BASES; you can visit its website at www.bases.org.uk. Summarise your findings.

Remember

- Health-related fitness consists of strength, aerobic endurance, muscular endurance, flexibility and body composition.

- All the components of health-related fitness are important for the sporting performance as well as from a health perspective.

- The athlete should avoid over-training through adequate rest and recuperation.

- Regular exercise can help with disease prevention, stress management, weight management and the ability to carry out daily activities.

- The current fitness guidelines for aerobic training recommend that we should exercise 3 to 5 times per week for 30 to 45 minutes in each session.

Assessment activity 10.2

Prepare and give to your group a 10-minute presentation using OHTs and/or handouts, covering the following points.

1 Introduce the term health-related fitness – making sure you mention the five components.

2 Pick two contrasting sports in terms of the components of fitness required. Produce two pie charts which show the importance of the

health-related fitness components for your two chosen sports (see the examples below). Justify the percentages you have given for both sports.

3 Discuss the purpose and importance of the health-related components of fitness for your two contrasting sports. For example, you could stress the importance of flexibility for gymnastics, as it allows the athlete to perform complex movements using the full range of motion.

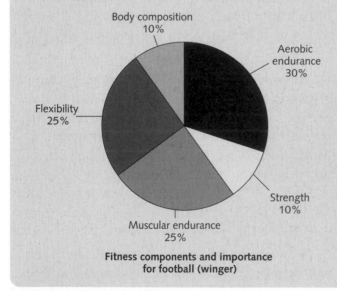

Fitness components and importance for football (winger)

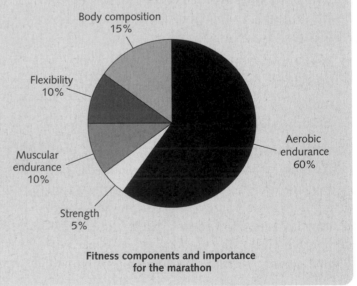

Fitness components and importance for the marathon

Fitness requirements

You should now be aware that health-related fitness includes the factors strength, aerobic endurance, muscular endurance, flexibility, and body composition. As briefly mentioned earlier, fitness can also be classified according to its skill-related components. This section will highlight

these skill components and discuss them in relation to the sporting performance.

Health–related and skill–related components

The health-related and skill-related components of fitness are summarised in the following table. As you can see, there is a clear difference.

Health-related fitness	Skill-related fitness
Strength	Agility
Muscular endurance	Balance
Aerobic endurance	Reaction time
Flexibility	Power
Body composition	Speed
	Co-ordination

Key concept

Skill-related components of fitness, for example reaction time, are predominantly used in relation to the sporting performance, although balance, for example, is needed for daily activities such as walking downstairs.

Think it over

Based on your understanding at this stage, work in groups to identify which components (health-related and skill-related) of fitness are required for 100-metre sprinters.

You will probably identify most of the components of fitness as being important for the 100-metre sprinter because of the demanding nature of the event.

Agility

Agility means the ability of an athlete to change direction many times quickly and accurately during the sporting performance. For example, a rugby winger sprinting for the try line may have

Which components of fitness are important for the 100-metre sprinter?

Agility and dynamic balance allow the player to avoid tackles

to dodge a number of defending players, by side-stepping them while moving quickly.

Balance

Often overlooked when considering the requirements of an activity, balance means being able to maintain stability or equilibrium while performing. There are two forms of balance:

● static balance, where the athlete is stationary, for example in a handstand in gymnastics

● dynamic balance, where the athlete is moving, for example a footballer sprinting with the ball.

Balance is also important in activities that require precise movements with a high degree of accuracy, for example archery or snooker. A lack of balance will often have a dramatic result on the sporting performance.

Think it over

In small groups, draw up a list of 10 sporting activities that need good balance (five requiring static and five requiring dynamic balance).

Reaction time

Reaction time is the time between the start of the movement and the stimulus, which may for example be a starting pistol in sprint events. After the stimulus (the pistol firing) the sprinter needs to react as fast as possible to leave the starting blocks. Reaction time is vital for a number of sports.

● In tennis, a player needs to react to a shot that has changed direction and speed because the ball has clipped the top of the net.

Good balance allows the gymnast to perform complex movements

- In football, the goalkeeper needs to react quickly to clear a shot.
- When a basketball has hit the rim of the basket, the players need to react quickly to regain possession of the ball.

Power

Power is strongly related to strength in conjunction with the speed of movement. It is the ability to generate and use muscular strength quickly. Athletes who are stronger tend to be able to produce a greater amount of power during the action. This can be seen with a boxer who is able to produce a fast punch, which shows good strength as well as power.

Speed

Team-based sports and certain individual sports (for example sprinting and squash) require a high degree of speed. Speed is the ability to move a short distance in the quickest possible time. A high level of speed can also have a significant influence on the result in team-based sports.

Co-ordination

Most of the sporting movements require the athlete to use a number of joints and muscles in a specific order or sequence. Consider the tennis serve, which requires movement of the ankles, knees, hips, upper body, shoulder, elbows and wrist. These complex movements require a high degree of co-ordination. Good co-ordination will mean the tennis player moves the right body parts at the correct time, while transferring force from the ankles through the body to the wrist joint.

Links to sports activities

Think it over

In small groups, match the following sporting activities with the most important components of fitness required for that activity. Discuss your answers with other groups.

Football   Strength
                            Muscular endurance
Golf   Aerobic endurance
                            Flexibility
Basketball   Body composition
                            Agility
Marathon running   Balance
                            Reaction time
                            Power
                            Speed
                            Co-ordination

Key concept

Each sport and exercise activity requires a different blend of health- and skill-related components of fitness because of the nature of the tasks involved.

Although it is clear that skill-related components have strong links with sporting movements, they are also required for everyday activities.

Theory into practice

Using a table like the one below, log your everyday physical activities including your sport and exercise for two days. Match them with the skill-related components, as shown in the example.

Relative importance of each component

Both health- and skill-related fitness components are vital for daily activities as well as the sporting performance. This is shown in the following case studies.

Case study

Tariq, a footballer aged 21, plays for the local team. Compared to the other players he has always had a high level of all the components of fitness. However, over the past six months the coach has not been training flexibility, so Tariq's flexibility has become poor. Lack of flexibility in the hamstrings leads to constant muscle tightness, and to strains and tears, which lead to him missing a number of key matches.

Sheila, a woman aged 50, has a good level of fitness for all components except strength in her triceps and biceps. This lack of strength influences her ability to perform basic activities such as opening a jar.

1 Explain why it is important for a footballer to have good flexibility.

2 Will missing a number of key games through injury have an effect on Tariq's other components of fitness?

3 What other daily activities will Sheila struggle with if she lacks strength in the biceps and triceps?

4 Explain why having good flexibility and aerobic fitness are important for someone of Sheila's age.

Remember

- Skill-related fitness consists of agility, balance, reaction time, power, speed and co-ordination.
- Everyday activities require skill-related components of fitness, for example balance is required when walking down the stairs.

Daily activity	Agility	Balance	Reaction time	Power	Speed	Co-ordination
Walking through college	✔	✔	✔			✔

Contrasting sports

This section looks at contrasting sports and their fitness requirements.

Think it over

In a small group, discuss the sports you take part in and the types of fitness you need for them. Mention both the health- and skill-related components.

Different sports require the development and training of different components of fitness. A 100-metre sprinter requires a high level of strength and speed, whereas a marathon runner requires excellent aerobic endurance. It is important to understand the differing fitness requirements for a variety of sports for the following reasons:

- Fitness tests should be matched with the component of fitness used in the sport or the position played. For example, a 1.5-mile run can be used to test for aerobic endurance.

- The coach or trainer needs to be able to train the correct components of fitness.

- When working with athletes as a sports practitioner, for example fitness trainer, it is important to show that you understand the sport they play by being aware of the fitness requirements.

This unit can discuss only a small number of sports, so you must expand your knowledge and understanding through wider reading and activities. It is also important not to forget that a number of the sports discussed require a high degree of tactical awareness and skilled execution, although we are concentrating here on the fitness components.

Athletics

Athletics encompasses a number of events split into track and field disciplines.

- Track events include the 100-metre sprint, 800-5000-metre races, etc.

- Field events include the shot put, javelin, long jump, etc.

In the sprinting events, the aim is to run as fast as possible over a short, specified distance and reach the finishing line before your opponents. The components of fitness required for sprinting differ greatly from those for longer distance races, for example the 10,000 metres. Sprinting requires good:

- reaction time – the sprinter must leave the block as fast as possible after the pistol has sounded

- muscle strength – especially at the start of the sprint to get the body moving from a stationary position in the blocks

- co-ordination – through good co-ordination the athlete can use the correct technique for sprinting and not waste energy and power

- speed – good leg and arm speed is required to move the body over the distance as quickly as possible

- power – required in the legs and arms

- body composition – a large percentage of fast-twitch muscle fibres is needed in the sprinter's legs. Fast-twitch fibres can exert a large amount of force over a short period of time, which is vital for producing high levels of power in the legs.

Theory into practice

Research the differences between slow- and fast-twitch muscle fibres, in terms of their colour, force-producing capacity, fatigue rate, trainability and percentage in the body. You may wish to illustrate some of your answers. Refer to Unit 5, The Body in Action, in the *BTEC National Diploma in Sport* core book, and Unit 11 in this book.

As you would expect, field events require a different blend of fitness components. The shot put is an individual event where the athlete has to push, rather than throw, the shot as far as possible. It requires good:

- body composition – shot putters normally have large amounts of both lean muscle and fat tissue to increase the power generated

- strength – required in the legs to generate the force needed to propel the shot

- co-ordination – the correct technique involves the use of the legs, waist, arms and hands, which must be co-ordinated correctly (see the illustration below)
- power – needed to apply to the shot to gain a good distance
- balance – dynamic balance is required for the athlete to remain within the designated area while putting the shot
- flexibility – this is vital in this discipline due to the range of movement shown by the athlete. The diagram below shows the range of movement required in putting the shot.

Swimming

In competitive swimming there are a number of events over distances from 50 metres to 1500 metres. Four different swimming styles are used:

- freestyle
- backstroke
- butterfly
- breaststroke.

The components of fitness and muscle groups required differ quite significantly because of the different techniques and distances covered. For example, for the 50-metre sprint freestyle event, the following are required:

- reaction time – the swimmer must react quickly to the start of the event, normally a bleep or pistol
- strength – a large amount of force is required in the leg muscles to push off the block with the aim of generating horizontal speed
- co-ordination – all muscle groups need to work together in the correct order; poor technique, especially when fatigued, will reduce the swimming speed
- muscular endurance – the swimmer must make continuous and repeated arm and leg movements over a significant period of time; for the 50-metre sprint, it is important for the trunk muscles to work at a high intensity propelling the swimmer through the water without fatiguing
- power – generated through the arms and legs to propel the swimmer through the water.

As the distance swum increases, there is a greater reliance on aerobic endurance and intensity decreases.

The correct technique for putting the shot needs co-ordination and flexibility

The ability to react quickly at the start is vital

Case study

Jackie, aged 16, has recently been promoted to the county swimming squad because of her excellent performances in the 100-metre freestyle event. She therefore has a new swimming coach, who has started to train different components of fitness. This has left Jackie confused, and she would like some clarification on the following questions.

1 Is the coach right in trying to reduce my body fat, and if so why?

2 The coach says he is tying to improve my power through training strength. Is this correct, and why?

3 He says that we should not train reaction time. Is this correct, and if not why not?

Gymnastics

Gymnastics has a number of different disciplines, for example the rings, beam and floor. It is quite unique in sport because it requires a combination of most health- and skill-related components of fitness.

Think it over

As a group, investigate the fitness requirements for gymnastics. Produce a spider diagram showing the links between the fitness components and the different disciplines. You may need to research the different disciplines to further your understanding before you produce the spider diagram. Some disciplines are:

● beam

● floor

● vault

● rings

● bars.

BISHOP BURTON COLLEGE

Dance

Dance includes a number of different disciplines and styles, for example:

- salsa
- tap
- ballet
- ballroom
- line.

Although they differ in their routines, moves and tempo, there are some common features in the fitness requirements of these different dance types:

- flexibility – vital for all forms of dance because the dancer has to move the body quickly into many different positions
- strength – dancing often involves lifting or carrying a partner, for example in ballet
- balance – the dancer sometimes has to hold a position for a number of seconds (static balance), and also requires dynamic balance while making complex moves
- co-ordination – in competition the judges will be looking for good co-ordination in executing a move correctly and with style
- aerobic endurance – dance routines are physically demanding and can often last up to an hour, therefore requiring aerobic endurance.

Combat sports

Combat sports normally involve a contest between two athletes. They include sports such as boxing, Olympic wrestling, sumo and some martial arts, such as karate. Professional boxing is normally contested over 12 three-minute rounds. Boxing requires the following components of fitness:

- strength – to produce power in a punch with the aim of delivering a knock-out blow; this needs to be sustained for 36 minutes, and so it is **strength-endurance** (the ability to produce power over a significant period of time)
- balance – poor balance will increase the chances of being knocked down, but good balance is also required to deliver a solid punch to the opponent

- muscular endurance – a boxer will throw up to 500 punches in a fight that lasts the full 36 minutes, so poor muscular endurance in the later stages of the fight is likely to lead to defeat, if the boxer is unable to punch the opponent consistently
- speed – a good level of hand speed is required; the better boxers are said to have quick hands, which ensures that their shots reach the target before their opponent can react
- aerobic endurance – the boxer is constantly moving around the ring, so aerobic fitness is important and is often trained through road running
- flexibility – see the case study below.

Case study

Although Kostya Tszyu (World Champion at welterweight) trains the traditional components of fitness for boxing, such as strength and power, he also concentrates on flexibility. The flexibility training is undertaken through gymnastic sessions that last for two hours within a six-hour daily training session.

1 Why do you think flexibility is important for boxing?

2 Why do some sportspeople tend to overlook flexibility?

3 If a boxer had poor flexibility, how would this influence the performance?

Invasion games

Invasion games include those listed below. The aim of the game is to score with the ball in the opponents' field of play, which has a net, basket, hoop or other designated target.

- football
- netball
- basketball
- hockey
- polo.

Basketball is classed as a team-based invasion game

The game of rugby has two codes, Rugby League and Rugby Union. League has 13 players, compared to 15 for Union. Because of their different rules, the two games differ in style; Rugby League is more flowing, and Rugby Union less so with its mauls and lineouts.

As with other invasion games, each positional role has different physical demands. A winger requires a great deal of speed, whereas a forward requires strength. The basic components of fitness for a rugby player are:

- upper and lower body strength – due to the contact nature of the sport, this is required in situations such as the scrum

- speed – when breaking with the ball and sprinting for the try line, it is important for players to have a good degree of speed

- power – both codes require a degree of jumping for the ball, so power in the legs is important

- agility – it is vital for the player running with the ball to avoid being tackled by the opposition, which means changing direction quickly

- balance – in changing direction at speed

- aerobic endurance and muscular endurance – a game lasts 80 minutes and players need to keep running throughout the game and make repeated sprints.

Net or wall games

Most net or wall games involve the use of a racquet and a divided court area, as in tennis and badminton, or a shared wall, as in squash. All the games listed below have the aim of getting the ball or shuttlecock into the opponent's area as often as possible without return:

- badminton
- tennis
- table tennis
- volleyball
- squash.

Squash is one of the most physically demanding games, and requires the following components of fitness:

- agility – the player must make rapid changes of direction constantly throughout the game to hit the ball
- strength – in the arm muscles to hold and use the racquet over a long period
- acceleration – speed when moving around the court is needed so the player can reach the ball before it hits the floor for the second time
- muscular endurance – in both upper and lower body, as the player has to make high intensity intermittent sprints throughout the game
- flexibility – on some occasions the ball must be played from the corner of the court, which requires a high level of flexibility
- balance – required when playing the shots and sprinting for the ball
- aerobic endurance – as some squash games can be more than an hour long, a good level of aerobic endurance is required for the continual running around the court.

Striking and/or fielding games

The basic principle behind striking and fielding games is that one team is attempting to score what are normally termed runs, while the other is trying to get them out and stop them scoring. Examples of striking and/or fielding games are:

- baseball
- rounders
- cricket.

Cricket contains three main disciplines – fielding, batting and bowling. They each require a mix of different fitness components. We will take batting as an example. Batting involves the player striking the ball with the aim of scoring runs and not getting out.

As with all sports the athlete needs good mental discipline to succeed at the top level. The mental attributes necessary for successful batting include:

- concentration
- focus
- decision-making skills
- alertness.

Batters are expected to run between the wickets to register a run, so they require:

- balance – poor balance when playing a shot will lead to a loss in power and may cause the batter to be out
- speed – when running between the wickets it is important to have good speed to reduce the chance of being run out
- strength – as the cricket bat can be quite heavy, the batter requires good strength in the arms, which also adds power to the shot
- aerobic endurance – some innings can last for six hours or more, so a good level of aerobic endurance is required to avoid fatigue later in the innings
- co-ordination – playing a shot in cricket requires a complex movement including most body parts. When hitting the ball it is also important to have good **hand-eye co-ordination**, which ensures the bat strikes the ball at the correct time.

Case study

Some players are classed as all-rounders – they are good at batting, bowling and fielding. An all-rounder will be expected to bat, bowl and field and on some occasions keep wicket. Andy Bichel is an all-rounder who played an important role in Australia's 2003 World Cup winning team. Bichel consistently produced world-class bowling, batting and fielding performances throughout the tournament.

1 What components of fitness are required for bowling?

2 What components of fitness are required for fielding?

3 What influences do you think the demands of being an all-rounder have on Andy Bichel's training regime?

Target games

Although the basic principle behind target games is the same – to hit or reach a target – target games can be quite different in nature, and include:

- golf
- bowls
- curling
- ten-pin bowling.

Golf is sometimes regarded as a game requiring little fitness, but this is far from the truth. The components of fitness for golf are:

- balance – good balance is central to any shot in golf, whether it is a drive or a putt

- flexibility – this is required throughout the body because the golf shot is a complex movement; good flexibility is needed in the ankle, knee, hip, shoulder and wrist joint as these form the basis of the golf shot

- co-ordination – linked to the need for good flexibility, co-ordination is also required to ensure the shot is executed in a skilful manner

- strength – a level of strength is required in the upper body to propel the golf ball further

- aerobic endurance – although golf requires a number of short explosive movements during the driving shots, there is a need for a good level of aerobic endurance because it involves walking for 4-5 miles depending on the course, and a round can take up to five hours. Poor aerobic endurance will mean that fatigue is likely to lead to a decrease in performance level over the closing holes.

Remember

- Each sport requires a different blend of health- and skill-related components of fitness, depending on the nature of the task.

- When considering which components of fitness are required, you should consider the sport, activity, and position played.

- In team-based sports, each position will require differing levels of fitness; for example in football, a winger will need more speed than a goalkeeper.

- Flexibility and balance are often overlooked when training in relation to most sports.

Assessment activity 10.3

This activity requires you to describe the fitness requirements of three contrasting sports.

1 As a group, produce a list on the whiteboard of all the different types of sports you play, watch or are interested in.

2 From this list, choose three contrasting sports with different fitness requirements (two may be the same as those identified in your pie charts in Assessment Activity 10.2 on page 82).

  For example, three contrasting sports could be:
  - golf
  - swimming
  - football.

3 Interview an athlete in each of your three chosen sports. The aim of the interview is to ascertain the fitness requirements for each sport. When you have gathered the information, complete a table like the following, linking the

sport to the component of fitness by placing a tick in the appropriate box.

Fitness component	Sport 1	Sport 2	Sport 3
Strength			
Muscular endurance			
Aerobic endurance			
Flexibility			
Body composition			
Agility			
Balance			
Reaction time			
Power			
Speed			
Co-ordination			

You may have to add to the table based on your own knowledge and research, if you feel a component of fitness has been overlooked in the interviews.

4 Type up the completed table and any other research you have identified as being important evidence for this assessment activity.

Health screening and fitness testing

This section will concentrate on the processes of health screening and fitness testing. Health screening must take place before any exercise or testing is performed by the client, and must be administered by the sports practitioner. It usually takes the form of a questionnaire and its aim is to identify any medical condition which would prevent the client from exercising safely; the aim is to ensure the health and safety of the client.

Case study

Barry, aged 42, is a computer specialist who has decided to start a training programme to lose a significant amount of body fat. Before being allowed to use the local gym, Barry is given a medical questionnaire during the induction process. The questionnaire has identified that recently Barry has been experiencing chest pains and shortness of breath. Also, last week while playing football he had pain in his left knee.

1 What is the aim of health screening in this case?
2 Would you allow Barry to start a training programme?
3 If not, which factors cause you concern about Barry's situation?

In an induction programme, as part of the health-screening process, the client should take a number of health-related fitness tests. These tests would evaluate blood pressure, cholesterol levels and lung function. The aim of these tests, as with the questionnaire, is to ensure that the client can safely undertake any type of exercise.

Practice

A number of organisations offer exercise facilities and programmes and are therefore involved in the practice of health screening and fitness testing. These organisations include:

- local authority-owned leisure centres
- health clubs
- fitness facilities
- primary care settings which offer facilities for special populations, such as the elderly.

Health clubs

In both the public and private sector, there are many health clubs in the UK providing facilities for fitness and exercise. As part of good practice, they need health-screening and fitness-testing programmes for all new members.

Screening and testing is normally carried out before the induction or during the induction process. At this stage the practitioner would complete the relevant paperwork, taking down personal details. Although each health club has different paperwork and ways of storing the information, the basic components will be as shown in the example on the next page.

Application form and health assessment

Section 1: Medical questionnaire

To be competed by all gym users

Have you ever suffered from any medical conditions? Have you had a surgical operation or injury in the past 3 years? If yes, please give details:

_____

Have you ever suffered from back pain? _____

Do you suffer from asthma? _____

Do you suffer with high blood pressure? _____

Have you or any member of your family ever suffered from coronary heart disease? _____

Do you have any allergies? _____

Do you suffer from epilepsy, dizzy spells or fits? _____

Do you take any drugs or medication? If yes, please state: _____

Please note: If you have answered yes to any of the above questions we may ask for a doctor's note of approval before a membership card or programme is issued.

Do you smoke? Yes/No   If so, how many? _____

How long have you smoked? _____   Would you like to stop? Yes/No

Do you drink alcohol? Yes/No   If so, how many units per week? _____

Doctor's name _____ Doctor's telephone _____

Doctor's address _____

Section 2: Declaration

I understand that if I use equipment or undertake exercise I do so at my own risk and I agree to accept such risk subject to the statutory duty owed to me by the Council.

Signed _____

Professional sports clubs

There is increasing use of health screening and fitness testing in professional sports clubs, especially in football, rugby, athletics, hockey and many more.

County-level clubs now use fitness testing as some tests are inexpensive and require only a limited level of experience to administer effectively. Professional sports clubs tend to use the tests to measure an athlete's fitness levels after injury or during pre-season training. Fitness tests are also used to assess fitness when a player is joining a club.

Case study

Wimbledon footballer Lionel Morgan returned to training after an injury and proved that he is fitter than ever. The 19-year-old left midfielder ruptured his knee ligaments in April 2002. At the end of October he underwent multi-stage 'bleep' testing for endurance, and improved on his personal best. His previous best was level 12, but after returning to fitness he reached level 13.6, and was delighted with the result.

1 Why is it important to use a fitness test after an injury?

2 Does it guarantee that the player has match fitness? What is meant by the term match fitness?

GP and medical referral schemes

Since the early 1990s, many areas of the UK have introduced GP referral schemes, also known as exercise-on-prescription schemes, with the aim of promoting a healthier lifestyle for individuals with certain medical conditions. The GP referral scheme works through a partnership of medical practitioners – GPs, practice nurses and other health care professionals – with local authority leisure centres. There are a number of specific conditions which may benefit from regular exercise, including:

● hypertension (raised blood pressure)

● obesity

● depression.

The process involved can be as in the following flowchart.

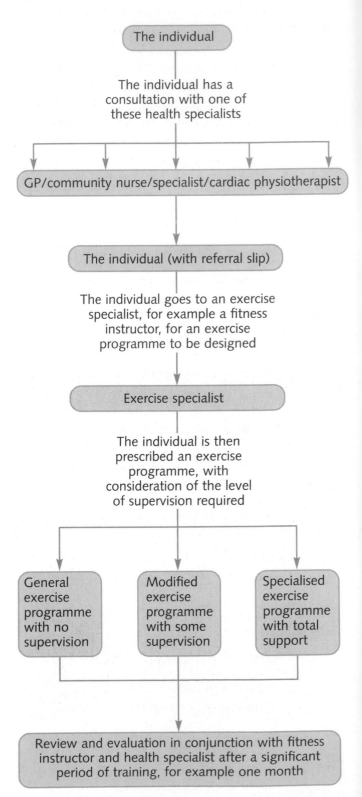

The referral process

An individual can be given a recommended exercise programme on the initiative of a variety of health specialists, for example the GP. The individual is then directed to a facility or professional who can design a specific fitness programme based on the individual's background. If the individual is deemed low risk by the health specialist, the programme will reflect this, with a reduction in the supervision required. A high-risk individual will require more supervision while working on the specific programme.

High-risk patients may have angina, established CHD or high blood pressure, for example. As shown in the chart on the previous page, the referral may come from a cardiac physiotherapist or specialist at the local hospital. For low-risk referrals, it is the GP's role to ensure the patient is medically fit to start the exercise programme, but in high-risk cases the specialist (for example the cardiologist) takes clinical responsibility.

Case study

In the area of Kelty and Cowdenbeath in Scotland a significant number of GP referral schemes have been introduced. These schemes have had the specific aim of reducing dependence on drug treatment by promoting exercise for specific patients who could benefit. These have proved to be very popular, and more GPs are now becoming involved.

1   As a group, discuss the advantages of using exercise rather than drugs to overcome certain conditions.
2   Identify the conditions which may benefit from regular exercise.
3   Discuss the reason for referral schemes becoming popular with some clients.
4   Some patients fail to complete the programme. Discuss possible reasons for this.

Health screening

Health screening is an important component of any exercise programme, and should be carried out with all individuals who are contemplating starting an exercise or fitness testing programme. It should be taken seriously by practitioners in the health and fitness industry, because it aim is to ensure the health and well being of clients.

The main role of the health screening process is to detect any diseases, illnesses or injuries. It also provides the individual with a number of baseline scores (for example, body fat percentage) so that any changes to health status can be monitored.

A high quality health-screening programme should involve a number of health checks, which may include the following components:

*   taking the client's past medical history
*   taking the family medical history
*   recording blood pressure
*   measuring lung function
*   checking cholesterol levels
*   measuring body composition
*   using an electrocardiograph (ECG) for monitoring heart conditions (used only in specialist facilities).

Think it over

In small groups, discuss and research the following questions.

1   When invited for health screening, many people do not attend. Draw up a list of the possible barriers to the screening process.
2   Discuss, with examples, why it is important for the sports practitioner to have a good level of competence and experience when involved in the health-screening process.
3   Describe the process of the health screening. Explain the roles of the client, medical practitioner and sports practitioner.

As specified by the ACSM, the aims of the screening process are to:

*   identify individuals who possess a medical condition, for example angina, which should exclude them from a testing or exercise session
*   identify individuals who require supervision or assistance while involved in a structured exercise programme

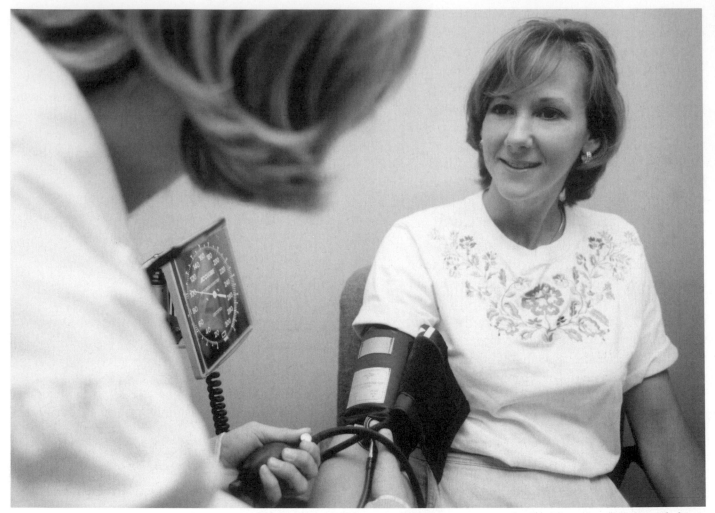

Health screening aims to ensure the health and well being of clients

- identify individuals who, because of their background and history, should have a medical check with their GP prior to having a fitness test or starting an exercise programme
- identify individuals who possess other special needs, for example Braille testing instructions for the visually impaired.

The following section will discuss the different methods used to screen individuals.

Lifestyle questionnaires

The practitioner must take into account a number of lifestyle habits when considering a client's health. This is normally done through a paper-based lifestyle questionnaire. The questionnaire should ask about:

- diet
- alcohol intake
- tobacco intake
- level of current physical activity.

The information provided should highlight any risks to the client posed by a fitness test or training programme. An example of a lifestyle evaluation form is shown on the next page.

Theory into practice

Try answering all the questions in the lifestyle evaluation form yourself.

Lifestyle evaluation

Smoking habits

1 Have you ever smoked cigarettes, cigars, or a pipe?   Yes/No

2 Do you smoke presently?

    Cigarettes _____ a day   Cigars _____ a day   Pipefuls _____ a day

3 At what age did you start smoking? _____ years

4 If you have quit smoking, when did you quit? _____

Drinking habits

1 During the past month, on how many days did you drink alcoholic beverages? _____

2 During the past month, how many times did you have 5 or more drinks per occasion? _____

3 On average, how many glasses of beer, wine or cocktails do you consume a week?

    Beer _____ glasses or cans   Wine _____ glasses

    Cocktails _____ glasses   Other _____ glasses

Exercise habits

1 Do you exercise vigorously on a regular basis?   Yes/No

2 What activities do you engage in on a regular basis? _____

3 If you walk, run or jog, what is the average number of miles you cover each workout? _____ miles

4 How any minutes on average is each of your exercise workouts? _____ minutes

5 How many workouts a week do you participate in on the average? _____ workouts

6 Is your occupation
   - ❏ Inactive (e.g. desk job)
   - ❏ Light work (e.g. housework, light carpentry)
   - ❏ Heavy work (e.g. heavy carpentry, lifting)

7 Tick those activities that you would prefer in a regular exercise programme for yourself:
   - ❏ Walking, running, or jogging
   - ❏ Bicycling
   - ❏ Basketball
   - ❏ Aerobic dance
   - ❏ Stationary running
   - ❏ Stationary cycling
   - ❏ Swimming
   - ❏ Stairclimbing
   - ❏ Jumping rope
   - ❏ Handball, racquetball, or squash
   - ❏ Step aerobics
   - ❏ Other (specify)
   - ❏ Tennis

Dietary habits

1 What is your current weight? _____ lb _____ kg Height? _____ in.

2 What would you like to weigh? _____ lb _____ kg

3 What is the most you ever weighed as an adult? _____ lb _____ kg

4 What is the least you ever weighed as an adult? _____ lb _____ kg

5 What weight loss methods have you tried? _____

6 Which do you eat regularly?
   ❏ Breakfast   ❏ Mid-morning snack   ❏ Lunch   ❏ Mid-afternoon snack   ❏ Dinner   ❏ After-dinner snack

7 How often do you eat out each week? _____ times

8   What size portions do you normally have?

❏ Small   ❏ Moderate   ❏ Large   ❏ Extra large   ❏ Uncertain

9   How often do you eat more than one serving?

❏ Always   ❏ Usually   ❏ Sometimes   ❏ Never

10   How long does it usually take you to eat a meal? _____ minutes

11   Do you eat while doing other activities (e.g. watching TV, reading, working)? _____

12   When you snack, how many times a week do you consume the following?

Biscuits, cake, pie _____   Sweets _____   Diet drinks _____   Soft drinks _____

Doughnuts _____   Fruit _____   Milk or milk beverage _____

Potato chips, pretzels, etc._____   Peanuts or other nuts _____   Ice cream _____

Cheese and crackers _____   Other _____

13   How often do you eat dessert? _____ times a day _____ times a week

14   What dessert do you eat most often? _____

15   How often do you eat fried foods? _____ times a week

16   Do you salt your food at the table?   Yes/No

❏ Before tasting it   ❏ After tasting it

It is important to note that the client may not be completely honest in his or her answers for a variety of reasons, such as feeling embarrassed. (You may be sympathetic to this after answering the questions yourself!) The practitioner must therefore refer the client to the GP, for the client's own safety, if there are any doubts. In addition, a less demanding fitness test may have to be used to flag up any health issues, for example poor aerobic endurance.

Key concept

If the practitioner is in any doubt regarding the suitability of the client, the client should automatically be referred to the GP for clearance.

Health-screening questionnaires

The health or fitness instructor should also use a questionnaire on health and physical activity. These questionnaires ask specific questions relating to past or current illnesses, for example angina. The instructor should use the information to select the correct level and types of exercises for the individual. The aim of the health-screening questionnaire is to identify any conditions which may worsen with exercise.

Medical history questionnaire

Demographic information

Last name _____   First name _____   Middle initial _____

Date of birth _____   Sex _____   Home phone _____

Address _____

City, county _____   Post code _____

Work phone _____   General practitioner _____

Section A

1 When was the last time you had a physical examination?

2 If you are allergic to any medications, foods or other substances, please name them.

_____

3 If you have been told that you have any chronic or serious illnesses, please list them.

4 Give the following information on the last 3 times you have been hospitalised. *Note:* Women, do not list normal pregnancies.

	Hospitalisation 1	Hospitalisation 2	Hospitalisation 3
Type of operation	_____	_____	_____
Month and year of hospitalisation	_____	_____	_____
Hospital	_____	_____	_____
City	_____	_____	_____

Section B

During the past 12 months:

1	Has a doctor prescribed any form of medication for you?	Yes	No
2	Has your weight fluctuated by more than a few pounds?	Yes	No
3	Did you attempt to bring about this weight change through diet or exercise?	Yes	No
4	Have you experienced any faintness, light-headedness or blackouts?	Yes	No
5	Have you occasionally had trouble sleeping?	Yes	No
6	Have you experienced any blurred vision?	Yes	No
7	Have you had any severe headaches?	Yes	No
8	Have you experienced chronic morning cough?	Yes	No
9	Have you experienced any temporary change in your speech pattern, such as slurring or loss of speech?	Yes	No
10	Have you felt unusually nervous or anxious for no apparent reason?	Yes	No
11	Have you experienced unusual heartbeats such as skipped beats or palpitations?	Yes	No
12	Have you experienced periods in which your heart felt as though it were racing for no apparent reason?	Yes	No

At present:

1	Do you experience shortness or loss of breath while walking with others your own age?	Yes	No
2	Do you experience sudden tingling, numbness, or loss of feeling in your arms, hands, legs, feet or face?	Yes	No
3	Have you ever noticed that your hands or feet sometimes feel cooler than other parts of your body?	Yes	No
4	Do you experience swelling of your feet and ankles?	Yes	No
5	Do you get pains or cramps in your legs?	Yes	No
6	Do you experience any pain or discomfort in your chest?	Yes	No

7 Do you experience any pressure or heaviness in your chest?   Yes   No

8 Have you ever been told that your blood pressure was abnormal?   Yes   No

9 Have you ever been told that your serum cholesterol or triglyceride level was high?   Yes   No

10 Do you have diabetes?   Yes   No

If yes, how is it controlled?

❏ Dietary means   ❏ Insulin injection   ❏ Oral medication   ❏ Uncontrolled

11 How often would you characterise your stress levels as being high?

❏ Occasionally   ❏ Frequently   ❏ Constantly

12 Have you ever been told that you have any of the following illnesses?

❏ Myocardial infarction   ❏ Arteriosclerosis   ❏ Heart disease   ❏ Coronary thrombosis

❏ Rheumatic heart   ❏ Heart attack   ❏ Coronary occlusion   ❏ Heart failure

❏ Heart murmur   ❏ Heart block   ❏ Aneurysm   ❏ Angina

Section C

Has any member of your immediate family been treated for or suspected to have any of these conditions? Please identify their relationship to you (father, mother, sister, brother, etc.).

A Diabetes _____   C Stroke _____

B Heart disease _____   D High blood pressure _____

Key concept

It is important that the completed questionnaires are kept in a secure place for reasons of confidentiality, and that they can be accessed only by authorised persons for details on a client's medical history.

Computer-based screening

A number of computer-based questionnaires can be found on the Internet, which give a basic assessment of health and lifestyle. These questionnaires aim to evaluate:

- activity levels
- nutritional intake
- body composition
- medical history.

After completing the questionnaire the individual can print out a copy of an evaluation, which should provide some form of comment on current health status.

Theory into practice

1 Visit a selection of the following sites and complete the computer-based assessments. Keep a copy of your results.

- www.amihealthy.com
- www.self.com/calculators/
- www.diabeticgourmet.com
- www.healthstatus.com
- www.jackswink.com

2 In your group, discuss the possible disadvantages of this type of health screening. A starting point may be to compare the service offered by a GP and that of a computer-based questionnaire.

Blood pressure

Measuring blood pressure is an important part of any test, and should be done with all individuals. Hypertension (high blood pressure) is a widespread health problem, affecting 20% of the world's adult

		16-24	25-34	35-44	45-54	55-64	65-74
Males							
	Normal (untreated)	98	97	93	83	58	47
	Normal (treated)	0	0	1	8	17	24
	High (treated)	0	0	0	2	8	13
	High (untreated)	2	3	6	8	17	17
Females							
	Normal (untreated)	100	98	93	84	62	42
	Normal (treated)	1	1	3	9	21	22
	High (treated)	0	0	0	2	6	15
	High (untreated)	0	0	3	6	11	21

Source: Health Survey for England, Department of Health 1997

population according to the World Health Organisation. If blood pressure remains high over a long period, there is an increased risk of heart attacks, strokes and kidney failure.

In the USA, 50 million people suffer from hypertension, which is approximately one in four adults. This causes a loss of 29 million working days per year, meaning a loss of $2 billion in earnings.

There is an increase in blood pressure as we age, as you can see from the table above, which shows percentages of people, by gender and age, who have the blood pressure indicated.

A number of factors cause hypertension, including:

- excessive amounts of body fat
- low levels of physical activity
- excessive intakes of salt
- excessive consumption of alcohol.

Blood pressure is normally measured using a mercury or digital sphygmomanometer. This measures systolic and diastolic blood pressure (see Unit 11, page 174 for a review of these terms). The average adult reading for blood pressure is 120 (systolic) over 80 (diastolic). The following table shows what different readings indicate.

Systolic	Diastolic	Result
<130	<85	Normal blood pressure
130-139	85-89	High/normal blood pressure
140-159	90-99	Stage 1 mild hypertension
160-179	100-109	Stage 2 moderate hypertension
180-209	110-119	Stage 3 severe hypertension
210 or more	120 or more	Stage 4 very severe hypertension

Case study

Martin, the local butcher aged 40, has been referred to your fitness centre in order to start a training programme. He was told by his local GP that his blood pressure was 165 over 100, and that he should start to exercise.

1 Comment on the blood pressure reading given to Martin, in terms of the possible health risks.

2 Which components of health-related fitness should you train, with the aim of reducing blood pressure? Why?

3 Are there any forms of exercise which Martin should not do for health reasons?

A number of sources of inaccuracies can influence the reading given. Poor technique by an inexperienced practitioner can invalidate the reading. The presence of a physician, nurse or practitioner can cause an increase in blood pressure because the client feels anxious, so an incorrect diagnosis of hypertension can be made. The protocol for measuring blood pressure is as follows.

- The client should be in a resting state, normally seated, for five minutes before measurement.

- The client should avoid intake of nicotine and caffeine for 30 minutes before measurement.

- The arm should be relaxed and at heart level.

- Place the rubber cuff around the upper arm so it covers the brachial artery (see the diagram below).

- Inflate the cuff, using the pump, above 170 mm HG – this stops the blood flow.

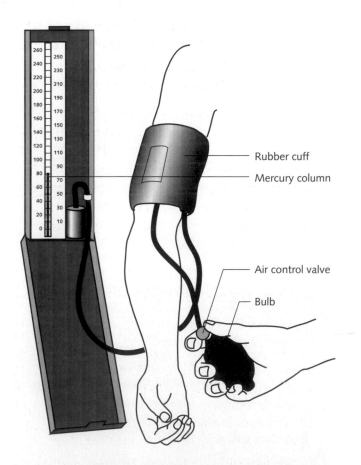

Preparing to measure blood pressure with a sphygmomanometer

Rubber cuff

Mercury column

Air control valve

Bulb

- Place a stethoscope over the brachial artery - there should be no sound because there is no blood flow.

- Release the pressure slowly by using the valve. At the systolic pressure the blood comes through the artery and a tapping sound is heard.

- Continue to reduce the pressure. When the sounds disappear this represents the diastolic blood pressure.

- Measure blood pressure twice within a three-minute period and record a mean average reading.

Think it over

In small groups, discuss the questions below about the following scenario. A middle-aged non-English-speaking woman has been invited for health screening at your fitness centre. Your screening programme involves taking blood pressure, measuring body fat and taking blood cholesterol measurements.

1 Identify three issues that should concern you as the sports practitioner in this situation.

2 Discuss ways to address the issues you have identified.

3 Draw up a list of other possible issues you may have to deal with while screening clients, for example wheelchair access to the health-screening equipment.

Lung function

The practitioner should assess the client's lung function during the health-screening process. Assessing lung function may identify conditions such as:

- asthma – lung disease which reduces the amount of air inhaled

- dyspnea – shortness of breath or laboured breathing, possibly due to various types of lung or heart diseases.

The normal measurement used when assessing lung function is known as **peak flow**. This is simply a measurement of how much a person can

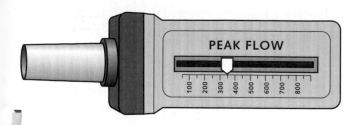

Peak flow meter used to measure lung function

exhale. Peak flow is measured by using a simple device known as the peak flow meter.

As with other tests, it is important that you use the correct procedures for measuring peak flow.

- Ensure the meter is set to zero or base level.
- Ask the client to stand, unless disabled.
- Ask the client to take a deep breath.
- Place the meter in the client's mouth ensuring the lips are placed around the mouthpiece.
- Instruct the client to blow out as hard as possible, which normally takes one to two seconds.
- Repeat this process so you have three readings. Take the highest value.
- Make sure you record the score on the evaluation sheet for the client.

Peak flow depends on age, height and sex. For example, a young boy who is 4 feet 10 inches tall should have a peak flow of approximately 350 litres per minute. A 50-year-old man of 5 feet 9 inches should have a peak flow of approximately 600 litres per minute. It is also important that you evaluate peak flow readings based on the client's previous scores – looking for any deterioration which may indicate a problem.

Cholesterol checks

Each client should be assessed for cholesterol levels prior to starting a fitness test or exercise programme.

Cholesterol is a waxy substance found within the cells and bloodstream, and it comes from the food

we eat as well as being made in the liver. High levels sustained over a period of time increase the chance of developing coronary heart disease. The measurement of cholesterol centres on three parameters: total cholesterol, low-density lipoprotein cholesterol, and high-density lipoprotein cholesterol.

- **Low-density lipoprotein cholesterol** is known as bad cholesterol and leads to atherosclerosis (thickening of the arteries).
- **High-density lipoprotein cholesterol** is known as good cholesterol and offers protection against heart disease.

Due to the complexity and the cost of the equipment involved, cholesterol assessment is likely to made by the GP. However, a number of high street stores now sell basic machines to measure cholesterol levels.

- Total cholesterol should be less than 200 milligrams per decilitre of blood.
- Low-density lipoprotein cholesterol should be less than 130 milligrams per decilitre of blood.
- High-density lipoprotein cholesterol should be above 35 milligrams per decilitre of blood.

Exercise can raise the levels of high-density lipoprotein cholesterol and can reduce the level of low-density lipoprotein cholesterol. However, it is important for you understand that changes in cholesterol are mainly brought about by changes in an individual's diet, especially if the client avoids foods high in saturated fat, for example deep-fried foods.

Theory into practice

High cholesterol levels are a major problem in the UK because of the high fat intake in many people's diets. This has a significant influence on the number of people who suffer from coronary heart disease. However, most people are unaware of their fat intake in comparison to protein and carbohydrate. This activity will allow you to measure the level of fat in your own diet.

1 Over a three-day period, write down all the foods you eat, together with the amount. You

could log the foods in a diary. See Unit 8 (pages 31–34) for more on methods of measuring your food intake.

2   Note the amount of carbohydrate, protein and fat (in grams) in the foods you eat. The nutritional content is clearly marked in grams on packaged food, and food tables can be used to assess others (see Unit 8 page 34).

3   Make a total for the three days in terms of carbohydrate, protein and fat (in grams).

4   Convert these totals into a percentage of total intake.

5   Compare your totals with the following recommended percentages:

   ● 60% carbohydrate
   ● 25% fat
   ● 15% protein.

Remember

● Fitness testing and health screening are used in many organisations, for example professional football clubs and local fitness centres.

● All clients should be screened for health problems before fitness testing, to ensure their safety.

● It is important that you measure factors such as height, weight, blood pressure, lung volumes and blood pressure to help you develop a picture of the client's health background.

● If you have any concerns regarding the health of your client, direct him or her to a GP before starting any form of exercise.

Assessment activity 10.4

For your assessment you are required to administer health-screening questionnaires to your two contrasting clients.

1   Prepare an appropriate health-screening questionnaire adapted to meet the needs of your clients. You can use the health questionnaire on pages 100–102 as a starting point, although you should make one of your own original design.

2   Ask your clients to complete the questionnaire after informing them of your aims.

3   Review the completed questionnaires to identify any possible health issues which may prevent a client from taking a particular fitness test. You may require tutor support to do this.

4   Store the information in a way that will ensure it is safe and confidential.

Fitness testing

Fitness testing has become more popular with the widespread recognition of the importance of fitness to physical performance and health. Fitness testing is used to measure and then evaluate a component of fitness, for example flexibility, for a variety of reasons. These may include the following.

● Identifying the strengths and weaknesses of a performer. For example, a speed test may find that a goalkeeper has poor speed, which influences his or her ability to clear a through ball.

● Identifying the stage of rehabilitation after injury or illness. The fitness test will inform the athlete about his or her recovery after any injury. For example, before an injury a runner could run one mile in five minutes. After months of rehabilitation, the runner records a time of 5 minutes 20 seconds. The test has highlighted the fact that the runner is still not at the level of fitness achieved before the injury and requires further aerobic training.

● Identifying talent. When testing a group of individuals, for example schoolchildren, it may be possible to identify talent in relation to a specific sport. If a child performs well in a test of upper body strength, he or she may be suited to the shot put, for example.

● As part of the health-screening process. Tests are regularly used as part of the health-screening process to identify issues that require further discussion with the sports practitioner or medical staff.

Key concept

Elite athletes continuously use fitness tests in their training programmes to assess their current fitness status and the effectiveness of the programme. Coaches at club level now regularly use a package of fitness tests, for example the multi-stage 'bleep' test (see page 114), with their athletes.

The following section discusses issues relating to the use of fitness tests.

Information about current states of health and fitness

The reasons for administering a fitness test include:

- identifying strengths and weaknesses, for example poor flexibility
- identifying the level of fitness for both health- and skill-related components
- setting individual goals to improve health and fitness
- identifying the exercises required for the exercise prescription
- developing a health and fitness profile.

Baseline scores

Fitness tests provide information on the level of the client's fitness before a training programme – baseline scores. Re-testing the client after a significant number of training weeks makes it possible to evaluate whether the programme has been a success. The practitioner should follow this procedure:

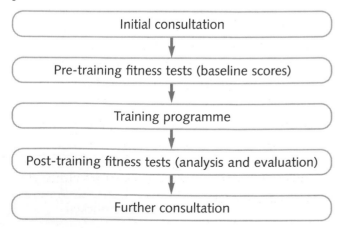

Initial consultation

Pre-training fitness tests (baseline scores)

Training programme

Post-training fitness tests (analysis and evaluation)

Further consultation

If the re-tested fitness levels are significantly higher than the baseline scores, this will motivate the client to carry on with the training programme.

Body measurements

Before starting any testing or exercise programme, the client's body weight in kilograms should be recorded. This is especially important when the client is training to reduce weight. Weight should be checked on a regular basis (every four weeks) to identify any changes. A variety of scales can be used to measure body weight, but all should be checked for accuracy. The client should be weighed at the same time of day to avoid any changes due to daily fluctuations in weight.

Height measurements

Height measurements are also taken at the initial consultation. Height is important data for some fitness tests. Height measurements are normally taken using a stadiometer (see the diagram opposite) with the client in bare feet standing as erect as possible.

Initial consultation

The initial consultation stage is very important for the practitioner and the client, as it builds the relationship between them. The initial consultation may take up to an hour, and involves a number of factors, such as:

- taking a record of personal details – name, contact number, GP's name, etc.

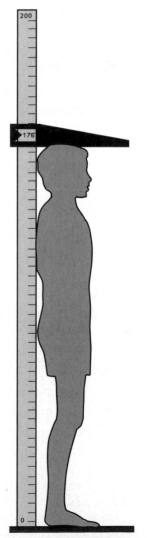

Stadiometer

- identifying and setting out the client's goals, for example assessing and improving aerobic fitness

- lifestyle evaluation

- health evaluation

- listing of any medications taken

- obtaining informed consent for fitness tests and programmes

- health-related fitness tests – for example blood pressure and body composition

- setting out your aims as a practitioner – what you will do, how you will approach the issue, etc.

Think it over

Many clients do not enjoy the initial consultation stage, for a variety of reasons. This means that some people are deterred from returning to the fitness or leisure centre. In groups, draw up a list of the possible reasons why people could regard the initial consultation as an unpleasant experience. In your discussions, include the possible communication issues between the client and the sports practitioner.

Pre-test procedures

Before starting a testing session there are a number of factors to consider. Although there is only a limited risk to health when fitness testing, the practitioner needs to act in a professional manner. The pre-test procedures should include the following checklist:

Test protocols

Each fitness test has a specific protocol. A test protocol is a system of rules which sets out the correct way of using the test. If the practitioner does not follow the correct protocol the results will not be valid and will not show a true picture of the client's fitness. The protocol for each test should state the following:

- the equipment to be used – for example treadmill

- the duration of the test – for example three minutes

- the correct technique for the test

- the type of facilities required – for example a gymnasium

- who the test is suitable for – for example schoolchildren only

- the sequence of activities – for example run for three minutes and then have the pulse rate taken for 15 seconds

- the data required – for example pulse rate or distance covered in metres

- how to calculate the results – some fitness tests require a specific equation to be calculated.

Validity and reliability

When choosing a fitness test, the practitioner must consider its validity and reliability. Only a test that has reliable results and is valid will provide useful information. When assessing for **validity**, the practitioner should try to answer the following question:

To do	✔
Select the correct piece of testing equipment for the test	
Make sure the equipment is well maintained and is safe to use based on the manufacturer's guidelines	
Ensure the practitioner is clear about the correct protocol	
Ensure health screening takes place prior to testing	
Perform a risk assessment taking into account the environment, equipment and protocol	
Ask the client to complete an informed consent form	
Have a contingency plan in place in case of an accident or incident – where to call, whom to inform, etc.	
Make sure someone is present who holds a full first-aid qualification and that the first-aid bag is fully stocked	

Does the fitness test or piece of equipment (for example heart rate monitor) measure what it is supposed to measure?

The component of fitness to be tested, for example strength, should be matched with a test. To measure strength you might use the one-repetition maximum test (see page 117).

Case study

The new coach of the local rugby team needed to test the players' fitness levels. He decided to test the players' speed, as this is important for rugby. After some thought the coach decided to time them in a 1.5-mile run.

1 Was this a valid test? Why, or why not?
2 Discuss the implications of this test for the players, coach and possible team selection.

A major part of whether a test and therefore results are valid is its **reliability**. Reliability means the consistency of the scores obtained while testing on different occasions.

In the table below we can see that the results of the second athlete's tests were highly variable, and we would class these scores as unreliable. Poor reliability means that the test is not valid and does not produce any meaningful or useful information. There may be a number of reasons for poor reliability, such as poor testing technique or a different practitioner being used. The first athlete's scores do seem consistent and valid, so the results could be used in relation to a baseline score.

Results obtained using a standard flexibility test		
Week number	Athlete 1	Athlete 2
1	20 cm	5 cm
2	22 cm	20 cm
3	21 cm	13 cm

Selection of appropriate tests

A number of tests are available for you to use, so it is obviously important that you select the appropriate test for your client, remembering that each individual is likely to have different requirements.

When choosing a test you should consider the medical and lifestyle history of the client. For example a patient who suffers from angina should not be given a maximal test for aerobic endurance as this may cause severe injury or illness. It would be advisable to select a low-intensity exercise test for this type of client, such as the Harvard step test (see page 116).

You also need to consider the main sport of your client. If the local rugby team wants you to test a player for aerobic endurance, this should be a test based on running and not swimming.

Key concept

The test must be specific to the client in terms of the sport and position played.

Test sequence

When you administer a number of tests it is important that you test in the correct sequence with adequate rest periods in between. If you do not test in a logical order the results are likely to be invalid. For example, if you test for aerobic endurance, which is physically demanding, this will lead to an increase in heart rate. If you then test for resting heart rate your results will be polluted. The ACSM produced the following guidelines in 1995 for test sequence:

1 Resting blood pressure and heart rate
2 Body composition
3 Aerobic endurance
4 Strength/muscular endurance
5 Flexibility.

Case study

Paulo, 17, is a new employee at the Sunshine Gym. He has recently performed his first set of fitness tests on a client, John Wallis. He performed the tests in the following order:

1 Flexibility
2 Aerobic endurance
3 Resting blood pressure and heart rate
4 Strength/muscular endurance
5 Body composition.

1 Why did John Wallis suffer a pulled abdominal muscle while performing a flexibility test?

2 Why were his resting blood pressure and heart rate readings higher than his normal values?

3 Why did John Wallis feel uncomfortable and self-conscious about having his skinfold measurements taken after an aerobic fitness test?

Recording of test results

It is vital that you record all the results from all your testing sessions as these form the basis of your analysis and interpretation. It is important to note that these results must remain confidential.

For recording your results you may want to use a simple paper-based method, using a table designed by yourself. However, it is advisable for safety reasons that you transfer these results to a computer programme, which will help you generate graphs and tables for analysis. You must keep your records in a safe place – asking the client to retest because you have mislaid the results would be very unprofessional. The results should be filed with the health and medical questionnaires in the client's own individual file.

Some of the tests you do will require a number of practitioners or helpers. It would be advisable for someone else to write down the results while you are involved in the testing to avoid confusion.

Analysis and interpretation

It is important to analyse and interpret the data you have gathered. The aim of the analysis and interpretation is to make an assessment of the client's fitness in terms of either a baseline score or progress in a training programme.

Compare your data against normative data for the specific test you have used. Normative data allows you to analyse how well the client has performed compared to others of the same age and gender. Classify your data according to the rating given, which normally ranges from poor to excellent. An example of normative data is shown for the abdominal curl test.

Abdominal curl test scores		
Fitness category	**Men**	**Women**
Very poor	below 15	below 10
Poor	15-24	10-15
Fair	25-34	16-25
Average	35-44	26-35
Good	45-50	36-40
Excellent	above 50	above 40

In addition to this you need to analyse the results in comparison with the client's baseline data or previous scores for that test.

Once you have analysed and interpreted the data, give either written or verbal feedback to the client.

Verbal and written feedback

The information you have gained from the fitness test should be given to the client as either verbal or written feedback. There are a few basic rules to follow when giving verbal feedback.

- Ensure the feedback is given in a quiet environment with no distractions, as some information may be confidential and personal.

- Don't baffle the client with science or technical jargon – unless he or she understands these terms – as this is likely to confuse the issue. For example, say 'aerobic endurance' rather than 'cardiovascular fitness'.

- Remember to link the results to the targets or goals set for the individual.

- If the client has made only small improvements below target, remain positive and stress that results are going in the right direction.

- If the results are poor, be ready to suggest other ways of improving fitness. For example, suggest changing from running to swimming, if this may be more suitable for the individual.

- It may be appropriate to reset goals or targets based on the results. For example, a person who now has good aerobic endurance may want to concentrate more on speed or flexibility.

Written feedback to clients can be produced in a number of formats. However, as with verbal feedback, it must remain simple and easy to understand and be applicable to the specific client. You can show a comparison of the client's data against normative data, either in a graph or a table. Graphs and tables can be generated through a computer programme, which will then provide a fitness profile for the client to show strengths and weaknesses.

Facilities and equipment

You are likely to need a wide range of facilities and equipment. Tests can be performed outside, in the fitness suite, gymnasium, laboratory, consultation room, local sports club or even in the classroom. It is your duty as practitioner to make sure that the facility is appropriate for the test; for example blood pressure readings should be taken in a relaxing environment.

Key concept

As all fitness tests have different protocols they require different equipment – some being as simple as a tape measure, some as complex as a machine that measures blood cholesterol.

As the practitioner you have three main duties regarding the equipment:

- Ensure on a regular basis that the equipment works as described by the manufacturer and that it is calibrated correctly (one kilogram on the scales should really be one kilogram).

- Through practice and guidance, you should be capable of using the equipment in a professional manner; for example, taking blood pressure readings requires a level of experience and expertise. If you do not possess this level of expertise your results are likely to be invalid and unreliable, giving the client the impression that you are unprofessional.

- Maintain the health and safety of the client.

Health and safety

As the practitioner you should have a good understanding and awareness of health and safety when testing a client. Maintaining good practice is paramount to ensure the health and safety of yourself, the client and others.

It is important to consider health and safety before, during and after the testing session. Throughout this unit we have identified a number of factors which must be considered in relation to

health and safety. The following checklist may help you ensure you have covered everything.

Health and safety checklist	✔
Risk assessment	
Health questionnaire	
Lifestyle questionnaire	
Informed consent	
Health screening e.g. blood pressure	
Warm-up	
Appropriate clothing (client and practitioner)	
Suitable testing environment	
Equipment in working order as per manufacturer instructions	
Experience in using equipment and protocol	
Cool-down	
After-test welfare of client	
First-aid provisions and training	

Informed consent

The client must complete an 'informed consent' form before testing. The form should explain the purpose and nature of the physical fitness tests the client is about to undertake. It should also detail any potential risks that may be present, and explain the benefits of the test to the client.

Key concept

If you are testing anyone under the age of 18, the consent form must be signed before testing by a parent or guardian.

A number of designs for informed consent forms are available. An example is shown on the next page.

Consent form

Informed consent for physical fitness test

In order to more safely carry on an exercise programme, I hereby consent, voluntarily, to exercise tests. I shall perform a graded exercise test by riding a cycle ergometer or walking/running on a treadmill. Exercise will begin at a low level and be advanced in stages. The test may be stopped at any time because of signs of fatigue. I understand that I may stop the test at any time because of my feelings of fatigue or discomfort or for any other personal reason.

I understand that the risks of this testing procedure may include disorders of heart beats, abnormal blood pressure response, and, very rarely, a heart attack. I further understand that selection and supervision of my test is a matter of professional judgement.

I also understand that skinfold measurements will be taken at a number of sites to determine percentage body fat and that I will complete a sit-and-reach test and curl-up test to evaluate factors related to lower back function.

I desire such testing so that better advice regarding my proposed exercise programme may be given to me, but I understand that the testing does not entirely eliminate risk in the proposed exercise programme.

I understand that information from my tests may be used for reports and research publications. I understand that my identity will not be revealed.

I understand that I can withdraw my consent or discontinue participation in any aspect of the fitness testing or programme at any time without penalty or prejudice towards me.

I have read the statements above and have had all of my questions answered to my satisfaction.

Signed _____

Witness _____

Date _____

(Copy for participant and for programme records)

Confidentiality

Those involved in testing or training have a duty of confidentiality regarding their clients. They should ensure any personal information such as medical history is stored in a secure place. Any information should remain confidential and should not be discussed with other instructors and clients. It is also recommended that when working in exercise referral schemes, exercise practitioners should have a policy on confidentiality included in their contract of employment.

Think it over

While working in his local fitness centre on a GP referral scheme, a fitness instructor is found to be discussing the personal issues of a client with other clients, workmates and friends. The topics involved include medical history, current illnesses and personal details of the client. After a time the client discovers the breach of confidentiality.

As a group, discuss the implications and consequences of this for the instructor, client, other members of staff, managers, the fitness centre and the GP.

Remember

- Each fitness test has a specific protocol or procedure, which must be followed to produce a good level of reliability and validity.

- Where possible, fitness test results should be compared against normative data, which allows a form of evaluation.

- It is important that all information is stored safely and remains confidential.

Assessment activity 10.5

Before you administer any fitness tests to your two contrasting clients, it is important to identify which components of fitness (health- and skill-related) they need to be tested for. You need to understand the individual goals and needs of the client.

1 Arrange interviews at convenient times for your two clients (the interview will probably last for around 15 minutes).

2 During the interviews, note down the key points (you will need to write these up for your assessment).

3 Ensure the interview concentrates on the individual goals and needs of your client. From these you should be able to identify some specific components of fitness to concentrate on. For example, your client may be a footballer, so his or her individual needs may centre on speed, aerobic endurance, power and muscular endurance, which are vital for football.

4 Identify four components of fitness for both clients (these are unlikely to be the same, because they will have different goals and needs). Complete a table like the following.

Component of fitness	Client 1 name: _____	Client 2 name: _____
1		
2		
3		
4		

Appropriate fitness tests

This section will identify the current protocols and testing procedures used to assess a variety of fitness components.

Aerobic or cardiovascular endurance tests

Aerobic endurance is the ability of the cardio-respiratory system to supply the exercising muscles with oxygen, which can be assessed through a variety of different protocols. Aerobic exercises are those exceeding one minute. In general, a person with a higher Vo_2 maximum will have a higher level of aerobic fitness (in $L.min^{-1}$). Aerobic endurance classifications were published in table form in Kenneth H. Cooper's *The Aerobics Way* (Bantam Books).

There are numerous maximal tests (where the client works to his or her maximum) and sub-maximal tests (where the client works below maximum) available to measure aerobic fitness, which the following section will describe.

Multi-stage fitness test

Owing to its ease of administration and the speed of results, the multi-stage fitness test (also known as the 'bleep' test) is widely used. This maximal test is ideal for testing in sports based on multi-sprint activities, such as football and rugby. The test is progressive in terms of intensity (speed) and is used to predict a client's Vo_2 maximum based on how far the client progresses during the test. The equipment required for the test is minimal, consisting of the multi-stage fitness test tape, audio cassette player, cones and a space in excess of 20 metres. Once the practitioner is clear about the protocol, the test normally takes around 20 minutes.

Before starting the test the client is advised to do a warm-up, which should include a stretching programme. The client is asked to run between cones placed 20 metres apart and keep in time with the bleeps emitted from the tape. The aim is

Multi-stage fitness test

to reach the cone when the tape bleeps, not before or after. After every minute the bleeps become progressively faster, which has the effect of increasing the speed at which the client must run. The goal is to run for as long as possible while keeping up with the bleeps, until fatigue makes it impossible to keep pace. If the client misses three consecutive bleeps, he or she is asked to stop the test. While the client is running the practitioner or helper should be monitoring the level and shuttle number the athlete has reached. The Vo_2 maximum score is converted from the last shuttle number completed.

From a health and safety perspective, the following considerations should be taken into account:

- ensure there is a non-slippery surface
- ensure the room is well ventilated
- check that running footwear is suitable, with adequate grip
- ensure the client has not eaten for 2-3 hours before the test
- avoid dehydration by ensuring a high fluid intake has been achieved over the previous day.

The test is ideal for testing a large number of people (for example, a class of schoolchildren) and produces results within a matter of minutes.

However, there is a possibility of inaccurate measurements if the practitioner miscounts the finishing level, and the tape requires calibration (one minute on the tape should be one minute in reality).

Cooper 12-minute run

The Cooper 12-minute run is a maximal test which estimates Vo_2 maximum based on the following equation:

Vo_2 maximum $(ml.kg^{-1}min^{-1}) = 11.2872 + (35.9712 \times$ miles covered$)$

The basic concept of the test is that the client is asked to cover the longest distance possible within 12 minutes, with the distance recorded in miles. If a client covered a distance of 1.5 miles, his or her Vo_2 maximum would be estimated at 65.24 $ml.kg^{-1}min^{-1}$.

This test is predominately used in schools and amateur clubs, because of its ease of use and the minimal equipment required. It is demanding, so it requires a significant amount of motivation from the athlete.

Although this test is simple to administer it has a number of limitations:

- it can be influenced by environmental conditions

- the correlation between the distance covered in miles and Vo2 maximum is r = 0.65 to 0.90, which can be described as being a fairly good level of correlation at best
- the test tends to overestimate Vo2 maximum scores
- a high level of motivation is required
- pacing can be a problem for less experienced athletes.

1.5-mile performance timed run

As with the Cooper 12-minute run, this test is widely used because it is easy to use and brings speedy results. The client runs the designated 1.5-mile distance as fast as possible. Unlike in the Cooper test, the practitioner does not need to use a formula as the time is simply assessed against a set of normative data scores. However, little comparison can be made between two clients who used two different courses, because of the environmental differences.

Harvard step test

Theory into practice

Using the Internet or sources identified at the end of this unit, identify the fitness scores and classifications (normative data) for the Cooper 1.5-mile run test.

This style of test allows adaptation by the practitioner in terms of the testing distance. If the client is a long-distance runner, he or she may wish to be tested over three miles, for example. Finding normative data would be difficult but the practitioner could evaluate the time against previous times recorded by the same athlete.

Harvard step test

Unlike the tests previously discussed, the Harvard step test is a sub-maximal test. It uses the athlete's recovery heart rate to estimate the Vo_2 maximum score. As this test is not too physically demanding, it can be used with special populations such as over 55s. The client is asked to step up and down on a bench (approximately 41.3 cm high) to a

specific beat (normally generated by a metronome) for a period of five minutes.

Males taking the test should step at 24 steps per minute, and females should step at 22 steps per minute. The heart rate is recorded for a 15-second period, between 5 and 20 seconds after finishing the exercise. The 15-second heart rate count should then be multiplied by 4 to calculate the heart beats per minute (b.min^{-1}). For example, 15 b.min^{-1} x 4 = 60 b.min^{-1}. The respective heart rate for males and females should then be put into the following equations to calculate the Vo_2 maximum:

- Male – Vo_2 maximum (ml.kg^{-1}min^{-1}) = 111.33 – (0.42 x heart rate)
- Female – Vo_2 maximum (ml.kg^{-1}min^{-1}) = 65.81 – (0.1847 x heart rate)

It is strongly recommended that this test is not used with elite athletes, who require precise results, because the validity of the Vo_2 maximum score is questionable. The test is sub-maximal in nature and predicts the score, so there are possible errors. It has been reported that there may be a variability in scores of ± 16%, which is considerable.

Theory into practice

Within your group, test each other using the multi-stage fitness protocol and record your results in a table like the one below. In the following week, at the same time of day to avoid biological fluctuations, test for aerobic fitness using the Harvard step test and again record your results.

Name	Multi-stage fitness test ml.kg^{-1}min^{-1}	Harvard step test ml.kg^{-1}min^{-1}

1 Calculate the differences between the two sets of raw data from the different protocols.
2 Compare and contrast any differences and offer any possible reasons.
3 Based on the reliability and validity of results, decide which protocol would be most suited to use with an elite athlete, explaining your reasoning.

Yo yo endurance test

This test should be used for sportspeople who perform endurance exercises, such as long-distance running. It converts the results to a Vo_2 maximum score. Similar to the multi-stage fitness test, this test is based on 20-metre running intervals. There are 20 different running speeds and a number of repetitions or intervals ranging between 7 and 15. From the tape, which omits a bleep, the client starts each interval and tries to reach the end of the interval before the next bleep. The client keeps going until he or she can no longer continue and a score is recorded, for example 17-8 (17 being the speed and 8 being the interval number).

Theory into practice

Prepare and deliver a five-minute presentation to the rest of the group on the different fitness tests which can be used to evaluate a client's aerobic endurance. Outline the protocols used by the different tests.

Muscular strength tests

Strength is the ability of a specific muscle or muscle group to exert a force in a single maximal contraction. We often think of the concept of strength in relation to athletes such as weightlifters and boxers. As with aerobic fitness, there are numerous methods of assessing a person's strength.

1 RM

The one-repetition maximum strength test (1 RM) is often used to measure dynamic strength in a specific muscle group. Simply put, the test measures the maximum mass the client can lift in one single movement and is normally performed on a fixed resistance machine.

The machine selected for the test should reflect the specific muscle groups used by the client in his or her sport. For example, a Rugby League player who requires a good level of lower body strength should use a machine such as a leg press.

After a suitable warm-up to avoid injury, the client attempts a mass which is well within his or her capability. After each attempt the client should increase the mass by no more than 5 kg. Between trials there should be a rest period of three minutes. The client continues to add mass until the one-repetition maximum is achieved. The score can be converted into a percentage of the client's body mass.

Example: A Rugby League player who has a body mass of 100 kg and had a one-repetition maximum of 110 kg would have a 1 RM percentage of 110%.

Fixed resistance weights machines are used to measure 1 RM

Dynamometers

The basic concept behind dynamometers is that the client has to squeeze, push or pull to measure isometric strength, which is measured in kilograms. The dynamometer is a mechanical device to measure the force generated in a specific muscle group. There are a number of different types of dynamometers, which test strength in the handgrip, back, and leg.

The handgrip dynamometer takes a direct measure of peak force generated by the client. It is important to understand that the result obtained from the handgrip test should not used to assess the muscular strength in other muscle groups.

Once the results have been obtained they can be compared against a table such as the following, which gives norms for 16–19-year-olds.

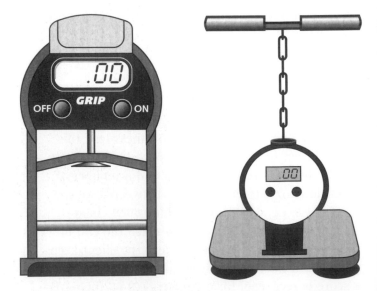

Grip dynamometer   *Back dynamometer*

Grip: muscular strength in kilograms	
Rating	Kilograms
	73.0
	69.5
Super	65.5
	64.0
	62.0
Excellent	60.0
	58.5
	56.5
Good	55.0
	53.0
	51.0
Average	48.5
	48.0
	45.5
Fair	44.0
	42.0
	40.0
Poor	38.0
	36.5
	33.0
Very poor	29.0

Back strength normative data (kilograms)		
	Male	Female
Excellent	180-161	120-101
Above average	160-131	100-81
Average	130-101	80-61
Below average	100-81	60-41
Poor	80	40

These types of dynamometers are relatively cheap to buy and maintain, and easy to use for the client and practitioner. One disadvantage of these machines is that they may lead to strained muscles if poor technique is used. From a health and safety perspective, individuals who have high blood pressure should avoid these isometric exercises as they increase blood pressure and may lead to medical complications.

Isokinetic machines

The measurement of muscular strength has evolved over recent years to include the use of computers to aid assessment. Isokinetic dynamometer

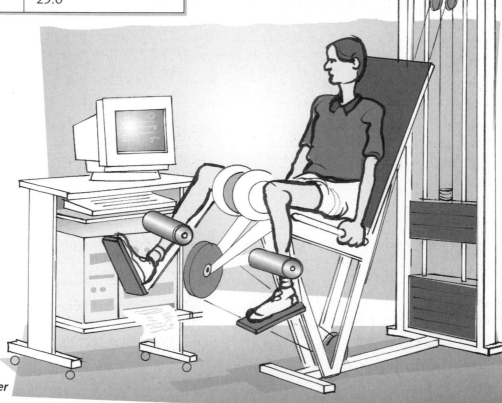

Isokinetic dynamometer

machines are controlled by a computer and are capable of varying the resistance (load). Although the load is variable the movement is constant in terms of speed (isokinetic movement).

A force transducer measures the force generated by the client over a specific time period and produces more reliable results than traditional dynamometer devices.

Muscular endurance tests

Muscular endurance, as we have seen, is the capacity of a specific muscle or muscle group to make repeated contractions over a period of time.

One-minute press-up test

The press-up test, also known as the push-up test, is used to assess muscular endurance in the upper body. To improve the validity of the results and avoid injury, it is important that the client uses the correct technique for the test. The hands should be shoulder-width apart and the back straight. The practitioner or a helper should place a fist below the client's chest on the mat or floor. For the press-up to be counted as one repetition, the client's

chest should touch the fist on the floor. The client is required to do as many press-ups as possible within one minute, based on the correct technique.

For some individuals who have less upper body strength, the technique can be modified. The client can flex his or her knees to 90° in a kneeling position, with the ankles crossed.

One-minute curl-up test

The one-minute curl-up test is similar to the press-up test in nature, as it measures local muscular endurance. It is also known as the sit-up or abdominal curl test. It is important that there is a helper for this test to hold the feet in a stationary positions. The client is positioned on the mat with the hips flexed and knees flexed to 90°, with the feet flat on the mat. The normative data table below is based on a protocol which requires the athlete to perform as many as possible until there is total fatigue. A full movement requires the elbows to touch the knees, and the shoulders must touch the mat after the downward movement. Clients with neck or back pain should not try this test. It should be preceded by a suitable warm-up of neck and leg muscles.

Press-up test – number of repetitions completed						
Age (years)						
Men	**15-19**	**20-29**	**30-39**	**40-49**	**50-59**	**60-69**
Excellent	39+	36+	30+	22+	21+	18+
Above average	29-38	29-35	22-29	17-21	13-20	11-17
Average	23-28	22-28	17-21	13-16	10-12	8-10
Below average	18-22	17-21	12-16	10-12	7-9	5-7
Poor	<18	<17	<12	<10	<7	<5

Age (years)						
Women	**15-19**	**20-29**	**30-39**	**40-49**	**50-59**	**60-69**
Excellent	33+	30+	27+	24+	21+	17+
Above average	25-32	21-29	20-26	15-23	11-20	12-16
Average	18-24	15-20	13-19	11-14	7-10	5-11
Below average	12-17	10-14	8-12	5-10	2-6	1-4
Poor	<12	<10	<8	<5	<2	<1

Curl-up test scores		
Fitness category	Men	Women
Very poor	below 15	below 10
Poor	15-24	10-15
Fair	25-34	16-25
Average	35-44	26-35
Good	45-50	36-40
Excellent	above 50	above 40

Flexibility tests

Flexibility is important for health and for all sports movements. It describes the possible movement around a joint or number of joints. Some methods for assessing a client's flexibility are detailed below.

Repeated sprint test

Unlike the curl-up test the repeated sprint test requires the client to use all his or her major muscle groups to complete the test. The distance the client sprints can be changed to match the demands of the sport involved, for example a footballer may sprint a 15-metre distance.

The athlete uses a one-metre flying start prior to sprinting over the specified distance; and the time is recorded using a stopwatch or timing gates. After completing one sprint the client jogs back slowly to the start again, and performs another sprint.

It is common practice to ask the client to perform 10 repeated sprints, with the test time period being around 10 minutes. The aim of performing 10 sprints is to evaluate the client's ability to make repeated sprints while maintaining a level of consistency in the recorded times. Based on the recorded times, the practitioner can calculate the level of fatigue through the fatigue index:

Fatigue index (%) =
$$\frac{\text{(fastest time} \times \text{total number of sprints)} \times 100}{\text{Total times of all sprints}}$$

Sit and reach

The most common test for measuring flexibility is the sit-and-reach test, which is designed to assess the flexibility of the hamstrings and lower back. The equipment required for this test is minimal – it consists of a yardstick and a bench. It is recommended that the client's legs should be 12 inches (30.5 cm) apart with the heels touching the bench.

Sit-and-reach test

The client should reach forward slowly and as far as possible without causing injury, keeping the hands parallel. The knee joint should not flex. The score is obtained by recording the furthest point obtained by the fingertips against the yardstick. If the client fails to reach the 0 mark then he or she is given a minus score, for example –14 cm.

The test should be done three times with a mean score being calculated. Evaluate the mean score against the following data.

Theory into practice

Perform the repeated sprint test and calculate the fatigue index for the person tested. In addition to this, plot the time in seconds against the sprint number using a line graph.

1 Based on your line graph, comment on the person's ability to maintain sprint times.

2 Which sports would be best suited to using this test?

Rating	Men	Women
Excellent	>17.9	>17.9
Good	17.0-17.9	16.7-17.9
Average	15.8-16.9	16.2-16.6
Fair	15.0-15.7	15.8-16.1
Poor	<15.0	<15.7

Shoulder and wrist

This test is similar to the sit-and-reach test, as it uses a one-metre rule to assess flexibility.

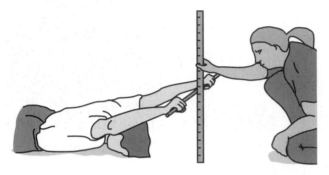

Shoulder and wrist flexibility test

The client lies on the floor with arms fully extended behind the back and a one-metre rule in the hands. The aim of the test is to raise the rule as high as possible, while ensuring the nose remains on the ground. The practitioner should measure the vertical distance (in centimetres) from the floor to the rule.

Rating	Men	Women
Excellent	>12.5	>11.75
Good	12.5-11.5	11.75-10.75
Average	11.49-8.25	10.74-7.5
Fair	8.24-6	7.49-5.5
Poor	<6	<5.5

Trunk and neck

As with the previous test the client should lie face down on the floor. The hands should be gripped at the side of the head. The client raises the trunk as high as possible, keeping the hips on the floor. A

Trunk and neck flexibility test

helper can hold the feet down while the test is taking place. The distance recorded by the practitioner should be the vertical distance from the ground to the tip of the client's nose.

Rating	Men	Women
Excellent	>10	>9.75
Good	10-8	9.75-7.75
Average	7.99-6	7.74-5.75
Fair	5.99-3	5.74-2
Poor	<3	<2

Direct measurement

Direct measurement of flexibility can be made using a goniometer, which is normally plastic or metal and comes in different sizes depending on the joint which requires assessment. The goniometer can measure the range of motion at a joint.

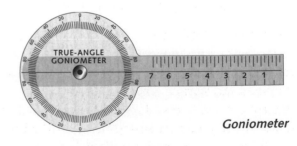

Goniometer

The centre of the goniometer is placed at the axis of rotation of the joint. The arms (similar to a basic ruler) are lined up the with long axis of the specified bones. After the athlete has made the movement, the change in position is recorded by measuring the angle in degrees on the goniometer. Although this method can provide a precise reading in terms of degrees, it is difficult for the practitioner to determine the axis of rotation or joint centre.

Body composition tests

The body composition of a client means the percentage of body fat and fat-free body tissue. A variety of methods are used for measuring body composition, and they have different levels of accuracy and cost. This section will discuss the different methods available to the practitioner. When assessing for body composition it is paramount to look for excessive amounts of body fat, as this has been linked to hypertension and diabetes type II.

Hydrostatic weighing

Hydrostatic weighing

Hydrostatic weighing, or weighing underwater, is fairly common in the research field and is the method often found in universities and specialist sports science facilities. Because of its cost and space requirements, however, it is unlikely to be found in the local fitness centre.

Research has proven that this method produces the most accurate results in terms of determining body composition. Other methods such as skinfold measurements can be assessed against it to determine the reliability of their results.

The dry weight of the subject is first recorded. Then, wearing a swimsuit, the client is lowered into a tank of water, after exhaling the air from the lungs. All parts of the body must be underwater. Fat is less dense than water and acts as a buoyancy force, causing the individual to rise. However, bone and muscle tissue are more dense than water, causing the athlete to sink. Therefore a client who has a greater amount of muscle mass and bone will weigh more underwater in relation to his or her dry weight.

Girth measurements

Using a tape to measure limb circumferences is another method of estimating body composition. This method is good for evaluating changes in the client's body shape, and any reduction in size due to a decrease in body fat. It produces quick and reliable results, and little practitioner experience is required. However, it provides no information on the distinction between fat and fat-free mass.

The sites usually measured are the waist, abdomen, hips and thigh.

Height and weight charts

This is the most widely used method of assessing an individual's body composition, and offers a judgement about the client's weight in relation to his or her height, although it makes no attempt to assess the percentage of body fat. It is common to see a graph displayed on a poster in local fitness centres and doctors' surgeries, suggesting

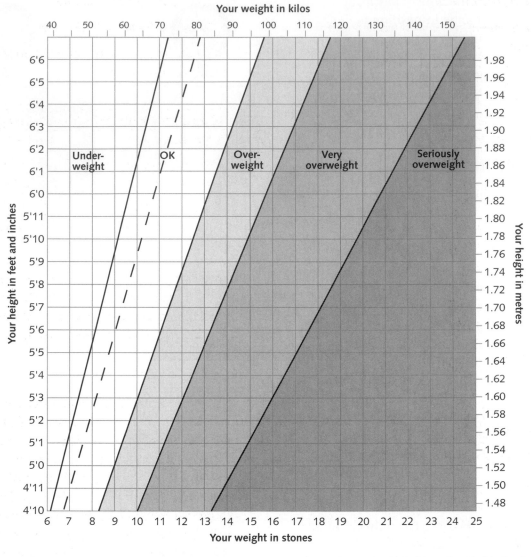

Your weight in kilos

Under-weight   OK   Over-weight   Very overweight   Seriously overweight

Your height in feet and inches

Your height in metres

Your weight in stones

Height and weight chart

acceptable weight ranges for each height. Numerous height/weight charts are available – an example is shown above.

Waist-to-hip ratio

Waist-to-hip ratio is a measure of the body's fat distribution. The ratio is used to predict the possible health risks associated with obesity. An increased amount of fat around the abdominal area is associated with an increased risk of conditions such as hypertension and diabetes type II. The following equation is used to calculate the ratio.

$$\frac{\text{Circumference waist}}{\text{Circumference hips}}$$

The measurements should be taken at the narrowest part of the waist and the widest part of the hips.

For men, a ratio above 0.85 to 0.90 would be deemed unsafe; for women a ratio above 0.75 to 0.8 is a cause for concern.

Skinfold measurements

Skinfold measurement requires a trained and competent practitioner who can make reliable measurements over a period of time. Skinfold measurement has a good correlation of r = 0.70 to 0.90. The skinfold callipers measure the amount of subcutaneous fat (fat immediately below the skin) in millimetres. The following procedure is used.

- Take measurements from the right side of the client.
- Use the thumb and finger to pinch the client's skin while testing.
- The reading should be taken from the gauge after 1-2 seconds.
- Make a second measurement – measurements within 1-2 mm of the previous reading indicate the results are reliable.

Numerous sites can be measured: abdomen, triceps, biceps, chest, calf, subscapular, suprailiac and thigh muscle. Most protocols use either three or four sites, for example:

- male: chest, thigh and abdomen
- female: triceps, suprailiac and thigh.

The measurements for the three sites are added together to produce a total in millimetres, which can be evaluated in terms of a percentage of body fat, using conversion tables that take into account the client's age. A body fat percentage of 15-25% is considered optimal for women, and between 10% and 20% for men.

Body mass index

Another method of evaluating body composition is to use the body mass index (BMI) method, which evaluates weight in relation to height using the following equation:

$$\frac{\text{Body weight in kilograms}}{\text{Height in meters squared (m}^2)}$$

This method assesses the appropriateness of an individual's weight in comparison to height. For example, if a client's height is 1.70 m and weight is 70 kg, then:

$$1.70 \text{ m} \times 1.70 \text{ m} = 2.89 \text{m}^2$$

$$70 \text{ kg} / 2.89 \text{ m}^2 = 24.22 \text{ BMI}$$

This can be evaluated using the following BMI classification table:

Classification	BMI score
Underweight	Under 20
Normal weight	20 to 24.9
Overweight	25 to 29.9
Very overweight	30 to 40
Seriously overweight	Above 40

However, as with girth measurements there is no distinction between fat and fat-free mass. This method cannot be used with pregnant women, or with clients who are very muscular.

Bioelectrical impedance

Another method of assessing body composition, which requires little in the way of practitioner skill and experience because it is easy to administer, is the bioelectrical impedance method. The machine passes a harmless electronic current through the client's body and records the impedance (opposition) to the current. The current will flow through tissues with a high water content faster than through tissue with less water, such as fat. A client who has more fat will record a slower speed for the current. The speed at which the current moves is measured and used to determine the body composition.

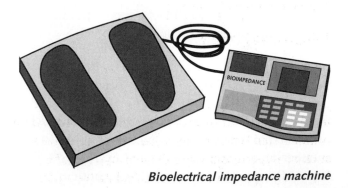

Bioelectrical impedance machine

One type of impedance machine requires the client to remove footwear including socks and stand on a plate. It produces a computer printout detailing the parameters of body composition, such as fat-free mass. Research has shown that this method has a good level of accuracy with only ± 4% error.

The following are the requirements for a bioelectrical impedance procedure.

- The client should not drink for 3-4 hours prior to the test.
- The client should not undertake physical activity of moderate or high intensity for 12 hours prior to the testing session.
- The client should not consume alcohol for two days prior to testing, and should avoid caffeinated drinks such as coffee.

Bioelectrical impedance readout

Name	Joe
Age	30
Height	1.70 m
Weight	87 kg
Fat %	34

Theory into practice

Consider the client reading shown above, and answer the following questions

1 Consider the percentage body fat and the age of the client. Is the percentage too high for an individual of this age and gender?
2 Using the height and weight chart on page 124, comment on the client's weight.
3 Identify possible health issues that may arise from an excessive amount of body fat.

Speed tests

Speed is the ability to cover a set distance quickly, and is explosive in nature. Speed is vital for a number of activities in sport and exercise, especially sprinting and jumping activities. It is also important for certain positions in team-based sports, such as a winger in rugby.

Sprint testing

A client can be tested for speed over various distances, depending on the demands of his or her sport. For example a long jumper may wish to test his or her speed over 15 metres, which is a relevant distance for long-jump technique.

On response to a stimulus such as a whistle, the client should sprint as fast as possible over the prescribed distance. The time is measured in seconds. It is common practice to give the client a one-metre flying start regardless of the test distance.

This test requires only a suitable surface, a timing device, cones and a measuring instrument. In the past, the timing device was always the traditional stopwatch, but with that method the practitioner's reaction speed influences the result, so it is now common to use electronic timing gates.

Theory into practice

Test members of your group for their speed over the following distances: 15 m, 25 m and 40 m. Record the results using a table like the following.

Student name	15 m (seconds)	25 m (seconds)	40 m (seconds)

Once you have collected your results, rank them in order for each of the three distances.

1 Are there any differences in the order of group members for the different times? If, so why do you think this is?
2 How reliable do you think the timings are, and how could the timing be improved in terms of reliability?
3 Which sporting activities require a high level of speed?

Illinois agility run

The Illinois agility run is a test which measures speed and agility over a prescribed course. This test is suitable for sports or activities that require a player to sprint while changing direction, for example a rugby winger running for the try line.

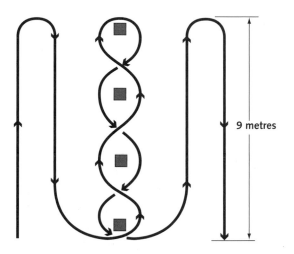

Layout for Illinois agility run

Mark out an area of 9 metres in length and place four cones 3.3 metres apart, as shown in the diagram. The client should be lying on the floor and on the command should sprint the course as fast as possible. The time should be recorded and assessed against the following data.

Agility run rating table		
Rating	**Men**	**Women**
Excellent	<15.2	<17.0
Good	16.1-15.2	17.9-17.0
Average	17.1-16.2	21.7-18.0
Fair	18.3-17.2	23.0-21.8
Poor	>18.3	>23.0

Balance – stork stand test

There are few tests to measure the balance of a client. The main test for this purpose is called the stork stand test. The client stands on one leg with the hands on the hips. The toes of the lifted leg are placed against the opposite knee. The athlete should try to hold this position for as long as possible. Ask the client to attempt this three times and take a mean average recording. The results can be compared against the following table:

Stork stand test normative data	
Rating	**Seconds**
Excellent	>51
Good	41-50
Average	31-40
Below average	15-30
Poor	<15

Power tests

Vertical jump

The vertical jump is a measure of anaerobic power and is specifically related to the leg muscles. The client reaches up against the wall and makes a clear mark (perhaps with chalk), which signifies his or her standing reach. The client then jumps as high as possible in order to make a second mark on the wall. The result is calculated by subtracting the lowest mark from the highest, and is known as the jump distance, measured in centimetres.

The client should make up to three attempts, and the highest jump should be recorded. A break of 30 seconds between jumps is advisable. A formula is applied to calculate power:

$$\text{Power (watts)} = 21.67 \times \text{mass (kg)} \times \text{vertical displacement (m)}^{0.5}$$

You can also compare results against a table of normative data such as the following.

Vertical jump test		
Rating	**Men**	**Women**
Excellent	>65 cm	>55 cm
Good	60 cm	50 cm
Average	55 cm	45 cm
Below average	50 cm	40 cm
Poor	<46 cm	<36 cm

Wingate test

The Wingate test is uses a stationary exercise bicycle to measure anaerobic capacity, and requires specialist equipment:

- computer with printer
- Wingate software
- motion sensor (to measure the frequency of the cycle wheel)
- power supply and adaptor
- Monark cycle – a special exercise cycle which can be adapted for this test.

The Wingate test calculates the client's mean power in watts (averaged over a five-second period), therefore measuring anaerobic fitness capacity. It can also measure the peak power (in watts), which is the highest power output during the test (normally after a couple of seconds).

A warm-up on the cycle of 3–5 minutes is advised, so that the heart rate rises above 130 beats per minute, usually with only a small load. The client's mass determines the load applied for the test: 0.075 kg per kilogram of body mass. For example, a 70 kg client would have a resistance or load of 5.25 kg.

After the warm-up, the client pedals as fast as possible without any resistance in order to get a flying start. This normally takes 3 seconds. On command a helper applies the mass and the computer starts collecting the data. The client cycles as fast as possible for a period of 30 seconds (although this can be changed). The client should then perform a cool-down. The computer will calculate the mean power, peak power and fatigue index. A graph can be produced to show the results. The peak power usually comes after approximately 2–3 seconds.

The Wingate test is often reported as being the toughest, both physically and psychologically. Some subjects feel dizzy, vomit or even faint after the test, so caution is required to maintain the client's well being.

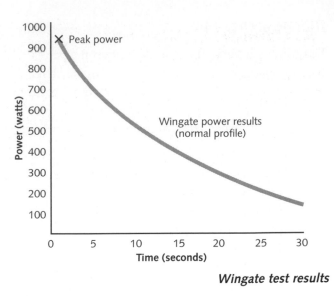

Wingate test results

Identify appropriate fitness tests

This summary section will re-emphasise the key points to consider when working with a client.

- Ensure that any test is suitable for the client – if an individual has a medical condition, it would be unsuitable to use the Wingate test, for example.
- Check that all the resources needed for the test, for example cones, are available.
- Check whether the cost of the equipment is within your budget.
- Use a health and safety checklist to ensure client safety at all times.
- Put tests in the correct sequence to avoid fatigue and false results.
- Check the relevance of tests – are they appropriate for the sport in question?
- Check the reliability of tests – do your tests produce reliable results?
- Analyse the results.
- Use normative data to decide what your results mean.
- Give verbal and written feedback about the outcomes of assessment and an estimate of levels of fitness – make sure they are appropriate and the client understands them.
- Make sure the results can be used to improve an individual's performance or well being.

Assessment activity 10.6

You are now ready to use tests to assess two clients' fitness.

1   Decide on the components of fitness that are important to each client and make a table like the one below.

2   Identify the fitness tests you are going to use with both of your clients (you may require teacher support for this).

3   Describe the fitness tests you are going to use to your clients. Tell them about:
    - the names of the tests
    - how they work (including any equation used for the results)
    - the equipment required
    - the time required
    - the normative data (if available).

4   Administer the fitness tests, making safety a priority. Record the results.

5   Provide feedback to your clients on the test results. You may require tutor support for this. You should consider:
    - using tables and graphs to express the data (remember to include the normative data)
    - giving written feedback in the form of a short report
    - giving verbal feedback to the client.

Component of fitness	Client 1 name: Jack Smith	Name of fitness test:	Client 2 name: Rohan Cole	Name of fitness test:
1	Strength		Speed	
2	Speed		Muscular endurance	
3	Balance		Agility	
4	Aerobic endurance		Flexibility	

Check your knowledge

1   What are the components of health-related fitness?

2   Why is it important to consider body composition in relation to the sporting performance, and also from a health perspective?

3   What are the guidelines in relation to aerobic training as recommended by the HDA and ACSM?

4   Briefly describe the six components of skill-related fitness.

5   What is the difference between a golfer and long-distance runner in terms of fitness requirements?

6   Why is it important to screen a client's health prior to starting a fitness test or training programme?

7   What is the difference between the reliability and validity of a test?

8   Outline the factors which may cause raised blood pressure levels in the long term.

9   Identify three tests which can assess a client's aerobic endurance.

10   What does the term Vo_2 maximum mean?

11   Describe three methods of measuring body composition.

12   Why is it important to evaluate test scores against normative data?

Assessment guidance

For this unit's assessment, you are required to produce evidence of your involvement in a testing programme with two clients (one can be a fellow student within your group). You must meet the following criteria for the different grades.

To gain a pass:

✔ explain the purpose and importance of health-related fitness for two contrasting sports

✔ describe the fitness requirements of three contrasting sports

✔ identify and describe the range of fitness tests that are suitable for two contrasting clients

✔ prepare and use appropriate health-screening questionnaires for two contrasting clients, with teacher support

✔ safely administer with teacher support four different types of fitness tests, recording your findings

✔ prepare and give feedback to a client following fitness testing, describing assessments and levels of fitness, with teacher support.

To gain a merit:

✔ compare the purpose and importance of health-related fitness for two contrasting sports

✔ compare the fitness requirements of three contrasting sports

✔ safely administer four different types of fitness test, summarising the main findings for future use by the client

✔ independently prepare and use health-screening questionnaires, identifying strengths and weaknesses of two contrasting clients

✔ independently prepare and give feedback to a client following fitness testing, explaining and commenting on assessment and levels of fitness.

To gain a distinction:

✔ critically evaluate the importance of health-related fitness for two contrasting sports

✔ critically analyse the fitness requirements of three contrasting sports

✔ critically analyse health-screening questionnaires, drawing valid conclusions

✔ safely administer four different types of fitness tests, analysing the main findings and providing recommendations for appropriate future activities and/or improved levels of fitness.

The assessment activities in this text have been designed to help you pass the unit. It is important that you follow them closely in order to generate evidence. To gain a merit or distinction, you will need to take note of the following points.

Merit

1 You will be expected to work more independently throughout the assessment activities. Therefore you should show a better understanding and awareness, and need less tutor support. You must be able to work on your own in most situations, making your own decisions.

2 Throughout your assessment you will need to use appropriate terminology, for example reporting on aerobic endurance, not stamina.

3 You will be expected to show more depth and breadth in your understanding. For example, rather than just describing the fitness requirements for three contrasting sports, you have to compare the three sports. Use comments such as 'gymnastics requires a good level of speed for some moves, whereas golf does not'.

4 You will also be expected to do more evaluation and analysis when assessing the test results of your two clients. There should be clear, constructive summaries of the test results, which are useful to the client.

Distinction

1 You will be expected to work totally independently throughout the assessment activities. You should show an excellent understanding and awareness, which means you require no tutor support. You must be able to work on your own in all situations, making your own decisions.

2 Throughout your assessment you will need to use appropriate terminology, for example reporting on aerobic endurance, not stamina.

3 You will be expected to show full depth and breadth in your understanding. For example, rather than just describing the fitness requirements for three contrasting sports, you have to critically analyse the three sports. Use comments such as: 'Gymnastics requires a good level of speed (Smith, 2000) for some moves, where as golf does not (Baxter, 1998). Speed of movement is not required to produce a golf shot because of the nature of the task, whereas power and upper body strength are.'

4 You will be expected to perform evaluation, analysis and synthesis when assessing the test results of your two clients. There should be clear, constructive summaries of the test results, linked to appropriate research, and these should be useful to the client.

5 You will also be expected to produce a high level of work in the classroom and in practical workshops, for example when answering questions, to show your understanding. You will show a professional attitude and application when involved in practical sessions.

Resources

Texts

Bird, SR, Smith, A & James, K: *Exercise Benefits and Prescription*,1998, Stanley Thornes (Publishers) Ltd

Carr, G: *Fundamentals of Track and Field*, 1991, Human Kinetics

Davis, B, Bull, R, Roscoe, J & Roscoe, D: *Physical Education and the Study of Sport*, 1997, Mosby

Dick, FW: *Sports Training Principles*, 1992, A & C Black

Heyward, VH: *Advanced Fitness Assessment and Exercise Prescription*, 1998, Human Kinetics

Howley, ET & Franks, BD: *Health Fitness Instructors' Handbook*, 1997, Human Kinetics

Jackson, AW, Hill, DW, Morrow, JR & Dischman, RK: *Physical Activity for Health and Fitness*, 1999, Human Kinetics

Maud, PJ & Foster, C: *Physiological Assessment of Human Fitness*, 1995, Human Kinetics

McArdle, WD, Katch, FI & Katch, VC: *Exercise Physiology, Energy, Nutrition and Human Performance*, 1991, Lea & Febiger

Morrow, JR, Jackson, AW, Disch, JG & Mood, DP: *Measurement and Evaluation in Human Performance*, 2000, Human Kinetics

Neder, JA, Nery, LE, Silva, AC et al: 'Short-term effects of aerobic training in the clinical management of moderate to severe asthma in children', 1999, *Thorax* 54, pp 202-206

Powers, SK & Howley, ET: *Exercise Physiology Theory and Application to Fitness and Performance*, 1997, Brown and Benchmark

Reilly, T, Secher, N, Snell, P & Williams, C: *Physiology of Sports*, 1990, E & FN Spon

Skinner, JS: *Exercise Testing and Exercise Prescription for Special Cases*, 1993, Lea & Febiger

Thomas, JK & Nelson, JK: *Research Methods in Physical Activity*, 1996, Human Kinetics

Websites

British Medical Journal (www.bmj.com)
Department of Health (www.doh.gov.uk)
Office of Health Economics (www.ohe.org)
Resources for Open University Teachers and Students (www.routes.open.ac.uk)
National Statistics Online (www.statistics.gov.uk)
The Wellcome Trust (www.wellcome.ac.uk)
The World Health Organisation (www.who.int)

TRAINING AND FITNESS

Introduction to Unit 11

This optional unit introduces you to the concepts of fitness training and programme design for a variety of client groups, from the elite athlete to the child athlete. The unit will provide you with the necessary background knowledge to work in a fitness suite or gym, under appropriate supervision. Specifically it will allow you to design and monitor individual customer fitness programmes for a wide-ranging client base.

There are clear links with Unit 10, Fitness Testing. To support your learning you should refer to this unit at certain points in your reading.

Assessment

Within the unit there are numerous activities to aid your learning and reinforce knowledge gained. A number of technical terms are used, and a glossary of these terms is provided at the end of this unit. It is good practice to make your own glossary of technical terms as you learn them.

This unit is internally assessed and requires you to provide evidence of your involvement in programme design and evaluation of training, based on a selected subject. Although there are no clear guidelines for the format of your evidence, it is suggested that a case study would be most appropriate. This approach would allow collection and presentation of evidence such as the training programme, log or diary, fitness test results, evaluation and recommendations for the subject's future improvement.

After completing this unit you should be able to achieve the following outcomes.

Outcomes

1 Examine the principles of training and their application to the design of training programmes

2 Investigate the various methods of fitness training

3 Design an effective fitness-training programme

4 Investigate the long-term adaptations of the body to fitness training.

What you need to learn

- The principles of training
- How to apply these principles in order to design appropriate fitness training programmes
- Different methods of fitness training to achieve relevant goals
- How the body adapts to fitness training.

Principles of training

Any fitness programme is based on the principles of training. They apply to anyone embarking on a programme, ranging from an elite athlete to an unfit over-55. These principles are vitally important because if they are followed, individuals will see an improvement in their fitness levels. If the principles are not adhered to, individuals will not maximise their possible improvement in fitness – fitness levels will remain fairly constant or possibly even decline. The principles of training are:

- individuality
- overload
- progression
- specificity
- reversibility.

These will all be discussed in the following pages.

The principles of training can be used to produce an improvement in a number of components of fitness:

- aerobic endurance/aerobic fitness
- muscular strength
- anaerobic fitness
- flexibility
- sports-specific fitness.

These components of fitness are explained in detail in Unit 10, Fitness Testing.

Key concept

When designing a training programme for any individual, it is important to consider all the principles of training – they are vital for success.

Theory into practice

Consider your own experience, or that of someone you know who has been involved in a training programme without a great deal of success. What do you think are the main reasons for this lack of success? Remember to include psychological factors.

Examples where people have not incorporated the principles of training include cases where:

- the intensity or the distance involved have been increased too quickly, for example running one mile the first week and trying to run five the next week – this will lead to a reduction in motivation due to lack of success
- the intensity or distance have not been increased at all, for example running one mile on two days every week – this will not encourage the body to adapt and there will be no change in fitness levels.

When exercising, it is important to consider the principles of training in order to maximise the benefits

Individual differences

The development and maintenance of fitness should be viewed as an ongoing project based on an adaptable programme which is specific to the individual. A tailored programme should be incorporated into the individual athlete's lifestyle, with consideration given to the following factors:

- short-term goals – e.g. go to the gym twice a week
- medium-term goals – e.g. lose 2 kg in body weight within two months
- long-term goals – e.g. win the county tennis championship
- current activity and fitness levels, which may change over a short period
- age
- equipment availability
- access to facilities – e.g. opening times of the local swimming pool
- work commitments
- family responsibilities
- other leisure or social commitments.

The practitioner (coach, personal trainer or fitness instructor) must consider the individual as a whole (this is called using a 'holistic' approach) rather than try to follow a standard approach. A tailored programme will allow the individual to increase his or her fitness levels to the maximum amount possible.

Goals

The first consideration should be the individual's goals. The programme must be flexible while still being capable of meeting these goals and personal needs. Listed below are examples of different individual goals that you may encounter while working in a local fitness centre:

- an amateur rugby player wishing to regain fitness after injury
- a middle-aged person wishing to improve flexibility
- an elite performer wishing to use the facility for fitness maintenance during the off-season period.

Each individual will have different ambitions and aspirations; your programme should reflect this.

Case study

Claire, aged 30, is the local librarian. She has joined the gym with the aim of losing a stone in body weight over an eight-week period. She also aims to improve her flexibility, as this is important for her job in the library.

1 Why would the standard training schedule at the gym, which focuses on strength, not be suitable for Claire? Base your answer on the principles of training.

2 When losing weight it is important to have short-, medium- and long-term goals, and that they are realistic. Set out three possible goals (short-, medium- and long-term goals) for Claire's weight loss programme.

3 Why is it important to consider the individual as a whole, in a holistic approach, when designing a programme?

Key concept

Although goals are of high importance, remember that some individuals will start a fitness programme or join the fitness club for social reasons, and may not have a distinct goal.

Examples of health- and performance-related goals are shown in the table below.

Health-related goals	Performance-related goals
Decrease body fat percentage	Win a competition
Reduce hypertension	Gain selection for the county squad
Slow down osteoporosis	Improve personal best running time
Decrease chances of coronary heart disease	Improve accuracy in a precision activity
Increase strength of muscles	Improve reaction time in swimming
Lower blood pressure	Increase power in legs for sprinting

Current activity level

The practitioner needs to consider the individual's current fitness level, levels of activity and lifestyle. If the individual is a beginner or has not trained for a significant amount of time, such as six months, he or she will need to start on a lower intensity training programme. With regard to the principles of overload and progression, the programme should be increased slowly in terms of intensity, frequency and duration. Trying to increase any of these too quickly could lead to injury or demotivate the individual. However, the changing programme should still involve overload and encourage an improvement in health, fitness and possibly performance.

It is important to understand the difference between the terms physical fitness and performance. Performance relates to the individual's ability to perform a given activity at a specific level, for example playing tennis at county or international level. Physical fitness involves a number of physical attributes, for example strength and flexibility, which everyone can achieve.

Previous activity level

When designing a training programme, the sports practitioner must gain a picture of the client's history, including any health-related issues such as a punctured lung. Previous activity levels are part of this picture. If the athlete has previously been involved in a structured programme and has a good level of fitness, assessed through fitness tests, then the programme should reflect this. The exercises prescribed should be at a moderate to high intensity. Another individual may not have exercised at all for a significant period (one month or more) for a variety of reasons, such as injury, illness or loss of motivation. In this case the programme should be set at a lower level to start with, in terms of number of sessions per week, duration and intensity.

Age

Older people can benefit greatly from the adaptations made through fitness training. However, these adaptations take longer to achieve in comparison to a younger person.

When designing a programme for an older individual, you should carefully consider the starting intensity and progression of the programme. It should start at an easier level, for example a brisk walk rather than a jog, over a reduced distance. Once the individual is comfortable with the exercises, progression should be minimal and increases in intensity should be made slowly during the training programme. The goals of the individual should be given careful consideration. A younger person may wish to improve upper body strength by 20%, whereas a realistic goal for an older individual may be to improve strength by 10% at first, and then possibly set a further goal. If an older person remains free of illness and injury, however, he or she should be able to do the same exercises as a younger person.

Healthy older people can do the same exercises as young people

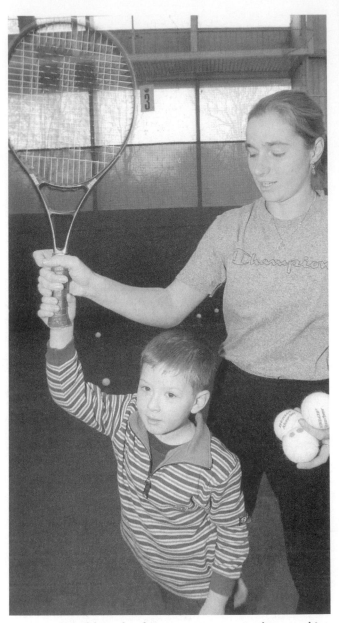

Health and safety are paramount when working with a child

Special consideration also needs to be given in the case of children. In the UK there is an increase in the number of children taking part in structured training programmes outside school, in such sports as basketball, football, rugby and cricket. When working with children it is important that you do not treat them like small adults, however. Because they are growing, their skeletal and muscular systems are constantly changing.

Health and safety are always paramount considerations when working with a child. It is

important that a child does not:

● train or play in an excessively hot or cold environment

● perform an extensive and over-long workout

● over-train or compete in too many competitions.

Over-training or excessive competition may lead to an overuse injury in the child. Excessive amounts of training can damage growth areas in the body, such as growth plates in the bones.

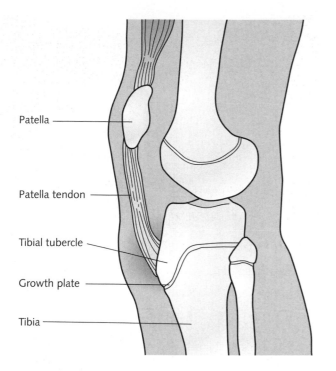

A child's knee. Osgood-Schlatter disease is caused by microscopic injuries to the growth plate

Patella

Patella tendon

Tibial tubercle

Growth plate

Tibia

A number of overuse injuries are specifically linked with child athletes, such as little league elbow, shin splints and Osgood-Schlatter disease (knee pain). These can be avoided by careful consideration of the training and competition schedule.

Despite the caution required when designing a training programme for a child, the benefits of exercise are huge. It is widely accepted that physical activity during growth periods can optimise physical and psychological development. Therefore, involvement in well-structured sessions, taking health and safety issues into account, will only be of benefit to the child.

Children are capable of training the cardiovascular system to improve aerobic endurance without any long-term damage. If you follow the basic principle of overload in training, the child's fitness levels will improve in a similar way to an adult's.

Key concept

A child should be encouraged to take part in well-structured sessions that do not place too much stress on the body over a long period of time.

Time available

When designing a training programme it is important to understand the individual's lifestyle, specifically the time he or she has available to dedicate to the training programme. People have various commitments connected with work and family life, and the time available for most people is very limited – it is concentrated in evenings and weekends.

The training programme should be slotted into the time available and fit with the individual's lifestyle. Elite athletes who receive lottery funding, sponsorship or prize money may not need to work, so they will have larger amounts of time to devote to training or travelling; but training for the working individual may have to be concentrated near home. Sessions may have to be as short as 20 minutes, and may involve performing basic exercises in the home or using exercise videos.

Equipment and access to facilities

In recent years much more equipment has become available, and much better access to facilities is now widespread. The local fitness centre or gym will now have a variety of equipment such as treadmills, rowing machines, cycles, step machines, resistance machines for improving strength, and a number of others.

Think it over

In pairs, choose a local fitness centre or sports facility, and visit it to draw up a list of the equipment used. You must ask permission from the management before you do this. Once you have compiled your list, compare and contrast the different pieces of equipment found by other pairs in your class who have visited other centres.

The availability of a variety of equipment means that the individual can be offered choice, and this can reduce boredom.

People who are interested in reducing body fat percentage should look for a centre that has a number of cardiovascular machines (treadmill, rower, stepper, etc.). People who want to improve their strength should train at the local gym on resistance machines and free weights. When designing a programme, therefore, you should match the goals of the individual with the equipment available to him or her.

For financial reasons, some individuals may not be able to afford to join the local facility and use the specialist equipment. But a number of options are still available to them at a lower cost. Walking, jogging and swimming are all cheaper options than those using specialist facilities.

Also, the home should be viewed as a possible exercise venue. A large number of exercise videos for all components of fitness are available to buy or rent. Some are more suitable than others, of course, and caution should be used when purchasing.

If an individual has no access to facilities, he or she can still make lifestyle changes to improve fitness, such as walking or cycling to work or to the shops.

Think it over

In small groups, devise a wide-ranging list of possible types of client who may enter your fitness or health club requiring a tailored training programme, for example disabled athletes. Discuss your answers with the other groups in your class.

Overload

Overload is an important principle of training. It involves exercising at an intensity (level of work) greater than that which has been used previously. An example of this can be seen in the graph opposite, which shows overload being used in a

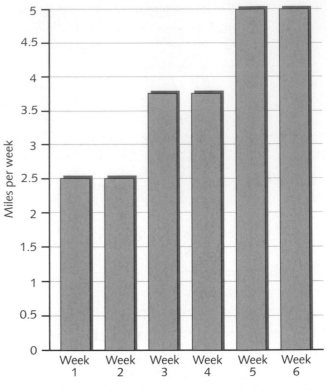

Overload in running

middle-distance runner's training programme. The athlete increases the distance gradually over a six-week programme.

Constant overloading of the body's systems will cause it to respond and adapt – this is known as **chronic adaptation. Acute responses** to exercise are the short-term adaptations, for example increased body temperature or heart rate. Chronic changes, such as decrease in resting heart rate, take from six weeks to a number of months to come into effect. The athlete is very unlikely to see an improvement in performance unless the overload principle is incorporated into the programme.

The following are the components that can be adapted to lead to overload:

- frequency – number of sessions per week, for example an increase from two to four
- intensity – the amount of energy needed to perform a particular exercise or activity

- duration – the total time an exercise session or activity takes, for example a 20-minute session could be increased to a 30-minute session.

Progression

Progression is achieved when there is a steady increase in the overload of the training programme, to bring an improvement in fitness over a period of time.

Beginners often stop their training programmes because of lack of motivation when they fail to achieve progression. Poor performances may be due to either too little progression in the programme, or more likely a training programme which overloads the system too much and has an excessive intensity. Excessive overloading may lead to a number of acute or chronic injuries, or even illness.

The human body improves its efficiency gradually, adapting to a sensible level of overload. The frequency, intensity or duration of exercise should be increased gradually over a period of time. For example, for running or swimming the flow chart below could be used. It demonstrates the concept of progression by overloading the system through changes in the intensity and the number of exercises performed.

Specificity

A common mistake that people make is not to train the specific muscles or muscle groups involved in the activity they perform. Change is also specific to muscle fibre type; for example, a 100-metre sprinter wishing to improve speed would use a speed-based programme which would train the fast-twitch muscle fibres required for sprinting.

The training programmes should reflect the specific requirements of the sport or activity. An athlete who needs to improve strength in the biceps should not develop a programme around extensive resistance work for the legs.

Key concept

The key to making training specific is to outline clear goals before starting the programme, which will allow the physical changes to match the desired outcome.

An individual who wishes to decrease body fat percentage should engage in a training programme that maximises low-intensity, high-duration aerobic work (in conjunction with a possible change in diet and lifestyle).

Adaptations that result from chronic overload take place at cellular level – this topic will be discussed later in the unit (see page 168). The instructor must link the metabolic/physiological responses and adaptations required with the training programme to ensure that the changes meet the individual's needs.

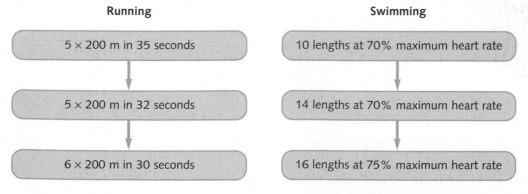

Running	Swimming
5 × 200 m in 35 seconds	10 lengths at 70% maximum heart rate
5 × 200 m in 32 seconds	14 lengths at 70% maximum heart rate
6 × 200 m in 30 seconds	16 lengths at 75% maximum heart rate

Flow chart showing progression

Case study

The local football team have been training for the past six weeks using the following training programme, with the aim of improving aerobic fitness.

Week 1
- Swim 400 metres freestyle
- Jog at 50% of maximum heart rate for 1 km
- Skills 1 hour

Week 2
- Swim 400 metres freestyle
- Jog at 50% 1 km
- Skills 1 hour

Week 3
- Swim 200 metres backstroke
- Jog at 50% 1 km
- Skills 1 hour

Week 4
- Swim 200 metres backstroke
- Jog at 50% 1 km
- Skills 1 hour

Week 5
- Swim 300 metres freestyle
- Jog at 50% 1.5 km
- Skills 1 hour

Week 6
- Swim 300 metres backstroke
- Jog at 50% 0.8 km
- Skills 1 hour

After a series of fitness tests they find that their aerobic fitness has not improved at all.

1 What do you notice about the training programme in relation to the concepts of overload, progression and specificity?

2 Why do you think there has been no improvement in fitness?

3 Why is it important to consider the principles of training when designing a programme?

Reversibility

Rest is essential within any individual's training programme to allow for repair and renewal of the body's tissues. However, a marked decrease in training or complete inactivity will lead to a decrease in functional capacity, for example maximal cardiac output or aerobic capacity, and will be detrimental to performance. This decrease in performance is due to the principle of training called reversibility, which is also known as detraining.

Key concept

If training is infrequent or not sufficiently intensive, the training effects will diminish, which can influence all components of fitness ranging from flexibility to power.

There may be numerous reasons for a training programme to be reduced in terms of frequency, duration or intensity, such as:

- injury
- illness
- decrease in motivation
- ending of the season – June and July are the off-season in football
- loss of facilities or equipment – e.g. closure of the local fitness club
- personal or social reasons – e.g. bereavement, peer pressure.

Reversibility leads to a dramatic and rapid reduction in fitness levels – faster than the improvements gained through overloading over a period of time.

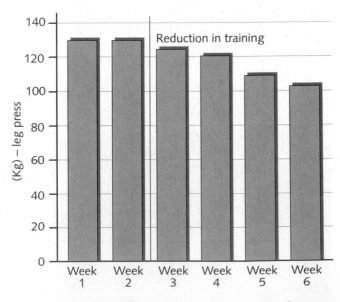

Billy's strength as assessed through 1 RM leg press

Case study

Billy, aged 16, plays for the local rugby team. Over the past four weeks he has reduced his training considerably. The graph on the previous page shows Billy's strength as assessed through a leg-press strength test over a six-week period.

1 What may have caused Billy to reduce his strength training?

2 What do you notice about the graph in terms of how quickly strength is reduced, and why do you think this is?

3 What influence may a reduction in strength have on Billy's performance?

4 Can you identify other components of fitness which are important for a rugby player?

Elite athletes aiming to achieve a peak performance at, for example, an Olympic games, avoid exercise burnout by reducing the training intensity, frequency or duration just before the important performance. This is known as tapering (reducing) the training, and helps the athlete maximise performance.

Individuality

All individuals have different needs, abilities, goals, skills and physical attributes. Therefore a training programme should be tailor-made for each individual.

It is important not to overlook the individual's preferences related to exercise, for example the mode (the method or piece of equipment used) of training. If an individual wishes to decrease body fat percentage using a bike rather than a treadmill, this is acceptable as both should allow the individual to meet the goal.

Elite athletes like Sir Steven Redgrave will reduce their training prior to competition to avoid burning out

Case study

Hassan, the local butcher aged 45, took up running a month ago with the aim of reducing his body fat. However, recently he has been missing some sessions through lack of interest. Hassan asks the following questions:

1 I am interested in using free weights to reduce my body fat percentage. Will they work and if not, why not?

2 What other aerobic exercises can I do to regain my motivation?

3 For how long and how often do I have to exercise to reduce my fat percentage?

Individuals with low levels of fitness will show a greater improvement than elite athletes because they have scope for larger amounts of improvement. But even though elite athletes will show a minimal improvement, this could prove significant in relation to other elite athletes. An example of this would be weightlifting. A previously untrained individual may increase his or her strength by 40 kg after a long period of training. An elite weightlifter, however, might increase his or her personal best by only 5 kg, but this could mean breaking the world record!

Potential for improvement is strongly linked to the individual's genetic make up. The instructor should expect the individual to show continuing progress over a long period of time, but at some point each individual will reach a genetic plateau for the specific muscle group or component of fitness.

Current fitness level

The current fitness level of the individual coupled with the person's goal will influence the type of training chosen. Elite athletes will have the aim of maintaining a high level of fitness and peaking for a major performance or competition. Recreational fitness participants may possess a good level of fitness and train simply to maintain their current level, even though they have not reached their maximal fitness level. An individual who has a poor health status or lifestyle may wish to start a programme to stabilise fitness or minimise deterioration of health.

Gender

The gender of an athlete is an important consideration. Women are capable of performing the same exercises as men, and of reaching high levels of aerobic endurance, strength and muscular fitness. However, there are special circumstances such as pregnancy and breast-feeding which will need to be considered when designing the training programme.

Performance potential

When designing and applying the training programme it is important to consider the

For elite athletes, small improvements can bring dramatic success

performance potential of the individual. Performance potential means the highest possible sporting ability and fitness level the person could reach after long-term training and coaching. The training programme should take this into account so that in the long term the individual can maximise fitness and ability. If the individual is young and has great potential for improvement, the programme should reflect this. It should be based on steady and consistent overloading, because the body is able to withstand the changes brought about by exercise.

However, if the athlete has a lower performance potential, possibly due to age or genetic factors such as muscle fibre type, then the programme should reflect this too. It should be based on more gradual and smaller increases in exercise intensity, time and frequency. The end result should always be the same for all individuals – they should aim to achieve their individual goals.

Remember

- When designing a long-term training programme you must consider the principles of training.
- The key principles of training are individuality, overload, progression, specificity and reversibility.
- If the athlete does not overload the body there will be no improvement in fitness and therefore probably none in performance.
- The training must be specific to the needs of the athlete and sport. For example a 100-metre sprinter should concentrate on speed drills, which will improve the power in the legs.
- You must consider your client as an individual – everyone will have different needs, goals, time available, financial resources and access to facilities.

Assessment activity 11.1

Imagine you are to be visited by a new coach who is interested in learning about the principles of training. Prepare a three-page summary which includes the following, to aid the coach:

1 An introduction to the concept of the principles of training, stating who can use them and how they form the basis of a training programme.

2 A table or spider diagram showing the principles of training.

3 A brief description of each principle of training (one brief paragraph for each principle). You may wish to use diagrams or figures to illustrate them.

4 A discussion of how the principles of training influence two contrasting sports, such as football and gymnastics (this can be in bullet point form). In football, for example, you would need to mention that the training should be specific and based on running, as this is what football involves.

Methods of fitness training

This section will discuss a number of methods of fitness training that relate to the different components of fitness, for example aerobic fitness. It will highlight the different methods the athlete may use to improve fitness, and analyse their effectiveness.

Aerobic fitness

Aerobic fitness is the ability of the cardio-respiratory system to supply the exercising muscles with oxygen to maintain the exercise. It is also known as aerobic endurance or cardiovascular endurance. In Unit 10, aerobic fitness is discussed in relation to its importance in sporting performance and from a health perspective.

Another common term related to aerobic fitness is Vo_2 maximum, which is the maximal amount of oxygen uptake that can be used by the athlete during aerobic exercise, such as long-distance swimming, running and cycling. In basic terms it is the ability of the athlete to use oxygen to provide energy during exercise. An athlete with a higher Vo_2 maximum will have a higher level of aerobic fitness.

Key concept

From a health perspective, aerobic fitness is important for everyday activities as well as reducing the chance of coronary heart disease.

Three methods used to improve aerobic fitness are discussed below. They are steady state training, interval training and Fartlek training. Evidence is insufficient to determine which method is the best for improving aerobic fitness; with the correct implementation of training methods, all three will lead to improvements in aerobic fitness.

Steady state training

Steady state training is also known as continuous or long, slow, distance training. It involves the athlete training at a steady pace over a long distance. The intensity of steady state training should be moderate to high (60% to 80% Vo_2 maximum) over a long distance and time. Using the principle of overload, the intensity should be high enough to lead to biological adaptation.

This method of training is suited to long-distance runners or swimmers. Because of the lower level of intensity, the athlete is able to train for a considerable period of time. This method of training at a lower intensity is ideal for:

- beginners who are first taking up structured exercise
- athletes recovering from injury
- 'special population' athletes – children or elderly people.

To overload the system and show an improvement in performance, the athlete should increase the duration or distance of training.

Interval training

The basic concept of interval training is that the athlete performs an exercise bout (work period) followed by a rest or recovery period, before completing another work period.

Interval training can be used to improve anaerobic fitness components (components that do not use oxygen, for example speed) and aerobic fitness (Vo_2 maximum) by varying the intensity and length of the work periods. Below is an example of an interval for improving aerobic fitness components.

Run two minutes (60% Vo_2 max.) – rest 30 seconds – run two minutes (60% Vo_2 max.)

Running   Rest   Running

Interval training alternates work periods with rest or recovery periods

This method of training allows clear progression and overload to be built into the programme. Listed below are possible ways of incorporating overload into the training session:

- increase the intensity of the work periods
- increase the number of intervals
- decrease the duration of the rest period
- make the rest period more intense – for example a slow jog rather than a brisk walk.

Theory into practice

Using the example of intervals on the previous page, change the set to show overload, using all four methods in the bullet points.

When designing a programme it is important that you consider:

- the number of intervals (rest and work periods)
- the intensity of the work interval
- the duration of the work interval
- the duration of the rest interval
- the intensity of the rest interval.

Case study

Amy, aged 23, is a local 200-metre freestyle club swimmer. She wants you (a local fitness instructor) to devise a one-week training programme to improve her aerobic fitness. She has been told that interval training should improve her aerobic fitness.

1 Devise a one-week training programme (three sessions of 45 minutes in duration) for Amy and use an appropriate method to display the programme, for example a timetable or logbook.
2 Show overload, gradual progression and specificity between the sessions, which will allow her to improve her aerobic fitness.
3 Include interval training over a variety of distances, making sure you clearly indicate the duration of the rest and work periods.
4 Show the number of intervals clearly.
5 Show rest days which should be taken to avoid over-training.

When designing a programme using interval methods, it is important that the rest intervals should be the same or greater than the work periods. However as you have already discovered, the rest period can be shortened especially if the individual has a good level of fitness and will be able to meet the extra physical and psychological demands. For aerobic training, the intervals should exceed one minute in length with an intensity level above 80% of the maximum heart rate.

The maximum heart rate can be calculated using the following formula:

Maximum heart rate (beats per minute)
= 220 – age

For example, a person aged 20 will have a maximum heart rate of about 200.

Fartlek training

Fartlek training is another method designed to improve an individual's aerobic fitness. It is based on running outdoors, and varies the intensity of work according to the requirements of the individual. The intensity of the training is changed by varying the terrain. The athlete may run on the following terrains:

- sand
- hills
- undulations
- soft grassland
- wooded areas.

Through increasing the intensity during training, the individual will be switching from aerobic to anaerobic energy supplies.

Key concept

Through Fartlek training the anaerobic component will lead to an improvement in aerobic fitness (Vo2 maximum).

In Fartlek training there is no rest period, but the individual has more control and is able to decrease intensity at any given time to take

Running up and down hills is a good way of improving aerobic fitness through Fartlek training

informal rest periods. The benefits of Fartlek training are:

- athletes control their own pacing
- the boredom of conventional training is reduced
- it is suitable for off-season training to maintain aerobic fitness.

Muscular strength

There is a clear distinction to be made between muscular strength, muscular endurance and power, which are discussed later. Strength is the ability of a specific muscle or muscle group to exert a force in a single maximal contraction. For example, if weightlifter A lifts 80 kg and weightlifter B lifts 100 kg, weightlifter B is said to have greater strength than weightlifter A (although perhaps only in the muscle groups used in this particular lift). Strength is often thought of as being related to athletes such as weightlifters or boxers, but it is important to understand that strength also relates to health and well being. Muscular strength is required for a variety of everyday tasks as well as sporting activities:

- picking up and carrying the shopping
- stacking shelves at the supermarket
- executing a throw in judo
- heading the ball in football.

Muscular endurance

Muscular endurance is needed where a specific muscle or muscle group makes repeated contractions over a significant period of time (possibly over a number of minutes). Examples are:

- a boxer making a repeated jab

- continuous press-ups or abdominal curls
- the 400-metre sprint in athletics
- a sprint finish in rowing.

Key concept

The ability to maintain a high level of muscular contractions, known as local muscular endurance, is vital for a number of sporting activities.

Muscular endurance is closely related to the ability of the athlete to perform in his or her chosen sport. For example, the 400-metre sprinter produces a high level of force in the leg muscles repeatedly over a number of minutes.

Power

Power is closely related to muscular strength in combination with speed of movement. It is the ability to generate and use muscular strength quickly. Athletes who are stronger tend to be able to produce a greater amount of power during the action. Generally, an individual interested in health-related fitness does not train power as it is specific, and is needed only by the elite athlete. Power is important for many track and field athletes, for example in:

- sprinting – the legs and arms need power to sprint as fast as possible
- jumping (triple jump, etc.) – the legs need power to gain a greater distance and/or height
- throwing (shot put, etc.) – strength is needed in the upper body and arms to propel the shot.

The equation for power is as follows:

$$\text{Power} = \text{force} \times \text{velocity}$$

The velocity part of the equation means the speed of the movement. To improve power, individuals should aim to improve strength.

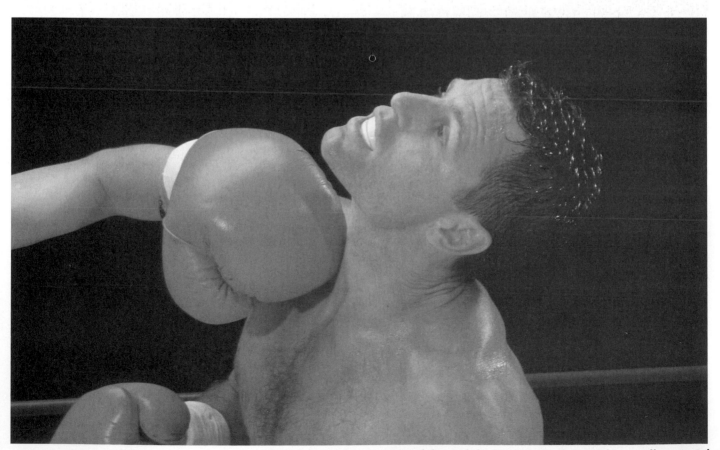

The boxer produces a powerful punch by having good strength as well as speed

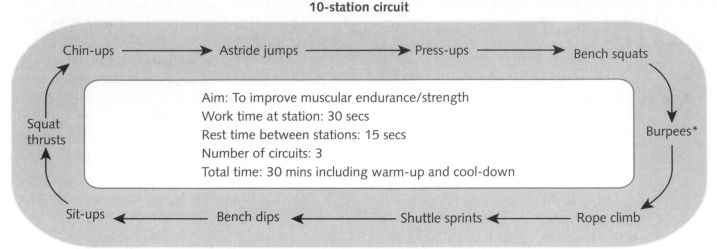

10-station circuit

Chin-ups ⟶ Astride jumps ⟶ Press-ups ⟶ Bench squats

Squat thrusts

Aim: To improve muscular endurance/strength
Work time at station: 30 secs
Rest time between stations: 15 secs
Number of circuits: 3
Total time: 30 mins including warm-up and cool-down

Burpees*

Sit-ups ⟵ Bench dips ⟵ Shuttle sprints ⟵ Rope climb

*A burpee is a squat thrust combined with a star jump

Example of a circuit session

Circuit training

In a circuit training session, a number of different exercises (or stations) are organised normally in rotations and athletes are usually under some time constraint to perform them, for example one minute per station. Between the stations there should be a designated rest period, of between 15 and 30 seconds.

A circuit can be specifically designed to improve aerobic fitness, muscular endurance, strength or a combination of these. To avoid fatigue the stations should be structured in a way that consecutive exercises use different muscle groups, for example repeated sprints (legs) may be followed by press-ups (upper body). To increase the progression and overload, the athlete may wish to:

- decrease the rest period
- increase the number of stations
- increase the number of circuits
- increase the time spent at each station
- increase the number of circuit sessions per week.

Theory into practice

Design a 40-minute session (to include a warm-up and cool-down) with the aim of improving a combination of aerobic fitness, muscular endurance and strength.

Once the athlete has obtained a good level of fitness, the rest periods may become light work periods, such as jogging on the spot or skipping. Circuits are a good method of maintaining a level of aerobic fitness, possibly during the off season period, and they offer the following benefits:

- they add fun and variety to the training
- they allow training of a combination of fitness components
- they allow the athlete to specialise in a specific movement pattern or muscle group
- they require minimal equipment
- sessions can involve a number of athletes
- they are designed to allow progression and overload.

Think it over

You have been asked by the local football manager to design a circuit session (for a squad of 14), which lasts 40 minutes in total. You have some basic gym equipment, for example skipping ropes, cones, benches, etc. In small groups, consider the following.

1 Warm-up and cool-down periods.
2 Rest periods.
3 The number of stations.
4 The time at each station.
5 The variety of exercises to make it enjoyable.

6 The training of fitness components important for football, for example speed.

7 The specific muscle groups required for football.

After you have designed the session, run the circuit with your fellow class members. Evaluate the appropriateness and suitability of the session you have designed.

Fixed resistance machines

Your local fitness centre should have a number of fixed resistance machines made by manufacturers such as Nautilus, which allow athletes to change the load based on their training programme schedule. The variable resistance ranges from 0-100 kg on most machines, allowing the programme to include overload and progression.

These machines are expensive, however, and are unsuitable for the home environment. Also, due to their design they are limited to specialist exercises such as a bench or leg press. On the positive side, they have an increased safety factor compared to free weights, and an individual is able to change the range of movement at a specific joint by adjusting the machine's settings.

Free weights

Free weights, also known as barbells or dumbbells, have been popular for a number of years. They allow the athlete to have a constant resistance during a dynamic action. The use of free weights has certain distinct advantages:

- research data provides some support for claims of increases in strength in the short term
- they allow an increased range of movement
- they allow the individual to specialise in certain movements or muscle groups
- some movements can aid the training of balance and co-ordination
- they are convenient for exercising in the home.

However, there is a greater chance of injury while using free weights, and when using larger weights helpers are required to oversee (or 'spot') for the athlete, for safety reasons.

Fitness centres have a number of fixed resistance machines

Free weights provide constant resistance during a dynamic action

There seems to be no clear advantage in using either fixed resistance machines or free weights in terms of results when training for strength. Each individual athlete will have his or her own preferences and experiences.

Plyometrics

Plyometrics is also known as jump training, and has been used to improve athletes' jumping over the past three decades – it is designed to improve explosive leg power. The basic concept is that it uses the stretch reflex to aid recruitment of additional motor units during movement. Plyometric exercise requires maximal force during the shortening stage of the muscle action (concentric contraction) and then immediate maximal force when the muscle lengthens

(eccentric contraction). Plyometric training is ideal for sports and activities that involve explosive jumping, such as basketball, netball and the high jump. It can be used to improve vertical jumping capacity.

A hurdle or box may be used in plyometric training. The individual jumps down from the box and immediately on impact jumps up. By jumping up after jumping down, the muscle is made to stop lengthening and is overloaded.

Repetitions

When the aim of the fitness programme is to improve muscular strength, muscular endurance and power, the number of repetitions in the training session is an important consideration. A repetition is equal to one movement; therefore if an athlete does 10 leg presses he or she has done 10 repetitions or reps.

Sets

A set consists of a series of repetitions. Therefore the individual may leg press for 10 reps followed by a rest period and then do another 10 reps; this is classified as two sets of 10 reps.

Plyometric training improves explosive leg power

Resistance

The resistance in a training programme is the load the athlete has to move. For example, when performing a leg press a 50 kg load is a larger resistance than 25 kg.

Athletes use a number of methods to improve their muscular strength, muscular endurance and power. Below are some basic guidelines. When training for strength:

- the general concept is low reps and high loads
- three sessions per week with a rest day in between sessions are required for optimal improvement
- the load should be increased gradually over a period of time
- high weights close to the individual's maximum should be avoided at the start of the programme
- repetitions per set should be either 10 down to 6 (therefore 5 sets) or 6 up to 10 (therefore 5 sets)
- apart from a general warm-up, aerobic exercises should be avoided on the same day as a strength session
- a record of sessions should be kept – using an exercise card like the one below.

When training for muscular endurance:

- the general concept is high reps and low loads
- three sessions per week with a rest day in between sessions are required for optimal improvement
- the number of reps and sets should be increased gradually over a period of time
- high numbers of reps should be avoided at the start (no more than 10)
- there should be a rest period before starting a new set to avoid a decrease in performance and build-up of lactic acid
- a record of sessions should be kept – using an exercise card like the one below.

Theory into practice

Design a four-week training programme for yourself to improve your strength (two sessions per week) using eight training cards and four different machines. The programme should show progression and overload while taking into account the health and safety factors, such as gradual increases in resistance.

Name			Date		
Resistance equipment	**1 RM**	**%**	**Reps**	**Kg**	**Cardiovascular equipment**	
Pec deck					Tread mill	
Shoulder press					Gyro	
Chest press					Gyro club	
Tricep pushdown					Stepper	
Lateral pulldown					Bike	
Arm curl					Reclining bike	
Abdominal board					**Comments:**	
Hip conditioner					1 Warm-up 5 mins	
Calf press					2 Stretch	
Leg press					3 CV workout	
Leg extension					4 Resistance workout	
Leg curl					5 Cool-down 5 mins	
Extra exercises					6 Stretch	

Anaerobic fitness

Anaerobic activity can be classified as any activity that lasts less than 60 seconds. 'Anaerobic' means without oxygen, and in these bursts of activity the muscles are not supplied with oxygen for power. Muscular strength, muscular endurance and power, which have been discussed previously, are classified as anaerobic in nature.

Speed and speed endurance are also classified as anaerobic. Speed is the ability to cover a set distance in the fastest time and is explosive in nature. Speed is vital for a number of activities in sport and exercise, especially in sprinting and jumping activities. It is also important for certain positions in team-based sports such as a winger in rugby. Speed endurance (anaerobic endurance) is the ability of the athlete to make repeated sprints over a long period of time. A midfield player in football often has to make 10-15-metre sprints continuously throughout the game.

The following section will detail the methods available to the athlete for improving speed and speed endurance.

Interval training

Interval training can be used to improve anaerobic fitness. The work intervals for aerobic fitness training would tend to be long in duration and low intensity so as to train the aerobic system. In contrast, for anaerobic fitness the work intervals will be much shorter but will be more intense (near to maximum). By its nature, interval training can help the athlete improve speed and anaerobic endurance (speed endurance):

- speed – short bursts up 5 seconds – rest – short bursts up 5 seconds
- speed endurance – short bursts up 15 seconds – rest – short bursts up 15 seconds.

The athlete should be working at a high intensity (85%-100% of maximum). The principles of overload and progression can be brought into the programme by making the changes described in relation to aerobic fitness, for example decreasing the rest period.

Acceleration sprints

Acceleration from a standing position is critical for success in sports such as sprinting. It is also important in team-based sports such as Rugby League, where the player has to accelerate with the ball past opponents, changing pace rapidly. Numerous acceleration drills can be used; three common methods are shown below.

- **Parachute sprinting:** the athlete attaches a small parachute to his or her back, which has the effect of increasing wind resistance.

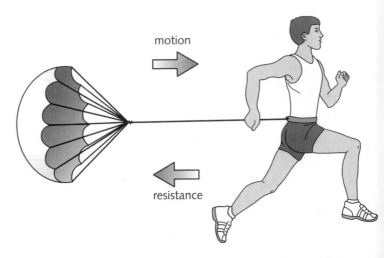

motion

resistance

Parachute sprinting

This helps to build leg-muscle strength. Once the parachute is removed, sprinting at a higher pace feels a lot easier.

- **Stair drills:** a flight of stairs (not house stairs, but ones with deeper steps) is used to train acceleration. The athlete has to sprint up a number of stairs for up to 10 seconds, with the aim of improving leg power and strength. Stride length is also improved because of the depth of the steps.

- **Resistance drills:** athletes can use some form of resistance, such as dragging a tyre, to improve their acceleration.

This is similar to the parachute method in improving muscle strength, which should aid acceleration.

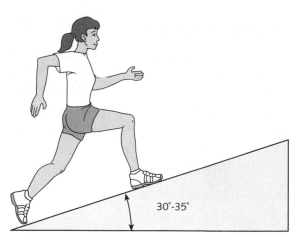

Uphill sprints develop power, acceleration, speed and balance

Hill sprints

Athletes have used hill sprints to increase their speed, co-ordination and acceleration for many years. These sprints can either be up or down a hill, depending on the content and aims of the session.

- Downhill sprints help to develop leg speed, co-ordination and dynamic balance. Sprinting downhill can be very demanding and requires a high level of technique to avoid loss of balance. Ideally, to start with the athlete should keep the distance short (about 15 metres) and use a hill that has only a small decline.

- Uphill sprints help to develop power, acceleration, speed and balance. The hill should ideally have an incline of around 30-35° when starting this type of exercise. Once again the distance should be short (15 metres) and rest periods should be built in between sets and reps.

Case study

Helen plays for the local hockey team and wants to improve her speed and acceleration, which is important for hockey. She has been training for two weeks using uphill and downhill sprints.

1 Helen wants progression in her hill sprint training. Draw up a list of ways in which Helen

can achieve overload and show progression, for example by increasing the number of reps.

2 Helen is also concerned about the health and safety issues involved in this type of exercise. Draw up a list of the possible hazards while hill sprinting.

3 Which other components of fitness are important for hockey?

Speed drills

There are dozens of drills designed to improve the speed of the athlete. Three common drills are described below.

- **Ladder sprints:** many coaches use a ladder laid on the floor as a method of improving leg speed and co-ordination. This is an ideal and fairly cheap method to use for activities that rely on footwork, for example boxing. The aim is to sprint through the ladder as fast as possible. The key to success is having a high knee lift, good technique and minimal ground contact.

Ladder sprints are ideal training for activities that rely on quick footwork

- **Basic sprint training:** two sets of cones are placed 10-25 meters apart, depending on the training session. The athlete should sprint between the cones then jog back to the start and sprint again. To incorporate overload, you can increase the distance, increase the reps, increase the sets, or add weights to the athlete.

BISHOP BURTON COLLEGE

Plyometric drills use the bounding principle

- **Bounds:** there are numerous drills that use a bounding principle and can increase an athlete's speed.

  The aim of the plyometric drill is to raise the free knee as high as possible while running. The knee should become parallel with and in line with the hip. The stride length should be increased compared to a normal running style. This method of training for speed will lead to an increase in the athlete's leg strength and power, while lengthening the stride.

Key concept

When you are doing sprint training it is important that you warm up thoroughly to avoid any muscle strains or tears. You should start with three sets of eight repetitions (each repetition being one sprint) and have a work to rest ratio of 1:5.

Flexibility training

Flexibility is important for all sports and also for health. It relates to the amount of movement possible around a joint or number of joints.

Poor flexibility may lead to:

- a decrease in the range of possible movement

- an increased chance of injury and stiffness
- a decrease in the sporting performance.

However, possible improvements in flexibility are limited by an individual's:

- body composition – for example percentage of body fat
- genetics – characteristics inherited from parents
- age – flexibility levels generally decrease with age
- gender – females tend to be more flexible than males
- muscle and tendon elasticity – the capacity to stretch before injury occurs.

It is important that any joint does not become too flexible because an excessive range of movement can lead to injury; for example, a dislocated shoulder is likely to recur in rugby because of an excessive range of movement.

The general principle of flexibility training is to overload the specific muscle group by stretching the muscles beyond what they are normally used to. The aim is to increase the range of movement, and work must be targeted towards the joints and muscle groups which require improvement. Of course, the movement should not exceed the tolerance level of the tissue, which may cause injury.

For improvements in flexibility, an individual should increase the time (duration) of stretching and the number of repetitions to allow overload to take place. Three different methods of stretching are described below:

● static (passive and active)
● ballistic
● PNF (proprioceptive neuromuscular facilitation)

Static stretches

Static stretches are controlled and slow, and are of two types: passive and active. The general principle behind the static stretch is that after stretching the muscle the individual remains in a constant position for a number of seconds. Once in position the individual then applies an internal force to overload the muscle so that it stretches beyond its normal range, thereby improving flexibility. Jerky movements should be avoided, and positions should be assumed slowly.

Passive stretching is also known as assisted stretching, as it requires the help of another person or an object such as a wall. The other person would apply an external force (push or pull) to force the muscle to stretch. An example of this can be seen in the illustration below. The floor is aiding the athlete to stretch and maintain the position.

In this passive stretch, the floor helps the athlete to maintain the position

Unlike passive stretching, **active** stretching can be achieved by the individual alone, and involves voluntarily contracting specific muscles. An example of this is where the individual raises his

or her lower leg by holding one foot behind the back, and stretches the leg in the new position.

Active stretching gives increased flexibility and strength

This type of stretching gives an increased flexibility and strength to the agonistic (stretched) muscles.

Ballistic stretches

Ballistic stretching also improves an individual's flexibility. With this form of stretching the individual has to make fast, jerky movements, usually taking the form of bouncing and bobbing through the full range of motion.

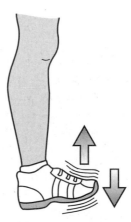

Ballistic stretching involves fast, jerky movements

This type of stretch improves dynamic flexibility, which is important for a number of activities – for example a goalkeeper making a save in football. Ballistic stretching should be specific to the movement pattern experienced in the relevant sporting activity. However, ballistic stretches can lead to soreness or may even cause injury such as strains, so must be undertaken carefully and with the correct technique.

PNF (proprioceptive neuromuscular facilitation)

PNF stretching is slightly more complex than static stretching – it involves two clear stages and requires two people. The athlete holds the muscle in isometric contraction (where the muscle develops tension but there is no shortening), and then performs a slow static stretch as previously described, aided by a second person. PNF stretches can be used to increase strength and flexibility while aiding muscle relaxation.

PNF stretching requires two people

In the stretch illustrated, the helper attempts to push the raised leg up and back, stretching the hamstring. The role of the helper is to aid in overloading the muscles; the athlete tries to push the leg back to the ground in opposition to the helper's efforts. The helper also prevents unnecessary movement, and therefore reduces the risk of injury.

General tips for stretching

- Warm up first to increase body temperature.
- Stretch all the major muscle groups.
- Stretching session duration should be 10–30 minutes.

- For improvements in flexibility, three sessions per week are needed.
- Remain in a stretch position for at least 10 seconds.
- To overload, increase the time spent holding the stretch.

Key concept

Static stretches rather than ballistic stretches should be chosen to decrease the chance of injury and muscle soreness.

Sports-specific techniques

The specificity training principle, as noted earlier in this unit, states that the effects of the training programme on the body are specifically related to the exercises performed. Remembering this principle, when designing a training programme you should consider movement pattern and metabolic specificity.

Movement pattern specificity

Many sports and activities require a number of very precise movements, which require good co-ordination and application of force. Consider the tennis serve; it involves all of the body at some point in the movement.

It is important that an athlete's training programme is specific and involves movements which are similar or identical to the movements performed in competition. The concept of matching training to performance is known as movement pattern specificity.

Precise training for the tennis serve will train the player for the speed, power, flexibility, co-ordination and balance required to make the serve effective. This type of movement pattern training also trains the muscle groups that will be used in competition.

The actions in the tennis serve

Metabolic specificity

Metabolic specificity relates the principle of specificity to the energy systems used by the athlete to produce a particular movement. The training programme should be matched to the energy system being used when the athlete is in competition. For example, a marathon runner uses predominantly aerobic energy to run over 26 miles. Therefore the training programme should centre on exercises that use the aerobic energy system, namely running, cycling and swimming. As we have seen, however, the cycling and swimming should be limited because we need to make the training movement pattern specific.

Remember

- Aerobic fitness can be improved through using various training methods such as steady state, interval and Fartlek training.
- For maximal improvements in aerobic fitness, the athlete should concentrate on exercising at a high intensity rather than for a long duration.
- Fixed resistance machines and free weights are used to improve muscular strength. Both produce positive results.
- Circuit training is an ideal method of improving a number of fitness components in the same training session.
- It is important from a health and safety perspective that individuals with high blood pressure and a history of coronary heart disease do not perform isometric exercises.

Theory into practice

A beginner athlete is unsure about the different training methods to improve aerobic fitness and speed. Prepare and give a 10-minute presentation outlining the differences between the various training methods. For example, you should distinguish between steady state, interval and Fartlek training. You may wish to use diagrams and pictures in your presentation. It should be supported by handouts.

Assessment activity 11.2

Produce an A3 poster which could be displayed at the local gym. The title should be 'Methods of flexibility training'. Your poster should distinguish between the following forms of stretching:

- static passive
- static active
- ballistic
- PNF.

The poster should be colourful and include pictures with the aim of being informative but not too technical. It should include key references and figures which support the points you are making.

The text should explain the differences between the forms of stretching with the aid of your diagrams.

Fitness training programme

FITT

When designing a training programme you can use the acronym FITT to help you remember the important points. FITT stands for:

- frequency
- intensity
- time
- type.

In general, as recommended by the American College of Sports Medicine (ACSM) people should:

- exercise on three to five days each week
- warm up for 5 to 10 minutes before aerobic activity
- maintain exercise intensity for 30 to 45 minutes
- gradually decrease the intensity of the workout, then stretch to cool down during the last 5 to 10 minutes
- for weight loss, undertake aerobic activity for at least 30 minutes on five days per week.

Frequency

Put simply, the frequency of a training programme refers to the number of training sessions per week. Most evidence suggests that for increases in fitness levels, the intensity and duration of training are more important than the frequency.

Key concept

For health and fitness reasons, the number of sessions per week should not exceed five. This will prevent over-training and burnout.

A beginner should not exceed two to three sessions per week to reduce the chance of injury and illness. After an increase in fitness over a long period (more than three months) the individual should be encouraged to increase the frequency of sessions to allow further overloading and physiological adaptation. Use the following diagram as a guide in terms of frequency of session:

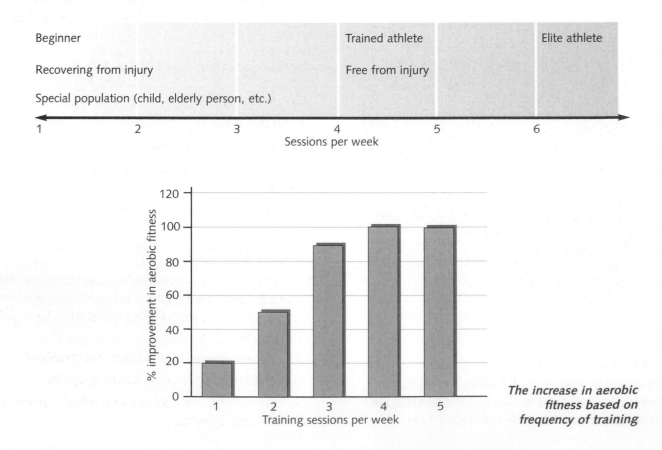

The increase in aerobic fitness based on frequency of training

People should not train for health and fitness reasons in excess of five sessions per week. The elite athlete may train on six or even seven days a week, but a number of these sessions will be light in terms of intensity or duration, and they may focus largely on skills or psychological training.

Intensity

The concept of intensity in the programme is closely linked with the training principle of overload. Research has identified that intensity is the most important factor for the sports practitioner to consider when designing a training programme.

There seems to be a widespread misconception that athletes must always be working at 100% Vo_2 maximum to induce changes in fitness levels. However, an athlete who works near to 60% Vo_2 maximum is likely to see some improvement in aerobic capacity over a long period of training, if the programme is designed to incorporate the training principle of overload. Furthermore some individuals, such as those recovering from injury, will gain health benefits for exercising below 60% Vo_2 maximum.

Theory into practice

As a group, devise and carry out a basic aerobic workout which includes four clear levels of intensity. To assess the intensity levels, for each activity measure the heart rate (in beats per minute) and compare it against maximum heart rate (220 minus age).

Once you have collected the raw data, this can be plotted on a line graph representing the heart rate in beats per minute or as a percentage of maximum heart rate. On completion of the graph you should be able to identify the four clear intensity levels of your chosen exercises.

Time

The concept of time in connection with a fitness session is also known as duration. To improve an individual's aerobic fitness through overload, the exercise period needs to exceed 20 minutes at the correct intensity level. Some studies have shown an improvement in aerobic fitness when training for only 10 minutes per day at a high intensity (above 80% Vo_2 maximum).

Key concept

Aerobic fitness can be improved by high intensity/low duration or low intensity/high duration exercise.

Type

The type or mode of exercise will depend on the individual's choice – for example it may be running, swimming or cycling. If the athlete wants to improve aerobic fitness, this can be achieved by using certain types of exercise, for example steady-state training.

The choice of exercise method may be based on access to facilities and equipment, as not everyone may have regular access to a swimming pool, for example. From a performance perspective, if the athlete is a runner he or she should concentrate a large percentage of training time on running, as swimming would train different muscle groups and movement patterns. When choosing the type of exercise, you should consider:

- the equipment/facilities available
- time available
- time of season
- the sport of the athlete
- the position played by the athlete – for example winger
- the personal preferences of the athlete.

Periodisation

Most professional and amateur coaches now use a training programme which is based on a structured cycle. This is known as **periodisation**. The training cycle can be split into:

- macrocycles – one- to four-year training cycles
- mesocycles – monthly training cycles
- microcycles – weekly or individually planned training sessions.

Key concept

Periodisation is the cycling of work to provide the chance to improve the fitness of the athlete and maximise performance potential.

The aim of periodisation is to divide the programme into smaller training cycles, for example the period of October to December may be used to concentrate on speed training.

Periodisation offers the following benefits in a long-term training programme:

- time to recover from training
- increased chances of performance peaking at the correct time, for example in national championships
- reduced chances of over-training
- overload and progression included
- reduced chances of injury.

The nature of the sport or activity will dictate how long the training period is.

Macrocycles

The first layer of a training programme may be based on a one- to four-year cycle, which is known as a macrocycle.

A football player will train based on a one-year cycle, from June–May, aiming to peak for a weekly or bi-weekly match. An Olympic athlete like the rower Sir Steven Redgrave will have a training period based on a four-year cycle, aiming for peak performance to coincide with Olympic games.

Mesocycles

The macrocycle is divided into a number of mesocycles (layer 2). These mesocycles normally consist of a number of months and depend on the structure of the season. A mesocycle in cricket would be the pre-season period and would include the months January, February and March. The second mesocycle would follow with the months of April, May and June. The aim of mesocycles is to distinguish the focus of training for the athlete. In the pre-season stage there will be a focus on

aerobic work, and in the second mesocycle there may be a change from aerobic exercise to speed and power work.

Microcycles

Each mesocycle is divided into a number of microcycles (layer 3). The microcycle adds more detail, and can be one week in length. For one microcycle the athlete will be performing the same exercises with the same intensity, duration and type.

The diagram below shows part of the training cycle for football. The year is split into four mesocycles (each mesocycle is three months). In the pre-season months June, July and August, the footballer will be concentrating on aerobic work to achieve a base level of fitness. This aerobic work will involve long runs and swimming. As the season starts (September, October and November) there is a change from aerobic work to more work on skills and drills.

Football training programme macrocycle		
June/July/Aug	**Sept/Oct/Nov**	**Mesocycles**
70% aerobic endurance	30% aerobic endurance	
20% strength	20% speed	**Microcycles**
10% skills	10% strength	
	40% skills	

Think it over

In small groups, devise a one-year training programme for a sport or activity of your choice. Use the football-training programme as a starting point. You should include:

- macrocycle
- mesocycles
- microcycles
- the components of fitness to be trained, for example aerobic fitness
- the percentage of training devoted to each component
- skills and drills work.

Once you have completed your programme you should discuss it with the other groups in your class.

Peaking

Due to the demands of training and ongoing competition, athletes are unable to produce their best performances (or 'peak') all the time. It is important for the athlete to match peak physical performance with the most important competitions, such as world championships. An Olympic athlete's training programme would be centred on producing the best possible performance on the day of the Olympic final.

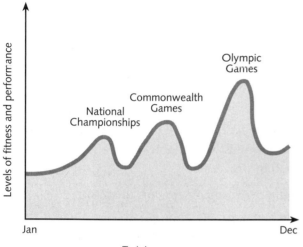

Peaking for major competitions

It often happens that the best athlete (in terms of world ranking) does not win the Olympics because he or she has peaked before the competition. It is impossible for the human body to be in its peak physical condition for more than a few weeks at a time. If the athlete tries to maintain this he or she will become stale, which produces a poor performance.

Key concept

It is important for an athlete to take into account the competition schedule when training to produce a peak performance at the right time, rather than burn out due to fatigue.

Training sessions

It is generally accepted that a training session should include three basic components: the warm-up, main workout and cool-down.

Warm-up

The warm-up is performed before the main exercise period and is done for a number of reasons that are important to the health and safety of the athlete. The warm-up prepares the athlete for the more intense main section of the training session. A warm-up is needed to:

- increase cardiac output
- increase the blood flow to the working muscles
- increase vascular blood flow
- increase the muscle temperature
- reduce the chance of injury – pulls or strains
- prepare the athlete for the environment
- improve the elasticity (stretchiness) of the tendons and muscles
- prepare the athlete psychologically for the exercise (arousal).

Warm-ups consist of two clear stages. The general warm-up is performed before the specific warm-up, and consists of jogging, stretching and other general exercises. The specific warm-up relates closely to the exercises to be done, and uses actions performed in the main workout section. Warm-ups should include:

- gentle loosening exercises – for example heel raises
- an aerobic phase (low intensity), for example light jogging, walking, cycling, etc.
- a stretching programme – specific stretches for the main activity.

The following shows how warm-up programmes may be designed.

1   General preparation stage/pulse raising/ mobilising (five minutes minimum). All at moderate intensity. Activities such as:
    - walking
    - jogging
    - cycling

- rowing
- callisthenics.

2 General/specific stretching phase (five minutes minimum).
  - All major muscle groups to be stretched using accepted stretches (hold for at least eight seconds).
  - Specific stretches for the sport – for example a football player may perform more stretches on the hamstring muscles.

3 Specific preparation stage: exercise/skills/drills that match the sport and activity in the main session (10 minutes minimum). For example, rugby players may pair up and run and pass the ball between the partners. This may then be advanced to some light sprint work.

Cool-down

Although the importance of a warm-up is generally known, a structured cool-down after the main workout is also paramount. The cool-down tends to be shorter than the warm-up and is based on low-intensity exercises. The main aim of the cool-down is to return the body to its resting state, and the main focus is on the aerobic component. There are a number of reasons why the athlete should perform a cool-down:

- to remove waste products from the working muscles, which are still receiving the oxygenated blood
- to stretch in order to decrease the chance of muscle stiffness
- to reduce the chances of fainting after an intense session.

Safe practice

Everyone should have a medical check-up before starting on a programme, but especially older people and those who have had cardiovascular complications. The sports practitioner should also take into account the following when considering health and safety factors:

- appropriate warm-up and cool-down
- implementation of the principles of training – gradual progression

- the exercise environment
- safe use of the equipment or facilities
- suitable clothing for the environment.

The exercise environment and athlete

Regardless of the exercise being performed, there are a number of basic rules to follow in order to ensure the safety of the athlete. Within the fitness suite there are a number of considerations while exercising.

- Exercise machines should be well spaced out and in proper working order.
- Any loose equipment, for example free weights, should be stored correctly when not in use.
- Appropriate flooring should be provided for the exercise to be performed – for example gymnastics requires a sprung floor.
- There should be sufficient fluids available.
- There should be suitable ventilation to aid the cooling process.

Clothing is an important consideration.

- Always wear the appropriate clothing for the exercise – for example tracksuit bottoms, not jeans.
- Make sure the footwear is correct for the exercise – failure to do this can lead to injury.
- If running outdoors, especially in the dark, make sure individuals wear bright reflective clothing so they can be seen by traffic.

The personal safety of individuals who run outdoors, especially if running alone, requires careful thought. Runners should:

- if possible run with a dog or running partner
- inform someone they are going running so that someone knows where they are
- avoid taking valuables with them – such as money or jewellery
- not wear headsets, as these can distract
- run on the same side of the road as oncoming vehicles, so that they can see approaching traffic
- vary their routes so that they don't develop a recognisable pattern

If possible, run with a partner for safety reasons

- make sure they know the route they are going to take
- only run in well-lit areas.

Theory into practice

In small groups, produce a three-minute video or an audiotape for the radio, which focuses on the health and safety aspects of running outside. Your project has the aim of reducing the numbers of injuries and deaths caused by running outside. Include the following in your video or tape:

- the importance of considering health and safety for the athlete
- the hazards associated with running outside
- the specific hazards for the female runner
- things to consider when running at night or in winter
- tips to reduce the chances of injury while running outside.

Good practice

In any exercise environment, the following points of good practice should be followed.

- Avoid dehydration – drink plenty of fluids, especially water, for two hours before exercise.
- Take some fluids during and after exercise.

- Avoid eating before training – try to have a light meal two to three hours before training.
- Make sure the warm-up is suitable for the session.
- Don't forget the cool-down, as this can reduce muscle soreness and aids the recovery process.

Key concept

If you feel dizzy, any pain, shortness of breath or excessive fatigue, stop or reduce your exercise immediately and see your GP before exercising again.

Safe use of the equipment

When exercising, equipment should always be used in an appropriate manner. Individuals should be shown the correct technique during the induction process, which should reduce the risk of injury. Follow the guidelines given by the manufacturer when using any equipment, and ensure the equipment is used only for the purpose it was designed for.

Key concept

If you are unsure of how to use a piece of equipment, ask for help.

Safety checks

The manufacturers of fitness equipment such as treadmills have a responsibility to make sure the equipment is safe to use. Most fitness and leisure facilities will have a maintenance contract with the supplier to provide regular servicing of the equipment. The service contract should cover:

- replacement of worn parts
- ensuring the weights are fixed
- oiling of movable parts
- checking the electrics where appropriate.

The individual also has a large responsibility regarding health and safety. Anyone who finds a faulty piece of equipment should report it immediately.

Use of repeat fitness tests

As described in Unit 10, fitness testing is now becoming more prevalent in the sporting, fitness and health sectors. It is used to measure and evaluate an individual's state of fitness at that specific moment in time. Due the number of components of fitness, such as aerobic endurance and flexibility, there are large number of fitness tests available to the sports practitioner.

Fitness tests can be used for a variety of reasons, such as evaluating fitness after an injury.

Theory into practice

It is important you know which fitness test evaluates which fitness component. Research a variety of tests and complete a table like the following by inserting the name of a suitable test for each fitness component.

Component of fitness	Test name
Aerobic endurance	
Muscular strength	
Speed	
Speed endurance	
Flexibility	

After you have completed your table, you may like to compare it with those of your classmates, and discuss any different tests they have chosen.

Fitness tests should be used throughout the training programme to evaluate its effectiveness and measure progress towards the goals set. The training programme should follow the following path:

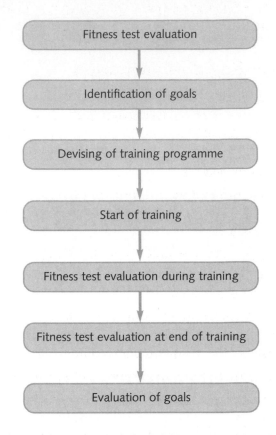

It is clear that fitness testing forms an integral part of the training programme. Correctly implemented and evaluated, fitness tests enable the sports practitioner to evaluate the training programme and any progress made. By using a single fitness test or number of tests, you should be able to judge whether any overload has been applied and any progression achieved in the athlete's fitness.

Key concept

If no or few changes to the athlete's fitness levels are shown by the fitness tests, it is strongly suggested that there should be a change in the training programme.

It is quite possible for an athlete to be training a couple of fitness components at the same time, such as speed and strength. The results of the fitness test may show, for example, an improvement in strength but not speed, so the training programme could be changed to have a greater emphasis on speed work or simply to alter the method of training designed to improve speed.

Recording documentation

The need to keep records of the training programme is often overlooked in the fitness industry, possibly due to the fact that it is time-consuming. However, it is paramount for a number of reasons:

- health and safety – records can increase a practitioner's awareness of previous injuries or illnesses
- progression – records allow the sports practitioner to see whether there is progression in the programme
- communication – records allow the practitioner to gain an understanding of the individual's history, which should aid communication
- evaluation – the information stored can be used as a part of the evaluation process

- professionalism – keeping records shows the sports practitioner has a level of competence and is following good practice.

The recording of information specific to the training programme can be done using a variety of methods, such as:

- basic programme cards (see the example below)
- brief note format
- training logs (for example a diary)
- timetables
- calendars
- personal organisers
- audio tape
- video recorder.

It is now becoming common practice for sports practitioners to record training details using information and communication technology, such as:

- databases
- spreadsheets
- word-processed documents such as tables
- on-line journals.

Programme card							
Client name		**Goals**					
		1					
		2					
		3					
Venue	**Date**	**Exercises performed (FITT)**				**Comments**	**Fitness test results**
		F	I	T	T		
		F	I	T	T		
		F	I	T	T		
		F	I	T	T		
		F	I	T	T		
		F	I	T	T		

Regardless of the method used for recording the information, it is important that this is done in a professional and systematic manner. The records should be updated on a regular basis, such as weekly, and should be filed securely using a logical filing system. The following information should be logged:

- dates of training sessions
- locations of training sessions
- frequency
- intensity
- time (duration)
- type (method of training, for example speed drills)
- sets
- reps
- rest periods (in interval training)
- competition results
- fitness testing results (before and after training)
- missed sessions
- any changes made during the programme for any reason, for example if the client suffered from a cold for a couple of days
- future needs, for example a need to concentrate on improving speed.

As well as the basic programme, the sports practitioner should keep a number of other records, including:

- personal contact details in case of emergency – stored confidentially for security reasons
- health questionnaires
- accident, injury or illness forms
- copy of any quality check questionnaires given to the client to assess the quality of service.

Think it over

As a group, discuss what details should be recorded when you are working with individuals. It may help you to draw up a spider diagram or checklist on the whiteboard with tutor support.

Evaluation

An athlete's training programme should be evaluated on a regular basis to gauge its success and effectiveness. Through appropriate fitness tests, the programme should be evaluated to assess whether personal goals and objectives have been met.

Key concept

Evaluation allows a judgement to be made as to the health or fitness status of the individual before, during and after the implementation of a training programme.

From the trainer and client

The evaluation should come from both the trainer and the client. The follow areas should be brought into focus:

- the overall suitability of the programme in terms of structure, goals, time, equipment
- achievements – physical, psychological, social and health-related
- negative aspects – issues such as boredom, lack of motivation
- future needs – new or modified goals
- whether the client has received value for money.

Key concept

A review half-way through a programme can help to pinpoint any problems and therefore indicate where valuable changes could be made.

For techniques and methods used when communicating with a client and giving feedback, see Unit 10.

Remember

- When considering the long-term goals of an athlete (e.g. winning the county competition) devise a training programme based on a long-term period (one year).

- The training cycle can be split into macro-, meso- and microcycles, which allow for planning of the training. This is known as periodisation.

- Regardless of the level of the individual, each session should contain a warm-up and cool-down to avoid injury.

- The safety of the individual should be paramount at all times. Consider the safety of the environment, equipment and exercise methods.

- Use fitness tests to monitor the training programme in terms of producing higher fitness levels and better sporting performances.

- Record the training sessions in terms of times, distances, frequency, type, equipment used and competition results.

Assessment activity 11.3

Select a client and ask him or her to agree to engage in a training programme with you. This may be a fellow student from your group, or a client you have previously identified, such as an older athlete you know.

1 Interview your client regarding the components of fitness he or she would like to improve through training. Decisions about this should be based on the needs and the goals of the client, for example a football player may wish to improve speed and aerobic fitness.

2 Gather information from the client about his or her commitments relating to work, family or study. Complete a timetable like the following, showing the client's commitments, for example study time. This will be important for identifying possible testing and training sessions.

3 Carry out fitness tests to establish a baseline score for the relevant components of fitness and form the basis of your evaluation.

4 Make a table like the one at the foot of this page which you can complete as the programme progresses. Consult Unit 10 when deciding which fitness tests to use with your client. This will also help you to make sure you are using the correct protocol and equipment.

5 Devise a six-week training programme for your client based on the relevant components of fitness, using a range of training methods. Log your training programme, for example by using a:
   - timetable
   - diary
   - database
   - spreadsheet.

Name:							
	Mon	**Tues**	**Weds**	**Thurs**	**Fri**	**Sat**	**Sun**
Morning							
Afternoon							
Evening							

Name:			
Component of fitness	**Name of fitness test**	**Result before training**	**Result after training**
e.g. Speed	30-metre sprint test	5.04 sec	4.56 sec

Remember to apply the principles of training, for example show constant overload over the six-week period.

6 Evaluate the effectiveness of the training programme. You should consider:
   - the suitability of the exercises
   - the number of training sessions
   - the intensity of the exercises
   - the duration of the exercises
   - the change in the client's fitness levels
   - whether the goals of the client were met
   - the client's own evaluation
   - any changes you would make in the future, for example including a swimming session to avoid boredom.

7 Monitor the programme of someone else who has been given a training programme, for example by a coach or fitness instructor. To do this you will need to make contact with a coach or fitness instructor who is willing to give you information about a suitable training programme (with the permission of his or her client). You may require a level of tutor support.

Consider the achievements, successes and future needs of the client on this programme. Think about:
   - the suitability of the exercises for the client
   - the number of training sessions
   - the intensity of the exercises
   - the duration of the exercises
   - the change in fitness levels (if available)
   - whether the goals of the client were met
   - the client's own evaluation (if available)
   - any changes you would make.

Long-term adaptations to fitness training

When an individual has been on a training programme for a number of weeks, several changes occur in the body. These changes are known as long-term adaptations or chronic adaptations and usually take place after six weeks. For example, with strength training there will be an increase in muscle size.

The changes generally improve the athlete's body efficiency at rest and during exercise. There is an increase in the athlete's fitness, which should lead to an increase in performance levels, perhaps evident in faster running times or heavier weights lifted.

The oxygen transport system

The oxygen transport system is comprised of both the circulatory and respiratory systems. This section will discuss the changes brought about by training to some components involved in the transport of oxygen.

Cardiac output

Cardiac output is the product of the heart rate and stroke volume, and is represented by the following equation:

Cardiac output = stroke volume × heart rate

Heart rate means the number of beats per minute. Stroke volume is the amount of blood pumped per heartbeat. Put simply, cardiac output is the amount of blood pumped while exercising.

After long-term training, cardiac output can increase quite dramatically – by as much as 25%. This increase is caused by an increase in stroke volume, in conjunction with a decrease in resting heart rate. The increase in stroke volume is caused by an increase in plasma volume (the fluid in the blood that transports nutrients).

Increased cardiac output can increase the duration for which the athlete can perform aerobic exercise, as more oxygen will be pumped around the body. This extra oxygen will be delivered to the working muscles.

Resting heart rate

Training decreases the resting heart rate as a chronic adaptation. This is linked to an increase in stroke volume, as discussed above. Because of this increase in volume the heart does not have to work so hard and has become more efficient, so resting heart rate can be lower. Highly conditioned endurance athletes often have resting heart rates around or lower than 40 beats per minute.

Training also brings a decrease in the sub-maximal heart rate at a given intensity. This can be expressed through the following graph:

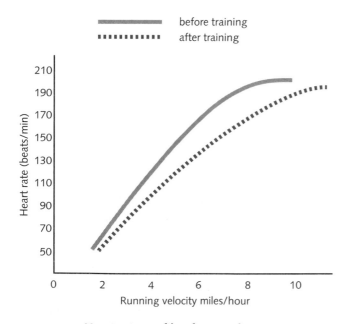

Heart rate profile after aerobic training over a three-month period assessed against an athlete's running velocity

Theory into practice

1 What do you notice in the graph about the sub-maximal heart rate after training?
2 Is there a difference between the speeds the athlete can achieve before and after training?
3 Name and describe three training methods which may have caused these changes.

This adaptation leads to an increase in the efficiency of the circulatory and respiratory system, as a conditioned heart performs less work than an unconditioned heart.

Capillary density

Capillaries are the smallest blood vessels in the body and are the site where there is an exchange between the blood and tissue cells. Through long training, the density of the capillaries increases, and also the number of capillaries in the muscle increases, allowing a larger amount of blood to flow to the working muscle. An increase in the blood supply within the muscle means an increase in oxygen supplied for movement – so the athlete will be able to perform for longer periods.

Blood volume

An increase in plasma volume gives the athlete a higher blood volume. As blood volume is vital for oxygen transport, this means an increase in the amount of oxygen delivered to the working muscles. An increase in blood volume is of particular benefit when exercising in a hot environment, because the extra blood volume can aid the cooling process.

Haemoglobin

Oxygen loading occurs in the lungs, and the direction of transport is from the lungs to the tissue cells. Erythrocytes (red blood cells) are dedicated to the job of respiratory gas (oxygen and carbon dioxide) transportation.

A single red blood cell contains 250 million haemoglobin molecules. Haemoglobin is the oxygen-transporting compound of the erythrocytes, taking oxygen to the tissues. Most oxygen carried in the blood is bound to haemoglobin. It is important to know that increases in blood volume caused by training are, as discussed, due to an increase in the plasma volume and not an increase in the haemoglobin concentration.

Lung volumes and capacities

Breathing is the act of gaseous exchange, and involves breathing out (exhaling) and breathing in

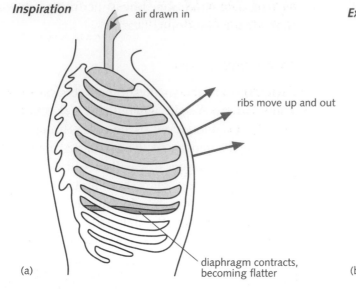

Inspiration

air drawn in

ribs move up and out

(a)

diaphragm contracts, becoming flatter

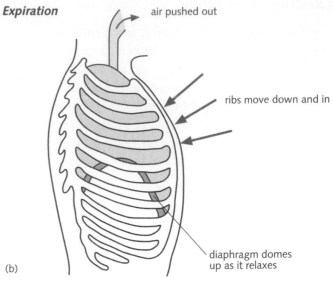

Expiration

air pushed out

ribs move down and in

(b)

diaphragm domes up as it relaxes

(inhaling) using the rib cage, intercostal muscles and diaphragm.

As a general rule elite athletes tend to have larger lung volumes (in litres) compared to non-athletes of the same body size, gender and age. They therefore have a greater pulmonary diffusion capacity, which means that more of the oxygen inhaled through the lungs enters the circulatory system. This increase in diffusion capacity is due to the larger lung volumes, which provide a greater surface area for diffusion.

Gaseous exchange process

Certain gases, for example oxygen, move between different body tissues such as the lungs, blood and exercising muscles. This is known as the gaseous exchange process. Movement of oxygen is through diffusion. High concentrations of oxygen cause high pressure in the lungs and therefore move to an area of low concentration (low pressure) in the muscle tissue. The muscles require the oxygen for energy production while performing aerobically (in the presence of oxygen). Through training, the amount of oxygen extracted by the muscle cell increases, and this may be due to an increase in diffusion capacity.

The muscular system

Long-term exercise causes many adaptations to occur in the muscular system in relation to the muscle fibre. Within 3-6 months, a 25% to 100% improvement in strength, measured as the one-repetition maximum, can be achieved. These reported increases in strength are due to a variety of factors:

- muscle hypertrophy (increase in muscle size)
- muscle hyperplasia (increase in the number of muscle fibres)
- changes to the nervous system
- psychological factors – increased motivation and confidence.

In addition to this there are a number of metabolic adaptations that take place in the muscle cells.

Muscle hypertrophy

Gains in muscle strength are accompanied by a gain is muscle size (hypertrophy) over a period of time. This increase means that the muscles can generate a larger amount of force. However, immediate increases in strength (in the first eight weeks of training) are related to a change in the neural component, as strength gains can be made without changes to the muscle.

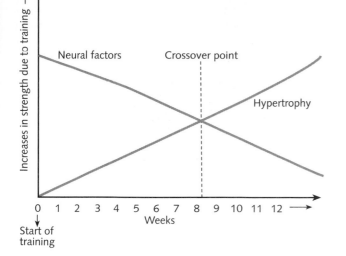

The causes of changes in strength due to training

may be able to lift 220 kg because of the long-term adaptation to the myofibrils.

Fibre type

Each muscle within an athlete's body will differ in terms of the structure and function. There are three types of muscle fibre:

● slow-twitch

● fast-twitch A (or I)

● fast-twitch B (or II).

Each type of muscle fibre has different characteristics, as shown by the table below.

These increases in strength due to neural factors may be caused by the following factors:

● extra recruitment of motor units (a motor unit is made of a motor neuron and muscle fibres)

● motor units being called on not at the same time but in intervals.

Hypertrophy of the muscle fibre is brought about by an increase in size and number of the myofibrils. The myofibrils are the contractile part the muscle cells and 80% of each cell is made up of them – within each muscle fibre there are hundreds of myofibrils. This increase after training occurs in both fast- and slow-twitch fibres. A weightlifter who could lift 200 kg before training

	Slow-twitch muscle fibres	Fast-twitch muscle fibres A	Fast–twitch muscle fibres B
Contraction speed	Slow	Fast	Very fast
Force production	Low	High	Very high
Capillary density	High	Medium	Low
Oxidative capacity	High	High	Low

Long-term aerobic fitness training enables fast-twitch B fibres to be converted to fast-twitch A fibres, which have more capacity for using oxygen. This conversion will lead to an increase in the capacity to perform exercises which rely on oxygen, such as swimming and walking. This is brought about by an increase in the number of mitochondria and capillary density.

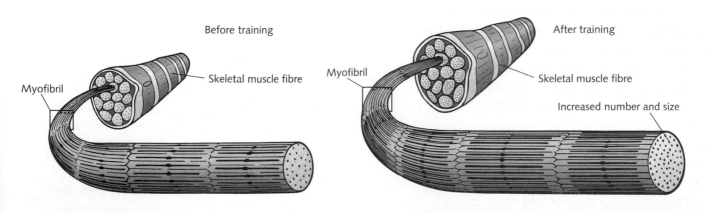

Myofibrils increase in number and size after training

Mitochondrial density

Through aerobic fitness training there is a change in the muscle and consequently the mitochondria. Mitochondria are found within the cells and are responsible for the production of ATP (adenosine triphosphate), the substance used to produce energy in the muscles when exercising. The mitochondria are the powerhouse of the cells. The density of the mitochondria relates to the amount of energy the cell requires. As muscles begin to need more energy, they require a greater density and number of mitochondria.

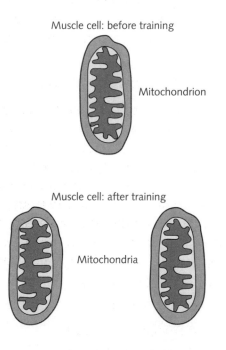

Muscle cell: before training

Mitochondrion

Muscle cell: after training

Mitochondria

Trained muscles require a greater density and number of mitochondria

This change to the mitochondria and an increase in capillary density cause an increase in the amount of energy that can be produced from oxygen. Therefore the endurance athlete is able to work at a higher intensity and for a longer duration, which should improve results.

Oxygen uptake at the muscle cell

The changes identified above to the mitochondria and capillaries result in an increase in oxygen uptake within the muscle cells. This can be represented as in the following table.

	Resting	Submaximal exercise	Maximal
Pre-training	0.275 litres	1.49 litres	2.70 litres
Post-training	0.275 litres	1.49 litres	3.20 litres

There is no change between pre-training and post-training oxygen uptake while resting and performing sub-maximal exercise, but there is a significant difference in relation to maximum effort. This allows the athlete to exercise for a longer period or at a higher intensity.

The energy systems

For any movement you make and even during sleep, your body needs energy. The body uses a substance called ATP (adenosine triphosphate) for energy, and it is stored in the cells of the body.

When an athlete starts to move, ATP stores are quickly depleted and must be replaced. ATP restoration or resynthesis takes place through the use of three energy pathways, which are called:

- the ATP-PCr system
- anaerobic glycolysis system
- aerobic metabolism system.

Key concept

Through aerobic training, the athlete should increase stores of ATP by up to 40%.

ATP-PCr system

This energy system is required for activities that are high intensity and short duration, for example the shot put, which lasts for only a few seconds. This energy system provides energy at high rates for around 20 seconds in total.

Think it over

As a group, draw up a list of 10 sports which involve high-intensity, short-duration work and therefore require predominantly the use of the ATP-PCr system.

In this system ATP is generated through the use of PCr (phospocreatine), which is a high-energy molecule stored in the body's cells. The flow diagram shows the process of energy production.

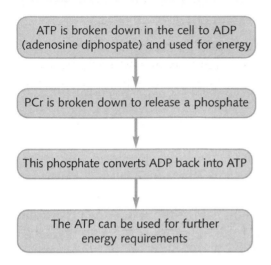

ATP is broken down in the cell to ADP (adenosine diphospate) and used for energy

↓

PCr is broken down to release a phosphate

↓

This phosphate converts ADP back into ATP

↓

The ATP can be used for further energy requirements

Key concept

ATP is vital for all movement and is broken down into ADP to be used by the body for energy for all movements.

Anaerobic glycolysis system

The term **anaerobic** means that energy required is supplied without the presence of oxygen. The anaerobic glycolysis energy system relies on the use of stored glucose in the blood, or glycogen stored in the liver, to provide energy. This system is used for high-intensity exercises that last between 30 seconds and 2 minutes, for example a 400-metre sprint.

Think it over

As a group, draw up a list of 10 sports which require high-intensity exercise for 30 seconds to 2 minutes, and therefore predominantly use the anaerobic glycolysis system.

This energy system produces a by-product called lactate. Lactate builds up in the body causing the Ph level to drop, which leaves the athlete with a burning sensation in the muscles. The athlete becomes fatigued and exercise becomes difficult as ATP energy production stops.

Aerobic metabolism system

ATP is also produced in the mitochondria within the muscles through the aerobic metabolism system. This system uses oxygen and is therefore known as **aerobic**. It produces energy for events that are low in intensity but long in duration, for example cross-country running or long-distance swimming. This system uses the fat, carbohydrate and protein we eat in our diet to produce ATP. It can provide energy for a number of hours.

Energy stores in the muscle cell

One benefit of long-term training is that there is a change in the levels of energy (ATP) in the muscle cell. After aerobic fitness training the muscles also store increased levels of glycogen, required for energy production. Training also causes the muscles to use fat stores more efficiently; increased reliance on the fat stores spares the glycogen stores, so that when required the athlete can use glycogen for high-intensity exercise.

In summary, training leads to:

- increased stores of ATP
- increased storage of glycogen
- increased reliance on fat stores
- glycogen stores being spared until required.

Impact on performance

The changes to the muscle, circulatory and respiratory system caused by fitness training over a long period of time lead to an increase in aerobic fitness (Vo_2 maximum). This means that the athlete can:

- exercise for longer (duration)
- exercise at a higher intensity
- exercise in more sessions (frequency)
- recover from exercise faster
- perform to a higher standard.

Health-related long-term adaptations

The impact of exercise and long-term training on the health status of the individual cannot be overestimated. For a more in-depth review, see Unit 10 (Fitness Testing). There is clear evidence that exercise can reduce the chances of developing, and aid the treatment of, numerous conditions such as:

- hypertension (raised blood pressure)
- CHD (coronary heart disease)
- asthma
- obesity
- stress
- some forms of cancer
- diabetes.

Weight management

Weight management is important for most sports but is vital in sports such as boxing and horse racing where the athlete's body weight is used for classification. The ideal body composition for each sport varies, because of the nature of the demands placed on the athlete.

The general rule of thumb is that an increase in body fat is likely to lead to a decrease in performance. It is important to understand that performance is not directly related to the overall weight of the athlete, but rather to the percentage of body fat. In certain sports, however, performance is not decreased by excessive amounts of body fat – an example is weightlifting.

Before discussing methods of weight reduction through exercise programmes, it is important to understand that weight loss can be achieved without exercise, through monitoring and changing the daily calorie intake of the individual. It is possible to reduce weight by ensuring there is a daily calorie deficit – that the body is expending more calories than it is taking in. Daily calorie needs can be calculated by working out a person's basal metabolic rate (BMR). This is the number of calories required to maintain the body in a normal resting state. Any activity requires further calories.

For males, BMR is:

$$\text{Weight in kilograms} \times 1 \times 24$$

For example, for an 80 kg man this would be 1920 calories per day.

For females, BMR is:

$$\text{Weight in kilograms} \times 0.9 \times 24$$

So BMR for a 55 kg woman is 1188 calories per day.

An exercise programme (at the correct intensity, duration and frequency) coupled with a change in diet will allow the individual to achieve weight loss through a decrease in percentage fat and an increase in lean body mass. Weight loss should be achieved through decreasing body fat rather than the fat-free mass.

Like any other person the athlete should avoid crash dieting (trying to lose a large amount of weight over a short period of time) as this will lead to a decrease in performance, and possibly:

- dehydration
- excessive fatigue
- eating disorders
- bone mineral deficiencies.

A combination of dietary control and a specific exercise programme will allow the athlete to take a sensible approach to weight loss. The athlete should aim to lose around 0.5 kg per week through exercise. Decreasing the daily calorie intake by between 200 and 500 calories (Kcal) should lead to a decrease of 0.5 kg in weight over a period of a week.

Blood pressure

Blood pressure (shortened to BP in most texts) is the pressure exerted by the blood on the arteries. When measuring blood pressure, the sports practitioner will assess systolic BP and diastolic BP.

- Systolic BP is the higher value and is the pressure in the arteries when contraction forces a volume of blood into the arteries.

- Diastolic BP is the lower value and is the filling stage in the heart.

BP is measured using a sphygmomanometer and is reported as the systolic pressure over the diastolic pressure, for example 130/80. When the individual is in a resting state systolic BP should measure between 100 and 140 mm HG (millimetres of mercury). Diastolic values should read between 60 and 80 mm HG. Classifications of blood pressure readings are shown in Unit 10, on page 103.

An individual with a systolic BP in excess of 140 mm HG over a period of time is deemed to have hypertension. Hypertension is linked to cardiovascular diseases, because of excessive pressure within the arteries.

Many factors can influence blood pressure levels, as shown in the diagram below.

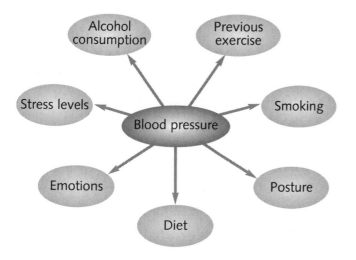

Exercise, through long-term fitness training, can reduce blood pressure and reduce the risk of developing hypertension. Individuals who suffer from hypertension can reduce systolic and diastolic BP by exercising three times per week at 40–60% Vo_2 maximum for a period of three months or more. Training should be based on dynamic exercises such as swimming, running, walking and cycling. However, resistance training has little effect on excessive levels of BP.

Blood pressure also changes in the short term in response to exercise. Systolic BP shows a slight increase when exercising, but diastolic BP remains fairly constant.

Key concept

From a health and safety perspective you should not allow individuals with hypertension to perform isometric exercises (where the muscles are in static contraction). Isometric exercises lead to a decrease in blood flow, therefore elevating BP even further.

Rehabilitation and recovery

Exercise plays an important role in the process of rehabilitation and recovery after injury or illness. Exercise forms only a part of the treatment, which can be a complex process that involves a number of specialist practitioners, such as:

- sports scientist
- fitness instructor
- physiotherapist
- doctor
- coach.

The final stage of recovery should see the athlete perform sports-specific training to ensure he or she is ready to meet the demands of the sport again. A range of fitness tests should be used during the rehabilitation process to assess the stage of recovery in terms of fitness levels.

Adaptations to different types of training programmes

After long bouts of training the human body adapts and becomes more efficient. This adaptation enables the athlete to produce better performances but also to improve health-related fitness, such as reduced body fat. The following sections will summarise the main adaptations brought about by training.

Aerobic fitness

Through training the athlete can expect to improve Vo_2 maximum (aerobic capacity) by 15%

over a three-month period. Sedentary individuals will increase their Vo₂ maximum more than a fit athlete because they have greater room for improvement. Aerobic fitness can be improved by long-term training, which results in:

- decreased working heart rate
- increased stroke volume
- increased cardiac output capacity
- increased mitochondrial number and density
- increased capillary number and density
- muscle fibre conversion
- increased oxygen uptake in the muscle cell
- increased stores of ATP
- increased stores of glycogen.

Muscular strength

Muscular strength increases after training because of the following adaptations:

- muscle hypertrophy (increase in muscle size)
- muscle hyperplasia (increase in the number of muscle fibres)
- extra recruitment of motor units
- motor units are not called on at the same time but in intervals – they become more efficient.

Muscular endurance

Muscular endurance can be defined as a specific muscle or muscle group making repeated contractions over a significant period of time (a number of minutes). As you would expect, training improves muscular endurance, because of the following changes to the body:

- increased glycogen storage
- reduced muscle glycogen usage
- increased glycolytic enzyme activity (the enzymes responsible for anaerobic glycolysis)
- increased removal rate of lactic acid
- reduced fatigue rate of muscle fibres.

Power

As strength is trained and improved there is an automatic increase in the power the athlete can generate.

Flexibility

When training flexibility over a long period of time, the following adaptations (some health-related) are made by the body:

- increased range of movement at the joint
- reduction in muscle soreness after exercise
- increased blood flow and nutrients to the joints
- improvement to posture
- prevention of lower back pain
- maintenance of healthy joints
- reduction in risk of injury
- better balance.

Health-related

The health-related benefits associated with exercise are numerous. These are some of the benefits of training:

- decreased body fat
- increased efficiency of the digestive system
- decreased stress levels
- increased removal of waste products (toxins, etc.)
- maintaining an independent lifestyle
- avoiding certain types of injuries – for example back injuries
- increased calorie usage
- increased uptake of fat.

It can also help reduce the chance of developing the following diseases:

- coronary heart disease (CHD)
- non-insulin-dependent diabetes mellitus
- some types of cancer
- osteoarthritis
- osteoporosis
- obesity.

Assessment activity 11.4

Previously you were asked to design and undertake a training programme with one client and to study the training logbook of another client. Now, you need to prepare and give a 20-minute presentation using visual aids, which will be addressed to both of those clients. The title should be 'Long-term adaptations to the body caused by training in the sport of …'.

- Keep it fairly simple and informative.
- Avoid too much technical jargon.
- Use diagrams and figures.
- Concentrate on the changes that relate to your clients; for example in golf you should describe the changes brought about by flexibility training (which is important to golfers).
- Identify how these changes will improve their performances.

Check your knowledge

1   List the five key principles of training.
2   Identify ways in which an athlete can change a training programme to allow for overload.
3   As a fitness instructor, what factors connected with individuality would you need to consider when designing a training programme?
4   Describe the similarities and differences between interval and steady state training.
5   Describe the advantages of using free weights in a training session.
6   How will training based on movement pattern specificity aid performance?
7   What does the acronym FITT stand for? Define each aspect.
8   Why is it important to taper training prior to an important competition?
9   Why is evaluation an important stage in relation to a training programme?
10   What does the term **chronic** mean?
11   After long-term training, why is the exercising heart rate lower?
12   Name the three energy systems in the body.

Assessment guidance

For this assessment you are required to produce evidence of your involvement in a six-week training programme with one client (this can be a fellow student within your group). You should design, undertake, monitor and assess a training programme, and aim to meet the following criteria for the different grades.

To gain a pass:
✔ describe the principles of training and their influence on two contrasting sports
✔ identify the different types of fitness training
✔ prepare a safe and effective training programme for a selected client with teacher support, incorporating the principles of training and using a range of training methods
✔ produce a training logbook for two contrasting clients that identifies their achievements, successes and future needs
✔ describe the long-term adaptations of the body to fitness training for two contrasting clients.

To gain a merit:
✔ compare different types of fitness training
✔ independently prepare a safe and effective training programme for a selected client, justifying your choice of training methods
✔ produce a training logbook for two contrasting clients that assesses their achievements, successes and explains their future needs
✔ explain the long-term adaptations of the body to fitness training for two contrasting clients.

To gain a distinction:
✔ critically evaluate the different types of fitness training, commenting on their fitness for purpose and suitability
✔ critically analyse your choice of training methods, providing alternatives and further recommendations
✔ critically evaluate the clients' achievements, providing recommendations for future training programmes

✔ critically analyse and compare the long-term adaptations of the body to fitness training for two contrasting athletes, drawing valid conclusions and recommendations.

The assessment activities in the text have been designed to help you pass the unit. It is important that you follow this closely in order to generate evidence. To gain a merit or distinction, you will need to take note of the following points.

Merit

1 You will be expected to work more independently throughout the assessment activities. Therefore you should take a more independent approach when designing and evaluating the training programme. You should show a better understanding and awareness, and need less tutor support. You must be able to work on your own in most situations, making your own decisions, and taking control of your assessment.

2 You will also be expected to show more constructive evaluation of the outcomes and success of the training programme. You will be expected to make recommendations for the future in relation to the testing and training programme you have designed.

3 Throughout your assessment you will need to use appropriate terminology, for example reporting on 'continuous running training' rather than 'running'.

4 You will be expected to show more depth and breadth in your understanding. You should be able to support your points with further research gathered outside the classroom, through using appropriate information sources such as training manuals.

Distinction

1 You will be expected to work totally independently throughout the assessment activities. You should show an excellent understanding and awareness, which means you require no tutor support. You should take a fully independent approach when designing and evaluating the training programme, and the training programme should also show a level of originality. You must be able to work on your own in all situations, making your own decisions.

2 You will be expected to show full depth and breadth in your understanding. You should use a wide range of appropriate information sources, for example reference books, training manuals, the Internet, magazines and journals. Information may also be gathered from contact with people in the fitness industry, but as with other material it should be fully referenced.

3 Emphasis will be placed on your evaluation of training programme design and of the training in relation to the expected and actual progress made by the client. You should be clear about the actual adaptations made by the client within six weeks, as some changes to the body take longer, for example hypertrophy.

4 You will be expected to produce a high level of work in the classroom and in practical workshops, for example when answering questions, to show your understanding. You will show a professional attitude throughout the assessment and especially when working with the client.

5 Throughout your assessment you will need to use appropriate terminology, for example reporting on 'continuous running training' rather than 'running'.

Resources

Texts

Bird, SR, Smith, A & James, K: *Exercise Benefits and Prescription*, 1998, Stanley Thornes (Publishers) Ltd

Brown, LE, Ferrigno, VA & Santana, JC: *Training for Speed, Agility and Quickness*, 2000, Human Kinetics

Davis, B, Bull, R, Roscoe, J & Roscoe, D: *Physical Education and the Study of Sport*, 1997, Mosby

Dick, FW: *Sports Training Principles*, 1992, A & C Black

Drews, CM: *Physiology of Sport Study Guide*, 2000, Human Kinetics

Heyward, VH: *Advanced Fitness Assessment and Exercise Prescription*, 1998, Human Kinetics

Howley, ET & Franks, BD: *Health Fitness Instructors' Handbook*, 1997, Human Kinetics

Marieb, EN: *Human Anatomy and Physiology*, 1995, Benjamin Cummings

Maud, PJ & Foster, C: *Physiological Assessment of Human Fitness*, 1995, Human Kinetics

McArdle, WD, Katch, FI & Katch, VC: *Exercise Physiology, Energy, Nutrition and Human Performance*, 1991, Lea & Febiger

Morrow, JR, Jackson, AW, Disch, JG & Mood, DP: *Measurement and Evaluation in Human Performance*, 2000, Human Kinetics

Powers, SK & Howley, ET: *Exercise Physiology Theory and Application to Fitness and Performance*, 1997, Brown and Benchmark

Wilmore, JH & Costill, DL: *Physiology of Sport and Exercise*, 1999, Human Kinetics

Websites

British Medical Journal (www.bmj.com)

Department of Health (www.doh.gov.uk)

Office of Health Economics (www.ohe.org)

Resources for Open University Teachers and Students (www.routes.open.ac.uk)

National Statistics Online (www.statistics.gov.uk)

The Wellcome Trust (www.wellcome.ac.uk)

The World Health Organisation (www.who.int)

Glossary

Acute responses – short-term responses (measured in seconds) made by the body after the onset of exercise

ADP (adenosine diphosphate) – a high-energy phosphate produced when ATP is broken down

Aerobic fitness – the ability of the cardiorespiratory system to supply the exercising muscles with oxygen to maintain the aerobic exercise for a long period of time

Anaerobic fitness – the ability to undertake short bursts of high-intensity activity

ATP (adenosine triphosphate) – a high-energy phosphate used by the body for energy

Chronic adaptation – changes that occur in the body after six to eight weeks of training

Duration – the amount of time spent performing an exercise or group of exercises

Flexibility – the ability of a specific joint, for example the knee, to move through a full range of movement

Frequency – the number of sessions or exercises performed by the athlete

Homeostasis – the body's ability to remain in or return to stability or normal levels, for example resting heart rate

Intensity – how hard the body has to work

Macrocycles – one- to four-year training cycles

Mesocycles – monthly training cycles

Microcycles – weekly or individual training sessions

Movement metabolic specificity – the energy system predominantly used with one particular sport or activity

Movement pattern specificity – the movement patterns associated with one particular sport or activity

Muscular endurance – a specific muscle or muscle group, such as the biceps, making repeated contractions over a significant period of time (a number of minutes)

Muscular strength – the ability of a specific muscle or muscle group to exert a force in a single maximal contraction to overcome some form of resistance

Overload – exercise or effort in excess of the athlete's normal amount

Periodisation – planning work in a fitness programme in cycles

Progression – progressive or steady achievement of overload in training

Resistance – the load the body must overcome while exercising

Reversibility – the principle that physical improvements caused by training will be lost if training is reduced

Specificity – the principle that training methods must match the desired outcomes

Vo$_2$ maximum – the maximal amount of oxygen uptake that can be used by the athlete during aerobic exercise

PRINCIPLES OF COACHING

Introduction to Unit 13

This is an optional unit which discusses how a sports coach can maximise the potential of performers through improving his or her own coaching effectiveness.

The unit explores the roles, responsibilities and qualities of a successful sports coach and identifies the skills and knowledge that are required to effectively coach an individual or team of performers. A good coach will not only know about these things but will also be able to adapt coaching to meet the needs of the performer, the situation and the environment. As you begin to understand what is needed to be a good sports coach, you will be able to identify the basic principles of the coaching process. You will be given the opportunity to put these principles into practice by planning, delivering and evaluating your own sports coaching session.

Assessment

Sport coaching is a practical process and a coach's effectiveness is best measured by observing him or her in practical coaching situations. You will therefore be required to demonstrate your practical coaching skills as part of this unit. So that you can be in a position to demonstrate these skills, the unit will provide you with appropriate underpinning knowledge about the principles of sports coaching and introduce you to the skills required to plan, deliver and evaluate your own coaching sessions.

The activities and tasks in this unit are structured to enable you to progress towards applying your knowledge of the coaching process in practical coaching sessions. First, you will be encouraged to draw on your own previous experiences of being coached or watching top coaches in action, in order to recognise the important roles and characteristics of a good coach and to identify areas of good practice. Next, you will work towards understanding the important skills that are required by an effective coach. This will be done through tasks and activities that explore how people learn and how you can structure coaching sessions to make learning safe and effective. This will lead to the identification of the major elements of a coaching session and the key elements of the coaching process.

After completing this unit you should be able to achieve the following outcomes.

Outcomes

- Investigate the roles, skills, techniques and responsibilities of successful sports coaches
- Explore the techniques required to improve the performance of selected athletes
- Plan and lead effective coaching sessions.

What you need to learn

- The different roles and responsibilities of a coach
- The range of skills and knowledge required by an effective coach
- The different styles and approaches to coaching
- The different elements of the coaching process.

The roles, skills and responsibilities of a successful sports coach

What is a sports coach?

There are many different ways to describe a coach and what a coach does. Some people suggest that a coach is involved in the **development** of people and works to help others get better at doing things. Others suggest that coaching is more about **change**, and that a coach is someone who brings about a change in some aspect of a person's life.

Describing what a coach is can be made easier by considering what coaches do. They may be required to do a range of things. The following section of this unit will identify the different roles a coach may be required to fulfil.

The roles of a coach

In order for a coach to effectively develop or change a performer, he or she will need to adopt a variety of different roles when coaching. These roles can be categorised as **educator**, **trainer**, **manager**, **innovator**, **role model** and **friend**. The following pages describe these roles in detail.

Think it over

In small groups, consider the different roles of a coach and try to identify examples of things that a coach might do when fulfilling each of the different roles.

The coach as an educator

The educational role of the coach can take a number of different forms. Principally, it will involve teaching people how to do things so that they can learn new skills and techniques. There are a variety of different teaching methods and styles, and coaches need to be able to match the appropriate teaching methods to the stage and experience of their performers. A coach working with a young beginner should use different teaching methods from those used with an expert performer.

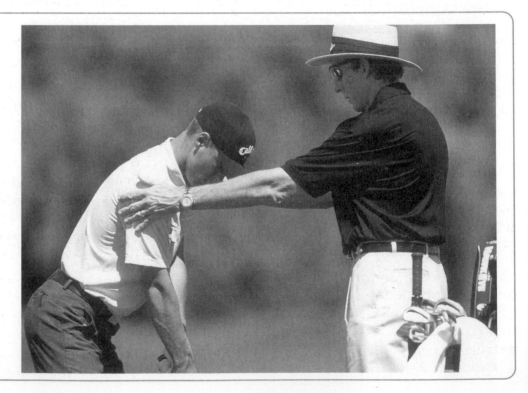

'A coach is somebody who develops, improves or promotes change in a person's ability and/or understanding within a specific context.'

'A sport coach is somebody who works with another person or group of people to develop and improve their understanding and ability in a sport and also to develop and improve them as people using sport as a vehicle for development.'

A coach must draw on experience and knowledge in order to demonstrate and explain

Young athletes and beginners who are not familiar with the skills of a sport will need to learn them and be given the opportunity to practise them. The 'educator' coach should be able to understand how people learn new skills, and be able to devise practices and drills that will allow skills to be developed so that they can be performed correctly in competitive situations. Similarly, developing performers or established competitors will require appropriate instruction to allow them to refine their skills. They may also need to be taught more advanced skills, which will make them more effective.

When teaching a skill, a coach will need to draw on his or her own experience and knowledge of sports skills and be able to demonstrate and explain how they are performed. In addition, the coach will need to educate performers about how the skills fit together and contribute to the overall performance of the sport. This will involve introducing performers to tactics, and patterns and styles of play.

An effective coach will not only teach somebody a new skill but also how and when to use it most effectively. A knowledgeable coach will be able to develop tactical awareness and strategy in performers in a way that is appropriate to their level of performance. Teaching detailed tactical manoeuvres and set plays in rugby to a group of young performers relatively new to the game would be inappropriate, yet a team which is looking for performance enhancement may benefit from new tactical inputs in training so that they can progress to a higher level of performance.

As well as the technical and tactical skills of a sport, a performer also needs to learn more general skills associated with sport participation. A coach needs to educate performers by teaching them how to control their emotions and develop self-esteem through sport, and also by helping them to develop social skills such as teamwork, co-operation, citizenship, fair play and being able to compete with others. Through sport, young people can also develop personally by being encouraged to consider their own welfare and by being empowered to learn life skills and develop their own values and attitudes.

Theory into practice

1 Use a dictionary to define the following words:

    To teach   Teacher

    To coach   Coach

2 Discuss with a partner what you consider to be the difference between teaching and coaching.

The coach as a trainer

Having educated their performers in the fundamental skills associated with their sport, coaches must then ensure that performers are able to meet the demands placed on them by the sport. In addition to the technical demands dealt with through the teaching of new skills, coaches must ensure that performers can meet the physical and psychological demands of their sport. The coach must therefore take on a trainer role and devise and run training programmes to develop the technical, physical and psychological abilities of performers.

The role of trainer is probably most commonly associated with the physical development of performers. Virtually all sports place a physical demand on participants, and there is plenty of evidence that suggests participants can improve their performance in a sport by developing their general and sport-specific fitness levels. The 'trainer' coach, armed with a good understanding of the different components of fitness (see Unit 10), a thorough appreciation of the physical demands of the sport and knowledge of the basic principles of training (see Unit 11), should be able to devise a training programme that enables performers to maintain good all-round health and develop appropriate fitness training routines to enable performers to improve their fitness levels.

With careful planning a coach should also be able to include in the training programme clear

progressions in technical development, and also routines and practices that help the performer to develop the psychological skills needed to meet the challenges of the sport.

Think it over

In small groups, discuss the following questions:

1 What do you think of when you think of a manager?

2 What do you think a manager does?

The coach as a manager

The role of manager can relate to the management of a number of different aspects of coaching. A good coach should be able to demonstrate good leadership skills and be able to manage and direct other people effectively. The success of a coaching session or programme will depend largely on the ability of the coach to manage the coaching environment in an authoritative and respectful manner.

This does not mean that a coach should always be shouting and telling people what to do. A well-organised coach who gives clear instructions in the most appropriate way will gain the respect of performers and achieve a well-managed coaching environment.

The management of people is about trying to ensure that they perform to the best of their ability. In individual sports, the coach is aiming to manage the development of the performer effectively and to ensure an appropriate relationship exists between coach and performer so that optimal performance can be achieved. In team sports, the management role of a coach involves selecting teams, and in this context the 'manager' coach not only has to select the best players but also has to ensure that the players fit together and the team is able to perform to the best of its ability.

In some sports and at high levels of coaching, the coach may not be the only person involved in the coaching process. There may be assistant coaches, specialist coaches or support staff working alongside the coach. In these instances the coach has to manage the contribution of other coaching staff while maintaining the development of the performer as the focus for coaching activities.

To some extent the role of trainer and manager can overlap. A good coach will be able to plan a training programme, deliver it, monitor progress against the plan and adjust the plan in the light of any problems. The coach, therefore, has to manage the implementation of a training programme as well as act as the trainer.

Depending on the structure of the sport or club within which the coach works, a coach may also have to adopt a number of administrative roles. These may include organising venues for practice and competition, registering and entering performers for competitions, co-ordinating the activities of other coaches and support staff, and dealing with parents and officials.

The coach as an innovator

Coaching is always about progressing and developing. A good coach will be able to maintain performers' interest in training by devising new ideas and practices that encourage continued development. This may simply be about finding new ways to do things, so that sessions do not become boring, or it may be that the coach comes up with new ideas for practices, match tactics and training methods to solve problems and make improvements.

A former Olympic champion once used the motto:

> If you always do what you have always done,
> You will always get what you always got.

This is a strong statement suggesting that coaches and their performers should be brave enough to try new things in an attempt to get different, and hopefully better, results. This is why a coach needs to access and use the latest scientific and technical knowledge to help inform coaching practice. New and innovative approaches to coaching can help gain the extra advantages necessary for success.

Effective coaches should also find time to reflect on their own coaching, and where necessary return to the role of student and further develop their own understanding and professional development, by learning from other coaches and other sports.

A new approach: the Fosbury Flop (bottom) has allowed greater heights to be jumped than the traditional straddle technique (top)

Case study

We have just seen that one of the roles of the coach is to be innovative and forward thinking in the search for new training methods and approaches to coaching. There have been numerous examples of athletes and their coaches experimenting with new ideas and paving the way for future developments in their sport. One good example is the story of the first man to run the mile in under four minutes.

In 1954 Roger Bannister was a medical student at Oxford University. He was also a very good middle-distance runner. The accepted training methods at that time required long periods of continuous running to build up stamina. This meant many hours of running. Bannister could not afford the large amount of time required to train in this way as it clashed with his medical studies.

He considered how he might be able to get the same effect without having to commit so much time to his training. This led him to try short-distance, fast-pace repetition training sessions at the local track in his lunch break. He would regularly do hour-long interval sessions on the track – focusing on high quality running, rather than a high quantity of mileage.

In May of that year Bannister ran the mile in under four minutes – the first man to do so. Much of his success could be put down to his innovative training regime, which arose from his courage in challenging what had always been done before.

Other innovations tend to be technique- or skill-based, and in many instances a new technique or skill is named after the first person to use it in competition, such as:

● the Fosbury Flop – high jump (see the illustration on the previous page)
● the Cruyff Turn – football
● the Tsukahara – gymnastics (see the illustration on page 211).

1 Select one of the above techniques or skills and, using the Internet or appropriate coaching manuals, identify:
 ● the key components and elements of the technique or skill
 ● how the technique or skill made an impact in the sport
 ● the nationality and major achievements of the person it is named after.

2 Find other examples of innovations in technique or skill in a sport you are interested in.

The coach as a role model

Performers need someone to guide them and be their role model, and a coach can be a very influential person. The coach who behaves in a way that earns and maintains trust and respect can become a positive role model. You need to ensure that the influence you exert as a coach is positive in this way. There are recognised standards and practices that a coach should adhere to, and some issues related to these are covered in more detail on pages 189–195. Behaviour will be observed by performers, particularly young performers, and they will seek to imitate it.

The coach as a friend

Coaches and their performers spend a lot of time together. They will share positive experiences as well as negative ones, and they need to be able to do this in a friendly and respectful environment. The sporting environment can be tough at times and performers will need someone to talk to in order to help them cope with the demands of training and competing. The 'friend' coach may need to be there to pick up the pieces if things go wrong and to be an outlet for emotions. The coach may also need to be there to help performers keep their feet on the ground if they are successful.

Theory into practice

One function of a coach is motivating performers.

1 Think about a coach you have either been coached by or worked with, and describe an example of how he or she motivated you to train.
2 What sort of things did the coach do to make the sessions fun?
3 Now think of a top coach who has been successful. Can you think of any examples of how he or she motivates performers to achieve?
4 What types of things might a coach do which could be demotivating, or put somebody off training with him or her?

The coach who acts as a friend may also be able to motivate a performer. In most instances the performers you will work with will be highly self-motivated. They will come to you for coaching because they enjoy the sport and the coaching experiences they get. It is up to you to ensure that you manage the coaching environment in a way that enables them to maintain this self-motivation.

To achieve this you should think about what motivates your performers to participate and what drives them to perform. If you understand why a person takes part in sport, you will be better able to create a coaching environment that allows him or her to remain motivated.

There are numerous factors that may motivate people to participate in sports. These include enjoyment, to meet other people, to improve fitness, to give themselves a challenge, to be in a competitive environment, to gain some form of reward or, in some cases, to please others.

Case study

The following is an extract from a *Sunday Times* interview with Paula Radcliffe published on the morning of her world record performance in the London Marathon in April 2003. Paula's coach, Gary Lough, is also her husband and fulfils a number of different roles.

We are sitting in an apartment above Gerard Hartmann's clinic on Limerick's O'Connell Street. Radcliffe and Lough have been here in this room so many times that they see the sprawling Kenyan flag on the wall as part of the wallpaper. It is eight o'clock on a midweek evening, 12 days before the London Marathon, and they are half-watching Eastenders.

'Gary is more into it than I am,' she says.

'That's not true,' he responds. 'You watch it more than I do.'

So they continue back and forth, neither prepared to back down. Spiky defiance is their way. 'We're both strong characters,' she says. 'We're also very secure with each other. We don't think, "Oh well, if I tell him what I really think, he might go off and leave me". That security probably comes from spending a lot of time together and being good friends even before we got together as a couple. We can say exactly what we think, and it will be taken like that.'

They disagree, too, on who's got the harder part. She says it is he. He has to be there all the time – training partner, facilitator, manager, personal assistant, media director and husband. 'You can't have the same motivation as I have, you don't get the end result', and when she tells him that, he realises she struggles to understand that his motivation is seeing her do it.

Lough may also be her greatest fan. He tells a story of what could easily have been a calamitous accident towards

Gary Lough and Paula Radcliffe

the end of their time in Albuquerque. Twenty minutes into a 24-mile training run, Radcliffe was overtaking a young cyclist when the girl unwittingly turned her bike and clipped Radcliffe's trailing leg.

Lough was right behind, and watched as she flew through the air and crash-landed on the cycle path. Bending over her, he was horrified by the extent of the damage. Her elbows and knees were cut and burned, her shoulders were bruised, her face was a mess. There was a gash on her chin and blood everywhere. Suspecting that she might be seriously injured, she cried.

He saw her now only as his wife and soul mate. 'Your face,' he said, 'your face is ruined.'

'I don't care about my face,' she cried.

'What do you mean, you don't care about your face?'

'I don't run with my bloody face.'

Why should we be surprised that alongside the ladylike calmness, there is a fiercely competitive athlete? How else could she have endured the years of near-misses and come through to enjoy the season she had last year?

Maybe we forget that this woman sat in the stadium at the 2001 world championships in Edmonton, held up a sign saying 'EPO Cheats Out', and wanted one of her fellow athletes to take the taunt personally. We talk about decision-making and how she likes to have control over her running. 'Well, I do, because it's my life. It's my career. I don't want Gary to have complete control.

'In a week before a big race, he will keep things from me so I am not distracted or bothered, but generally I like to know what's going on. Sometimes he might think he knows, and then he might get a shock when we discuss it, because I want to do it differently. He's very good about it, because he knows that at the end of the day, it's me going out and racing.

'We discuss things, I will say, "What do you think I should do?" but it's me that has to make the decision. On the business and commercial side I bow to his greater expertise, but on the side of running, the decision must be mine. After winning the 10,000 metres in the European championships at Munich last year, I thought of running in the 5,000 metres. We discussed it a lot, but he wouldn't tell me what he thought, because he knew it had to come from me.'

1 Identify the different roles that Gary Lough plays.

2 What are the disadvantages of having to play so many different roles?

3 What are the advantages?

How and when a coach needs to play these different roles will depend on many factors, such as the aims, ability, experience and age of participants and also the situation they are in. Coaches who work with young beginner athletes will be required to fulfil different roles from coaches working with elite adult athletes.

Primarily, coaches working with young people will have a trainer or educator role to play because the emphasis may be on learning and developing new skills. They may also need to adopt a more personal, friendly and role-model type approach. However, an elite adult athlete will probably have mastered the skills of his or her sport and require the coach to play the roles of manager and innovator more than those of educator.

Remember

- A sports coach is somebody who works with individuals or teams to develop their understanding and ability in a sport and to develop them as people.
- A coach has many roles to play – educator, trainer, manager, role model, innovator and friend.
- These roles can vary according to the aims of performers, their ability, experience and age and the situation.

Assessment activity 13.1

Coach:	Mary Hughes
Sport:	Squash
Performer:	Julia Marsh
Performer's age:	14
Experience:	Beginner

Coach:	Alex Ferguson
Sport:	Football
Performers:	Manchester United
Performers' ages:	20–30s
Experience:	Professionals

Look at the coach profiles above.

1 Identify the three most important roles that you think each coach will play with their respective performers.

2 How will the coaching roles of Alex Ferguson and Mary Hughes be different?

3 Are there any things that these two coaches will do that are similar?

4 Draw a table with the headings shown below and identify a top-level coach from a sport of

Role	Task
Manager	Selecting the team according to players' strengths and weaknesses and with consideration to opponents' strengths and weaknesses

your choice. Make a list of all the different roles that you think the coach performs. Give some examples of when and how these roles are performed.

5 Draw another table and do the same for a coach you know who works with a local club and coaches young people.

6 Compare the two lists and consider why some of the roles may be different.

Knowing your responsibilities as a coach

Whatever role a coach undertakes, he or she has a responsibility to ensure that sport is safe and ethical and meets the demands of those participating in it. Given the crucial part that coaching plays in the development of a sport and of the performers within that sport, coaches have a duty to ensure that a person's experiences of sport are positive and long lasting.

To fulfil this duty coaches face a number of responsibilities towards their performers, their sport, their profession and themselves. These responsibilities fall into several categories:

- coaching responsibilities – the delivery of appropriate coaching sessions to aid the development of performers
- health and safety – the maintenance of a safe environment for performers
- professional conduct – the demonstration of proper personal and professional behaviour and conduct in the light of legal responsibilities.

A good coach will always seek to meet these responsibilities and will try to set a good example and be a positive role model.

Coaching responsibilities

Coaching is about coaching people and not necessarily a sport. Coaching sessions should meet the needs and abilities of individuals, regardless of their level of performance. The aims of effective coaching may range from improving a person's

ability to hit a ball through to achieving international success on a world stage. Indeed, the number of people who achieve world success is minimal compared to the number of people who regularly play sport and simply get better at playing it.

The main function of a coaching session or series of sessions is to provide performers with the opportunity to develop and maximise their potential. Each session should be well organised and planned and offer participants the opportunity to develop an appropriate range of skills.

Sessions should be constructed so that they meet the demands of the performers, and if they are part of an ongoing programme they should show clear progression from one session to the next. Prior discussion and planning with the performers will allow the coach to identify their desired goals and to plan coaching sessions to enable the performers to work towards achieving those goals. In some instances their performance levels and therefore their coaching needs may be beyond the level of you as their coach. In such instances you should seek to identify other opportunities that will allow performers to progress and develop.

Case study

Chris is a level 2 tennis coach who enjoys coaching young beginner tennis players and teaching them the fundamental skills of the game. He has never played top-level tennis himself and recognises that he does not know enough about some of the advanced skills, tactics and drills needed to coach at a higher level. He is content to work on introducing and developing young players to gain enjoyment from the game, and he does not have the time to advance his coaching skills to allow him to coach young players to a high level.

One of Chris's young players, Craig, has just won a regional under-14 tournament – his first major success. After the match Craig's opponent's coach, Simon, approaches Chris. Simon is more qualified than Chris and has experience of coaching junior players to national level. The conversation ends with an invitation for Craig to join Simon's coaching group. Chris is not sure whether Craig should join Simon's group. He decides to draw up a list of positives and negatives to help him decide.

1   What might be some of the things Chris includes on his 'positives' list?

2   What might be on his list of 'negatives'?

3   Should these issues be considered in relation to Chris or to Craig?

4   What would be your advice to Chris?

A coach has the duty to encourage performers to progress and develop

In order for performers to gain the most from coaching, coaches should try to ensure that coaching sessions are enjoyable and rewarding. A performer who has had a positive and enjoyable experience is more likely to keep attending and be motivated to develop skills and performance. It is a coach's responsibility to engage and motivate performers to maintain their involvement. By doing this coaches will maintain a high professional standard.

Coaching sessions should be accessible, equitable and free from fear and harassment. A coach has a responsibility to ensure that coaching sessions are accessible to all those who wish to be involved, and they should take place in a non-threatening environment built on trust and respect. There should not be any barriers to prevent people from taking part and developing their ability.

Health and safety

All coaching sessions should take place with health and safety in mind. They should occur in a safe environment that maximises the benefits and minimises the risks to performers. The health and safety responsibilities of a coach can be split into three essential components.

- **The safety of the facilities** When you are preparing a coaching session you must consider the facilities in which the session is to take place. You must ensure that the activities you are planning can be done safely with the space and equipment available. You must also make sure that you are aware of any emergency procedures that may need to be followed and what should be done in the event of an emergency. In short, a coach must undertake a full risk assessment of the venue and make sure that he or she can deal with any incidents that could arise.

- **The safety of the activities** A good coach will select practices and activities that are safe and technically correct. They should pose no risk to the performer. In selecting activities the coach needs to consider the following:
  - performers should always undertake a warm-up before attempting any demanding activities
  - performers should not be required to perform activities of which they are not physically or technically capable
  - performers should always undertake activities which remain within the rules of the sport
  - coaches should not allow activities that are unsafe or technically incorrect.

Good practice makes the safety of performers paramount

- **The safety of the participant** If a coach appropriately addresses the safety issues related to the coaching venue, the equipment and the selected activities as identified above, the safety of the participant will have been addressed. However, there may be some instances where the safety of the performer can be compromised if the coach fails to adhere to good practice guidelines.

Theory into practice

You have been asked by your head coach to undertake a risk assessment of a coaching venue that you use regularly. This may be a local football pitch, local sports hall, swimming pool or some other venue where your coaching might take place.

1 Draw a plan of the venue detailing all the important features that may be used in any coaching that goes on there.
2 Identify any features that you consider to be unsafe.
3 How can you make these safe for coaching?
4 What facilities (e.g. first aid box, telephone) are available for use in an emergency?
5 Draw up an emergency plan that you would follow if an accident occurred while you were coaching at the venue.

Professional conduct

A coach is often viewed as a person of authority who has a certain amount of power. It is important that a coach knows how to use this authority and power appropriately and not to abuse it. Unfortunately, some coaches use their power to achieve inappropriate gains. A coach should know what constitutes good and bad practice and be able to ensure that coaching is within the boundaries of good practice rather than in danger of becoming inappropriate or even illegal behaviour.

Coaches should always ensure that what they do is in line with acceptable standards and good practice. All coaches should demonstrate a professional approach to performers that is fair, honest and considerate to their individual needs. As with many professions in the UK, coaching promotes its own code of conduct to ensure that coaches practice in the most ethical and professional manner. Across all levels of coaching it is stressed that coaches 'must demonstrate ... a high degree of honesty, integrity and competence'. Sports coach UK, the governing body for sports coaches in this country, has produced a Code of Conduct for Sports Coaches, and this forms the basis for good coaching practice. It is underpinned by the following key principles, with which all coaches should familiarise themselves:

- **rights** – to respect and champion the rights of every participant in sport
- **relationships** – to develop open and honest relationships with participants
- **responsibilities** – to demonstrate appropriate personal behaviour and conduct and achieve a high level of competence through qualifications and continued professional development.

An integral part of coaching is the responsibility of a coach to keep his or her knowledge up to date. This will ensure that what coaches are doing is accurate and has not been superseded by new information, and will help coaches to continue to provide a safe coaching environment and maintain the respect of participants and colleagues.

Most national governing bodies provide courses for coaches to update and develop their coaching knowledge, and gain professional recognition for their knowledge and expertise. New developments within coaching may soon require coaches to be registered or licensed to practise. To achieve such status coaches will be required to show evidence not only of an initial coaching qualification, but also any courses or learning experiences that they have undertaken as part of their ongoing professional development.

Legal obligations

As well as the need for maintaining professional standards, coaches need to be fully aware of their legal responsibilities. We are all governed by the rules of the society we live in, and these laws apply regardless of whether we are on the playing field or in the local pub. In addition, in order to maintain fair play in competitive sport, coaches and performers are subject to the rules and laws of their sport.

As well as being aware of what is and is not allowed in their sport, coaches must also be aware of how the law can affect coaching. Coaches should make every effort to ensure that they and their performers do not do anything that may be considered illegal or unethical.

Many different sources of liability may affect a coach. The most directly relevant areas include:

- common law
- negligence.

Common law relates to the fundamental laws of the society we live in. Sport does not exist outside of real life, and thus real-life laws still apply. The most obvious example of this can be seen by considering the laws of common assault. Eric Cantona's flying 'kung-fu' kick at a Crystal Palace supporter during a Premiership match was considered as an assault no different from a similar attack in the street. Assault during the course of play – there are numerous examples of rugby players punching opponents – is not beyond the law. Coaches should ensure that their players, and indeed their own conduct, do not encroach beyond the boundaries of acceptable behaviour.

Other areas where common law applies include rights of entry and occupiers' liability, equal opportunities, race relations, disability discrimination and the Children Act. There is now a demand for coaches who wish to work with children to undergo a police check via the Criminal Records Bureau. Coaches should make sure that they are familiar with the appropriate aspects of common law and manage their, and their performers', behaviour accordingly.

Negligence is another important area. Coaches must understand that should a performer suffer an injury, loss or any damage to property due to a coach's negligence, that coach may be held liable. Negligence can be a result of both actions and omissions – what you do and what you don't do. As a coach you will have what is termed a 'duty of care' towards your performers. A coach has a duty to be:

- safe – in relation to coaching, the equipment used, the environment for work, the size of the group and the activities involved
- qualified – coaches should hold relevant, current qualifications which are at the appropriate level for the group they are working with
- insured – coaches should hold insurance cover appropriate for the sport they are involved in and for their employment status (self-employed coaches need public liability insurance)
- competent – to select appropriate activities to match the age and ability range of performers.

With good planning and careful coaching, negligence can be avoided. Much of the key information to underpin good practice is outlined in this unit.

Theory into practice

1 Using the Internet, undertake a search to find details of the following laws:
- Disability Discrimination Act
- Race Relations Act
- Children Act
- Equal Opportunities Act
- Occupiers' Liability Act.
2 Write a short summary of how you think these acts impact on the work of a coach.

In addition to the general areas of liability identified above, there are two major areas of the law that the coach needs to be able to deal with. These areas, drugs in sport and child protection, pose ethical and moral dilemmas as well as legal ones. There are some grey areas when dealing with these issues, and coaches need to be able to make their own moral judgements based on a good understanding of the rights and wrongs of each issue.

The role of **drugs in sport** is widely discussed, but coaches need to base their coaching philosophy on the known facts rather than rumour and hearsay. Some drugs are illegal and the issues surrounding their use are not up for discussion. However, some drugs are legal within society but deemed to be performance-enhancing when used in a sporting context. For example, some asthma and common-cold medications are legal but are considered to be stimulants when taken to enhance performance.

Coaches should be aware that the use of illegal performance-enhancing drugs not only gives performers an unfair advantage, but also puts them at risk of being banned from their sport and in many cases suffering adverse medical effects. Coaches have a responsibility to educate performers on issues relating to the use of performance-enhancing drugs in sport, and to co-operate fully with anti-doping agencies and policies.

Case study

In Germany in 1998, four coaches and two doctors, former employees of the Dynamo Berlin Club, were charged with inflicting grievous bodily harm by administering drugs to 19 minors between 1974 and 1989. They were accused of being responsible for long-lasting physical damage to young sportswomen in their care. According to German investigators, these former East German coaches supplied performance-enhancing drugs to the performers throughout their careers in sport. Evidence also suggested that doping was conducted regularly on 2000 of East Germany's elite sportspeople. Routinely, anabolic steroids and other drugs were given to 13- and 14-year-old adolescent girl swimmers – some evidence suggested that children as young as 10 were also given performance-enhancing drugs.

1 What happened in 1989 that allowed this information to become public knowledge?

2 What performance-enhancing effects do anabolic steroids have?

3 Access the world records for the women's 400 metres, 800 metres and 1500 metres in athletics since 1960. Plot a graph of how each of the records changed in that period of time. What do you notice about the times? What do you think accounts for the graph?

4 Who holds the world record for 10,000 metres for women? What is questionable about this record?

Many coaches may also find themselves spending a great deal of time coaching **children and young people**. This means they will develop relationships with performers and in some instances fulfil some of the more intimate roles of coaching – be a friend, parent, consoler. In these instances, and throughout their coaching, coaches must avoid engaging in any form of inappropriate contact or behaviour with young performers that may breach child protection guidelines.

Recent additions to the Children Act introduced a requirement that all people working with children should be checked for any previous offences related to children. The Criminal Records Bureau undertakes such checks on behalf of employers, so

Coaches often spend much time working with children

most coaches being employed to coach children will have to be checked by police before taking up any position.

Case study

An NSPCC report, 'Child Maltreatment in the United Kingdom', was published in November 2000. This major research report included the following statistics:

- 43% of the young people surveyed identified bullying or being discriminated against as the most common source of distress or upset
- bullying occurred as a result of some personal feature (e.g. size, race, speech or dress)
- 14-15% of the young people said they had been physically attacked while being bullied, and many reported that they had had possessions stolen
- 6% of boys under 18 and 4% of girls under 18 reported a serious lack of supervision
- 6% of boys under 18 and 8% of girls under 18 reported serious physical abuse.

1 What would you do as a coach to prevent bullying and physical abuse from taking place in your coaching sessions?

2 With a partner, design a poster or leaflet that you would give to your performers to warn of the dangers of bullying.

Coaches who adhere to the basic principles of good practice and maintain high professional standards protect themselves from slipping into bad practice and do not put themselves or their performers at risk. Most coaches work under the auspices of the governing body of their sport and the governing body qualifications, registration or membership entitle them to insurance cover as an added mechanism for protection. It is a major responsibility of a coach to ensure that he or she is appropriately qualified and/or registered and has suitable insurance cover.

Theory into practice

1 Access the sports coach UK website (www.sportscoachuk.org) and download or note down any information you can find about codes of conduct, legal issues, child protection and any other ethical issues related to sports coaching.

2 Prepare a short summary document for your classmates focusing on the key messages.

3 What educational opportunities does sports coach UK offer coaches on ethical and legal issues?

4 Access the website for the governing body of your sport. Does the national governing body have any additional information?

5 Does the national governing body have a child protection policy?

6 Access the Child Protection in Sport website (www.sportprotects.org.uk). Use the information available on this site to produce a single A4 sheet of information that you could give to parents of children you coach.

Remember

- Coaches have a responsibility to ensure that their coaching is safe and ethical and meets the demands of their performers.
- Coaching sessions should be organised, planned, progressive, enjoyable, and accessible to all, and should offer participants the opportunity to develop their skills.
- Coaches should undertake a full risk assessment of the coaching environment to minimise the risks to performers.
- Coaches should be familiar with the desired standards of good coaching practice and adhere to them at all times when coaching.

The skills of a coach

In order to fulfil the different roles discussed above and to meet the required responsibilities, a coach needs to have confidence in a wide range of skills. These skills fall broadly into three categories:

- communication skills
- organisational skills – including the organisation of sessions, analysing and problem-solving, evaluation, time-management, and health, safety and security skills
- sport-specific skills – including a knowledge of sports, tactical skills and basic sport science.

Communication skills

Some coaches feel that effective communication is all about talking and telling performers what to do. But communication is a two-way process, with the sending of a signal (verbal or non-verbal communication) being as important as the receiving of a signal (listening and understanding). Coaches should think carefully about their ways of communicating, and spend as much time listening as they do talking.

How a coach sends a signal to a performer can have a huge impact on the effectiveness and interpretation of that signal. Communication is of two types – verbal and non-verbal. **Verbal communication** is characterised by use of the spoken word, and most coaches are certainly able to talk! Varying the tone, pace and volume of the spoken word is an important means of conveying specific messages. A coach needs to remember that constant shouting does not make communication more effective – in fact it may become less effective, as a performer may begin to ignore the shouts.

Non-verbal communication involves alternative methods of sending signals, which might include

Monica Seles's coach uses verbal and non-verbal communication

body language, facial expressions and gestures. In general coaches are less adept at using non-verbal communication. Remember, a well-timed facial expression can say more than a thousand words. In competitive situations, non-verbal communication may be the only way to communicate with your performers.

Theory into practice

Non-verbal communication is a powerful way of conveying messages. Try the following tasks and see how much you can learn about the use of body language and non-verbal communication. Use a dictionary, encyclopaedia or the Internet to help if necessary.

1 What is semaphore? Who might use it?
2 Obtain a copy of the semaphore alphabet. Make two flags and practise sending a message to a partner.
3 What is British Sign Language (BSL)? Who might use it?
4 Obtain some examples of the signs used in BSL, and practise signing.
5 Watch a video clip of a sporting activity, with the sound turned down. Observe who uses body language and try to work out what message people are trying to convey.
6 How might a referee or umpire use body language?
7 Can you give some common examples of body language or signs that are used in sport? What do they mean?

Listening is an important feature of good communication. Effective listening can serve two main functions. First, it is a good way to check understanding; it is important for a coach to be sure that performers have understood the information they have been given. By questioning performers and listening to their responses, a coach can assess whether or not a message has been received correctly.

Second, listening can be a good source of useful information. Listening to a performer's opinions and how he or she feels during a practice or a drill may help the coach identify errors that are not immediately obvious through watching the performer.

Think it over

In small groups, discuss the difference between hearing and listening. What are the important characteristics of listening? How can you tell whether somebody has been listening to what you have said?

Organisational skills

If a coaching session or training programme is to be effective it has to be organised well. This requires a range of skills that may include organisation, analysing and problem-solving skills, evaluation, time-management, and health, safety and security skills. How and when a coach requires these skills is related to the different stages of the coaching process.

Think it over

You have been asked by your head coach to organise the next coaching session. Working in pairs, write a list of all the things that you need to do before the next session starts to ensure that it is effectively organised.

Even before a coaching session begins, a coach has to be well organised. He or she will need a clear idea of the equipment and facilities required and available for use, the activities to be undertaken, and who is to be coached. Good organisational skills prior to a coaching session will ensure that during the session the performers are doing the right thing, in the right place, at the right time.

Most coaches find the administrative aspects of their role the least enjoyable part of their work. However, these are of equal importance to the other aspects of coaching. Obviously, a coaching session cannot take place if the facilities have not been booked; similarly, performers cannot use their newly developed skills in a competitive environment if they have not been entered for a competition. Some coaches will seek to involve other club members or parents in these organisational aspects associated with coaching. This is a good idea as it will reduce the amount of time that a coach has to allocate to basic administrative duties, and it also involves other people who may be better at this work than the coach!

Analysis and problem-solving

Coaching is as much about analysing people's actions as it is about instructing them what to do. The careful observation of a performer while practising a skill, undergoing a training session or competing gives the coach a lot of useful information. The ability to observe performers and then to compare the observed performance with the desired performance is the basis of analysis. The ability to develop appropriate coaching practices to address any differences is a key aspect of the coaching process.

Coaching will not always go smoothly – things will go wrong and problems will arise. A coach must be able to identify when things have gone wrong and be able to determine the exact nature of the problem. He or she should then be able to assess the situation and try to identify appropriate solutions to the problem. This requires logical thinking and reasoning, and being prepared to rethink an approach to a particular coaching situation.

Problem-solving can be the most challenging part of coaching but it can also be the most rewarding. The problems a coach faces may take a variety of different forms.

- The problem may lie with the performer – a performer may be unable to carry out a particular skill being taught. In this case the coach will need to try to identify why the performer is being unsuccessful and then try a different set of practices to help the performer grasp the skill.
- The problem may be associated with the coaching environment – a particular pitch or court may not be available at certain times and the coach will need to plan alternative arrangements to solve the problem.
- There may be a problem in the competitive arena – a team may have difficulty dealing with a particular opponent or with a tactic used by opponents. The coach will have to use tactical

knowledge to find a strategy for dealing with the opponent and overcoming the problem.
- The coach may struggle to grasp a scientific concept or some aspect of the planning process, and may need to seek advice from others or attend a coaching course to gain the required information.

Evaluation

Coaches are always keen to assess and pass comment on their performers' abilities and performances. However, they are rarely prepared to reflect on their own performances, and if they are they will tend to focus on what worked well. Effective evaluation of a coaching session should be impartial and identify not only what went well but also what worked less well. The key to good evaluation is honesty, and this will allow the coach to learn from mistakes and improve coaching skills.

Time management

Coaches often complain that they do not have enough time with their performers to achieve the desired outcome. This can sometimes be a poor excuse for bad time management. Coaches must try to use the time they have available effectively. Careful planning of a session should minimise the time wasted and maximise the learning opportunities. Coaches must try to strike an appropriate balance between providing enough time on a practice or a drill for the performer to learn and improve, and spending too much time on activities which do not provide new learning opportunities.

Sport-specific skills

A coach needs to be able to understand and execute certain skills associated with the technical and tactical aspects of the sport. Some people argue that a good coach can coach a person in any sport because the fundamental coaching skills are the same across all sports, and it is only the context that differs. This is partly true, but a coach also has to have a good knowledge of a sport and its demands in order to effectively teach the skills of that sport. A coach needs to know what the correct technique looks like in order to teach a beginner how to perform it.

Most coaches operate within a sport they are very familiar with. Many are former performers or have been coaching in that sport for many years. As a result they will be familiar with the specific techniques, skills and tactics of their chosen sport. The coach will be able to observe and analyse a performance and compare it to a desired ideal performance.

Theory into practice

Different sports use different terms and descriptions. It is important for a coach to be able to understand the different terminology used in his or her sport. Try the following tasks to see how much you know about the different terms that are often used in sport.

1   Below is a description of a passage of play in cricket. Read through it and rewrite it using non-cricket terminology to describe how the ball was bowled, how exactly the batsman hit it and where the ball ended up.

It was Wahid's last delivery of the over. He used his usual bowling approach – left-arm over the wicket. This time he bowled a 'yorker' that was somewhere between middle and leg and just short of a length. Jackson came down to meet it and hit a wonderful cover drive through the leg side just missing the square-leg umpire. Smith, fielding at cover point, made a brilliant stop and returned the ball underarm missing the leg stump by inches. Unfortunately, the wicketkeeper missed it and Jenkins had to run round from silly mid-off to field the overthrow. The running between the wickets was slow and Jackson only took a single – enough to prevent Wahid from getting a maiden.

2   Copy and complete the following table:

Term	Sport	Explanation
Full-toss	Cricket	
Volley	Tennis	
Volley	Volleyball	
Half-volley	Football	
Interval	Athletics	
Flic-flac	Gymnastics	

Using demonstrations to convey thoughts or teach new skills (e.g. teaching a group of novice tennis players how to serve) is an important means of modelling the desired performance to a learner. Therefore it is desirable for coaches to have some of the basic sport skills themselves so that they can do effective demonstrations. It is important however that a coach makes sure that demonstrations are correct – otherwise performers will learn poor techniques and pick up bad habits.

A large number of factors can affect performance in a sport and a coach cannot realistically expect to be knowledgeable in all of them. Knowledge of the specific skills of a sport is, however, important to a coach, as is an understanding of the physical and mental demands placed on their performers. This means that a coach has to have some understanding of the sport science aspects of the sport. For example, coaches of team sports should have an understanding of the typical distances that their players run during a game and also the intensity of activity. This will help them to decide whether their sport places predominantly aerobic or anaerobic demands on players.

Sport science is one area where coaches are probably not familiar with up-to-date information. However, it is important that a coach has some understanding of these factors and how they can influence performance, so that they are aware of the additional tools that might be available to aid performance development. Some sport scientists compare the scientific development of performance to completing a jigsaw puzzle. All the different aspects of sport science fit together like the pieces of a jigsaw puzzle to create a final picture. Some of the main pieces of the sport science and sport medicine jigsaw are shown in the diagram on the next page.

In some instances a coach may be able to draw on the expertise of others to help out in these areas. Sport science is becoming increasingly available to all levels of coaching and not just to top coaches at the elite level. Some coaches and clubs are able to pay people to provide scientific, fitness and sport medicine advice and support, while others

Performers can undertake a wide range of simple fitness tests in a field-based environment to assess how well they meet the physical demand of their sport. For more detailed assessment coaches could access specialist laboratory-based testing procedures to accurately assess the fitness levels of their performers.

New techniques associated with weight training, agility training and plyometric training have been shown to effectively enhance the development of basic fitness, strength and power in performers.

Execution of the correct technique cannot always be determined by watching a performer at 'normal' speed. Biomechanics can allow the analysis of a technique through video imaging and precise tracking of limbs and joints as the body performs a skill. This is useful not only to identify and correct technical errors but also to identify potential injury risks and to correct posture.

FITNESS ASSESSMENT

FITNESS and CONDITIONING

BIOMECHANICS

SPORTS PSYCHOLOGY

PERFORMANCE ANALYSIS

NUTRITION

Performers not only have to meet the physical demands of their sport but also the mental demands. Sport psychology can introduce performers to techniques that enable them to relax and control their emotions and anxiety prior to competition and enable them to cope with stressful situations.

Coaches are able to purchase specific software programmes that can be used in conjunction with household computers and video cameras to undertake performance analysis of techniques and tactics.

There is always a need for performers to maintain a healthy lifestyle and careful management of their food and fluid intake can ensure that they remain healthy and have sufficient energy and water levels to allow them to train and compete effectively.

The pieces of the sports science jigsaw

may be able to access this through their national governing body or their local authority. Some coaches may be lucky enough to have people within their coaching group or parents who have some knowledge and experience in these areas – such people can be used as part of a coaching team to provide specialist additional input to assist the coach.

Theory into practice

Sport science is an important component of sports performance and coaches should have an understanding at least of some of the basic principles and issues.

1   Access the website or prospectus of a university that offers sport science degrees and try to identify which aspects of the curriculum might be helpful to a coach wishing to learn more about how sport science can help with coaching.

2   Access the sports coach UK website (www.sportscoachuk.org) and make a list of the workshops that they offer to help coaches understand sport science.

3   How does the governing body of your sport provide sport science information to coaches?

In addition to these more obvious aspects of a sport, coaches should have a good knowledge of the way their sport is organised and managed and also of how coaches are updated on the latest technical, tactical, regulatory and scientific knowledge. It is one of the responsibilities of a coach to keep abreast of developments within the sport. Some of the important questions you should regularly seek answers to include the following.

- Have there been any rule changes?
- What coach education and qualification opportunities are available?
- Does the sport have guidelines and policies related to child protection, performance-enhancing drugs and other legal and ethical issues?
- What scientific or training developments have occurred that might affect my sport and the way it should be coached?

Remember

- In order to fulfil their responsibilities coaches need a wide range of skills including communication, organisational and sports-specific skills.
- Communication is a two-way process in which the coach should listen to the performer as well as talk to him or her.
- Coaching sessions and training programmes will be more effective if they are well organised and a coach has well-developed organisational skills.
- Coaches should ensure that they have a good knowledge and understanding of their own sport and how the latest innovations in sport science can help develop performance.

Assessment activity 13.2

1 Identify the coach of a top performer or team in your chosen sport. List the different roles, responsibilities and skills that he or she has. Try to give examples of when and how these roles, responsibilities or skills are demonstrated.

2 Identify a local coach – it may be someone who coaches with you or who has coached you in the past. Repeat the above process and list the different roles, responsibilities and skills that he or she has.

3 Create a series of tables that compare the different roles, responsibilities and skills of the two coaches identified above.

Coaching techniques

Your aims as a coach

Coaches come from all different walks of life and there may be many reasons why a person decides to take up coaching. They may be former performers who want to stay involved in their sport and 'give something back', or they may be parents of children who are involved in a sport. Whatever coaches' reasons are for being involved in sports coaching, they should always act in the best interests of their performers. A person who coaches for personal satisfaction and gain alone is unlikely to be effective and will soon become disappointed and frustrated.

Think it over

Consider your own aims as a coach. What are the main reasons why you wish to become a coach?

Your motives for and attitudes towards coaching will probably have an effect on the style of coaching you adopt.

Coaching styles

Because every coach is different there are likely to be many different styles of coaching. Individual coaches will develop their own style. In most cases this style will be influenced by a number of factors, including the following.

- **Personality** Some coaches are outgoing and lively and their coaching style may reflect this. Others may be quiet and prefer to get on with the job without being the centre of attention. It really does not matter, as long as the coach has the right coaching skills to be able to fulfil the required roles effectively.
- **Knowledge** Coaches will have a wide range of knowledge about, among other things, their sport, their performers, how people learn, sport science, session planning and tactics. The knowledgeable coach will adopt a different style than the coach who lacks knowledge in certain areas.

● **Reasons for coaching** As we saw above there are many reasons why people take up coaching, and their style of coaching will reflect some of these reasons. Coaches who want to help people develop may adopt a more developmental approach than those seeking to coach championship-winning teams. They will have different measures of success, and probably seek to work with different age groups and abilities.

● **Previous experiences of being coached** People may adopt the same style as the person who once coached them. They may feel that they were successful as performers under a certain style of coaching and therefore choose to adopt the same approach. It may also work the other way – a coach may have had a negative experience of being coached in a particular way, and actively choose to coach in a different style.

Some people suggest that there are distinct styles of coaching and all coaches fall into one of several clearly defined categories. It is perhaps too simplistic to categorise coaching styles in this way. It is more accurate to suggest that coaching styles exist as a pool of behaviours and approaches, with coaches selecting different aspects of behaviour and hence different coaching styles at any given point according to the group or situation they are working with.

Typical coaching styles range from the **autocratic** coach – someone who is the only decision maker and who tells performers what to do and when to do it – to the more **laissez-faire** coach, with a relaxed and flexible approach to coaching. This relaxed approach can sometimes appear to be indecisive and may leave performers unsure of what is required. More balanced variations of these extremes also exist, with some coaches being considered to be **democratic** in nature because they invite performers to suggest solutions to problems and allow them to become part of the decision-making process. The coach may ultimately make the final decision as to what is required, but the performers are involved in the process. More recent developments in coaching

styles have given rise to an **empowerment** style of coaching, whereby coaches and performers outline the problem together and performers are encouraged to use their own knowledge and experiences to make decisions themselves.

Those styles in which the coach tends to make the decisions and uses his or her authority to instruct are often termed **coach-centred** approaches, while styles that allow performers some influence and input to the coaching experience are termed **performer-centred** approaches. No single style is right or wrong, and each of the different styles mentioned here can have a place in a particular situation. It is important for coaches to be able to adopt aspects of each style at appropriate points so that the coaching style matches the performers they are working with and the situation in which they are operating.

Certain approaches are not recommended for certain situations. For example, a democratic approach is not advisable in situations where safety may be compromised. In such instances a coach needs to be authoritative to ensure that accidents do not happen. Also, younger performers tend not to want to be involved in decision-making, and thus a democratic approach may not be appropriate, with the young performers preferring to trust the coach to identify a way forward.

Regardless of which style of coaching you choose to adopt, it is important that your coaching is safe, within the accepted standards of good practice, and in the best interests of your performer.

Theory into practice

Revisit the case study on page 187 and consider these questions in light of the discussion above.

● Who makes the decisions?
● Is this a performer-centred approach or a coach-centred approach?
● What style of coaching do you think Gary Lough adopts?
● What style of coaching do the two coaches you identified in Assessment activity 13.2 adopt?
● What style of coaching do you think you adopt?

Young players may need the coach to make the decisions

Key concept

- There are many different reasons why somebody takes up coaching and these motives may influence the way a person behaves as a coach and his or her coaching style.

- A number of different styles of coaching can be adopted. Good coaches will be able to change their style of coaching to meet the needs of their performers and the situation.

Whether your objectives as a coach are to coach a team to championship success or to help a beginner learn the basic skills of the sport, your ultimate coaching aims will be essentially the same. The fundamental aims of coaching are:

- to understand how individuals learn so that you can create an effective learning environment

- to improve sports techniques and develop skills

- to recognise areas for improvement.

Coaches need to address a number of different issues and processes in order to achieve these aims. The following sections will discuss some of these and consider how a coach can best employ them to aid the development of performers.

Creating an effective learning environment

In order for performers to gain the maximum benefit from the coaching experience, the learning environment has to be right. Coaches have a responsibility to help their performers develop, and one of their coaching aims should be to create and maintain an effective learning environment for their performers. To achieve this they have to:

- understand how individuals learn

- understand the conditions in which performers learn best.

Theory into practice

Think back to a recent situation in which you have been a learner – this may be in a classroom situation or a sporting context.

1 Make a list of the things you think enhanced your learning experience.

2 Draw up a separate list of things that you think made learning more difficult.

3 Use these lists to describe the conditions in which you feel you learn best.

4 How would you structure a learning experience to ensure that you met these conditions?

For coaches to be effective in teaching performers new skills and techniques it is important that they have an understanding of how people learn. Such an understanding will help coaches plan their sessions and devise the practices and drills that they think will be of most benefit to their performers.

There are three accepted stages to the learning process, and performers of all ages and levels will progress through the different stages as they learn and master new skills.

- **Stage 1 Learning what is required** For performers to learn what is required to perform a new skill they will need to sort through their previous experiences and try to identify experiences and movement patterns that could be useful for the new skill. They will then have to learn new movement patterns and try to integrate these new patterns with the previously learnt ones in order to create the whole skill.

To assist the performer in stage 1, the coach should:

– provide a general description of the task and what is required – a simple explanation

– show the performer what the desired outcome should look like – a demonstration

– help the performer execute the task well enough to begin practising it. This may involve physically executing the task with performers by moving their limbs for them or 'walking' them through the task.

Once they have an initial idea of what is required, performers can begin to practise the task. Throughout the learning stage the coach should be placing emphasis on the process rather than

Backhand drive shot in squash

STAGE 1
Learning what is required

A player will have learnt skills associated with the forehand drive including how to hold the racquet, how to stand, the necessary hand-eye-ball co-ordination and the necessary movement patterns to move the racquet to the ball.

In the first stages of learning the backhand, players need to decide which of the previously learnt forehand skills are of use – some aspects of gripping the racquet, some aspects of the hitting process, etc. They must then learn the new things exclusive to the backhand and finally put them all together to create the whole skill.

STAGE 2
Practice

Our example squash player may now be able to adjust his or her hand position on the racquet or adjust the position of the racquet at the point of contact to prevent the ball going out and perhaps begin to see how the force and speed of the racquet may influence the shot. Repeated practice of the backhand shot will enable the player to 'feel' the shot and recognise errors.

STAGE 3
Mastery

The advanced squash player who has mastered the backhand shot will be able to play it from any position on the court and also be aware of where the opponent is and where the ball is likely to end up after the shot – the player can think two or three shots ahead without having to worry about how to execute the backhand shot.

The stages of learning

Once performers have mastered a skill, the coach needs to make minimal interventions, as for Clive Woodward in rugby

the outcome – it does not matter if the squash player hits the ball out in the first few attempts provided that the grip, stance, racquet movement and positioning are correct. Practices should be kept short and simple and the amount of information should be minimal.

- **Stage 2 Practice** In order to progress their learning, learners need a sufficient grasp of the basic idea of the task in order to be able to practise it. At this stage the number of errors is likely to reduce and performers may begin to make their own corrections as they begin to understand the relationship between their actions and the outcomes.

The coach should now be able to add more detail to the instructions and begin to fine tune the skill by offering feedback about what is being done correctly or incorrectly, and reinforcing correct performance. Coaches should also encourage the performers to analyse their performance and use their own internal feedback mechanisms to identify errors and correct mistakes. There should be an increased focus on the outcome of the task.

- **Stage 3 Mastery** In this phase performers are able to execute the skill competently and efficiently. They have no need to think about what they are doing and thus the skill sometimes appears automatic. Any errors are minimal and can easily be detected and corrected by the performer. Performers at this stage of the learning process are able to perform the skill in a variety of different contexts and are able to concentrate on other aspects of their performance without having to worry about the execution of the skill.

The coach has a limited role to play when a skill has been mastered. There should be minimal intervention from the coach, other than to perhaps make minor adjustments or to deal with highly specific aspects of the task. Performers should be encouraged to continue to practise the task in order to maintain their mastery of the skill.

The rate at which individuals progress, and thus the amount of time spent on each stage, will vary from one person to another. It is important that the coach, once aware of the different stages, is able to identify how each performer behaves and responds to the different stages. Some people may progress quickly through the early stages and struggle with the final stage, while others may struggle early on and then develop quickly. What is important to remember is that each person learns at a different rate and a coaching session must take into account these different learning rates. Coaches should avoid progressing too quickly as some people may not have achieved mastery of a skill, yet if progress is too slow some people may become bored. The coach has to achieve a good balance and progress at a rate that is appropriate for the performers.

Conditions in which individuals learn best

Knowing how to create effective learning environments is important. It is generally accepted that individuals learn best when they are:
- interested and motivated
- actively involved in their learning
- able to build on their own previous experiences
- able to see how things fit together
- able to see improvements in their performance.

Maintaining interest and motivation

Performers who are enjoying what they are doing and are interested in their activities will remain motivated for longer and are more likely to learn things. The coach should therefore seek to deliver coaching sessions that are interesting and exciting, so that the attention of the performers is maintained. This is particularly important when coaching children, as their attention span is limited and they can become bored easily.

Coaches should avoid spending too much time on the same activity and should be prepared to change the practices and drills they are using. This does not mean introducing lots of new ideas – coaches should provide a range of different tasks that enable individuals to practise the same new skill but in different contexts.

Managing the groups you are working with will also help maintain interest and motivation. Getting people to work with, and practise with, others of the same ability will prevent them from being intimidated by better performers and feeling demotivated because of a perceived lack of ability. Having small practice groups will also mean that people will be involved more and will get more practice opportunities.

Think it over

What things can you do as a coach to maintain interest and motivation in your performers?

Active involvement

Sport is a practical pastime and people get involved in sport because they enjoy doing it. A coaching session in which there is limited opportunity to actually perform the sport will not be interesting, motivating or effective in developing skill.

Individuals learn from doing things rather than being told about them. As we have seen above, there will be occasions when the coach has to spend time explaining things or demonstrating things, but these should be kept to a minimum. Coaches should spend as little time as possible explaining activities and create as much opportunity as possible for performers to do things. Explanations should be simple and the instructions for practices or drills should be easy to understand so that performers can get on with practising rather than trying to understand what it is they are supposed to be doing.

An ancient Chinese saying sums up the need for practical involvement as an important component of learning:

'Tell me and I forget, show me and I remember, involve me and I understand.'

Building on experiences

Performers will learn best when they are able to build on their own experiences and skills. Coaches should seek to introduce techniques progressively and show how they are linked to previous skills whenever possible. This relates to a performer's progression through the different stages of learning (see page 204). A performer will not progress to the practice stage if he or she only learns skills in isolation. Performers should be encouraged to build on their previous experiences of a skill and be given the opportunity to try fitting things together.

Fitting things together

Performers will get a better understanding of the skills and techniques they are learning if they are given the opportunity to see and practise how they fit into the wider context of their sport. A coach should always ensure that when introducing and teaching a new skill there is some explanation and opportunity to practise it in a game situation or wider context.

For example, teaching young performers how to hold a discus and move across the discus circle will have limited benefit unless they can see the likely end result and actually throw the discus. Allowing this opportunity will contextualise the skill being learnt and allow some performance-based feedback to be gained.

Seeing improvement

Success is a major factor in sport and performers will constantly be looking to achieve some form

Children need to experience success in their coaching sessions

of success in order to remain motivated and interested. When individuals are able to see that they are improving they will gain personal satisfaction and want to continue. A coach should try to structure coaching sessions in order to allow performers to see their own improvements. This does not always have to be in competitive terms, but can come in the form of the successful execution of a new skill for the first time.

Coaches should aim to structure their practices in a way that allows performers to experience some form of success and thus gain satisfaction from their achievement. This is of particular importance when coaching children. Learners should be praised when things go well and when they achieve something; constant criticism will act as a demotivator and is the quickest way to persuade someone to give up a sport.

Understanding these key principles and integrating them into coaching sessions will help the coach maintain the interest of performers and, most importantly, enable performers to develop new skills and techniques in a positive learning environment.

Key concept

Individuals learn new techniques and skills in stages. The rate of progression through these stages will vary from one person to the next.

Improving sports techniques and developing skills

Having given thought to creating an effective learning environment, a coach needs to decide how to go about teaching a performer a new skill. The teaching of new techniques and skills requires a systematic process so that the skill is taught in a way that can be easily understood and learnt by the performer. There are a number of stages to this process:

- introduction and explanation
- demonstration
- practice
- analysing and correcting errors.

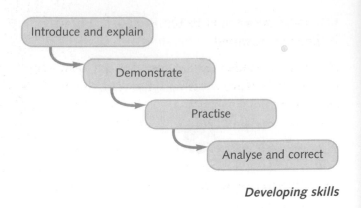

Developing skills

Theory into practice

Understanding how to break down a skill into its constituent parts is an important aspect of coaching. Try the following activity with a partner to see how well you are able to teach a basic skill.

1 Identify and list the constituent parts of writing – i.e. break down the physical skill of writing.

2 Now devise a series of practices to teach your partner how to write using the non-dominant hand (the left hand if he or she is right-handed, and vice versa).

3 Coach your partner how to write his or her name.

4 Evaluate how effective you were.

Introduction and explanation

An introduction to a skill should inform the performers what they will be learning and why it is important. It should also tell them how the particular skill fits in with other skills and techniques they have learnt and when it might be useful. To maximise the effect of an introduction and explanation, coaches should ensure that:

- they have planned what they are going to say
- they have the attention of the performers
- the performers are in a position to be able to see and hear what is going on
- they do not give too much information and keep the explanations brief
- they maintain the attention and interest of the performers

- they relate what is being taught to any previous learning.

Many sports skills are more easily explained, and consequently learnt, if they are broken down into smaller component parts. This allows the coach to point out the relevant aspects of the skill.

One way of breaking down a skill is to consider the order of the components and to address them according to **preparation, action** and **completion.** For example, a novice squash player who is learning to play a backhand drive shot may require the skill to be broken down into its constituent parts – the required grip and foot position would constitute the preparation component, the backswing and contact with the ball would constitute the action component, and the follow-through (or not) and final body position would mark the completion component.

Theory into practice

In your chosen sport, select a complex skill that is fundamental to performance (e.g. the lay-up shot in basketball). With the aid of a coaching manual, identify the constituent parts of that skill.

This skill may be simple enough for a player to learn as a complete skill and the sub-divisions may be needed only for the purposes of explanation. However, some skills are more complex in nature and the coach may decide to teach the skill in its 'broken-down' format. This involves the **whole** and **part** methods of teaching skills.

Effective coaches will be able to break down complex skills to their component parts and then introduce and teach the skill in this way. Coaches must first define the whole and the parts of a skill. The whole skill could be any one of the fundamental skills associated with a sport, and the parts could be defined as any aspect of that skill which can be isolated and practised on its own. The triple jump would be a good example of a skill that can be broken down in this way (see the illustrations on the next page).

The teaching of the individual components can be

approached in one of five different whole–part approaches.

- **Part-whole method** This approach would involve teaching all of the different component parts separately before attempting the whole skill. This method is most effective when the components do not form a natural sequence of actions.

- **Progressive-part method** With this approach a performer is taught one part and then a second part. When the two parts are learnt they are combined and practised together. The third part is then taught by itself and then the three parts are combined and practised together, and so on.

- **Repetitive-part method** This approach is similar to the previous method but involves teaching and practising a part until it is learnt and then combining a second part and practising and learning the two parts together until they are learnt.

- **Whole-part-whole method** This approach involves teaching the whole skill first and allowing the performer to practise it. One of the parts is then isolated, taught and practised, and when this has been effectively learnt the whole is practised again. The process is then repeated, adding the different parts to the whole.

- **Whole method** This simply teaches the whole skill without breaking it down into its constituent components, and is probably not effective for complex skills.

There are no rules as to which method to adopt and some coaches will find particular methods easier than others. When deciding which approach to adopt, coaches should consider whether the skill can be taught as a single whole skill or whether it is too complex and should be broken down into smaller parts. Teaching a skill as a whole is generally easier and quicker provided the skill is not too complex and the performer is able to learn it without being confused. Adopting one of the different 'part' approaches for complex skills may be a more motivational approach, as performers may be able to gain success more quickly as they learn and master each part.

In the triple jump the whole skill involves, as the name suggests, three phases, and effective performance results from correct combination of the three phases. Most coaches would recognise that this is too complex to teach as a single skill and it should therefore be broken down into its constituent components. The diagrams show how the skill can be broken down.

1–9 The run up

10–18 The hop phase

19–26 The step phase

27–36 The jump phase

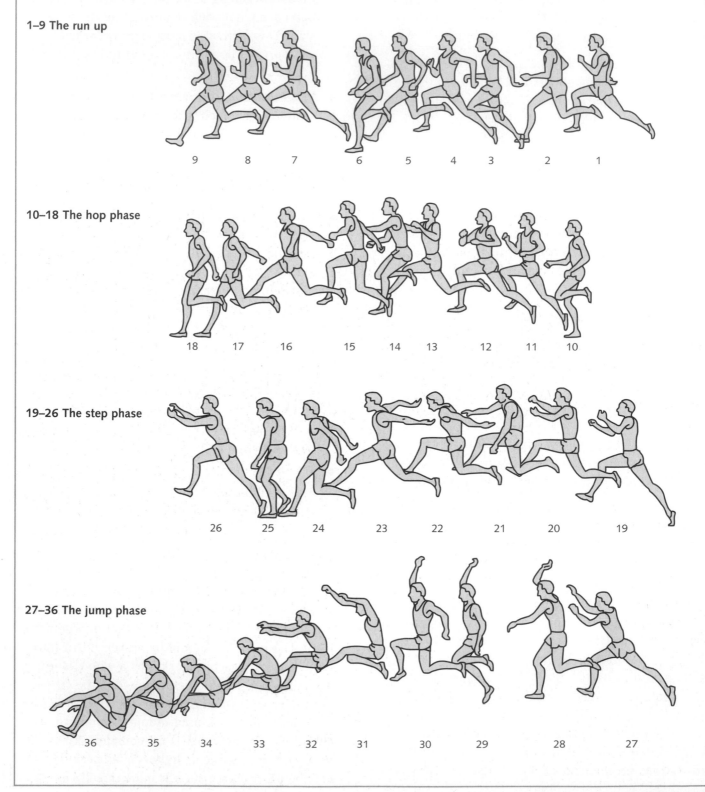

The triple jump

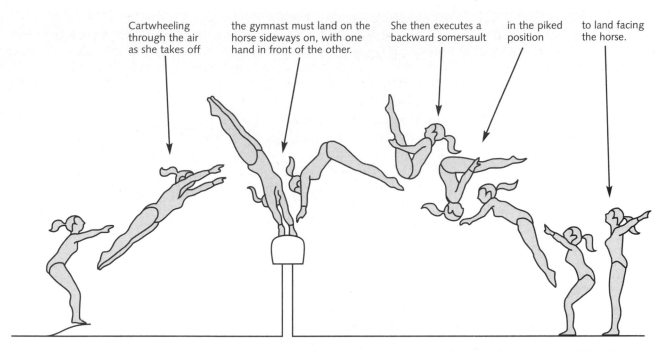

Cartwheeling through the air as she takes off

the gymnast must land on the horse sideways on, with one hand in front of the other.

She then executes a backward somersault

in the piked position

to land facing the horse.

Cartwheel, one-and-a-half backward piked somersault (Tsukahara)

Judging when, how and at what rate to teach a skill or technique is an important decision to make. A coach needs to know which techniques and skills are the most appropriate for different situations and when they should be introduced.

Techniques need to be coached in the correct sequence. For example, when coaching a young swimmer it is important to secure the basic technique of effective stroke execution before the swimmer is taught the complexities of a tumble turn. As the abilities and experience of the performer improve, the range of options can be increased. Coaches must be able to help their participants develop techniques at an appropriate rate of progression.

Theory into practice

Use the skill you identified in the previous activity (page 209).

1 Identify the best method to teach the component parts of the skill.

2 Identify drills and practices that you might use to help teach these component parts.

Demonstration

When learning a new skill a performer needs to be able to see the skill being performed correctly and to have a model of the required actions. It is almost always easier to show somebody an action than to describe it in words.

Effective demonstration of a skill should create a technically correct visual image for the performer to copy. It is important, however, that the demonstration is completely correct. If a coach is to perform the demonstration he or she has to be confident of being able to recreate the desired image, otherwise performers may imitate a technically incorrect model.

Some coaches who may not feel technically competent in a skill may use video images to demonstrate, or may ask experienced performers who are technically competent to perform the demonstration on their behalf.

However it is performed, a demonstration will be most effective if it follows these simple guidelines:

● make sure the performers are paying attention and that all are able to see

Skill demonstrations need to be at a level appropriate to the performers

- ensure that the demonstration emphasises the key coaching points of the skill
- ensure skills are demonstrated at the appropriate level for the performers
- repeat the demonstrations enough times for performers to understand what is required.

Practice

No amount of introduction, explanation or demonstration can replace the need for practice. The repeated execution of a skill is the only way of effectively learning that skill. As a coach it is your role to introduce a skill and follow this up by identifying drills and routines that give your performers the opportunity to practise it. You must devise sessions that offer performers the greatest learning potential.

Research suggests that for most skills, practice is most effective when it is **massed** – that is, it occurs continually with no rest, or only very short rest periods, between each practice. This approach to practice allows performers the greatest amount of time.

However, some skills and drills may be more demanding in terms of energy consumption, and the ability to perform repeated massed practice is limited when fatigue is possible. In such instances coaches may build in longer rest periods between practices and thus have a more **distributed** practice session.

An important part of the coach's role when introducing new skills is to construct practice sessions of appropriate intensity, duration and frequency to promote optimal learning.

Theory into practice

1 How will fatigue affect a person's ability to perform a skill?
2 When might it be appropriate to practise a skill under fatigue conditions?

A coach must provide support to the performers while they are practising. No performer should be left to practise alone. The coach must observe practice sessions and, where appropriate, offer interventions that help and guide the performers as they practise a skill.

Guidance

In some instances, a performer practising a skill may require additional guidance from the coach to help develop the appropriate movement patterns associated with the skill. This guidance may take one of three forms.

- **Visual guidance** This occurs when a coach follows up an initial demonstration with a more detailed, step-by-step demonstration of the skill and the performer is required to mirror the actions being performed. The coach should demonstrate a movement as slowly as possible and the performer is encouraged to imitate the action immediately after having observed it.

- **Verbal guidance** The coach tells the performer what to do and the performer follows instructions. This approach is most effective when the coach adds verbal cues to each different part of the movement and then repeats these in subsequent executions. For example, a series of verbal guidance cues for a squash player learning the grip and movement pattern for the backhand shot may be: 'Shake hands … swing back … look … swing through … hit and follow!'

- **Manual guidance** This involves the coach physically moving the performer through a particular movement pattern and encouraging him or her to 'feel' the action. After several repetitions the performer should be asked to perform the movement without the coach's guidance.

The coach should demonstrate an action slowly, and encourage performers to imitate it

Feedback

It is important to provide feedback to ensure that performers are aware of their progress. Some coaches behave in a way that suggests that criticism is the only form of feedback; but feedback should be constructive and provide information that helps with the learning process.

Feedback can come from a variety of different sources. Performers will gain their own **internal (intrinsic) feedback** as a natural consequence of their performance based on their interpretations and feelings when performing a skill. They can also receive feedback from external sources – **external (augmented) feedback** – which is in addition to what they would normally receive from their performance. The coach is usually the main source of external feedback.

Performers will gain internal feedback from their own sensory mechanisms. They will be able to see (as the ball goes into the net) or hear (the sound of the ball against the frame of the racquet rather than the strings) the outcome of their actions and make their own adjustments based on what they see or hear.

Also, performers will be able to 'feel' their performance and gain what is called **kinaesthetic feedback**. Performers gain feedback from their body either in terms of their balance, contact with an object or movement through water or air. They will be able to feel whether the performance was effective or not, and make the necessary adjustments to subsequent performances.

The external feedback that a coach gives a performer should be **positive** and corrective, yet also sufficiently accurate to support future learning. Performers will not learn if they are constantly being told that they are rubbish. **Negative** feedback should be avoided, as it could be demotivating. A coach should find an appropriate form of words to signal that something is being performed incorrectly without being too critical. Which would you rather hear as a beginner golfer?

'You're holding the club all wrong and the ball is going all over the place.'

'If you hold the shaft a little tighter the club face will not open out when you hit the ball and the ball will go straighter.'

The latter comment offers some constructive advice as to how to correct the fault.

Coaches should aim to offer feedback as soon after an event as possible, but not before performers have had the opportunity to process their own internal feedback. In most instances coaches will be able to provide **concurrent** feedback at or near the time of an error occurring.

Sometimes, however, it can be useful to supplement this with **delayed** feedback. The use of video to show performers how they have performed a skill can be an effective form of external feedback. This allows performers to watch themselves in action. It is particularly useful in sports where actions are performed very quickly and it is difficult to see or feel the skill at normal speed. Visual feedback from a video allows performers to see for themselves where the errors are occurring and what may be causing them.

Whether the feedback comes from themselves, the coach or a video, it is important that performers receive it clearly and are able to learn from it.

Theory into practice

With a partner, undertake the following experiment, using either a basketball or netball shooting task.

Identify a point from which to shoot and make sure that all shots are from the same point.

Trial 1 – Shoot 10 shots at the basket or net and record how many successful shots you had.

Trial 2 – Shoot 10 more shots, but this time with your eyes closed or with a blindfold on. Your partner must not tell you whether you scored or how close you were – there should be no feedback. Record how many successful shots you had.

Trial 3 – Shoot 10 more shots, again with your eyes closed or blindfolded. This time your partner should give you very precise verbal feedback between each shot. This feedback should contain information about a) how close you were (e.g. you hit the left-hand side of the ring); b) what your partner thinks you did wrong (e.g. you threw the ball too hard); and c) what your partner thinks you should do differently next time (e.g. throw the ball a little less hard and slightly more to the right). Record how many successful shots you had.

Discuss your scores.

● Which trial produced the highest score? Why?

● Did the amount of feedback affect your score?

● Was the verbal feedback useful?

Analysing and correcting errors

Inevitably, as performers practise a skill they make mistakes and there may be errors in their performance. A coach needs to analyse the performance in order to identify which features need to be corrected or improved.

The main requirement for this analysis process is for the coach to have a good understanding of the different techniques and skills required in the sport and to be able to recognise the correct technical aspects of a skill – to have a clear picture of the right way to perform a skill. This is one of the reasons why a coach has to have a good technical knowledge of the sport. Experienced coaches and those coaches who are ex-performers may have a slight advantage here because they are likely to be familiar with all the different technical aspects of a sport. They are therefore better able to recognise what the correct execution of a skill looks like.

Once a coach has a clear picture of the correct way to execute a skill, he or she needs to be able to contrast the actual execution by the performer with the ideal execution. This is one of the keys to good coaching – being able to identify the differences between how a performer executes a skill or technique and how that skill or technique should be performed.

To do this well coaches need to have good observation skills. Good coaches will watch their performers many times before they reach a conclusion as to whether anything is wrong or

needs correction. Once an imbalance between the actual and the ideal technique has been identified, the coach must consider the most appropriate way forward and whether an error needs correction.

In some instances the way a performer executes a particular skill may not be 100% technically correct, yet it may still yield effective results and simply be part of his or her individual style. The coach has to decide whether the error has an impact on the effectiveness of the skill or its safety. If correcting the error is unlikely to make any significant difference, it may not be necessary to correct it.

A good example is the case of Michael Johnson, who was arguably the world's best 400-metre runner. Many considered Johnson's running style to be unorthodox, and the way he held his arms

Michael Johnson won many titles, although his running style was considered unorthodox by some

when running looked clumsy to some observers. Yet he still managed to break world records and win Olympic and World championships. Trying to correct his arm carriage and running style would have served no purpose and had little impact on his effectiveness.

If, however, the safety of the performer or his or her ability to remain within the rules of a sport are at risk, style-related errors might need to be corrected. A cricketer whose arm action suggests throwing the ball rather than bowling it may be challenged by opponents for breaking the rules of the sport. A gymnast whose head is insufficiently tucked during a somersault may run the risk of injury. In both cases the coach would be wise to try to correct the errors.

Once an error or series of errors has been identified and the coach feels that there is a need to make corrections, the exact cause of the error needs to be identified.

Finding out what causes the error is the key to being able to correct it. There may be many causes of incorrect technique, including the following.

- **Forgetting** A performer may simply forget the correct way to perform the technique. If a technique or skill is new, remembering all the important aspects of it can be difficult. To correct errors which result from forgetting, a coach should allow performers the opportunity to practise the skill and should support the practice with regular reminders of the key points.

- **Lack of overall technical competence** When learning complex skills a performer may not have mastered the basics and thus will struggle to complete the complex skills. For example, a young footballer who has not mastered the basic ability to keep the ball under control at his or her feet may struggle when trying to run with the ball. Allowing performers to master basic skills before progressing to more advanced ones is one way in which a coach can prevent these types of errors occurring.

- **Lack of physical ability** Some performers may not have developed the appropriate strength levels or body control, or have the required

range of flexibility to execute certain skills. They therefore may not be able to get their body into the correct positions for a skill to be performed effectively. An athlete who does not have sufficient flexibility to bend a leg to right angles to adopt the hurdle position will struggle to clear hurdles effectively when running at full speed. Developing the right physical attributes to meet the demands of the sport would address this issue. The coach therefore needs to consider the physical development of a performer as well as the technical development.

- **Incorrect preceding technique** In some instances the error may not be at the point that the coach first identifies. Some error in a preceding part of skill execution may result in a subsequent error. For example, a triple jumper who lands in the pit and falls forwards may not have a problem with the actual jump. The error may lie in too much forward rotation or loss of balance during one of the previous two phases. The coach who observes the whole skill will be able to pinpoint the errors on landing as being due to errors in the hop or step phase. Correction of the earlier error will correct the landing error.

Only when the coach has identified the likely cause of an error or series of errors can he or she begin to develop drills and practices to correct and improve performance. It is important that the coach does not try to correct all errors at once. As we have seen, people learn in different ways and too much information at one time can be detrimental to learning. Having identified the errors and the areas for improvement, a coach should seek to prioritise the learning and correct or improve one area at a time. Deciding which area to address first can be difficult, but there are some basic guidelines to follow.

Some errors, as we have seen, can lead to other errors, and there may be a related 'chain of errors'. When choosing which area to focus on first, a coach should seek to identify the first error in the chain. If this is addressed and corrected, the subsequent errors may correct themselves or may need only small amounts of work. Similarly, in time-phased skills such as the triple jump, correcting and refining those skills that occur towards the beginning of the chain is likely to have a positive impact on subsequent events.

If errors seem to be unrelated, the coach should aim to correct those that are the easiest to learn and show the greatest progress. Performers like to see success, and significant improvements early on in the learning process will enhance their motivation.

Remember

- When teaching and developing skills, coaches need to use a range of techniques and procedures.

- When performers are practising a new technique or skill, the coach needs to support the learning process by providing appropriate forms of guidance and feedback.

- Coaches should make sure that they have sufficient knowledge of the techniques and skills required in their sport to be able to analyse and correct errors made by performers.

A good coach will continue to observe performers even after they have learnt and mastered a skill. This will enable the coach to refine the actions of performers and help them to continue to improve. The ongoing observation and analysis of performers will enable the coach to recognise areas for improvement that may be skill-related or may be linked to broader aspects of performance.

Equipment

The introduction of new technologies and new understandings in sport science make the task of identifying areas for improvement somewhat easier. Coaches no longer need to rely solely on their own observation skills, as they can now draw on a wide range of equipment to assist them and draw on other experts to aid the process.

The increased availability of videos and computers has meant that their use in sport has become an integral part of the observational analysis process.

Videos and computers with integrated software packages are effective tools for recording and analysing individual technique and team performance. A coach can capture performances and view them after the event, and undertake slow-motion or freeze-frame analysis to identify technical faults that may not be obvious in real time. Coaches may also be able to undertake tactical analysis of their team's performances and identify the patterns of play and tactics of future opponents.

In addition to observational analysis tools, coaches can now draw on physiological assessment equipment to determine fitness profiles and identify the physical strengths and weaknesses of their performers. Athletes from most sports can undergo fitness assessment, allowing coaches to access data that can tell them how well the performer meets the physical demands of the sport. This information can inform the training process and enable coaches to develop individualised fitness training programmes and reduce injury risks.

The information that is available to coaches through the increased use of technology and sport science will ensure that they are appropriately informed as they continue their search for areas for improvement.

Key concept

Coaches should use a wide range of technological and scientific knowledge and equipment to assist them to recognise areas for improvement.

Assessment activity 13.3

1 Watch a coaching session taking place at your local sports centre, swimming pool or playing field. Make a list of all the different techniques, styles and tools that the coach uses when coaching.

2 Repeat this with a different coach, ideally with a different sport.

3 Compare and contrast the range of techniques, tools and styles of coaching used by the two coaches.

The coaching process: planning and leading

In previous sections we have identified the roles and responsibilities of a coach and begun to describe some of the different ways in which a coach may introduce and teach new skills to performers or seek to improve performers' abilities. This process of teaching skills, along with all the other aspects of a coach's work – fitness development, tactical instruction and performance development – takes place within the time constraints of a coaching session. Whether the coach works with a different group of performers each session or with the same performers over a series of sessions there are a number of fundamental things that must be considered in order for the coaching session to be effective.

This section explores the issues associated with the successful planning and delivery of coaching sessions, and considers the processes and actions that a coach should undertake in order to ensure that coaching sessions are effective.

A coaching session can be sub-divided into three different aspects – before, during and after. Dividing a coaching session in terms of time is very simplistic but can help the coach ensure that he or she addresses all the main features of the planning and delivery process. This will help make it more likely that the session goes as well as the coach wants it to.

The 'before' aspect is the **planning** phase, the 'during' aspect is the **delivery** phase, and the 'after' aspect is the **evaluation** phase. Some people also call this the 'plan-do-review' process.

Successful planning will mean that coaching sessions are effective as well as enjoyable

As the diagram below suggests, this process is a cyclical one with a coach using the information gained from the evaluation phase to inform the planning for the next session. The whole circle of events is commonly termed the **coaching process**, and good coaches will continually go through this process as they plan their coaching sessions, deliver them and then evaluate how well they went.

The coaching process

The planning phase

The planning stage usually represents the starting point of the process and is arguably the most important part of the process. A coach needs to plan well otherwise all other aspects of the coaching process will be ineffective.

Most coaches plan each coaching session in advance. This is easier when you have been working with performers for some time and the sessions follow on from each other. You will already know a little about the performers and their aims, abilities and behaviours, and be able to build on your existing knowledge and experience of the group.

On some occasions coaches may be working with a group for the first time and know very little about them. In this case coaches should take some time to collect relevant information about the performers and try to build up a picture of what their aims and abilities might be. When planning to coach a group for the first time, it is advisable to use the first part of the session to get to know the performers and their current levels of ability.

Whether you are coaching your usual group or working with performers for the first time, there are a number of things you need to take into consideration when planning a session. These include:

- coaching aims for the session
- available resources, and equipment and facility use
- health and safety issues.

Coaching aims

The first thing a coach needs to think about when planning a session is the desired outcomes of the session. Knowing what it is that you are aiming to achieve in a session will make planning the practices within the session easier.

You will need to set goals for your performers to work towards (see Unit 11, page 134). These goals should be measurable and you should be able to see whether your performers have achieved the goals at the end of the session. They should also be achievable, so that your performers are able to see their own progress. Most importantly your performers should have some input into deciding on the goals. When trying to identify the desired outcomes of a coaching session, coaches should consider:

- the specific needs of the performers and what their goals may be
- the ability level of the performers and whether they can realistically achieve the desired goal
- their own goals for the session
- whether their goals match the performers' goals and abilities
- whether the session builds on a previous session and/or prepares performers for the next session.

When deciding the aims of a single session it is likely that the coach will set short-term goals – things to be achieved by the end of the session. Coaches planning for a series of sessions may also set medium- or long-term goals, which may be things they want performers to be able to do by the end of the series of coaching sessions. Progress towards these long-term goals may be measurable by the achievement of short-term goals along the way.

Resources and equipment

Once you have planned what you are aiming to achieve in a coaching session, you can begin to think about the resources you will need. When planning a session, the coach needs to know what facilities are available and what equipment is on hand. If you are coaching basketball and are planning to teach shooting skills, you will need to know if an appropriate facility is available allowing you to access the required number of baskets so that your performers can practise effectively.

If you are planning a regular session you will already have a good idea of what is available and whether other people use adjacent space or have particular requirements that might impact on your coaching. If you are coaching somewhere for the first time, visit the venue and get an idea of the size of the space and the resources available. If you do not have your own equipment you will need to make sure you know where you can access it, where it is kept and how much of it is available when you need it. Imagine planning a basketball shooting session for 15 people and arriving to realise that there is only one basket available and only one ball!

One of the most important requirements for your coaching plan is to have alternative ideas available. Coaches who are good planners will plan for every eventuality and will be able to resort to alternatives if problems arise with their original plan. This is particularly important when coaching outdoors – what happens if it rains? You should have contingency plans for an alternative session indoors. What if you have planned a rugby session that is designed to develop passing skills, and you find that the weather is too cold for your young performers to be able to handle the ball effectively? Your alternative plan should suggest a more active alternative.

Health and safety

The equipment and facilities, as well as the numbers and ability of performers, need to be considered with respect to health and safety.

Coaches will need to ask themselves some important questions about whether the practices they are planning are safe. A checklist of health and safety questions might include the following.

- Can the performers perform the required practices in the space available?
- Is there enough room for a large group to practise all at the same time?
- Is there a risk of injury from using the equipment in a limited space?
- Are the performers able to perform the skill safely, or are they not ready yet?

Coaches should make sure that they consider all the different aspects of safety when they are planning their sessions.

Theory into practice

Refer back to the risk assessment activity you undertook on page 191. Is there anything else you may need to add?

The lesson plan

Different coaches will undertake planning in different ways but it is always advisable to write down your plan. Various planning sheets or lesson plan formats exist for coaches to use – some of them are now even available in electronic form. But some coaches find it difficult to fit their planning into someone else's format, and therefore develop their own versions.

Experiment with different versions of planning sheets and perhaps develop your own. It does not really matter what your planning sheet looks like as long as it contains the key 'signposts' to help you remember what you need to cover in your session. The following gives you an idea of some of the important things you will need to note down on your planning sheet:

- **Session goals** What are you aiming to achieve in the session?
- **Coaching styles and techniques** How are you going to deliver the session? Does the session

require you to adopt an autocratic approach or is it more appropriate for you to adopt a different approach?

- **Warm-up/cool-down** What warm-up activities will you include? How will you allow the performers to cool down at the end?

- **Theme** What skill, tactic or fitness aspect will you be working on in the session? How will you introduce the session?

- **Sequencing of activities** What order will you adopt? Does the skill need to be taught as a whole skill, or might a whole-part-whole approach be more effective? Will you end the session with a game?

- **Practices and drills** What practices will you use? How long will performers be given to practise? Will practice be massed or distributed?

- **Monitoring and feedback** How will you monitor progress? When and how are you going to offer feedback?

- **Teaching points** What are the important teaching points for the skill?

- **Resources** What equipment is needed for each practice? How many balls are needed? Will performers practise alone, in pairs or in small groups? Will there be other coaches around to help you?

You will also need to ensure that you take into account the amount of time available and make sure that you allocate enough time to each activity. Try not to spend too much time on any one activity, as participants may become bored. Also, do not rush through practices without giving performers enough time to practise.

A lesson plan that contains this information will reflect a good level of planning and you should be able to deliver an effective coaching session.

Given that planning should take place in advance of a coaching session, there may be a need to make adjustments to the plan as new information or ideas become available. In the time immediately before a coaching session, usually once the participants have arrived, a coach needs to prepare for the session. This will involve ensuring that you have information about the exact number, gender and ability of the participants you will be coaching, and confirming whether any of them have special needs which you must address. Also, in this time you will need to check the equipment and facilities that are available and ensure you have enough to allow you to carry out your planned activities safely and effectively.

You will also need to make any last minute safety checks and, if using the venue for the first time, familiarise yourself with the emergency procedures. Check also whether there are any contingency measures that you may need to take. Once you have made the final preparations, you can put your coaching plan into operation.

The delivery phase

For many coaches this is the fun part of coaching – standing in front of a group of performers and teaching a skill or leading a training session. There are, however, still a lot of things to do and delivering a session requires more than simply reading out your lesson plan.

The coach has to be able to organise the group to ensure that they are doing the right thing, at the right time, in the right way. This will require the coach to use communication skills to make sure that he or she is delivering messages correctly and that the performers understand the information being given to them and learn from it.

Throughout the delivery of a session, coaches should be watching what is going on and observing how performers are undertaking the required tasks. They should be checking progress against the identified teaching points and analysing performance to identify any errors that may be occurring. The effective coach will be able to observe, analyse and correct errors as a session continues, as well as begin to think about future activities and future developments.

While delivering a session, a coach should be putting together all the aspects of coaching that have been addressed in this unit. A range of different coaching roles may be required, and varied skills and knowledge are necessary to ensure that the session runs smoothly and achieves the desired outcomes. Coaches will need to identify appropriate techniques to enable their performers to learn, and may have to adopt different coaching styles to achieve this. In short, the coach is doing a lot of different things at the same time and is trying to perform a complex juggling act.

The evaluation phase

The coaching process does not stop when the session stops. Coaches must take time after a session to evaluate it and decide what worked well and what worked less well. The evaluation process is best done immediately after the session, when it is still clear in the memory and the coach can recall incidents and issues more readily. The accuracy of recall can be enhanced if the session is video taped, as events can be reviewed again later.

Evaluation should not be done solely by the coach; the participants will have a different view of the coaching session and the coach, and they should be invited to comment on how well they feel the session went and how much they think they learnt or progressed during the session.

It can also be useful for another coach or an observer to comment on the session. They too will have a different viewpoint and may well have noticed things that neither the coach nor the performers noticed.

It may not be practical to invite the comments of participants or observers after every coaching session, but it can be useful occasionally to gain a different view. How you do this is up to you. Some coaches ask participants to complete short questionnaires after a session. These may contain simple questions about the session, about the coach or about the practices and drills being used. Observers could be asked to complete a checklist while they are watching a session. This may be a list of different coaching behaviours and the observer is required to tick a box each time a

particular behaviour is shown. Some coaches use this to try to identify their dominant coaching behaviours, and use the findings to modify undesirable behaviour.

Videoing yourself coaching may not always be practical and some coaches find it uncomfortable to watch themselves on video. It can, however, be an effective way of evaluating how well a coaching session went, and also how well a coach performed.

Theory into practice

Using a checklist like the one below, observe a coaching session and identify which behaviours the coach is using, and how often. Simply place a tick in the box each time you witness a particular behaviour. Write down some examples of what the coach did which made you notice that behaviour.

Coaching checklist		
Coach:		Observer:
Date of session:		Venue:
Aims of session:		
Behaviour	✔	Example

As well as the coach, the performer and the coaching session itself ought to be evaluated after a session.

Evaluating the performer is best done by measuring the progress he or she has made during the session. If a performer was able to meet the desired outcome of the coaching session, the session could be considered a success. If a performer can perform a skill at the end of the session that he or she could not do at the beginning, the session has been effective in developing performance.

On a larger scale and over a longer term, if the competitive performance of an individual or a team has improved and there has been an obvious benefit to performance, a coach can be said to be successful. In professional sports the success of the team is a measure of the success of the coach.

Conversely, the failure of a team usually reflects failure by the coach. How many professional soccer managers or international rugby coaches lose their jobs after a run of poor results?

When evaluating the effectiveness of the session itself, a coach needs to consider whether or not the aims of the session were achieved. If not, the coach needs to try to find out why. It may be due to bad planning, inappropriate amounts of time allocated to key practices, tasks being too demanding for the performers, poor coaching technique, lack of attention and effort by the performers, or a variety of other reasons.

In the same way as coaches identify errors in performers' actions, so they must identify errors in their coaching and try to find out the cause of the problem in order to rectify it next time. A coach may also wish to consider whether any aspects of the coaching session worked particularly well or particularly poorly. Was there one specific practice that performers enjoyed? What was it about that practice that made it enjoyable? Was there a particular drill that did not work well? Why did it not work so well? Was it explained clearly? Did performers understand what was required? These are the kinds of questions a coach should ask about a coaching session in order to evaluate it thoroughly and use the information gained to benefit future coaching.

Most coaches find evaluating the progress of the performer and the effectiveness of the session fairly easy, but when asked to evaluate themselves they struggle. It is always difficult to be honest about your own performance – it is human nature to maximise the positives and minimise the negatives, and to make excuses. Trying to identify things you can improve in your own coaching is difficult, but good coaches learn to be reflective about their performance and recognise some of their faults and errors. Once you are able to identify what you are less effective in, you are a long way towards becoming more effective.

Because the coaching process is a cyclical one, the final phase will always lead you back to the first phase. The results of the evaluation phase should inform the next cycle of planning. If your evaluation of a coaching session reveals that a performer has been unable to learn a particular skill, the planning of the next session should begin by identifying the problems the performer faced and planning a new approach.

If, however, a performer has mastered a technique, in the next phase of planning the coach can build on this newly learnt technique and develop the performer even further. In applying the coaching process, the effective sports coach will be able to plan appropriate sessions for performers, deliver effective sessions, evaluate the progress made in the sessions and then use the information to plan further sessions to build on the progress made.

Remember

- The coaching process is a cyclical process of planning, delivering and evaluating coaching sessions.
- When planning a session, the coach should take into account a number of factors including the needs of the performer and the resources available.
- Coaches should have a well-organised lesson plan to help them deliver the session. This should include all the necessary details required to deliver the session effectively.
- When delivering a coaching session, coaches should strike an appropriate balance between all the different roles required.
- All sessions should be evaluated, and positive and negative features should be noted and used in the planning of future sessions.

Assessment activity 13.4

Now that you have been introduced to the coaching process and had the opportunity to observe coaching, you should be in a position to lead a coaching session yourself.

With your tutor's support, plan, deliver and evaluate a coaching session for a group of your peers. Remember all the different features that have been discussed in this text and ensure that you undertake all the important stages of effective coaching. Consider the following points:

1 What issues do you need to consider when planning a session?
2 What are the potential risks?
3 What should a session contain?
4 What practices are you going to include?
5 How will you know if you have been successful?

Check your knowledge

1 What are the main roles of a coach?
2 For each of the main roles, give an example of a situation when a coach may be required to fulfil that role.
3 What are the main responsibilities facing a coach?
4 What are the three main categories of health and safety considerations for a coach?
5 Where can a coach go to get information about codes of conduct for coaching?
6 Name three laws that coaches must be aware of when they are coaching.
7 What are the main components of communication used by sports coaches?
8 What are the characteristics of an 'autocratic' style of coaching?
9 What are the three stages of learning?
10 Under what conditions do individuals learn best?
11 Describe the key features of the 'whole–part–whole' method of teaching skills.
12 What is meant by the term 'visual guidance'?
13 What are the different types of feedback that a coach may use when coaching?
14 What does the term 'augmented feedback' mean?
15 Draw a diagram that represents the key stages of the coaching process.
16 What questions should you ask yourself when evaluating a coaching session?

Assessment guidance

For this unit's assessment, you are required to produce evidence of having planned, conducted and evaluated a coaching session in a sport of your choice. You must meet the following criteria for the different grades.

To gain a pass:

✔ describe the roles, skills and techniques of two successful sports coaches

✔ identify the different techniques that are used to support athletes

✔ prepare and use an observation checklist in order to identify the different types of techniques that can be used to encourage, support and motivate four different athletes

✔ prepare a lesson plan for delivering an effective sports coaching session

✔ lead an effective coaching session, taking account of the needs and aspirations of the participants, with teacher support

✔ monitor the coaching session, providing feedback regarding your own and participants' performance.

To gain a merit:

✔ compare the roles, skills and techniques of two successful sports coaches

✔ compare the success of different types of techniques that can be used to encourage, support and motivate four different athletes

✔ independently lead a coaching session, taking account of the needs and aspirations of the participants

✔ explain the success of a coaching session, identifying areas for change and/or improvement.

To gain a distinction:

✔ critically evaluate the skills and techniques of two successful sports coaches

✔ critically evaluate the different types of techniques that can be used to encourage, support and motivate four different athletes, providing alternatives and changes as appropriate

✔ critically evaluate the needs and aspirations of the participants, justifying the choice of activities and offering alternatives as appropriate

✔ critically analyse your own role and that of participants and provide priorities for further and future activities.

Merit

1   You will be expected to work more independently throughout the assessment activities. Therefore you should show a better understanding and awareness of the coaching process and related issues, and need less tutor support. You must be able to work on your own in most situations, making your own decisions.

2   Throughout your assessment you will need to use appropriate terminology, for example when discussing sports science issues, coaching techniques and styles, and phases of the coaching process.

3   You will be expected to show more depth and breadth in your understanding. For example, rather than just describing the coaching styles and behaviours of two coaches, you should be able to compare the two people's styles and behaviours. Use comments such as: 'Sir Alex Ferguson works with highly motivated, elite performers, whereas Mary Hughes works with beginner players who find it difficult to remain motivated.'

4   You will also be expected to do more evaluation of your coaching session. There should be clear statements about what worked well and what worked less well, with some suggestions as to what you could have done better.

Distinction

1   You will be expected to work totally independently throughout the assessment activities. You should show an excellent understanding and awareness of the coaching process and related issues, which means you require no tutor support. You must be able to work on your own in all situations, making your own decisions.

2   Throughout your assessment you will need to use appropriate terminology, for example when discussing sports science issues, coaching techniques and styles, and phases of the coaching process.

3   You will be expected to show full depth and breadth in your understanding. For example, rather than just describing the coaching styles and behaviours of two coaches, you should be able to critically analyse the two people's styles and behaviours. Use comments such as: 'Sir Alex Ferguson works with elite performers, who are better able to motivate themselves (Smith, 2001). His coaching style encourages players to work hard and remain focused. Mary Hughes, however, works with beginner players who often, according to Smith (2001), find it hard to motivate themselves. Mary's coaching style takes this into account and she ensures that practice activities are short and hold the players' attention and interest.'

4   You will be expected to perform evaluation and analysis of your coaching session. There should be clear statements about what worked well and what worked less well, with some suggestions as to what you could have done better. Additionally, there should be clear examples to illustrate your analysis and you should make reference to the techniques, styles and behaviours recommended by coach educators and the literature.

5   You will also be expected to produce a high level of work in the classroom and in practical workshops, for example when answering questions, to show your understanding. You will

show a professional attitude and application when involved in practical coaching and adhere to good practice guidelines.

Resources

Texts

Dick, FW: *Sports Training Principles*, 1989, A & C Black

Foxon, F: *Improving Practices and Skills*, 1999, sports coach UK

Galvin, B & Ledger, P: *Planning Coaching Programmes*, 1998, sports coach UK

Hagger, M: *Coaching Young Performers*, 1999, sports coach UK

Martens, R: *Successful Coaching*, 1996, Human Kinetics

Sports coach UK: *How to Coach Children in Sport*, 2003, sports coach UK

Sports coach UK: *How to Coach Disabled People in Sport*, 2003, sports coach UK

Sports coach UK: *How to Coach Sports Effectively*, 2003, sports coach UK

Sports coach UK: *How to Coach Sports Safely*, 2003, sports coach UK

Sports coach UK: *What is Sports Coaching?*, 2003, sports coach UK

Whitmore, J: *Coaching for Performance*, 1994, Brearley Publications

Videos

Working with Disabled Sports People – sports coach UK, Coachwise

Planning and Practice – sports coach UK, Coachwise

Mind over Matter – sports coach UK, Coachwise

Improving Techniques – sports coach UK, Coachwise

Safety and Injury – sports coach UK, Coachwise

The Body in Action – sports coach UK, Coachwise

The Coach in Action – sports coach UK, Coachwise

Websites: sports councils

UK Sport (www.uksport.gov.uk)

Sport England (www.sportengland.org)

Sport Scotland (www.sportscotland.org.uk)

Sports Council for Wales (www.sports-council-wales.co.uk)

Sports Council for Northern Ireland (www.sportni.org)

Sports coach UK (www.sportscoachuk.org)

Websites: national governing bodies

Athletics (www.ukathletics.net)

Basketball (www.basketballengland.org.uk)

Football (www.the-fa.org)

Gymnastics (www.british-gymnastics.org)

Netball (www.england-netball.co.uk)

Swimming (www.britishswimming.org)

Tennis (www.lta.org.uk)

Websites: other related organisations

British Association of Sport and Exercise Sciences (www.bases.org.uk)

British Olympic Association (www.olympics.org.uk)

Child Protection in Sport Unit (www.sportprotects.org.uk)

Child-Safe (www.child-safe.org.uk)

Women's Sport Foundation (www.wsf.org.uk)

ENTERPRISE IN SPORT

Introduction to Unit 14

Businesses are set up every day and, unfortunately, every day many go out of business. There are no hard and fast rules for succeeding in a business enterprise, but there are essential areas such as knowing your customers and having a well-researched business plan with a cashflow forecast. Those organisations that succeed have well-thought-out plans and regularly evaluate and monitor their progress.

Within the sports business market, many types of organisations provide products and services for customers. The format of a business can range from an individual working on his or her own (a sole trader) such as a personal fitness trainer, to a national or multinational organisation that allows the public to buy its shares (a public limited company) such as Manchester United football club.

Successful business enterprises spend time researching the market and getting to know their customers. They use management assessment tools such as SWOT analyses, which examine the strengths and weaknesses of the organisation and explore the opportunities and threats or competition that are in the market. They can then develop their 'marketing mix', which ensures the products/services, price, place, promotion, and the process that customers may go through in using the organisation are appropriate.

All businesses have to fulfil legal and financial requirements. You should have a broad understanding of key legal and financial responsibilities and where you can access support. Most organisations use a cashflow forecast on which to base business decisions. This helps to anticipate any shortfall and ensure there are sufficient finances throughout the year to cover outgoings.

The business plan encompasses many of the areas identified above, and helps to keep an enterprise on a planned course. The business plan is also essential for showing banks or investors about the viability of a proposal in order to raise finance.

Business people also need to ask the question: 'How will we know if we are successful?' This is a more complicated question than it first appears, and will be explored in this unit.

Assessment

This is an internally assessed unit. At the end of the unit you will be asked to produce a business plan for a sports enterprise. You will have to provide evidence of how you generated the idea, including evidence of exploring the sports business market. You will need to produce a clear business plan that takes into account the key legal and financial requirements for your business to succeed, and include a marketing plan. You will also need to demonstrate how you intend to evaluate your business plan.

This unit will guide you through what you need to know in order to put this work together successfully. Your grade for the assessment will be your grade for Unit 14. After completing this unit you should be able to achieve the following outcomes.

Outcomes

1 Investigate a suitable sports business enterprise
2 Explore the market for a sports business enterprise
3 Determine the legal and financial requirements for the selected sports business enterprise
4 Develop and present a business plan for the selected sports business enterprise.

What you need to learn

- What are sports business enterprises?
- How to investigate markets for sports businesses
- The legal and financial issues for sports businesses
- How to develop a business plan.

Sports business enterprise

The growth of the leisure and sport industry since the 1960s has resulted in a diversity of products and services being offered to the public. The number of organisations supplying sports products and services has also significantly increased in this period. The following pages describe some examples from the range of products and services that are available in sport. Having an understanding of the types of work available will also provide you with an insight into the type of business you may want to choose for developing your enterprise in this unit.

Many organisations specialise in one area, such as outdoor activities. Others have grown to encompass a portfolio of leisure and sport activities. All suppliers have to be aware of the needs of customers and conscious of socio-economic and technological developments. This includes recognising that not all people in our society have the same income and standard of living, which affects their choices when purchasing goods and services. Also, technology constantly changes the way we produce things. Having an understanding of these factors can help organisations produce and supply products that reflect the needs of different groups in our society.

Theory into practice

The growth of the sports industry has been significant since the 1960s. Changes in technology, increases in people's leisure time and disposable income, and changes in fashion and demography have all been contributory factors. In small groups, brainstorm as many types of sports businesses as you can think of. Give examples – you might draw them from one part of the industry, such as football.

Types of jobs and enterprises

The sports industry has an enormous variety of opportunities for employment. These jobs exist in the public, private and voluntary sectors and, like all jobs, need different levels of skills and experience. There are opportunities for people to become self-employed by starting their own business. The following is a brief outline of some of the types of jobs and opportunities that are available in the sports industry.

Groundsperson

Sports pitches, grounds and parks have to be maintained to meet the needs of users and providers. For a groundsperson preparing a Premiership football team's pitch or a local authority playing field, many of the basic skills and knowledge are the same. These include knowledge of soils, seeds, grass and artificial surfaces. Specific skills are also needed for each type of sports ground, such as golf courses or hockey pitches. Hours of work are often unsocial as games and activities take place at weekends. Work may also be seasonal, and the nature of the sport will also dictate when the ground is used – cricket pitches will be used mainly in the summer, for example.

Health and fitness instructor

Within the growing health and fitness sector there are several specialist jobs, including fitness instructor, aerobics instructor and personal trainer. The essence of all these jobs is to help individuals develop their health and fitness. Instructors will:

- lead fitness services, run circuits and teach classes
- advise customers on health and fitness
- develop health and fitness programmes for individuals and teams
- support clients during their exercise.

Instructors may work with individuals, teams, large classes and often with mixed ages and abilities.

Outdoor pursuits instructor/educator

The outdoor pursuits sector offers a range of facilities and providers. Those in the public sector play a role in educating and developing people, and others, for example in the private sector, run leadership and management activities. Instructors

A groundsperson needs knowledge of soils, seeds, grass and artificial surfaces

lead activities including canoeing, sailing, climbing, pot holing, orienteering and walking.

There are also management roles within the industry, because outdoor centres, like sports centres and clubs, need managing. Apart from developing individuals' confidence and skills, educationalists use the outdoors to instruct others in areas such as geography, natural history, ecology, biology and the environment.

Professional sportsperson

This appears a glamorous occupation and can bring huge financial rewards. In reality this is limited to a very small number of people, and they need to commit to continual hard work and application to earn those rewards. Age, injuries and inconsistent performances make the career of a professional sportsperson a relatively short one. The opportunities are limited, especially for women, and becoming a full-time sportsperson can be an impossible dream.

Many more opportunities exist for sports performers to play at a semi-professional level. Here they can combine playing with receiving income from another job with a more long-term future. For example, a semi-professional Rugby League player may also work in sports development.

Sports science/medicine

This is a very broad area that has many specialist disciplines. These include:

- sports scientist, psychologist, physiologist, biomechanics specialist
- exercise scientist
- sports dietitian
- physiotherapist
- osteopath
- sports therapist.

In all areas an understanding of the parts and movement of the human body is essential. The specialist applies these basic principles to clients' individual needs, enabling them to meet their objectives and fulfil their potential.

Sports consultant

Sports consultants can be found in many areas of the industry, advising public and commercial organisations on areas such as planning, marketing and funding. Their training and expertise will be in the field they advise upon, but they will also have a wide knowledge of sports issues.

Working with children

Many people enter the sports business because they enjoy working with children. Jobs can vary in format and duties, from coaching and educating to entertaining and caring. Working with children involves developing their skills, confidence and ability to work with others. Work with children is available in:

- play centres
- crèches
- youth clubs
- leisure centres and play schemes
- activity centres
- hotels.

Theory into practice

Working in pairs, select a component of the industry (such as health and fitness) and undertake an investigation into provision in your local area. Include a description of facilities and providers, and describe the range of public, private and voluntary sector organisations.

As well as providing a clear description of the provision, identify and explain key factors that have contributed to the current structure of the industry in the area you have selected.

The information that each person collects should be presented in a form that can be used in an exhibition, and displayed in your resource room or classroom.

Facility provision, maintenance and management

People participating in sport normally do so either in purpose-built facilities, such as a sports centre, or in natural facilities such as lakes for sailing. Each facility varies in size and provision, but its success is largely dependent on how it is managed and maintained.

Some facilities are run by commercial organisations, while others are publicly owned. Some voluntary organisations, such as the guides and scouts, also own and run a range of outdoor and indoor facilities.

Swimming pools

Swimming continues to be, along with walking, the activity with the highest participation rates for adults and young people. In leisure centres, swimming is normally the most popular facility, appealing to men, women and families. Estimates of the number of swimming pools vary, but there are approximately 1,400 public indoor swimming pools, and approximately 3,000 pools in schools and universities. Most health and fitness clubs and hotels also have swimming pools.

Swimming pools vary in size and design. Competition pools are normally rectangular in shape and can be 25 or 50 metres in length. There can be up to eight lanes. Leisure pools come in all shapes and sizes, including kidney-shaped, and may have wave machines, slides and waterfalls. Children's pools are also common, and some pools have diving facilities.

The Ponds Forge International Centre in Sheffield, built in 1991, is one of the most modern pools in the world. It has the ability to change its size and the depth of the water depending on usage.

Indoor sports halls and leisure centres

Over the past 30 years there has been a dramatic increase in the number of indoor sports halls and sport and leisure centres. Lottery money for public and voluntary organisations has

Leisure pools come in all shapes and sizes

encouraged this growth. Finding an exact figure for the number of indoor centres is difficult, but there are approximately 1,500 indoor sports halls and centres.

Sports halls vary in size and provision. The main hall is often measured by the number of badminton courts it has, three or four being the most typical. Other facilities can include:

- ancillary/small hall
- indoor bowls
- ice skating
- racquet sports, e.g. squash courts
- fitness facilities
- bar and restaurant/café.

Sports stadiums

Many major cities in the UK now boast a sports stadium, such as the Arena in Newcastle and the Manchester News Arena in Manchester. These are designed for both sporting and entertainment events such as concerts. Basketball and ice hockey have benefited most from these arenas. Stadium managers are constantly looking to increase usage, to help contribute to the running costs.

Each facility can have capacity for 6,000 to 15,000 spectators, and provide modern services with a range of bar and food facilities.

There has also been a rise in provision of sports stadiums for cities wanting to host international

Many major cities in the UK now boast a modern sports stadium

events, such as Manchester hosting the Commonwealth Games. Wembley remains our national stadium, hosting football and rugby matches, but is undergoing redevelopment to modernise its provision.

Athletics tracks

Most athletics tracks are owned by local authorities. There are approximately 415 in England, 50 in Scotland and 24 in Wales. Most modern tracks have synthetic surfaces, which is a basic requirement for competition, both domestic and international.

The governing body of UK athletics is very keen to develop a national stadium that can host major events such as the Olympics. Recent proposals to

incorporate athletic provision within Wembley stadium have been halted.

Golf courses

The number of 18-hole golf courses in the UK continues to grow in line with demand, and many hotels now provide courses. Farmers have also begun to offer land for golf courses in an attempt to diversify. Most clubs are for members only, but each local authority will operate a number of municipal courses open to the public.

Playing pitches

The government introduced legislation requiring all state schools to seek the consent of the

Education Secretary before disposing of any playing fields. Despite the government's commitment to halt the sale of playing fields, however, the numbers continue to decline. The number of sites is around 25,000, with the majority of pitches being used for football, cricket, rugby and hockey.

The number of artificial grass pitches is approaching 400. These pitches are growing in popularity because of their flexibility of usage and the fact they can be used in all weather all year round.

The National Playing Fields Association, established in 1925, has tried to work with local authorities and central government to identify minimum targets for outdoor playing space. In 1986 this was identified as 6 acres per 1,000 population.

Management of sports facilities

Privately owned facilities have always been managed in accordance with commercial aims, such as increasing usage and generating profit. Traditionally, publicly owned sports facilities have been required to meet the needs of the local community and less emphasis has been placed on financial viability. The Local Government Acts of 1988 and 1999, and the Citizen's Charter of 1991, have made public providers responsible for improving the quality of public services and giving greater value for money through expanded competition.

Sporting goods

Spending on sports goods increased by 40% in real terms in the last five years of the twentieth century. Sportswear such as fleeces, walking boots and tracksuits are fashionable as leisurewear, as well as for sporting activities.

High street sports retailers continue to have widespread presence in most cities and towns, and they provide branded clothing and equipment for fashion and active use. Manufacturers include multinationals such as Nike, Adidas and Reebok, with others such as Champion and Fila developing niches in the UK market.

Sports retailers

With the rise in popularity of sports clothing for leisure wear, many organisations now consider themselves to be a part of the leisure and sportswear market. The supermarket Asda, for example, sells football kits and sports equipment. Some of the department stores have sections dedicated to sport and leisure clothing. Many of the sports retail outlets stock clothing, footwear and equipment, with some retailers becoming sports-specific and offering goods for running, skiing, football, martial arts or golf.

The rise in popularity of football and replica kits has seen the rise in football clubs operating their brand of merchandise, such as Leeds United and Manchester United. Independent retailers have been put under pressure by the growth of out-of-town shopping centres and multiple sports shops. They continue to be located in towns and city centres and try to offer a specialist service.

Multiple sports and clothes shops continue to grow, such as JJB, JD Sports, Athletic Attic and Sports Division. They appeal to active sportspeople as well as the fashion market. The Intersport stores still offer their traditional clothing and equipment while offering new styles of sports fashion, such as Rawcliffes Intersport.

Many retailers offer services via the Internet or mail order. Some are able to offer competitive prices as they do not have stores, and therefore do not bear the costs of operating retail outlets.

Sports manufacturers

Large multinationals dominate the market, mainly due to the growth in popularity of sport and the rise in sportswear as fashion. These include Nike, Adidas, Reebok and Russell Athletic. Manufacturing of equipment such as footwear is mainly done in the Far East and Europe. The leading manufacturers and their brands are:

● Adidas, based in Germany, which produces a wide range of clothing and equipment for sports such as football, rugby and athletics. It has recently bought Salomon and Taylor Made and is developing its sports equipment section, offering for example skiing and golf products.

- Nike continues to provide a range of clothing and sportswear, including goods for football, fitness, tennis and running. It is a US-based organisation.

- Reebok was the UK leader in sports clothing and footwear, and is now behind Nike. Originally it was a British company, but it is now based in the US. It has developed products from aerobics and fitness wear to outdoor clothing. It remains very popular for sports footwear.

- Dunlop Slazenger is the UK's leading sports equipment company. It has tended to produce cricket goods, such as the Stuart Surridge brand, and golf balls under the names Dunlop and Maxfli. Slazenger has world presence in tennis balls and hockey sticks.

- Pentland Group is based in the UK. Its brands include Mitre, Speedo for swimming, and Pony in football and American football equipment. Ellesse is an Italian designer brand and Reusch is the brand for goal-keeping and skiing gloves. Pentland also distributes a number of other brands such as Lacoste, Berghaus and Kickers.

- Umbro UK is a football specialist, making clothing and footwear. It provides clothing for many national and international teams.

- Hi-tech is a UK firm which is strong in racquet and sports footwear, and has developed a healthy market share in outdoor footwear.

- Fila originated in Italy and now has a firm presence in the UK, focusing on football, running and women's fitness. It is very popular in the UK in basketball footwear.

- Spalding Sports is based in the US, with Spalding Sports UK distributing primarily golf and American sports equipment here in the UK. Basketballs and golf balls remain very popular lines.

Theory into practice

What is the difference between a sports retailer and a sports manufacturer? Provide examples of each.

Sports coaching

The essence of sports coaching is to help others become better performers in their chosen sport. The sports coach requires specific skills and knowledge in his or her sport, and the ability to gain the best performance from athletes.

Sports coaching can be done on a full-time, professional basis, for example at a professional football or cricket club. However, most coaches in the UK work part-time or on a voluntary basis, such as working with young children in gymnastics, athletics, or at a local tennis club.

The National Coaching Foundation was established in 1983. It has gone through a number of structural changes including changing its name to sports coach UK, but its objectives remain to improve the quality of coaching via coach education. Sports coach UK is based in Leeds with 10 regional offices, and has coaching units in the sports councils of Northern Ireland, Scotland and Wales. It works with further and higher education colleges and schools as well as the national governing bodies of sport.

Coaching qualifications are provided by the national governing bodies of sport. There are many levels of coaching qualifications, which sports coach UK is trying to standardise. The National Occupational Standards for Sport, Recreation and Allied Occupations provide a benchmark for coaching qualifications in the UK.

Commercial coaching organisations also exist. They are usually sports-specific, such as for football or basketball. They run courses for children, after school or in the school holidays. They are led by qualified coaches from the national governing body of the sport.

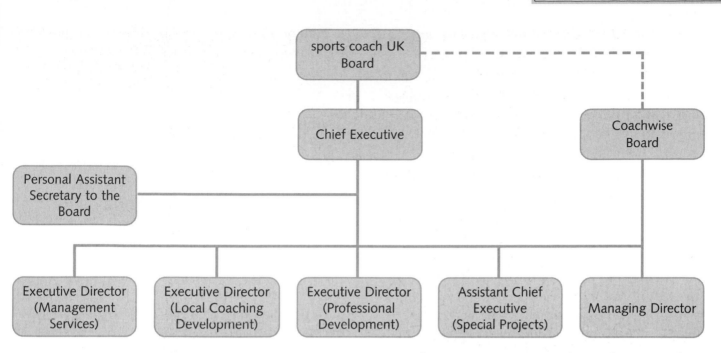

The corporate management team of sports coach UK

Sports development

Central government has continued to support the development of sport through the Sports Council, now UK Sport, and the national councils – Sport England, Wales, Northern Ireland and Scotland.

The government published a policy statement in 1995 called 'Sport: Raising the Game'. The essence of this is an attempt to achieve excellence in traditional and team sports, for example winning medals in Olympic finals. This has brought a different emphasis from the previous policies of sport for all.

Local authorities continue to provide facilities and opportunities for people to participate. Many authorities have a sports development team, which can be made up of officers with different roles, such as:

- community officers, who focus on developing sport and recreation in targeted communities, e.g. inner city areas
- income generators, who develop opportunities, events and courses that are commercially viable
- sports developers, who focus on developing specific sports and often work closely with governing bodies of sport, for example in swimming; their goals are to increase opportunities for people to develop from participation to excellence
- targeted officers, who have defined roles but may differ from authority to authority. These include youth, women and special needs officers, as well as those who link with schools or for lottery applications.

Sports tourism

Tourism continues to be one of the world's growing industries, and people travel more than ever, domestically and overseas. A prominent feature of tourist destinations is the provision of sports facilities.

Facilities

Many hotels and resorts recognise the demand for sports facilities and now include them as part of their package of attractions. These can include:

- squash courts
- golf courses
- tennis courts
- swimming pools
- health and fitness club

- water-based activities such as canoeing and windsurfing
- outdoor pursuits such as cycling.

The emergence of such facilities is directly related to the rise in awareness about the importance of health and fitness. Many providers have had to extend their facilities to cater for this increase in demand. The Greenalls Group in the UK, for example, offers health and fitness facilities as well as golf courses in many of its hotels.

Sport vacations

Tourists may travel specifically to participate in or watch sports activities. They could go to summer camps, on sport tours, or on golfing or fishing breaks. Club Med offers a cruise taking golfers to exotic locations, and tennis clinics are run around the world by renowned players.

Many tour operators have always provided vacations for major sports such as golf, skiing and tennis. More recently, specialist companies have emerged to meet specific needs, such as tours connected with:

- football matches in Europe
- boxing in the US
- cricket in the West Indies, Australia and South Africa.

A growing number of sports attractions are visited by tourists. These include museums and halls of fame such as:

- the Football Association Hall of Fame
- the British Golf Museum at St Andrews
- the Lawn Tennis Museum at Wimbledon
- the National Horse Racing Museum at Newmarket
- the Cricket Museum at Lords.

Sports halls of fame, which celebrate our sporting heritage, have been well established in the United States for many years, and are becoming popular in this country.

Sports festivals and championships

Hosting large sporting events has become a major

goal for many of the world's cities. This is primarily because of the economic impact of attracting hundreds of thousands of visitors, in addition to the 'feel good' factor created for residents. The longer-term effects for cities hosting events and the sustainability of facilities remain contentious issues. Sheffield, for example, is having to meet the costs of erecting several sports facilities as a result of hosting the World Student Games.

Large sporting events continue to attract huge numbers of visitors. Events include:

- World Cup football
- Olympic Games
- Commonwealth Games
- African Games
- World Student Games
- Special Olympics
- Tour de France
- Wimbledon tennis.

Many tour operators organise vacations around a sporting event.

Professional sport

Some sports and their governing bodies have fought to keep their amateur status, while others, such as in boxing and horse racing, have a history of paying people to perform. Rugby League and more recently Rugby Union at the highest level now pay players on a full-time basis.

Performers

The more popular sports offer great financial rewards to successful, full-time professionals. Some sports such as football and cricket also pay players on a part-time basis so that they can become semi-professional. Their wages depend on market forces – that is, how much they are in demand and how many others offer similar skills in their chosen sport.

Professional football has recently seen a massive increase in players' salaries at the highest level, because of market forces and the effect of the Bosman ruling, which allows sportspeople in

Europe to move freely between clubs at the end of their contracts. Salaries of £50,000 per week are becoming more commonplace.

Players are able to supplement this with sponsorship earnings by endorsing products and services – David Beckham wears Adidas football boots, for example. The influence of the media, in particular television, has led to an increase in the amount of money involved in sporting events, and therefore the money available to organisations and performers. The Lawn Tennis Association is able to offer substantial prize money to Wimbledon winners, although women still do not receive as much as men. Athletics has also moved clearly into the professional arena, with the athletics circuit offering a million pounds in gold bars for a champion who can win his or her event at each competition on the circuit.

Professional sports clubs and organisations

The growth in income and expenditure for many professional clubs has meant that a more professional approach to management is now essential. Many clubs depend on television income and sponsorship as well as their supporters. The commercial manager for such a club now plays a key role in its success.

This move to professionalism has seen a growth in the numbers of professional administrators and organisers in sport, for example in top basketball, football and ice hockey. Many of these organisations have incorporated American principles of entertainment into their events and matches. In fact, many sports performers consider themselves to be entertainers.

Sports agents and promoters

The complexities of contract negotiation between players and their clubs and the growing opportunities for endorsements have encouraged the rise of the sports agent.

Agents represent their sportspersons in contract negotiations. Some are also promoters of their sports, organising events – the most famous of these is the American Don King. He has often been

proclaimed by the boxing fraternity to be the greatest promoter in history, with some fights such as Mike Tyson versus Evander Holyfield being watched worldwide by more than two billion people.

Successful promoters and agents in the US include Mark McCormick with his IMG organisation, and Leigh Steinberg. Within the UK Frank Warren and Barry Hearn's Matchroom Sports primarily represent snooker players and boxers. Many other sportspeople, especially in football, rugby, cricket and golf, have agents who promote and represent them.

Sports-related gambling

Gambling has been associated with sporting events throughout history. In the twentieth century gambling became more socially accepted. With the National Lottery, the growth in spread betting and telephone and online betting, the gambling industry continues to grow overall in terms of the amount placed in bets.

Gambling activities

Sports betting is dominated by horse-racing. Estimates of the market vary, but it accounts for about 60% of all bets placed. The betting on football, mainly spread betting, is on the increase. De-regulation of the industry as a whole has aided sectors such as bingo and allowed advertising for the high street bookmaker.

Gambling organisations

Sports betting has traditionally been handled by high street bookmakers. This is changing rapidly with the growth of telephone betting and on-line gambling on the Internet. This has had the effect of reducing the number of smaller high street bookmakers and increasing the size of national chains such as Ladbrokes and the William Hill Organisation.

The new suppliers in the sports betting market are mainly in offshore, telephone and Internet betting, and include Bet Online and Net Bet. City Index provides a spread betting service.

Sports medicine

It is universally recognised that the general public and sports professionals are becoming more aware of the importance of health and personal well being. Many professional sportspeople and clubs employ specialists to help maximise their performance. This includes advice on prevention of injury, treatment of injuries and nutrition.

Advice and expertise is also available for all general medical problems in sport, including respiratory illness, diabetes and environmental factors that affect performance such as heat acclimatisation. Sports medicine professionals can be found in the public sector through local health authorities, and in the private sector with for example physiotherapists and sports injury clinics.

Physiotherapists

Physiotherapists are trained in the anatomy and physiology of the human body. They diagnose problems when we are not functioning as we should. They provide a treatment programme appropriate to the condition, which can include:

- massage, mostly used with injured soft tissues, to help increase circulation to soft tissues in the muscle and relieve muscle spasm such as a hamstring pull

- electrotherapy, using ultrasound and laser treatment to help stimulate blood circulation, reduce muscle spasm and relieve pain

- mobilisation of one or more joints to help free them and relieve pain and spasm – often used on the spine.

Rehabilitation exercises are one of the most important aspects of any treatment plan. These aim to stretch and strengthen the appropriate muscles. This can help prevent the recurrence of the injury; for example weak ankle joints can be supported by increasing the strength of the supporting muscle in the calf.

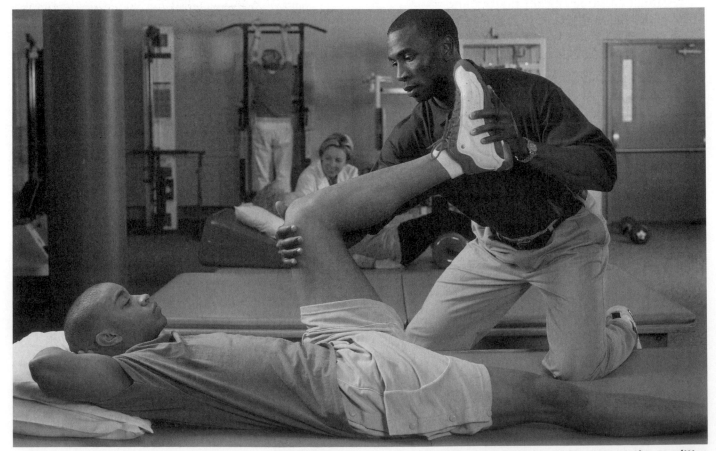

Physiotherapists provide a treatment programme appropriate to the condition

Sports injury clinics

The main function of a sports injury clinic is to diagnose, treat and rehabilitate athletes as quickly and safely as possible. They will also try to prevent the injury recurring. Most clinics offer a number of services, including:

- physiotherapy
- personal injury assessments
- training and recovery programmes
- podiatrists (specialists who treat problems occurring within the foot or lower limb).

Sports nutritionists

The importance of diet in relation to sports performance has been well documented. Nutritionists are able to offer assessment of individuals' dietary needs. A balanced diet is essential for providing the energy and nutrients needed for training, recovery and performance. Nutritionists are able to design dietary intake to meet the needs of individuals, for example long-distance runners and cyclists who often take extra carbohydrates before competition to help give the energy they require.

Nutritionists also examine an individual's lifestyle and offer suggested menus, depending on the training programme and time of the season.

Sports medicine organisations

Many organisations are part of the sports medicine industry. Most treatment requires products such as tape, for example, and Tysons Sports is one company supplying many of the leading football and rugby clubs with equipment needed for sports medicine.

The main organisation that represents those involved in sports medicine is the National Sports Medicine Institute of the United Kingdom. Its aim is to improve the quality of exercise medicine and sports sciences in the UK. It provides education and development for those involved in delivering sports medicine services.

Outdoor and adventure sector

Many outdoor activities such as walking are popular pastimes in the UK. Others have been developed into competition sports, such as canoeing and mountain biking.

Several clothing and equipment suppliers specialise in the outdoor and adventure activity market. Similarly a growing number of organisations offer facilities, leadership and instruction in outdoor and adventure activities. This area has become more regulated following the introduction of the Activity Centres (Young Persons' Safety) Act 1995.

Outdoor and adventure activities

These activities mainly involve journeying over 'wild' terrain and overcoming natural obstacles. They include the following.

- **Walking, running and climbing.** Hill walking or fell walking and rambling are very popular. Mountaineering includes rock climbing and is a growing sport because of the availability of climbing walls in sports centres. Orienteering involves running and using a map to find points as quickly as possible.
- **Cycling.** This has experienced massive growth and includes mountain biking, downhill and uphill racing and cyclo-cross-country racing. Mountain bike sales have increased dramatically over the past ten years.
- **Caving and potholing.** Like cycling, these are associated with danger and risk. They involve the exploration of caves and potholes underground and require special skills and training.
- **Water sports.** Traditional sports such as canoeing and sailing are now joined by white-water rafting, surfing, water skiing and windsurfing.
- **Snow sports.** These are popular in Scotland and abroad. Activities include downhill skiing, cross-country skiing and snowboarding.
- **Hunting and field sports.** These continue to be controversial. Recent government legislation

has reduced gun ownership and there are constant moves to ban fox-hunting. Fishing remains one of the most popular outdoor pursuits. It includes coarse fishing, game fishing and sea fishing.

Other activities can be included in this section, although participation figures remain low:

- hang-gliding
- forms of parachuting
- mountain range vehicles, e.g. quad biking.

Outdoor adventure organisations

A variety of organisations provide products and services for outdoor and adventure activities. They include those providing 'activity holidays', those selling equipment and clothing, and the outdoor adventure activity centres.

Most outdoor adventure activity centres offer some or all of the following services:

- environmental education, including practical exploration of the environment
- education programmes, primarily related to field-based humanities and science
- outdoor and adventure activities for people with physical or learning difficulties
- management programmes for those in industry, which focus on individual and team development.

A number of governing bodies and organisations represent the sector. These include the Countryside Agency, a non-governmental organisation; the National Trust from the voluntary sector; and the British Canoe Union, a governing body.

Theory into practice

In pairs, select two sports of your choice and prepare a presentation on them. Briefly describe where each is played, such as indoors on courts for squash. Identify the different sectors that provide facilities for your sports and any coaching, tourism, development, gambling and professional organisations or individuals associated with them. Collect items associated with the sports such as equipment, photos of stadiums, etc. which you can use as visual aids.

In pairs, present this information to the rest of the group.

Health and fitness

The health and fitness industry continues to increase its facilities and initiatives, focusing on participation in exercise to improve our health and general fitness. There has been a substantial rise in health clubs, especially in hotels, in personal fitness training and in schemes such as exercise referral from medical professionals.

Participation figures for gyms and health clubs tend to vary. There is no doubt that more people have joined clubs since the 1990s, but there is still evidence that many give up attending clubs soon after joining.

Health and fitness clubs

Health and fitness clubs continue to grow, as do organisations providing related services. There are over 40 prominent private organisations in the market. Also, each local authority provides or develops its own health and fitness facilities. A number of private organisations run local authority-owned facilities on a management contract basis. The total number of clubs in the UK is over 2,500.

Mergers, acquisitions and flotations among private organisations in the market have been frequent. The size of health and fitness clubs varies, with some extending to over 50,000 square feet. Membership numbers can be less than 500 or more than 3,000. The facilities offered by clubs include:

- fitness rooms with weights
- cardiovascular fitness rooms
- indoor/outdoor tennis
- squash
- saunas
- cafés and bars
- crèches and children's activity rooms
- aerobics studios
- swimming pools

- steam rooms
- restaurants
- beauty salons
- physiotherapy facilities
- solaria
- toning rooms.

There have been many advances in beauty and health treatments as well as in fitness equipment.

Personal fitness trainers

There has been a rise in qualified fitness trainers who offer a personalised service, usually in the client's own home. They help assess and work through a training programme with their client, motivating them to continue their programmes and to work optimally.

Trainers are usually self-employed and predominantly work on a part-time basis. The more successful providers are able to work full-time, and clients tend to be those who can afford the cost of a personalised service.

Case study

Funbury racquet and fitness club prides itself on offering excellent customer care and meeting the needs of its customers. This includes offering a comprehensive fitness assessment, designing a suitable programme and offering continuing advice and support during workouts. Personal trainers, who are self-employed, offer one-to-one training.

A new member joins the club and has a fitness test. During the preliminary questioning the fitness instructor discovers the member has a history of back problems and is concerned about his weight, which is well above normal for a man of his height. The instructor refers him to his doctor for a complete medical check. The doctor suggests a diet and gentle exercise programme including outdoor walking.

1 What organisations could instructors access to enable them to offer advice and support to the new member, on matters such as nutrition?
2 What equipment might the new member require, and where could he get this?

Personal fitness trainers help clients to work optimally

241

BISHOP BURTON COLLEGE

Technological developments

Every sport, facility and activity has been affected by developments in technology. For example, since the 1970s the following technological changes have affected the Wimbledon tennis championships:

- new methods and equipment for players' training
- new materials and designs for tennis racquets
- advances in treating, preparing and protecting grass and playing surfaces
- new television cameras and media coverage
- changes to the pressure and material in tennis balls
- introduction of beams and other electronic devices for line calls
- improved scoreboards
- computer scoring
- improved sports medicine and treatment of injuries.

Every sport has experienced similar changes. There is a popular belief that not all advances in technology have been for the benefit of sport. In tennis, the increased power of players, racquets and balls have all contributed to the grass-court game becoming dominated by the serve, and perhaps less of a spectacle. The debates will continue.

Suitable ventures

Feasibility

An idea or proposal for a new enterprise may come from an individual's inspiration, from a group's brainstorming, or be directed by management as part of an organisation's overall strategy and business aims. Once an idea has been identified, the first step is to undertake a feasibility study. This process tries to answer questions about content, finance, objectives, resources, staffing and time scale.

Wimbledon now has electronic devices at courtside for line calls

A feasibility study often takes the form of a business plan, and clearly identifies any problems and how they may be overcome. Several people will need to be involved in the study, such as bank managers, health and safety representatives, accountants and legal experts.

Aims and objectives

The plan must clearly and concisely state the overall purpose of the enterprise. In some organisations this takes the form of a 'strategic overview statement'. This is a general statement which covers:

- what is being done
- why it is being done
- the benefits it will bring to the organisation
- the unique selling point of the product or service (see page 256).

All plans will identify their aims and objectives.

Aims are broad statements of the overall intent of the project. They are likely to relate closely to the overall aims of the organisation. They are relatively short and should be clearly expressed. Examples are:

- to introduce potential customers to our facilities and services
- to identify the most cost-effective method of giving information about our products and services to potential and existing customers
- to design and create a database of all our customers
- to identify opportunities for funding and income generation
- to improve the services we offer to the community
- to review existing working practices to ensure we are environmentally friendly.

Objectives are more detailed statements defining what must be accomplished for the overall aim to be achieved. They will normally include time parameters and specific outcomes that can be measured to identify whether the project has been a success. The principle of SMART can be used when deciding objectives for a project. SMART objectives should be:

Specific – have identified targets, for example to introduce systems for recycling waste

Measurable – have criteria for judging whether the project was a success; for example, an event must attract 300 visitors of whom 50% must be pensioners

Achievable – with the resources that are available

Relevant – to the overall aims of the organisation

Timed – each objective has a specific time by when it should be achieved.

Analysing competitor activity

Any organisation must not only meet the needs of its customers, but do so better than its competitors. Organisations must therefore study and analyse their competitors as well as their customers.

Competition analysis starts with defining who your competitors are.

- Direct competition comes from those who offer similar products or services to the same customers.
- Indirect competition comes from those who sell different products within the same sector, or the same products within a different sector. A personal trainer does not have the facilities of a health club but may be competing for the same customers who wish to be motivated to keep fit. A private health club and a community centre which offers fitness services are not directly competing, because their potential customers will be different.
- Implicit competitors are indirect competitors who may seem quite unrelated to the sports industry. Some families may choose to go on holiday, decorate their house or buy a new car, instead of spending money on joining the local health club. The organisations trying to persuade them to spend their money in these ways are implicit competitors of the health club.

In many cases, organisations that provide different sports and leisure products or services such as cinemas, bowling centres, restaurants and shops are located on one retail site. This offers greater choice for customers, in the hope that they will combine two or more leisure activities in a day or evening.

In all cases, competitor analysis is about being aware of competitors' prices, products, services and selling points. Identifying their strengths and weakness and designing and implementing strategies to respond to these can help keep you ahead of the competition.

Theory into practice

What is the difference between indirect and direct competition? Use a realistic example in sport to illustrate your answer.

Private sector

Most enterprises are set up by private organisations as commercial businesses that aim to make a profit. They tend to be sports specific (such as professional sports clubs, ski centres or adventure sports) or private health clubs such as exercise facilities in hotels. In most cases facilities and equipment are modern, and strong competition often means that the quality of service has to be high.

Large public limited companies like the Hilton Group and Manchester United are dominant in the industry. However, many organisations are run by individuals, partnerships or small limited companies.

Options for ownership

Sole traders

Becoming a sole trader is perhaps the simplest way to set up in business. There are few formalities to complete and the decisions are made by you alone. Any losses you incur are your responsibility and therefore your personal assets such as your house and car are at risk. It can be difficult to raise money initially to start your business.

Conversely, all profits are yours, you are not answerable to anyone else (apart from customers) and little paperwork is required. It is essential, however, to keep accurate records of all financial transactions as you must register with the Inland Revenue within three months of setting up business and submit details of income and expenditure.

Although sole traders often start by running the business on their own, they can employ staff to help as the business develops. However, many sole traders find it difficult to work alone and often have to put in long hours. Expanding the business can be problematic as funding can be hard to find.

Theory into practice

What makes sole traders different from other business structures?

Partnerships

In a partnership two or more people set up in business together and share the financial consequences (debts and profits) and the management duties.

Partners share personal liability for business debts. If one partner cannot meet any debts the other partner must take on the burden. It is important to draw up an agreement that clearly states the role of each partner, how the organisation will be run, and how any proceeds will be split.

Partnerships do not need their accounts to be audited and often have lower tax and National Insurance liabilities than limited companies. Partnerships can also be successful because each partner brings different skills and knowledge to the enterprise. However, problems may arise if there are disagreements between the partners or if individuals make decisions without consultation.

Limited companies

A limited company has a separate legal identity from its owners. The owners of a limited company have limited liability for the debts of the business, up to the value of their shareholding; they are not personally liable for the company's debts. If the business fails, the shareholders simply lose the amount they have invested in the company. However, banks may require personal guarantees from directors for loans, and if the company fails and you have not carried out your duties as a company director, you may be disqualified from acting as a director in another company.

To set up a limited company, you need to create documents called a memorandum of association and articles of association, which have to disclose issues such as who will be performing what tasks in the business, what it will do and where it will be based.

Limited companies pay corporation tax on their profits and must have their accounts audited.

Markets and customers

All organisations use marketing methods to attract customers and visitors to buy their products and services, as opposed to those provided by competitors. This process starts with establishing clear marketing objectives and analyses the influences, external and internal, on the organisation.

The needs of the customer are monitored so that the marketing methods used are the most effective. In the present climate of changing markets and competition, this process needs to be regularly evaluated to ensure that customers' needs are being satisfied.

Before objectives can be set, any organisation needs to be clear on exactly what market it is aiming at and what products and services it has to offer.

The market

Most organisations try to identify customers and potential customers and provide products and services designed for this clientele. Organisations often compete for customers by providing alternative products and services. For example, most towns and cities have a choice of sports shops. The size of the market for sports equipment would be the total amount of sales of all the stores in a year. Each retailer would be trying to capture as much as possible of that market, and its proportion of the total amount of sales is known as its market share. The market can also be expressed in terms of the number of customers or transactions.

A few organisations operate in an environment where they are free from competition. This situation is called a 'monopoly'. An example might be a company offering diving facilities in a region where no other organisation offers this service.

Often a few firms will dominate the market, and this is referred to as an 'oligopoly.' This is the situation nationally in the brewing industry, where a few suppliers dominate the market.

Competition usually brings benefits for the consumer. For example, an area that has several private health clubs may see price reductions, incentives and greater value for money as each supplier competes for a share of the market.

Products and services

There can be distinct differences between the marketing process for products as opposed to services.

Products are tangible goods which have been manufactured and can be distributed to the customer. These include sports equipment or drinks from a bar. When purchased by customers these goods are then owned by them. Products are easily measured in terms of stock in storage or sold. Many sports facilities offer products that complement their main service, such as sportswear or health products in a fitness club. These are often known as 'secondary sales'.

Services differ from products as they are intangible – they cannot be touched. They include the help and assistance given by trained people such as a coach. Practitioners sometimes refer to their services as 'sports products', which can be misleading. Many organisations in the service sector market extra services as 'added value' to their core service. For example, a golf club's core service is the golf course, but it is likely to offer a range of other 'sports products' to attract targeted customers, including hosting corporate events, and providing golf lessons and caddying services.

Key features of services are the following.

- **Intangibility.** The service does not result in the customer owning anything. Furthermore, the service is worth nothing unless a customer uses it. It can be difficult for the customer to evaluate the service before purchasing it, and experiencing a service is an important part of a consumer's choice as to whether to continue to use a particular service. Marketers know the importance of word-of-mouth recommendations and creating a positive first impression.

- **Perishability.** This has particular relevance to the marketer. Leisure services cannot be 'stored'; a badminton court that remains unused one day is a sales opportunity gone for good. Most services experience fluctuations in demand. Sports centres experience times of peak demand between 5 pm and 9 pm and must work hard to service that demand and not disappoint customers wanting to book activities. However, they must find ways of increasing demand in off-peak times, during the hours of 10 am to 4 pm, when occupancy is well below its maximum.

- **Heterogeneity.** This describes the variability in quality and consistency of a service. A visitor to an outdoor activities centre may have two totally different experiences on two successive visits, if the services that staff provide are different. This has implications for consistency in customer service. Everyone must work to ensure the marketing and service are both tailored to meet the individual requirements of customers, and to emphasise quality in ensuring that customers' needs are consistently met.

Market segmentation

All customers are different. If you treat all customers alike you can guarantee most will be less than satisfied. Market segmentation has virtually replaced the mass market method, where

economies of scale were sought by communicating the same message on each product or service to as many people as possible. Research has shown that if the market is divided into smaller groups called segments, then it is easier to satisfy needs. This in turn makes each market communication method more cost effective.

Each sports organisation operates within a market which consists of customers who have similar needs, such as improving and maintaining their levels of health and fitness, but they are not all the same. Therefore, organisations try to segment the market into smaller groups that have more similar characteristics. In this way they hope to be able to:

- research specific needs and provide products and services that match these needs
- improve profits by matching products and pricing strategies according to the identified segments
- focus communication strategies by using the most appropriate promotional strategy for each segment
- research the size of the market, by identifying the viability and cost effectiveness of providing services for certain sections of the market.

It is worth noting that the market and its segments often change due to social and economic factors. Many sports providers have recognised that the 'family' has changed in recent years with the rise in divorce and separations. A segment classified as 'lone parents' has been identified. Many organisations are also targeting a growing segment known as the 'grey market', which includes older people who have retired, especially as they may have private pensions and therefore are more likely to have money and time to spend.

Theory into practice
Explain market segmentation and why organisations try to segment markets into smaller groups. Give examples related to sports organisations.

The following are the most common types of segments used by sports organisations.

Geographic segmentation

This is perhaps one of the simplest methods of segmentation – separating the market into areas of the country or perhaps regions of the world. This pre-supposes that there are different tastes, usage patterns and other variables specific to an area. Organisations can then tailor their sales campaigns and services to particular regions. There are also obvious differences between urban and rural areas, especially in terms of access.

ACORN (A Classification of Residential Neighbourhoods) is an information service for geographic segmentation which takes into account demographic as well as socio-economic factors. It identifies different living accommodation and neighbourhood types.

Demographic segmentation

This method attempts to segment the population based on the following categories.

- Age – some organisations have targeted certain age groups, such as fitness programmes targeting over 50s.

- Gender – some organisations focus their products and services on either men or women. The new wave of men's magazines which focus on men's fitness and health is an example.

- The family has been a market for many organisations. Many sports facilities have adapted their facilities to cater for the family, but the family also has sub-segments including single parents with children.

- Ethnic segmentation means targeting specific communities; for example the Football Association had a campaign to encourage young Asians to participate in football.

Socio-economic segmentation

This covers a number of variables based on education, occupation and social class. The most commonly used method of classification is the Joint Industry Committee for National Readership Surveys (JICNARS).

Social grade	Social status	Head of household's occupation
A	Upper middle class	Higher managerial, professional, administrative
B	Middle class	Intermediate managerial, administrative, or professional
C1	Lower middle class	Supervisory or clerical and junior managerial, administrative or professional
C2	Skilled working class	Skilled manual workers
D	Working class	Unskilled manual workers
E	Lowest levels of subsistence	State pensioners or widows, casual and unemployed workers

This method of segmentation is usually used in conjunction with other methods. It is used in advertising as the media (especially newspapers) provide socio-economic breakdowns of readership figures.

Psychographic segmentation

This is based on the motives and attitudes that influence buyer behaviour. Marketing strategies take into account the motivations of consumers. Some customers may decide to buy because of price, others because of quality.

- Lifestyle segmentation is a method commonly used by sports organisations. It groups together the activities, interests and opinions of certain types of people. Young upwardly mobile professionals ('yuppies') tend to join private clubs and buy the latest equipment and fashionable clothing, for example.

- Personality is not such a common method of segmentation, but extroverts could be targeted for adventurous sports, and introverts may be the focus where sport is marketed as a way to develop social interaction.

Behaviourist segmentation

This method analyses people's product or service usage statistically. People may be frequent, occasional or one-time users. The level of brand loyalty is another behavioural characteristic. Football clubs experience a high level of brand loyalty, where individuals support the team throughout their lives. Sports shoe purchasers may change brands depending upon promotional offers or changes in technology.

Think it over

In small groups, visit a fast food restaurant. Assess the different market segments that the restaurant tries to appeal to. This can be done through observing customers, looking at special offers, the pricing structure, the products and promotional material.

If you go as customers you do not need to arrange the visit with the management. Obtain examples of any literature such as promotional leaflets that you can use as evidence. This evidence could be compared with the evidence gained from advertisements in the media for the same restaurant.

Having developed a profile of the restaurant's customers explain, with examples, to the whole group how the restaurant segments its market.

Assessment activity 14.1

Working in pairs, create three ideas for a new sports business venture. These should ideally be in three different areas such as clothing, sports equipment and outdoor activities. Identify each main idea, the type of product or service, and what type of business format might be suitable for it. Provide a brief feasibility study detailing the strengths and weaknesses of each proposal. Finally, outline the markets and potential customers.

Present your findings to the class in a talk lasting no more than 20 minutes.

The market

For most modern organisations, marketing is not a stand-alone function or department but a continual process. Marketing is the process by which people's needs and wants are discovered and products and services are produced to satisfy those needs. The customer should be at the centre of any marketing strategy, whether in the public, commercial or voluntary sector.

Marketing has many different facets, ranging from market research to communicating messages to potential customers. Although marketing is a management function it is also the responsibility of all employees.

The growing competition in all sectors of the sports industry makes it essential that marketing methods are used effectively and then evaluated in order to continue to attract new customers, and retain existing ones.

Establishing marketing objectives

All organisations exist for a reason, whether it is to make a profit for shareholders or to help the environment. Organisations have to communicate these objectives to all staff to help ensure they are fulfilled. Many organisations produce a 'mission statement', which is a broad summary of overall purpose and aim. It also should aim to identify key stakeholders whom the organisation aims to satisfy. Stakeholders are people and organisations with an interest in the enterprise, including customers, suppliers, employees, investors and so on. Many organisations now also produce vision statements, which describe the organisation, and what it sees its role to be in the future.

Each area within marketing needs to set objectives against which to measure performance and to provide a focus for all staff. Marketing objectives must have flexibility to meet the demands of customers. Under the SMART principle (see page 243), each objective should be specific, measurable, achievable, relevant and timed.

Think it over

In small groups, discuss examples of SMART marketing objectives that a sports organisation might set for itself.

Theory into practice

Working in pairs, select a sector of the sports industry such as health and fitness, outdoor recreation or sports facilities. Develop a profile of the providers of the sector within your area. Include those from the commercial, voluntary and public sectors. Describe the facilities and main services which the organisations provide and find out their objectives and mission statements, and how they promote themselves.

Each sector of the sports industry should be covered by the work of the whole group. The location of the facilities could be displayed on a large map of the area. Information on the nature of the facilities, the prices and any promotion the organisation has undertaken should be compared to help identify the differences in the mix of organisations. This information can be in the form of a video, leaflets, brochures, newspaper advertisements or price lists.

Market research

Market research can take various forms and often provides the essential information enabling organisations to develop their strategy and operational policies.

Market research often starts by examining the different segments into which customers can be classified. These segments can then be targeted for primary and secondary research. Once data has been collected it must be analysed to extract the appropriate information for developing the marketing strategy.

Conducting primary research

Primary research is the process of gathering new information. It is often used by organisations which want to discover consumer attitudes towards their products and services. The most common methods are observation, experimentation, questionnaires and focus groups. Each method has its own strengths and weaknesses and is appropriate for obtaining certain types of information.

Observation can be done through either participant observation or non-participant observation. A non-participant observer finds a suitable position to watch, such as a balcony to observe an aerobics class. A participant observer would join in the class and observe from a participant's perspective. Participant observation is less common but can be used by some organisations through the device of mystery shoppers. These are people who play the role of customers in order to test services.

Audits are another method of observation, usually done daily by organisations which sell products, to identify sales and forecast trends.

Closed circuit television (CCTV) is used mostly as a system of security, but it can be used to observe people's behavioural patterns: for example which equipment is most popularly used in a health club. It is important to remember ethical considerations when using this method, as many people do not like to be observed in this way.

Counting devices, either manual or electronic, can also be used. Retail outlets and sports facilities such as football clubs have them built into entrances and turnstiles, monitoring the number of visitors to the facility.

Observation can be used to discover which equipment is most popularly used in a gym

Experimentation can be used to measure consumer responses to variables in the marketing mix. Organisations which have several facilities may experiment with different services, activities or promotions to compare responses. The most successful methods can then be used across all facilities. This information must be used in conjunction with segmentation analysis and therefore take into account geographic, demographic and psychological factors.

Questionnaires aim to elicit responses from targeted people to relevant questions. Questionnaires can be administered in face-to-face interviews, by post, telephone or via a computer.

Face-to-face interviewing may take place in people's homes, at their place of work or in the sports facility being researched. Shopping centres are also a common venue for face-to-face interviews. The questionnaire may be carefully structured by having a series of specific questions, or semi-structured where further questions may be asked depending on the interviewee's responses. Interviewers must be specially trained to select suitable subjects to interview, elicit honest responses and record them accurately.

Postal questionnaires are generally used in conjunction with segmentation. Customers on existing databases may be mailed to ask for information about their views on the service provided and how aspects of the service might be improved. They may also be asked for more personal details to help better segment the market. Postal questionnaires are a cheap method of gathering information but they have a low response rate (often below 10%) and often incentives such as a prize draw are used to increase the likelihood of a return. A prepaid envelope also increases the response rate.

We are committed to finding ways of improving our service. Please take a few moments to complete the following questions, to help us achieve this aim.

Name: _____ **Customer no.** _____

1 Where did you first hear about our insurance services?
❏ National press ❏ Local press ❏ Radio
❏ PR ❏ Word of mouth Other _____

2 How did you first contact us?
❏ By telephone ❏ By meeting an advisor ❏ On the Internet Other _____

3 If you used the telephone, how many times did you try before your call was answered?
❏ Answered first time ❏ 2-3 tries ❏ 3-5 tries Other _____

4 How well were the insurance advisors able to answer any questions you had?
❏ Answered all questions ❏ Answered most questions
❏ Answered some questions ❏ Unable to answer

5 Did the insurance advisor offer to complete the application form for you?
❏ Yes ❏ No

6 Overall, how well do you feel we handled your enquiry?
❏ Very well ❏ Well ❏ Acceptably ❏ Poorly

7 How satisfied were you with the written information you received?
❏ Very satisfied ❏ Quite satisfied ❏ Dissatisfied ❏ Very dissatisfied
If you were not satisfied, please say why:
_____
_____

8 How easy did you find it to complete the application and other paperwork?
❏ Very easy ❏ Easy ❏ OK ❏ Difficult

9 What can we do to improve further the service you have received so far?
_____
_____

10 Would you recommend our services to one of your colleagues/friends/family?
❏ Yes ❏ No

Any further comments:
_____
_____

A questionnaire form

Focus groups or user panels target a particular segment of people, who are invited to participate. They are led by a researcher to discuss aspects of service or ideas for forthcoming changes. The sessions are often recorded to allow the researcher to lead discussions without having to note down all the responses.

Theory into practice

Summarise the different types of primary research and where each method might be used.

Conducting secondary research

Secondary research involves accessing information or data which has already been published. It is sometimes known as 'library' or 'desk' research. Data can be found within an organisation or outside it.

Internal data is information already gathered by the organisation. Many sports organisations record the total number of users and sales information. Details on a database can be used to identify the number of off-peak users of a health club in comparison to the number of peak-time visitors.

External data is information available from outside the organisation. This could include searching the Internet for data on competitors, or gathering leaflets detailing their programmes of activities. The government, via Her Majesty's Stationery Office, produces many publications used by market researchers. These include:

- annual summaries of statistics, such as information on the value of goods purchased in a sector
- economic trends, providing information on the general economic situation
- social trends, giving social statistics
- census information, which gives the most detailed information on all aspects of the population and is published every 10 years.

Libraries normally hold this information, and it can be used to examine market segments and their

potential. For example, the fact that people are living longer means the 'grey' market is growing and may be a useful target. Organisations can also work out the size of their markets in order to set market share objectives.

Non-official sources of data are also published by specialist research organisations such as Mintel or in the trade journals.

Theory into practice

Working in small groups, undertake primary research on the sports provision at your school or college. Before you start your research, identify your objectives and specifically what you hope to find, such as younger students' opinions on sports facilities. Each person within the group should select a different method, such as observation, telephone interview, personal interview, direct mail or focus group. Record all the problems and difficulties you encounter in gathering your information, and compare your findings with those of other groups.

Qualitative research

The essence of qualitative research is that it is based on people's perceptions and opinions about products, services and organisations. It attempts to discover why customers exhibit certain kinds of behaviour, for example brand loyalty. It is subjective and as such is not conclusive.

However, this method can provide unique insights into consumer behaviour that cannot often be gathered through statistical evidence. These insights might lead to more creative approaches to marketing strategies. This method is often used when new programmes and activities are tried by organisations. Typical questions posed by the qualitative researcher are:

- What do you think of the new service?
- If you could change something, what would it be and why?
- What are the positive and negative aspects of the service?

Quantitative research

This method deals in numbers. The research produces statistical findings on the consumers, the market and the performance of the organisation. It is often easier to gather this information; it can be simpler to count the number of members or visitors to an outdoor activity centre than to find out what they thought of their experiences during their visit.

Statistical information on market share, sales and numbers of visitors can be used by marketers to quantify objectives, such as increasing turnover by 10%. Quantitative data can be used to help measure whether objectives have been met, but may not always identify why.

Sampling

Sampling is one of the main methods used by researchers. It would be impossible to discover the opinions of *all* those in a targeted segment, such as the grey market. Sampling collects data from small, representative groups and uses the theory of probability to suggest that the findings will reflect the whole group from which the sample was taken. 'Taking a bite out of a cake will tell you what the whole cake tastes like' is the rationale often used to justify this method. The two main methods used are random and quota sampling.

- **Quota sampling** is the non-random selection of a sample based on certain basic population characteristics such as age, gender, those with children or perhaps those in employment. The researcher selects the sample according to the quotas allocated to different groups. For example, a personal interviewer may ask the opinions of ten women and ten men who visit a sports centre, where the total numbers of female and male visitors are equal.

- **Random sampling** means that everyone has an equal chance of being selected for study. For example, telephone interviewers attempting to gather information may select every fiftieth telephone number to call.

Classification of data

Once the information has been gathered it should be organised into groups or classes with similar characteristics. Non-statistical information, such as the opinions of users on customer service, could be classified according to positive and negative results and whether these were from men or women or from a specific age group.

There are many methods of processing data, both manual and electronic.

Analysing findings

Once the data has been collected, stored and classified, the process of analysis must take place. This is where the information is interpreted to identify significant findings or possible relationships, for example to discover if there is a correlation between those using a facility during off-peak hours and their employment status.

The analysis of data from samples, questionnaires and surveys may produce averaged percentages and a variety of findings. Statistical methods such as correlation analysis, often found in specialist computer software programmes, can be used. The difficulty is always transferring the findings to your marketing strategy. Data analysis allows you to do this with a greater degree of confidence.

Case study

The local football club wants to offer new facilities and entertainment in the hope of attracting a wider audience. It undertakes some secondary market research to establish what other football teams are doing, and also undertakes primary research to establish a profile of existing customers.

1 How could the club discover which segments of the market it could aim its new ideas at?

2 What other information would it need to help it achieve its new objectives?

Analysing influences on the business environment

Internal factors

An organisation may wish to analyse its current strengths and weaknesses – not only its products and services, but how it organises and carries out its marketing. A SWOT analysis (strengths, weaknesses, opportunities and threats) can be used at any stage or level within the marketing function.

The team will attempt to identify the strengths and weaknesses of the organisation, in this case specifically in relation to marketing. They will then explore the opportunities available and the threats from outside the organisation. Within the SWOT analysis it is essential that the organisation evaluates its products and services as well as its overall structure and methods of marketing.

- **Strengths** could include qualified and experienced staff, a well-resourced facility with modern equipment, and an established place in the market.

- **Weaknesses** may include a shortage of skills in a specific area, a small market share, an unknown logo, a bureaucratic management structure, or poor accessibility for customers.

- **Opportunities** may include new products to offer to customers, or products for new markets. Links with other organisations to exchange information may be possible.

- **Threats** may come from a product becoming outdated, a possible reduction in the marketing budgets or a competitor developing more sophisticated systems of operation.

Once the SWOT analysis has been written it must be used by senior management to modify objectives and create a marketing plan where appropriate.

External factors

Many organisations focus exclusively on the internal factors that affect their marketing, because they have more control and influence over these. However, there are many factors external to the organisation which, even though they are outside its control, must be addressed because they may have a significant impact on core business.

The business environment is constantly changing at home and abroad, and very often these changes have an effect on the organisation. This study of the external influences on an organisation can be divided into four elements and called a PEST analysis. The four elements are:

- political
- economic
- social
- technological.

A fifth element, environmental factors, is often included. The findings from such a study can help prepare the organisation by providing the information necessary for planning.

Political elements include the laws, regulations and guidelines that affect every company. These may be focused on protecting people, consumers and communities. Changes in the law, as we have seen recently with the Children's Act and the Disability Act, have necessitated changes in procedures and in many cases to the physical structures of facilities. Organisations may have to invest capital and re-train staff to ensure new legislation and regulations are adhered to.

A change in the political parties in power at central and local government level can result in very different business conditions. Some local authorities and councillors are very keen to develop sport and leisure facilities and bid to host international events, such as the World Student Games in Sheffield and the Commonwealth Games in Manchester. It is therefore common sense to have a sound knowledge of the national and local political parties and the issues on their political agenda. Even though these are external issues, an organisation can influence decision making through lobbying and pressure groups.

Economic factors are inextricably linked with political ones. Basic economic principles, especially the factors of supply and demand, are central to any organisation. The market should be analysed in terms of demand for sports products and services, and who and what is being supplied. The level and nature of demand can change due to increases or decreases in:

- disposable income, through higher or lower unemployment or wages
- competition
- taxes and other expenses.

The level and nature of supply can also change due to:

- increases in the cost of raw materials or funding
- changes in interest rates
- changes in market demand.

The economic activity of the nation, and in particular the community in which the organisation is situated, can have dramatic effects on provision, pricing and services offered. David Lloyd Health Clubs actively target areas where there are people with more disposable income.

The **social** environment is made up of a number of issues that affect the way we behave in the societies in which we live. Attitudes, desires, education, beliefs and customs all change behaviour in society. In the sports industry, the facility manager needs to be aware of the demographics of his or her community, in particular the structure in terms of age, family, ethnicity, gender and class.

A clear picture of general social trends and those locally will help providers to meet the needs of individuals. A simple example is a rise in the numbers of single parents, which has resulted in facilities providing crèches. Changes in social behaviour include increased interest in health and fitness, which has led to many new providers offering facilities, and others changing their existing provision.

Technological developments can have a significant impact on any organisation. Technology affects the way we design, produce, sell, distribute and communicate all our goods and services.

Businesses must continue to be aware of technological developments and changes in methods of operation which affect their products and services. Failure to do this can result in the competition providing more up-to-date services.

Environmental factors are also taken into consideration by many organisations. This is because of the increasing influence of environmental pressure groups as well as a general increase in awareness on the part of the public about environmental issues. In response to these issues, organisations produce environmental policies which often support projects such as those improving their local landscape.

The PEST analysis is difficult to undertake if each factor is dealt with in isolation. Very often one issue, such as a rise in local unemployment, can have an impact in all four areas. It is best used as a method to ensure there is some ongoing analysis of the external environment, and consideration of how this may affect the planning and operation of the organisation.

Theory into practice

Produce a report on the marketing strategies of two sports organisations. These should be in two different sectors of the industry. Use primary and secondary research techniques to discover each organisation's overall missions and objectives and its marketing objectives. Undertake SWOT and PEST analyses of each organisation, as well as identifying the research techniques each uses.

Develop a marketing mix

In developing the marketing mix, managers make decisions relating to the 'four Ps': product, price, place and promotion. All of these are focused on achieving objectives. Most marketing in the service sector takes into account seven Ps: the four already mentioned, plus the people involved, the physical resources, and the process – the experiences of customers.

The seven Ps of the service sector marketing mix

The development of the mix often reflects the organisation's mission statements and objectives. The boundaries between the voluntary, public and commercial sectors have become less distinct, as all sectors strive for growth and efficiency by reducing overheads and meeting the needs of their customers, visitors, members or community.

The traditional mix

It is important to note that in deciding the details of the traditional marketing mix, the four Ps are not taken in isolation. Market research (including customer and staff feedback and details from SWOT and PEST analyses) greatly influences the components of the mix. A change in product or service can influence the price, where it is sold and how this is communicated to the market.

Product or service

In the sports industry products and services can be complex and multidimensional.

Products can be packaged and stored. They may have a sell-by date and be subject to quality checks, and are more likely to be standardised across production. They will have a clear unit cost so that customers can see they will pay more for a better quality product. Management have to decide, based on the needs of customers, on:

- features
- presentation
- name
- design.

These marketing decisions can have a dramatic effect on consumer decisions. Features that no competing products offer are known as 'unique selling points' (USPs). A USP may be the focus for advertising and the overall promotional campaign.

Services are performed, and unlike products are difficult to measure. They can be owned only temporarily; services are therefore perishable, such as an aerobics class. Your purchase only lasts for the duration of the class.

The International Organisation for Standardisation offers standards, such as ISO 9000, to help ensure quality in service provision. ISO 9000 is a family of standards concerned with quality management. It offers standards and guidelines relating to management systems – what an organisation can do to ensure its products and services conform to customer requirements.

The goal of an organisation is to ensure that services are of a continually high standard for each customer and for each time the customer uses the service.

Services are packaged to meet targeted groups of customers. For example, families who join a health club may be attracted to the package of services such as a crèche, swimming lessons for the children and family changing facilities.

A **product item** is a specific product or service that has its own price and function, such as a swimming session for £3, a gym session for £3. A **product line** is where a group of products or services are marketed closely together as they have similar characteristics, such as use of fitness services in a sports centre, including swim and gym, for £5.

Branding

Most suppliers of products and services want them to have a clear identity differentiated from competitors. This is achieved by 'branding'. The brand is the visual, emotional and overall image that you associate with a company or a product.

Brands often have a logo, such as the 'tick' associated with Nike. The supplier will try to create awareness and preference among customers for its brand. As well as the brand name and logo, this is achieved through brand associations such as Michael Jordan with Nike.

Product life cycle

Products, services, activities and programmes have a life span; they are introduced to the public and go through stages. The traditional life cycle is considered to have four stages.

- **Introduction**, where the product is introduced to the public, usually with an aggressive promotional strategy. This is a period of slow growth as products become known by the target markets.
- **Growth**, where there is a more rapid growth in sales and market acceptance, and branding is developed.
- **Maturity**, where there is a period of a slowdown in sales growth and profit margins

fall, and where competition is perhaps most intense.

- **Decline**, the period where sales fall because the product no longer meets the needs of the target market.

In sport there is evidence that not all products go through the full cycle as identified in the diagram. Some never take off into the growth stage, and some products with 'fad' status do not go through maturity, but straight into decline.

Products should be reviewed regularly to identify where they are in their life cycle and whether they are meeting the needs of customers. All products and services try to maintain **core values**. These may include aspects such as:

- value for money
- reliability
- durability
- support
- consistency.

These core values are often the reasons for customers to revisit the facility.

Price

The price the customer pays for products and services includes direct and indirect costs.

- Direct costs are the purchase price for the product or service, for example the admission fee for a swimming pool.
- Indirect costs are costs associated with the purchase, which could include travel fares or parking and petrol costs, and food and drink consumed on the premises.

Organisations select their pricing policies and strategies in accordance with their objectives.

Commercial sector organisations may want to make a quick profit, or even a quick loss, such as offering greatly reduced prices in an attempt to attract new customers to their facilities. The public sector may have to take into account subsidy and equity in the pricing of products and services.

There are basically two ways to determine price: cost-focused pricing and economic-focused pricing.

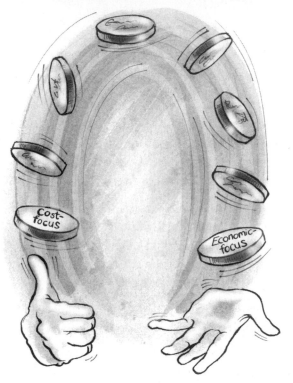

There are two ways of determining price

- **Cost-focused pricing** is based on the total fixed and variable costs associated with producing and delivering the products. Fixed costs are the same, irrespective of the number of customers, and may include rent, rates, lighting, heating, equipment and insurance.

  Variable costs fluctuate with the number of people using the facilities, such as raw materials, staff and cleaning costs.

  The total cost is then calculated to include a profit margin in order to arrive at the price of the product.

- **Economic-focused pricing** is based on the management's perceptions of the value which the customer will place on the product or service. The cost of a service may be £10, but the perception might be that a customer would be willing to pay £30. A good example can be found in many sports footwear products with a strong brand image. People are willing to pay over £100 for branded trainers which are produced at a cost much lower than this.

Economic-focused pricing decisions are based on factors of supply and demand. When demand is high, especially where there is limited competition, prices can be high. When demand is low, prices are often low irrespective of the total costs of production.

Sports organisations are greatly influenced by fashion, the time of the year, competitors, their targeted groups and their products. Their pricing policies reflect the characteristics of their services, such as perishability, and may include the following factors.

- **Seasonality.** The time of year has a direct influence on the costs of products and services. An organisation offering services during holiday periods, such as Christmas, may have increased costs such as staff overtime, and may charge extra for its products. Skiing is only available when there is snow, and therefore its costs reflect the fact that the season for skiing is relatively short.

- **Discounting.** This is a method used to meet any discrepancies between supply and demand. It involves reducing the original stated price if facilities have not been booked or items have not been sold. Discounting also takes place where customers buy in bulk or make long-term bookings, such as hiring astro turf for a full year. Discounts can be given because an income is guaranteed rather than relying on individual bookings or sales.

- **Discrimination pricing.** This is where different prices are offered for the same service. Leisure centres may offer prices based on the different segments, such as reductions for pensioners, or for activities at off-peak times. Football and rugby clubs may charge different prices based on the location of seats in their stands.

Westgate Climbing Wall

User prices	
Registration fee: Adults £2 Concessions/Under 16s £1	
Adults	£6.80
Concessions	£5.80
Under 16s	£4.50

Regular user prices		
Regular user fee £20	Peak	Off peak
Adults	£5.50	£4.50
Concessions	£4.50	£4.00
Under 16s	£4.00	£3.50

Lunchtime sessions		
12 noon–2 pm	User	Regular user
Adults	£3.25	£2.50
Concessions	£2.75	£2.25
Under 16s	£2.25	£2.00

Student term tickets
£65 per term.
Three term tickets for £170
Tickets run:
1 October – 31 December
1 January – 31 March
1 April – 30 June

Course prices
Junior beginners: £20
Beginners: £70/£65 concessions
Improvers: £60/£55 concessions
Taster sessions: £15 per person (min. charge £25)
Birthday parties: £15 per head including food

Annual membership prices
Adult £250
Junior £175
Full family £500 (2 adults and up to 2 kids)
Half family £350 (1 adult and up to 2 kids)
Same address: £425 (2 adults)

Sports facilities' pricing structures must take many factors into account

Pricing is a complex part of the marketing mix. It is a difficult task attempting to satisfy customers, work with the forces of supply and demand and cover the costs of delivering the product or service.

Theory into practice

What is the difference between variable and fixed costs?

Place

This is a critical element of the marketing mix – people may want the product at the price quoted, but choose not to purchase at the location where it is offered.

This is a topical issue with the continual growth of the sports business, especially out-of-town developments. Sports centres are highly dependent on people being prepared to travel to use their services. Many organisations target certain locations based on demographics. They would consider:

- the cost of the site
- the number of residents within a certain distance
- the socio-economic status of the community
- the infrastructure, including accessibility by road, bus routes and parking.

The 'place' aspect also includes the organisation's physical resources. The place may be a park, gym, or sports centre and will have a visual image, certain resources and a particular atmosphere. It is common sense to provide facilities which are welcoming and attractive. Once inside the facility the location of services is important, especially those which complement each other, such as children's activity areas and spectator seating.

Distribution is an important element of place. This refers to the channels whereby products are purchased, either directly from the producer or via an intermediary. The greatest influence on distribution has been the development of technology. It is commonplace nowadays for customers to purchase tickets and consumer items via the Internet.

Distribution strategies depend on the nature of the organisation and the size of the business. Businesses operating solely within a community and managed by the public sector may decide to distribute their facilities and programmes to targeted or disadvantaged groups. Conversely, larger commercial organisations may aim to standardise their distribution channels to gain economies of scale.

Promotion

This includes all forms of communication methods that are used to persuade customers that their needs can be satisfied by using your organisation's products and services. The 'promotion mix' is the chosen use of the types of marketing communication available, namely advertising, direct marketing, public relations, personal selling, promotions and sponsorship.

- **Advertising** means communication that is paid for and transmitted via the media, such as on television or radio, in newspapers and magazines.

- **Direct marketing** is where mail, telephone and computers are used to contact prospective customers and existing customers.

- **Public relations** is the way the organisation attempts to control and manage the publicity it receives via the media, for example by issuing press releases.

- **Personal selling** normally involves face-to-face communication, where trained salespeople persuade customers to purchase and use their services.

- **Promotions** are used by many organisations to attract attention, and often free publicity. They may involve holding an event and/or giving away sample products.

- **Sponsorship** is where the organisation provides finance and/or goods in return for exposure of its name or brands. This is popular in sport, such as with football teams.

Many organisations use the AIDA acronym to classify their marketing aims; they aim to create in their customers Awareness, Interest, Desire and Action.

- **Awareness** means ensuring that the targeted customers are aware of the services being offered. Careful selection of the media to be used to create this awareness is essential, and marketers are well aware of which segmented groups read which newspapers and magazines, and which television programmes they tend to watch.

- **Interest** must be gained once the customer is aware that the service exists. This can be achieved by having something eye-catching and appealing that is closely associated with the brand.

- **Desire** is where the promotional method has established an interest and provided information that makes the potential customer want to purchase the product or service.

- **Action** is the final stage, and all communication must clearly inform the potential customer of how he or she can act to purchase the product or service.

The service sector mix

The service sector marketing mix focuses on the performance of the service in terms of the people involved in supplying and consuming the service, the physical resources used, and the process, which is the customer's experience of using the service.

People

Managers in the sports industry are constantly looking at the people involved in providing the service and those customers at whom the marketing mix is aimed.

The people providing the service are employees, who might be full-time, part-time, casual, or perhaps volunteers. Everyone involved should be trained to provide a service which meets and exceeds customer expectations.

They need to be kept informed as to the organisation's objectives. Most employees will be dealing with customers face-to-face and therefore they need to have detailed knowledge of products, prices and promotions. This can be communicated through meetings, staff bulletins and memoranda.

The customers and potential customers should be the focal point of all elements of the marketing mix. Market research underpins any developments of the mix. For example, a sports centre wanting to change its programming by offering swimming for the disabled will need information on the potential market as well as the needs of the targeted group. The prices and timing of such activities and how the information is to be communicated to the targeted group are also crucial factors. The facility manager would work with disability and special needs groups to decide whether the existing staff are sufficiently trained to provide an appropriate level of service.

Physical resources

This element of the mix reviews the physical elements of service provision. It will examine the environment where the products and services are sold and the effect the physical environment has on provision.

For example, a health club may provide a range of services such as fitness testing, fitness advice, aerobics classes and circuit training, and offer them to a high standard. But there may be a lack of atmosphere caused by poor maintenance of public areas, poor layout of equipment, lack of air conditioning and other environmental factors which affect the service.

Many managers who organise sports events are very conscious of the importance of creating a visually attractive and welcoming facility. Many organisations use specific colours in flooring, uniforms and lighting which research has shown appeal to service users. It is worth noting, however, that sports facilities are often restricted as to the colours they can use – governing bodies of sport may impose requirements regarding surfaces and walls.

It is important to create a visually attractive and welcoming facility

Process

This is an essential element of the service sector mix. It follows the experience of the customer from the first contact with the organisation, through the use of the service and the after-service experience. A stadium manager may feel the company is providing a good choice of events at a selection of prices, and have trained staff to deal with customers. However, a customer may have experienced difficulty in parking, had to queue for a ticket and received no help when asking directions.

Process therefore looks at the whole of customers' perceptions and experiences of using the services. It is not feasible to expect that an organisation can satisfy each individual person's needs, but exploring the full experience of a customer should identify any areas that need improvement.

Theory into practice

What are the elements of the service sector mix, and how do they differ from the traditional mix?

Case study

The Devine Hotel, situated on the outskirts of a city, has 85 bedrooms and has begun work on building a leisure club to be used by residents and non-residents, who can become members. The facilities are to include a cardiovascular area, 15 resistance training machines, a kidney-shaped pool, jacuzzi, steam room, sauna, standing sunshower, aerobic and multipurpose room, and a food and bar area.

The management team have carefully laid out their marketing strategy and identified some SMART objectives they wish to achieve within the first year of opening. These include targets on membership numbers, quality of service and turnover. They have also undertaken SWOT and PEST analyses and believe they have the right marketing mix that will appeal to residents as well as the local community. There are other health and fitness facilities in the area run by the public sector, primarily consisting of a sports hall and a small

multipurpose room attached to the swimming pool. There is also a privately owned tennis and fitness centre in the area.

1 What methods can the management team use to calculate its pricing policies?

2 What could the organisation do to try to develop a brand that would be easily recognised by the general public, and in line with its objectives?

Assessment activity 14.2

Undertake some primary market research that will provide feedback on your chosen business idea. It should provide information that can be recorded and presented in diagram form. Produce a marketing plan that identifies all aspects of the marketing mix, paying particular attention to promotion and product. Include at least three different visual ideas for promotional methods such as a logo, poster or brochure.

Finally, produce a report on your proposed organisation and its environment, using PEST and SWOT analyses.

Legal and financial requirements

When starting a business, many legal and financial aspects must be carefully researched and planned. Once an idea has been clearly established it is a good idea to consult with legal and financial specialists. Financial advisors, banks, and business start-up advisors often don't make direct charges for this advice but make their profit in the prices for products or services business people may use in the future, such as an overdraft facility at the bank.

Statutory requirements

There are many legal duties placed on those wishing to start a business enterprise in sport. In the day-to-day running of any organisation it is the responsibility of all concerned to provide a healthy, safe and secure environment for those working on site, for customers and any visitors.

Health and safety

There are many statutes and guidelines covering health, safety and security. It is important to keep up to date with changes in legislation and always to seek specialist advice where appropriate, especially for those involved in the voluntary sector, such as coaches and event organisers.

The **Health and Safety at Work Act 1974** is the main piece of legislation. It has been expanded in European legislation, first by the Management of Health and Safety at Work Regulations 1992. These have been superseded by the Management of Health and Safety at Work Regulations 1999. The overall aims remain the same:

- securing the health, safety and welfare of people at work

- protecting people other than those at work (e.g. participants) against risks to health and safety arising from the activities of people at work

- controlling handling and storage of dangerous substances

- controlling the emission into the atmosphere of noxious or offensive substances from premises.

The main aim of the Health and Safety at Work Act is to involve everyone – management, owners and employees – and to make them aware of the importance of health and safety.

It is the duty of employers, as far as is reasonably practicable, to safeguard the health, safety and welfare of the people who work for them as well as that of non-employees (customers, visitors, members of the general public) on the premises. These duties are:

- to provide and maintain plant, equipment and systems of work which are safe and which are not a risk to health

- to provide safe storage, handling and use of substances that could cause a risk to health

- to provide appropriate information, instruction and training for employees in regard to health and safety

- to make certain the workplace is monitored and maintained in a safe condition.

Under the Health and Safety at Work Act, the employee also has responsibilities. Employees must:

- take reasonable care of their own health and safety

- take reasonable care of the health and safety of others who may be affected by their actions

- co-operate with the employer and other relevant organisations to ensure that the requirements of the act are met (this includes notifying supervisors of unsafe equipment or practices)

- not misuse equipment provided to maintain health and safety.

Key concept

The Health and Safety at Work Act imposes responsibilities on both employers and employees.

The Health and Safety at Work Act also requires that an organisation has a safety committee, safety representatives and devises a policy statement containing the following information:

- the organisation's commitment to health, safety and welfare at work

- the hierarchy within the organisation

- those responsible for health and safety

- all relevant codes of practice and advice covering the particular functions carried out at the premises. These include emergency first aid, pool and ice activities.

The **Management of Health and Safety at Work Regulations 1999** incorporate legislation on pregnant women and young workers. The following areas are covered and need to be addressed when commencing any business:

- risk assessment

- preventative and protective measures
- health and safety arrangements
- health surveillance
- procedures for serious and imminent danger
- information and training
- new and expectant mothers and young workers.

Even though much of the legislation covers organisations of five or more employees, smaller businesses are not free from liability for civil action for any damages suffered due to negligence.

The **Control of Substances Hazardous to Health Regulations 2002** are relevant to sports business because it is highly probable that even in the smallest of sport organisations such substances will be in use. These can include chemicals for cleaning and disinfecting, treating water or marking out grass pitches. Employers are required to identify, assess, monitor and control all substances hazardous to health under the regulations. Failure to comply constitutes an offence under the Health and Safety at Work Act 1974. Any risks in handling dangerous substances should be identified, and clear systems of work should be developed. Approved and recommended precautions will prevent exposure.

Substances have many different properties and potential to cause harm. The human body may be at risk through inhalation via the nose, ingestion via the mouth and absorption via the skin. All potentially dangerous substances must be handled and stored correctly.

Theory into practice

For a sport of your choice, investigate which potentially hazardous substances are used in connection with the sport, its equipment or the premises where it is played. List these substances together with the precautions necessary for their use. Share your findings with the rest of your group.

The **Health and Safety (First Aid) Regulations 1981** are found under the general duty of care in section 2 of the Health and Safety at Work Act. The duty of employers extends to the duty to provide first aid. The regulations cover three broad areas.

- The duty of the employer to provide first aid. These provisions must be 'adequate and appropriate' to the organisation. This depends on the number of employees, the type of work, and the location of employees. A general rule is to have at least one first aider for every 50 employees. Most sports organisations have more than this to cover different sites, outdoor/indoor and wet/dry provisions, as well as shift rotations. First aid boxes and first aid rooms must be identified. The overall aim is to ensure every employee has reasonably quick access to basic medical care.

- The duty of the employer to inform the employees of first aid arrangements. This includes a clear notice of the regulations and procedures involving first aid, as well as identification of people qualified as first aiders, and where first aid equipment is located.

- The duty of the self-employed person to provide first aid equipment. This is applicable

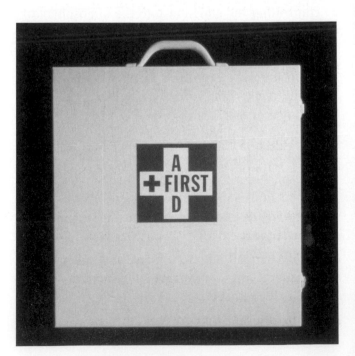

to those who run their own coaching programmes or any other self-employed person.

There are many other legal duties regarding health and safety that you need to be aware of when setting up in business, and if at any time you are unsure of your legal duties you should seek professional support.

Employment law

People and organisations who employ staff also have other duties. The next section briefly outlines the main duties and responsibilities of employers.

The Fitness Industry Association describes the three types of employment applicable to the industry as follows.

- **Regular workers** (full- and part-time) are contracted to work and required to carry out their duties, or an agreed number of hours, on a regular basis. These contracts are open ended and remain in force until terminated by dismissal, resignation or retirement.
- **Fixed-term workers** are employees who work an agreed number of hours for a specific time. The recommended maximum length of a fixed-term contract is five months.
- **Casual workers** are hired as and when required and for a fixed term. These contracts are sometimes referred to as 'zero-hours' contracts.

The Part-Time Workers (Prevention of Less Favourable Treatment) Regulations 2000 give part-time workers the right to the same terms and conditions of employment as comparable full-time workers. A part-time worker can claim he or she is comparable to a full-time worker if both:

- work for the same employer, at any workplace
- work under the same type of contract
- do similar work
- have similar skills, qualifications and experience.

Under the **Employment Rights Act 1996**, every employee is entitled to:

- not be discriminated against on the basis of sex, race or disability

- not be unfairly dismissed
- receive written reasons for dismissal
- receive and give a statutory minimum period of notice
- maternity leave – qualifying employees also have the right to receive statutory maternity pay
- receive a Statement of Particulars of employment (see below)
- receive statutory sick pay.

People who employ others must be careful about what they offer to prospective employees from the start. When advertising, don't imply terms and conditions that cannot be honoured. Make offers conditional on the receipt of satisfactory references and confirmation of medical fitness.

The offer of an employment contract can be revoked if it has not been accepted. Once accepted, termination of the contract would require payment for the contractual notice period. The employer must issue a contract to new employees within eight weeks of their start date. Contracts can contain:

- express terms – those set out in writing by the parties
- implied terms – assumed to be in the contract due to the parties' actions, custom and practice, common law duties or statute
- incorporated terms – brought into the contract, explicitly or implicitly, usually from collective agreements or works rules.

Key concept

An employment contract is not just the written statement of particulars that the employer supplies. It includes express terms, implied terms and incorporated terms.

Under the Employment Rights Act, employers must provide written details of employment (also called a Statement of Particulars) to any worker to be employed for a month or longer, and they must provide it within the first two months of employment. It should include:

- names of the employer and employee
- employee's job title
- date of commencement
- details of salary or wages and when paid
- normal hours of work
- details of any pension scheme
- details of period of notice
- rules for disciplinary and grievance procedures
- terms and conditions regarding injury and sickness
- place of work
- entitlement to holiday (in sufficient detail for the entitlement to be exactly calculated)
- if the period of work is temporary, the period for which work is expected to continue.

The **minimum wage** for an adult aged 22 and over is £4.50 per hour from October 2003. The 'development rate', for workers aged 18-21 inclusive, is £3.80 per hour from October 2003.

The **Working Time Regulations 1998** implement the EU Working Time Directive. Introduced to ensure the health and safety of workers, the regulations stipulate minimum rest periods and a maximum limit on working hours. The regulations apply to all employees over the minimum school-leaving age with a contract of employment, and to agency and freelance workers who are under contract. They do not apply to workers in the air, railway or sea transport sectors, nor to doctors in training.

The regulations state that there should be minimum daily rest period of 11 consecutive hours out of every 24-hour period. In addition, there should also be a rest break every six hours, of 20 minutes, during the working day, and a rest of 24 consecutive hours per week. Agreements may be made between workers and employers varying the rights to rest periods and rest breaks, with workers receiving 'compensatory rest'.

The regulations set a maximum average working week of 48 hours, but under certain circumstances the average can be extended if an agreement is made between workers and employers.

The average working time of a night worker is set at eight hours in each 24-hour period, averaged over four months. Workers are entitled to a health check before performing night work, and further checks thereafter.

Statutory Maternity Rights include:

- the right to time off for antenatal care
- the right to maternity leave
- the right to maternity benefit (Statutory Maternity Payment or Maternity Allowance).

In addition to statutory maternity rights, women are also entitled to:

- protection against unfair treatment or dismissal
- health and safety protection (from their employers) while pregnant, recently after birth and while breastfeeding
- protection against sex discrimination.

The above rights are a minimum standard which employers must meet. In the absence of such arrangements, an employee is free to claim statutory maternity rights.

Self-employed and unemployed persons are not covered by statutory maternity rights.

Under the Working Time Directive, full-time employees over the age of 17 who have worked for an employer for three months or more have **holiday entitlements**. They have the right to four weeks' paid holiday per year, including public holidays. Temporary and part-time workers are entitled to paid holiday on a pro-rata basis.

Employees are expected to give employers a notice period twice as long as the holiday they intend to take. For example, two weeks' notice is needed for a one-week holiday. An employer can object to a request for a holiday by giving counter-notice of the same period as the requested holiday, for example, giving two weeks' notice that the request has not been granted where two weeks' holiday was asked for.

Discrimination against anyone on the grounds of sex, race, disability, or trade union membership or non-membership is illegal, and this applies not only when recruiting or dismissing staff, but also during the course of their contract. Wages, promotion chances, training, fringe benefits and the allocation of work are all areas where a company must ensure that discrimination does not take place. The key Acts of Parliament that outlaw such discrimination are:

- Sex Discrimination Act 1986
- Equal Pay Act 1984
- Race Relations Act 1976
- Disability Discrimination Act 1995
- Trade Union and Labour Relations (Consolidation) Act 1992.

Employment tribunals are government bodies that deal with disputes about employment and industrial relations. The tribunals are organised on a regional basis and governed by the Employment Tribunals Act 1996 and the Employment Tribunals (Constitution and Procedure) Regulations 1993.

Employment tribunals deal with a wide range of individual aspects of employment law including:

- the written particulars of employment
- redundancy payments
- equal pay
- race relations
- time off work
- dismissal.

Insurance

The security of people, property, information and money all need to be clearly arranged. A security risk assessment should be carried out for your business. For example, you may want to hold stock in a storage facility. This will obviously need to be insured. Any insurance company will want to know what the security arrangements are before quoting on premises. Extra arrangements may have to be included, such as an alarm system that is linked to the police.

The level and type of insurance will depend upon the nature of the business and the findings from the health, safety and security risk analysis. Insurance can be purchased for:

- public and personal liability
- personal accident
- cancellation
- fire and theft
- medical cover.

The insurance will normally be arranged through an insurance broker, who would need to know all the details of the business, including numbers of visitors, hazards such as any fire and water that may be involved, and other organisations involved and their roles.

Licensing

Any business enterprise requires a license to sell alcohol or provide public entertainment, and there are many associated legal duties. About 111,000 premises in England & Wales hold on-licences, allowing them to sell alcohol for consumption on or away from the premises. About 45,000 premises in England & Wales hold off-licences, allowing them to sell alcohol for consumption only away from the premises. About 23,000 registered members' clubs hold a registration certificate, allowing them to supply alcohol to members and guests on their club premises.

The Department for Culture, Media and Sport is responsible for the law relating to alcohol and public entertainment licensing in England and Wales. Currently, alcohol licensing is governed primarily by the Licensing Act 1964, while public entertainment licensing for areas outside London is primarily governed by the Local Government (Miscellaneous Provisions) Act 1982, and for areas in London by the London Government Act 1963.

The Licensing Act 2003 attempts to provide a balanced package of freedoms and safeguards. It aims to clamp down on crime, disorder and anti-social behaviour perpetrated by a minority, and give the responsible majority more freedom and choice about how they spend their leisure time.

Key measures contained in this act are as follows.

- Flexible opening hours, with the potential for up to 24-hour opening, seven days a week, subject to consideration of the impact on local residents. This aims to minimise public disorder resulting from fixed closing times.

- A single scheme for licensing premises which sell alcohol, provide public entertainment or provide refreshment late at night. This will bring together the six existing licensing regimes (alcohol, public entertainment, cinemas, theatres, late night refreshment houses and night cafés), cutting down on red tape.

- A new system of personal licences which allow holders to sell or serve alcohol for consumption on or off any premises possessing a premises licence.

- Personal and premises licences to be issued by local authorities.

Planning

Any building of new premises or conversion of existing ones will have to follow strict guidelines on building and also on usage and opening and closing times. Local authority planning officers will consider access, potential noise problems, the present character of the area and other issues before judging applications.

Case study

Dryland Council has a number of community pools which are all nearing the end of their useful life and recognises the need for a comprehensive strategy which would avoid piecemeal replacements as pools close, and might result in a totally different pattern of provision. Research shows the following:

- many of the city's pools are operating at well below the regional average usage levels, when compared to capacity

- although there is suitable provision in Dryland to meet the demand from city residents, several of the pools are under-performing against model forecasts of usage
- Dryland is probably 'exporting' demand to better pools in surrounding areas, because pools outside the city generally have higher usage than estimated by the model, while Dryland pools have lower usage.

Sport England was consulted and they tested a number of 'what if' scenarios, including a number of pool closures, improvements to certain other pools, and major investment in new pool provision.

The findings of this local assessment led to a number of options which formed the basis of a major public consultation exercise. The council has since published its Pool Strategy and aims to double the number of swimmers in Dryland through the provision of a network of attractive and accessible pools.

1 Identify three examples of good practice by Dryland Council in the planning of sports provision.

2 What issues need to be considered if existing pool facilities are extended?

Byelaws

Local authority byelaws that have their basis in statutes. They impose further legal duties within a particular authority's area. Local authorities pass byelaws on such matters as the use of open spaces, and the hours in which school-age children may be employed.

Key concept

Anyone setting up a business enterprise must seek advice on complying with the relevant byelaws.

Self-employment

If you are self-employed, you must register as such with the Inland Revenue within three months of starting up. You will be responsible for paying your own tax and National Insurance. You will have to fill in a tax return each year and you will be taxed on your profits.

Correctly working out what your business has spent is just as important as how much money has come in. You will need to keep records of all your income and expenditure in order to fill in your tax return each year and pay the correct amount of tax. To work out your profit, you take allowable expenses away from your revenue. There are complex rules governing what you can claim as expenses.

Allowable expenses include the costs of any goods or materials bought as stock and then resold, rent and running costs for premises, marketing costs, costs of travel to see customers, financing costs and general running expenses such as postage and telephone. Costs which are not allowed include personal expenses such as travel to work, clothes or living expenses, entertaining clients and fines such as parking tickets.

The cost of buying equipment or premises (and any reduction in value following the purchase) is not allowed as a business expense – these areas are covered by the capital allowances system.

Finance

When setting up your own business you will have initial set-up costs, then costs to keep the business running, offset by sources of income. If the money coming into the business exceeds the costs of running it you will have made a profit.

You may need to obtain finance to help set up the business or develop it in the future. Financial management skills are essential to enable you to assess your present financial status and help forecast revenue and expenditure. A business may be very successful in terms of sales, market share and growth but still have cashflow difficulties if customers fail to pay on time and suppliers cannot be paid.

Finance required for start-up costs

This can vary considerably depending upon your business idea. Becoming a personal fitness trainer or soccer coach will require spending on items such as marketing and stationery. However, setting up your own fitness gym has considerable initial outlay and will need careful planning.

Theory into practice

Using the items listed below, investigate the start-up costs for the two business enterprises. Total them to find how much finance is required before the business commences.

Start-up costs	Football coach	Fitness gym
Legal/professional fees		
Research		
Premises		
Security		
Insurance		
Equipment		
Transport		
Business stationery		
Fixtures and fittings		
Clothing		
Phone: mobile, land line, answer machine		
Computer		
Utilities		
Council tax		
Premises alterations		
Promotional material		

Operating costs

These costs, sometimes known as running costs, are the day-to-day business expenses, and will vary according to the nature of the business. They include fixed costs and variable costs.

Fixed costs are costs that do not vary as the level of business activity changes, e.g. rent, some insurances, and overheads such as heating and lighting.

Variable costs vary in line with trading activity, e.g. postage and stationery. If you are selling sports equipment you will need to purchase more stock as sales increase, so these costs will vary with the level of sales.

The total of fixed and variable costs provides you with the total costs of the business. It is good practice to break these costs down into monthly figures, which will help when you calculate your cashflow.

Operating profit is the figure which remains after deducting all operating costs (except capital expenses) from sales revenue.

Sources of finance

Businesses are usually financed by equity, debt, grants or a combination of these.

Equity is investment by you, your family or friends, or profits that you retain in the business. It can also come from external sources such as venture capital provided by professional investors, by individuals, or by another business (this is known as corporate venturing). External equity involves raising money by selling shares in your business, in exchange for giving someone else a share of control in the business and a proportion of the profits and future value.

Debt finance can be money borrowed or bank overdrafts, or it can be based on the assets of your firm, such as factoring and invoice discounting, or hire purchase and leasing. The debt is usually secured against the assets of the business, or personally guaranteed by you or others. Your business must be able to generate enough cash to make both interest and capital repayments.

Depending on the nature of the business, it may be possible to obtain finance packages combining debt and equity.

Grants may be available from central or local government, or sports governing bodies. The government does not invest directly in small businesses, but provides incentives to individuals or institutions investing amounts of less than £1 million in unquoted companies.

There are opportunities for start-up businesses that allow you preferential rates on loans and assistance with training, especially if you are located in a government target area.

Venture capital can provide long-term, committed capital to businesses. Venture capitalists purchase shares in growing businesses on behalf of institutional investors. Venture capital investors are tied in to the long-term success of the business, obtaining their return by way of dividends but principally by selling their shares in the business in due course.

Venture capitalists seek businesses capable of growing rapidly within (say) five years. These businesses must be able to demonstrate a competitive advantage in a chosen market and be managed by experienced and ambitious teams who are capable of turning their business plan into reality.

Venture capitalists do not usually get involved in the day-to-day management control of a business but will assist with longer-term strategy. The combination of capital and experienced input from venture capital executives can help businesses to achieve their growth plans and increase value to shareholders. Although the management team may own a smaller 'slice of the cake', this can be compensated by the growth in the overall value of the business.

The British Venture Capital Association (www.bvca.co.uk) provides a detailed guide to the venture capital process, from targeting the appropriate investor to exit choices. This includes advice on preparing a business plan and venture capital terms.

Financial techniques

Financial techniques help assess your financial status and forecast future events. In many instances these techniques will be required in order to secure finance, such as a cashflow forecast prepared for a bank when requesting a loan.

Financial planning is necessary to assess how your business is doing and where it is going in the future. It will also assist in decision making, because purchasing decisions may well hinge on how much cash is available to the business at a given time.

Cashflow forecast

This records when you expect to receive money and when you have to pay it out. You not only have to try to predict sales, but exactly when you might receive the money into your bank. This is done on a month-by-month basis and will inform you of exactly how much money you need each month to ensure your enterprise is sustainable.

Cashflow is the cornerstone of any business and must be reassessed on a regular basis. Your business may be profitable but can experience difficulties if it runs out of cash due to late payments by customers. You can make arrangements to cover this through an overdraft facility at the bank or a loan, but you will have to pay for this, which in turn affects your profit.

A cashflow statement normally has a column for each month and a list of all receipts and payments. See the example on the next page.

The **opening balance** will show the initial money used to open the account, or that has been raised to start the business. Thereafter the opening balance should equal the closing balance of the previous month or statement.

Receipts list all the money coming into the business, including sales to customers, capital coming into the business such as an investor or bank loans, any tax or VAT rebates, or sale of any assets.

Payments include all the money that is paid out of the business including the cost of stock or materials, bank charges, maintenance fees, etc. Each organisation will have different payment terms. Some will allow you to pay monthly but make extra charges. Some organisations will give you 30 days to pay, while others will expect payment by pro-forma, which means you will

Cashflow forecast

	January	February	March	April	May	June
INCOME						
Sales		340	1,900	7,220		920
Finance						
Grants/loans					180	
Other/stock				2,000		
Total income (A)	0	340	1,900	9,220	180	920
EXPENDITURE						
Direct costs						
Stock			200			150
Materials						
Contract labour						
Capital expenditure						
Overheads						
Wages	100	50	50	3,740		50
Other charges					985	
Motor expenses						
Fuel	50	50	50	200		50
Car tax						
Car insurance						
Repairs/MOT						
Other						
Premises						
Rent				2,295		
Rates						
Heat/light/power						
Other						
Travel						
Printing/stationery		500			400	
Postage	550	40	40	40		550
Advertising			200			150
Telephone: landline						
Telephone: mobile	30	30	30	30	30	30
Repairs/renewals						
Insurance			80			
Loan repayments				1,050		
Professional fees	200					
Your drawings						
Total expenditure (B)	930	670	650	7,355	1,415	980
Net in-flow (A-B)	(930)	(330)	1,250	1,865	(1,235)	(60)
Opening balance	0	(930)	(1,260)	(10)	1,855	620
Closing balance	(930)	(1,260)	(10)	1,855	620	560

A cashflow statement

have to pay first before you receive goods. This is especially likely to be the case where you are a new business and do not have a trading record.

At the end of each month the table will calculate the closing **monthly balance** by taking the opening balance, adding receipts and subtracting payments. This figure will tell you what type of business overdraft you are likely to need and whether you can give extra credit terms to customers or whether you need to ask for payment up front.

The monthly figures will also give you feedback that will allow you to plan for each year and will enable you to identify seasonal trends in your business.

Profit-and-loss forecast

This can be used in conjunction with your cashflow statement. The profit-and-loss forecast shows you the amount of profit you can expect to make, taking into account sales, the cost of producing goods or services, and your expenses.

This can be calculated monthly but is often done quarterly, especially as start-up businesses put more emphasis on their cashflow statements. The main purpose of a profit-and-loss forecast is to show how viable your business is going to be. The following are normally included.

- **Sales:** your expected sales forecast. For example, a personal fitness trainer would quote the number of sessions booked with clients for a month, multiplied by the amount charged for each session.

- **Cost of sales:** the calculation of how much it costs your business to provide the services or goods. For example, if you are selling football kits the cost of sales will include the cost of the kits purchased (direct costs) which will increase as sales increase.

- **Gross profit:** the calculation of sales minus the cost of sales. For example:

Month:	January	February	March	April
Sales (turnover)	1500	2000	2500	3000
Cost of sales	750	1000	1250	1500
Gross profit	750	1000	1250	1500

If the sales volume increases, the cost of sales increases. However, quite often suppliers may reduce the amount you have to pay for each unit if you purchase more.

In the example above, the profit margin for January is £750 on a turnover of £1500, or 50%.

- **Expenses:** your costs for running the business, which are not directly related to the cost of producing the goods or services. An example is illustrated opposite.

	Month:	January	February	March	April
1	**Sales (turnover)**	1500	2000	2500	3000
2	**Cost of sales**	750	1000	1250	1500
3	**Gross profit**	750	1000	1250	1500
	Expenses				
	Rent & rates	180	180	180	180
	Heat & light	30	30	30	30
	Insurance	25	25	25	25
	Security	20	20	20	20
	Postage	15	15	15	15
	Maintenance	10	10	10	10
	Motor expenses	50	50	50	50
	Distribution	25	25	25	25
	Telephone	45	45	45	45
	Professional fees				
	Promotion	100	100	100	100
	Bank charges	10	10	10	10
	Interest	5	5	5	5
	Council charges	25	25	25	25
	Depreciation	30	30	30	30
	Miscellaneous	10	10	10	10
4	**Total expenses**	580	580	580	580
5	**Profit/loss (3-4=5)**	170	420	670	920

- **Net profit:** your gross profit minus the total of your expenses. This may well be liable for deductions in tax by the Inland Revenue.

Break-even forecast

The profit-and-loss forecast should provide information to show when your business is breaking even. The break-even point tells a firm what the lowest possible output is at which it can operate without losing money.

Firms use break-even analysis to:

- calculate in advance the level of sales needed to break even
- see how changes in output affect profit
- see how changes in price affect the break-even point and profit

● see how changes in costs affect break-even point and profit.

Break-even analysis can be too simplistic, and many assumptions made are unrealistic. For example:

● it assumes that all output is sold

● it assumes that no stock is held

● it does not account for sudden changes in wages, prices or technology

● it depends on the quality and accuracy of the data.

The margin of safety

When a business is producing output above the break-even point it is useful to know by how much sales could fall before a loss is made. This is called the margin of safety; it is the range of output over which a profit can be made.

This can be calculated by the formula:

Budgeted sales – break-even sales = margin of safety

Theory into practice

In 2002/2003, two enterprising students from a sixth-form college decided to run a pools competition for fellow students.

The price of entry (the selling price) was £2, and the cost of each game to the business was 50p (variable cost). In order to attract as many people as possible they offered a cash prize of £25 to the winner and £10 to the runner-up (fixed costs).

1 How many students did they need to attract to break even?

2 What was the margin of safety if target sales were 50?

To calculate the break-even point for the above scenario using the 'contribution' method, the following equations would be used:

Contribution per unit = selling price per unit – variable costs per unit

Fixed costs/contribution per unit = break-even quantity

The selling price was £2 and the variable cost 50p, so the contribution per unit was £1.50. Fixed costs were £35. Divided by the contribution per unit of £1.50, the result is:

Break-even number of students = 23.33 = 24 students.

Balance sheet forecast

The balance sheet shows the overall trading position of your business. On one side it shows what your business owns, and on the other what it owes. It gives you the amount of assets and liabilities and therefore the net value of the business. The balance sheet forecast can be produced monthly. It will contain the following.

● **Current assets:** assets that have a life span of less than a year, such as stock, cash at the bank and money you are owed (known as debtors).

● **Current liabilities:** money that you owe which is due for payment within a year. Items would include the money you owe to suppliers (known as creditors), tax or overdraft fees.

● **Fixed assets:** assets which normally have an expected life of more than one year, such as motor vehicles, property and large equipment.

● **Net current assets:** the figure you calculate by subtracting current liabilities from current assets.

● **Long-term liabilities:** loans repayable over more than one year.

● **Net assets:** the calculation that adds current and fixed assets and subtracts liabilities.

● **Capital and reserves:** the business's net worth. It is where your net profit (or loss) is shown, plus any money that you have invested in the business.

Key concept

Once these figures have been calculated on your balance sheet, your net assets (less liabilities) should equal your net worth (capital and reserves).

Working capital analysis

This calculation lets you know how 'liquid' you are. Liquidity means the ability of your business to pay its current liabilities. This is calculated by

Debtors + stock + cash – creditors

Ideally your working capital should cover the cost of any purchases before customers pay what they owe to you. This can be quite difficult if sales of products have gone well, and more capital is required.

Budgets

Budgeting is the planning of finances over a given period of time. An individual might plan a budget in order to be able to afford a holiday. For businesses, budgets are financial statements and/or quantitative statements prepared and approved for a defined period of time. They show the policy to be pursued during that period for the purpose of attaining a given objective.

Budgets are used for:

● planning and forecasting
● co-ordination between departments or partners
● keeping control and gaining feedback.

The two key questions to ask when preparing budgets are:

1 **Can revenues be increased in any way?**
   ● Would raising prices affect demand?
   ● Could demand be increased – would advertising be cost-effective?
   ● Could added value be provided, e.g. new services?

2 **Can costs be reduced in any way?**
   ● Can capital costs be reduced?

Theory into practice

Make a list of all the information you would need in order to budget for a week's holiday abroad.

- Should suppliers be changed?
- Should wage rates be lowered?
- Can power costs be reduced?
- Can maintenance costs be reduced?

The various types of budgets are:

- **sales budgets** – forecasts of sales volume at anticipated sales prices
- **expense budgets** – forecasts of direct expenses
- **stock budgets** – forecasts of requirements for stock
- **cash budgets** – forecasts of cashflows
- **marketing budgets** – forecasts of spending on marketing.

Theory into practice

Using the following table as a starting point, set your own budget for a month or term. You goal is to reduce your overdraft (or increase your savings).

Item	Month/term:
Balance at bank	
Income	
From loan	
From family	
From work	
Total income	
Expenses	
Rent	
Loan repayments	
Overdraft charges	
Council tax	
Electricity and gas	
Telephone	
Travel	
House, e.g. repairs, insurance	
Food	
Subscriptions	
Entertainment	
Pension contributions	
Other	
Total expenses	
Balance at bank	

Assessment activity 14.3

1 Briefly identify the main statutory requirements particular to your business idea, including key health and safety issues, insurance, employment laws and licensing.

2 Prepare a proposal that identifies how your business idea can be financed. Identify where the finance will come from and how it is to be repaid.

3 Produce one of each of the following for your business idea:
- break-even forecast
- budget
- cashflow forecast
- projected profit-and-loss account
- projected balance sheet.

Business plans

The writing of a business plan helps to put forward ideas and financial calculations in a conventional format. There are many different formats for writing business plans, some more detailed than others, but all describe the following:

- the idea
- the market
- the people
- market research and promotion plans
- sales forecasts and pricing policy
- premises and equipment
- costs and cashflow.

A business plan gives the first yardstick by which to measure success. It also shows evidence of planning to demonstrate to potential investors, or a bank, that finance issues and the market have been investigated fully. This gives confidence to such investors and increases the likelihood of acquiring financial support.

The business plan also gives an initial idea substance and shows how feasible ideas are. It needs to be as accurate as possible, which means researching some of the sections and seeking support where necessary.

Writing a business plan

The idea

This section describes the business. It should clearly identify the following information.

- **The name of the business.** This is extremely important. The business will almost certainly want e-mail and website addresses, and it needs a name that reflects the type of business but also one that does not already exist as a website. This should be checked in advance.

- **Location.** Where is the business to be located? The full address is needed, for example of a unit that is to be leased. Details of any leases and their penalty clauses should be included. Consideration needs to be given to the kind of premises needed now and what may be needed in the future. What are the business rates? And what insurance and security are needed? In many cases free estimates can be obtained, or information can be gathered from landlords.

- **Proposed activities.** This is essentially a description of the products or services to be offered. These must be described in as much detail as possible; for example, if the business is to organise football competitions, the plan needs to give details of the exact services offered and when the competitions will be run. Customers should be briefly identified, and also what it is that will make the idea successful. Competition, both direct and indirect, should be described, and the unique selling point(s).

- **Type of business.** This identifies the nature of the business and whether it will be trading as a sole trader, partnership or limited company. The nature of the business should dictate the format of the business. For example, new businesses trading as limited companies may find it difficult to obtain trading terms such as credit, whereas this would not be a problem for a sole trader, who has personal liability.

- **Why start the business?** This question will probably be asked by a bank manager and it is always good to have the reasons in writing. A description of skills and any business knowledge or previous experience that may be relevant should be included.

- **Business and personal goals.** Normally banks will ask about the goals for the business, such as to generate profit after six months, to increase market share, etc. Strategic consultants also start by asking people to identify their personal goals, such as to retire early, or work a shorter day. It is important to think about this and record personal goals before identifying business goals.

Market analysis

This should start by identifying who potential customers are, and describe what they may be like, such as male, 35-45, married with children, and in a full-time managerial post. All customers do not have to fit this description but it provides the reader with a clear picture of who the product or service is aimed at.

This section will also include the size of the market and the trends associated with the industry. It could provide some forecast of demand and more detail on the competition. Information on price, what competitors charge for similar products, and how sensitive the market is to price should be included. Competitors' details should be shown in list format. It is also useful to identify competitors' strengths and weaknesses, the organisation's own strengths and weaknesses, and unique selling points.

Management section

This identifies who is going to be involved with or employed by the organisation. Even if some activities, such as delivery, are outsourced, suppliers must be well researched for cost and quality.

Each employee will need a curriculum vitae (CV) and job description, and even if there are only two or four employees it is useful to draw an organisational chart that illustrates the hierarchy and people's roles and responsibilities. Each person who will be part of the organisation needs to record their skills and experience and any contacts or leads they may have in the business.

Financial data

This should include personal banking data and three to six months' banking history (bank statements).

The following are also needed:

- one-year projections for the profit-and-loss account
- start-up balance sheet
- cashflow forecast
- capital expenditure forecast.

Marketing plans

A marketing plan identifies the following:

- customer needs
- features and benefits of products/services
- the target market
- analysis of market research
- promotional plans, including sample materials such as leaflets, etc.

This information should be encapsulated in a plan showing a time frame, and with costs apportioned. See the flow chart opposite.

Resource plans

A resource plan clearly identifies the following, and their associated costs:

- the premises where the business will be located
- the equipment needed, to be purchased or leased
- the materials needed
- human resources such as skills and knowledge, and who will supply them
- financial resources and how they will be sourced.

Time management

Perhaps the most important resource other than financial and human resources is time. Time management is about using time effectively, managing what you do and having some control over how you live and work. In this way you are

To write an effective marketing plan you need to:

Conduct a market audit

Produce a mission statement for your business

Analyse your current marketing position

Formulate a marketing overview

Write a SWOT analysis

Use your knowledge and experience to make assumptions

Develop clear objectives

Broadly state how these objectives will be achieved

Consider your human and financial resource requirements

Decide how you will track progress and measure success

Write an introductory paragraph and executive summary

more likely to meet deadlines and have a successful business. Poor time management can lead to:

- stress caused by missing deadlines
- a feeling of failure
- having to put in maximum effort and often achieving minimum results
- procrastination

Day:					
Time	Number of minutes	Activity	Key area	Priority 0-5	Ideas for improvement
0700					
0800					
0900					
1000					
1100					
1200					
1300					
1400					
1500					
1600					
1700					
1800					
1900					
2000					
2100					
2200					
2300					

A time management plan

- an unhealthy lifestyle if your needs for rest, exercise and healthy eating are neglected.

Good time management leads to:

- confidence and a 'feel good' factor
- achievement in meeting deadlines
- freedom from stress
- minimum effort bringing maximum results
- new opportunities.

Perhaps the best method of managing time is to create a timetable for the week. Record the time taken up by travelling, relaxing, eating, social activities, part-time work and studying. The time left is the time you have available to complete tasks, hold meetings and research information.

You need to set goals and prioritise them. Work back from set deadlines, using a personal diary and weekly timetable, to ensure that you plan your time so that they are adhered to.

Identifying sources of help

You may find you need support in acquiring the resources identified in your resource plan. There are many organisations that work to support and develop other organisations and their members. There are also profit-making organisations that can assist you. A simple example is sponsorship. The following steps will help you to identify sources of help.

- Identify your objective – is it to obtain finance, equipment, free gifts, posters?
- Decide how far you are restricted by finances. Can you afford to pay external consultants or suppliers?
- Use known sources and contacts, such as the Internet, your library reference section, the sports councils, the national training organisation SPRITO, and the Institute of Leisure and Amenity Management.

- Create your own information library with useful telephone numbers, e-mail addresses and Internet details.

- Get to know key people. People are generally very busy but it is worth taking note of those in a position to help.

- Make contact. How you do this depends on the nature of the request – it will vary from a simple telephone call asking for addresses of potential partners, to arranging a formal meeting in order to present a corporate sponsorship bid.

Theory into practice

1 Identify your tasks and functions within your enterprise, and place them in order of priority. Undertake a time management exercise which clearly shows when you will be achieving and performing your tasks.

2 Compile a database or list of all the key partners and sources of help you may need to complete your project successfully. Draft a standard letter which describes what you are doing. A paragraph can then be created requesting the help you require from each person or organisation.

Evaluation

Although reviewing and evaluation appears at the end of this section, it is a task that should start at the beginning and continue all the way through the process of planning a business enterprise. Evaluations are normally made by measuring results against objectives. If a system of review and evaluation is in place throughout the start-up of the business, it may be that changes can be made or objectives adjusted to ensure that overall aims are met.

Evaluation criteria

All information can be in a quantitative or qualitative format, depending on its purpose. Quantified financial data may be important for those responsible for budgets, whereas qualitative feedback from customers and visitors may be useful for the marketing team.

Key concept

Before gathering information at the objective-setting stage, decisions must be made about:

- a suitable format for the information
- how success will be measured.

Traditional performance indicators tend to focus on the outcomes of events, such as the total number of visitors. However, evaluating the process, and individual, team and business performance, will give much more useful information on which to base an overall assessment. Criteria should include the following.

- **Achievement of aims and objectives.** This is perhaps the most important as it will cover the reasons for the work taking place.

- **Meeting deadlines.** How well has time been managed?

- **Effectiveness of the planning process.** This measures how well the planning stages helped achieve the aims of the enterprise and overall performance. It will review decision making, meetings, methods of communication and allocation of tasks and responsibilities.

- **Project success.** This not only assesses whether aims and objectives were met but explores effectiveness from the viewpoint of all involved, such as sponsors.

- **Individual performance.** It is important to have criteria for self-assessment, but managers need to establish the strengths and weaknesses of other individuals to help improve their effectiveness and to decide and allocate future roles.

- **Team performance.** This develops from individual assessment and must establish factors that affect the team's performance, such as clashes of personality, and whether being part of a team helped or hindered the performance of individual tasks.

- **Financial criteria.** These would include return on capital employed, profit margins and sales growth.

Evaluation techniques

A range of evaluation techniques can be used to gather the required information, depending on who is providing the information.

- **Team 'de-briefs'.** All stakeholders should be given an opportunity to provide feedback. This can be done through a meeting if it is well managed. Team members should be encouraged to contribute constructive comments from their own perspective. Issuing an agenda in advance will help structure the meeting and should include opportunities to comment on key assessment criteria.

- **Individual appraisal.** This must be encouraged, and used to identify areas for individual development such as skills training, perhaps in computers or problem solving. Identified standards or criteria can include:
  - motivation
  - problem solving
  - task achievement
  - meeting deadlines
  - communicating with the team
  - communicating with customers.

- **Peer feedback.** Often how you feel you have performed is not how others perceive you. The key to peer feedback is to focus on constructive points which will help the individual being assessed to develop. Feedback must be given with clarity and sensitivity, as negative or poorly worded comments will not be listened to, however accurate. Feedback can be given in informal meetings or more formally in pre-designed forms.

- **Customer/supplier feedback.** This is normally collected via questionnaires and surveys like those used with customer care. Questions set against a rating scale or with pre-determined choices can provide quantitative data. Open-ended questions may also elicit useful qualitative information. These forms should be simple for customers and may be slightly more detailed for suppliers. Typical areas to ask customers about include:

- where they heard about the organisation
- what they can recall about promotional material
- what they thought of the overall service/product
- what they might like to see in the way of improvements in the service/product.

Assessment activity 14.4

If you have worked through the activities in this unit you will have brainstormed an idea for a sports enterprise and researched information on its feasibility, your market and the legal and financial requirements.

You are now to produce a detailed business plan and evaluation for your project. Your business plan should include the following:

- a feasibility study of the project
- marketing plan
- resource plan.

Identify the different elements that make up the plan and break them down into specific tasks. For example, the feasibility study needs to include:

- finance and budgeting
- facilities and equipment
- legal issues, including health and safety
- administration plans.

Provide evidence of research in each area; it should be accurate, logical and clearly presented.

Finally, show how you will evaluate whether your business has been a success.

Check your knowledge

1 Identify five different types of opportunities for business enterprises in the sports industry.
2 What are the main components of a feasibility study?
3 When setting up in business, what potential options are there for ownership?
4 Why is it important to analyse the potential market? Provide three examples of how the market may be segmented.

5   What are the main legal requirements you must address before starting up in business?

6   Where might you obtain finance to assist your business start-up?

7   Why is cash flow one of the most important aspects of any business?

8   What type of information do you need before you start to write a business plan?

9   Identify five sources where you might access support or help for your business enterprise.

10 How will you be able to identify whether your enterprise has been a success?

Assessment guidance

For this unit's assessment you are required to produce a business plan for a sports enterprise of your choice. You can choose any style of ownership, such as sole trader, but it is advisable to select an enterprise in which you have both an interest and some knowledge, for example a football coaching business or personal training. You must meet the following criteria for the different grades.

To gain a pass:

✔ describe a range of options for a sports business enterprise, selecting with teacher support the most appropriate

✔ conduct with teacher support appropriate market research related to the business enterprise, listing suitable methods and results

✔ identify the legal and financial requirements for the selected enterprise, listing possible sources of finance

✔ complete appropriate financial techniques for the selected enterprise

✔ present a business plan for the selected option, including promotional material to launch the sports business enterprise.

To gain a merit:

✔ independently select and justify the choice of sports business enterprise

✔ independently select appropriate market research techniques, explaining the results and conclusions

✔ explain the implications and effects of the legal and financial requirements of the proposed sports business enterprise

✔ present a business plan justifying and explaining the proposals and choice of promotional material.

To gain a distinction:

✔ critically evaluate a range of sports business enterprises, selecting the most appropriate

✔ analyse the market research results, drawing valid conclusions and recommendations

✔ analyse the financial requirements of the proposed sports business enterprise, providing appropriate alternatives

✔ evaluate the business plan, providing modifications and changes as appropriate.

Merit

1   You will be expected to work with more independence throughout the assessment activities. You must be able to work on your own in most situations, making your own decisions.

2   In your business plan you should demonstrate a depth of understanding of the different elements that make up a business plan.

3   There should be clear evidence of research to support your business plan, and it must be clearly presented.

4   There should be a logical approach to evaluating your business plan and this must be clearly linked to your business goals.

Distinction

1   You will be expected to work totally independently throughout the writing of the business plan. You should show an excellent understanding and awareness, which means you require no tutor support.

2 Throughout the business plan you should demonstrate an in-depth understanding of the different elements that make up a business plan.

3 There should be very detailed evidence of research from a range of sources to support your business plan, and it must be very clearly presented.

4 There should be a critical approach to the evaluation of your business plan and this should clearly link to your business goals.

Resources

The High Street banks publish relevant information texts and CDs.

Texts

Adams, P: *155 Legal Do's (and Don'ts) for the Small Business*, 1996, John Wiley

Beech, J & Chadwick, S: *Business of Sport Management*, 2004, FT Prentice Hall

Becket, M: *The Daily Telegraph Small Business Guide to Starting Your Own Business*, 2003, Pan Macmillan

Cook, Kenneth J: *AMA Complete Guide to Strategic Planning for Small Business*, 1995, Ntc Business Books

Edmunds, H: *AMA Complete Guide to Marketing Research for Small Businesses*, 1996, McGraw-Hill/Contemporary Books

Nicholas, T: *43 Proven Ways to Raise Capital for Your Small Business: Where the Money is and How to Get It*, 1992, Enterprise

Norman, J: *What No One Ever Tells You About Starting Your Own Business: Real Life Start-up Advice from 101 Successful Entrepreneurs*, 1999, Upstart Publishing

Stone, P: *Accounting for the Small Business: Understand Financial Accounting and Stay in Control of Your Business*, 2001, Essentials

Journals

Sports Management

Leisure Research

Magazines

Business Week

Sports Business

Websites

The Sports Industries Federation (www.sports-life.com)

Start Ups (www.startups.co.uk)

Graduate Prospects (www.prospects.ac.uk)

SPORTS DEVELOPMENT

Introduction to Unit 16

This is an optional unit for the qualification, which will introduce you to the ways in which sport is promoted and developed, and the work of sports development professionals. Sports development has grown to become an important part of the sports industry, whether it be for a facility, a specific sport or a target group of participants.

In this unit you will learn about the key concepts associated with sports development, and the methods and strategies used by professionals working on behalf of local authorities, sports governing bodies or sports clubs, for example.

Assessment

This unit is internally assessed, so guidance on preparing for the test aspect of the unit is included. Students are also reminded that during the completion of activities and tasks there will be opportunities to enhance key skills evidence.

After completing this unit you should be able to achieve the following outcomes.

Outcomes

1 Explain the key concepts that are used in sports development

2 Explore the role of local authority sports development departments

3 Investigate the role of organisations involved in sports development

4 Examine the effectiveness of an organisation involved in sports development.

What you need to learn

- How organisations are structured to deliver sports development

- How plans are implemented

- The use of resources in order to deliver sports development aims

- Factors which influence delivery, such as performance assessments for local authorities

- How partnership arrangements work to deliver objectives under sports development schemes.

Background to sports development

Historically, sports development began with the Central Council for Physical Recreation in the 1950s and 1960s, with a team of 'outreach workers' working at community level. The emphasis was moved to facilities in the 1970s as the Sport Council and local authorities led the way with provision.

By the 1980s it was clear that facility provision alone was not going to work, and a shift in policy brought more targeted efforts aimed at groups who rarely participated, particularly in urban areas. In the late 1980s and 1990s, 'Action Sports' programmes led the way, getting out into the community and taking sports opportunities to the people.

Sports development has been through a tough development period itself. The responsibility seemed to lie with sports governing bodies for their own sport's development, but they had few resources and little expertise to meet the challenge. They were criticised for being too preoccupied with setting up coaching and management structures. However, once the national centres for excellence were established, such as Bisham Abbey and

Crystal Palace is one of the longest-established national centres

Crystal Palace, and the National Coaching Foundation was set up, the pendulum swung back to a focus on sports development for target groups in the late 1980s and 1990s. A lead was given by the Sports Council.

This proactive approach prevails today, with programmes aimed across the spectrum of participants, non-participants and specific target groups, and a distinctive professional sports development career pathway can be identified.

Although sports development activities have been with us for about 40 years, it is still quite a broad area. Sports development does of course cover a great deal of work in local authorities, sports facilities and clubs. This is not always driven by a single policy; like the provision of sport, it varies from city to city and region to region depending on politics, resources and applications of sports strategy.

The purpose of sports development continually changes focus, with emphasis on social, recreational, or health factors. It is clearly, however, as Collins states (ILAM report 1995), about 'getting more people to play more sport'. The motives may differ among the providers, as do the structures, processes and opportunities for delivery.

The modern sports development professional needs not only knowledge of sports but the skills involved in planning, managing and delivering sports development schemes to the satisfaction of the participants and the policy makers or funding agencies.

Many other people contribute to sports development:

- coaches – who may be volunteers
- teachers – who run after-school clubs
- instructors – who run a few sessions per week
- parents – who give of their time freely to support children, clubs and teams

- volunteers – who provide support systems such as transport, catering, administration, and fundraising.

A great deal of knowledge and expertise has been built up over the years, which has given more structure to schemes, ensured a better network of provision and developed criteria for judging success. Key concepts have also been identified, along with a better understanding of client needs.

Key concepts and delivery methods

Concepts

The sports development continuum

The modern sports development programme is usually based on a four-part model called the sports development continuum, first developed in Scotland in the simple form shown below:

- The foundation level emphasises gaining basic motor and perceptive skills and assumes this will happen at school level.
- The participation level is concerned with providing opportunities to participate, the primary aim of local authority services.
- The performance level emphasises improvement from one level to the next, through competition and practice, with the onus on governing bodies and networks of clubs to deliver this.
- The excellence level focuses on preparation for competition at the highest level.

This model gave coherence to both ideas and applications, and began to clarify the fact that strategies and projects had to be devised for the whole of the continuum, rather than in discrete pockets for schools, facilities or elite athletes, as had been the case. It emphasised the relationship and interdependence between these areas.

Further research and feedback from demonstration projects made it necessary to revisit the model to produce a slightly more sophisticated version. This reflects the relationship which was emerging between participation and performance, with the former supporting the latter, and allows for the factors changing people's lifestyles at different life stages.

Additionally, government changes in the 1990s brought a shift in policy, because of a desire to reverse unwelcome social trends. The emphasis was on trying to engage with contemporary problems, using sport as a vehicle. The advent of local financial management of schools, and Compulsory Competitive Tendering for local authorities, diverted attention away from sports development agendas and funding. New programmes were developed, but they were often not sustainable past their funding period, so many of the problems re-emerged. As a consequence, a more sophisticated version of the continuum model was created to clarify additional factors such as movements in, out and within it, based on players' decisions to stay at the same level, or leave and return.

Target groups

Over the years a number of groups and areas have been targeted for sports development, some more successfully than others. In some categories, targets have been set year on year but never really achieved.

In the early 1980s the Sports Council set participation targets in its strategy document 'Sport in the Community – The Next Ten Years'. The aims were to:

- close the gap between men's and women's participation
- increase participation in middle and older years
- prevent a large drop-out rate in late teenage years.

When these aims were reviewed in the next main strategy document, 'Sport in the Community – into the 1990s', it was found that nearly 1 million more women had been attracted into sport (but not into the traditional sports – more into indoor fitness activities). There was a general increase in participation among the middle to older age groups (particularly for men), but less success with the younger age groups.

In 2000 some of the original target groups were still on the list for continuing development:

- women
- young people
- the over 50s.

These were joined by:

- disabled people
- ethnic groups
- the socially excluded
- health targets
- performance and excellence targets
- excellence for elite athletes.

Taking these in turn we can identify the reasons for their inclusion.

Women

Since records have been kept about sports participation, the gap has always been large between men's and women's rates. Sports development programmes aimed at changing participation rates take some time to achieve their targets, so a five-year or even ten-year strategy might be needed to bring about a cultural change in attitudes, lifestyle, expectations and opportunities. In 1987, after a great deal of research into women's participation, some aims were devised and promoted by the Sports Council in its strategy document 'Sport in the Community – Into the 1990s'.

- Encourage women to engage in more organised leisure activities more frequently.
- Improve relations between recreation managers/staff and women customers.
- Encourage women into more leisure venues.
- Facilitate more free time for women.
- Improve the general physical and social environment.
- Improve and expand equal opportunities initiatives.
- Expand awareness and knowledge of gender inequalities.

Think it over

Discuss with your group whether you think these long-term aims have been achieved today. If not, why not?

In 1994 another landmark stage was reached with what was called the 'Brighton Declaration', which set the direction for developing women's sport all over the world.

Subsequent work done by the Women's Sports Foundation and the Women and Sport Advisory group produced an action plan which has tried to 'roll out' the targets for women's sport. The plan involved working to get governing bodies to review their equal opportunities policies; getting more women promoted to top jobs in sport (administration and coaching); eliminating all discriminatory clauses in clubs' and associations' constitutions; and making sports facilities more

Much has been achieved in attracting women to traditional 'male' sports

friendly for women. Over time much has been done along these lines, but it is an ongoing task.

Think it over

As a group, list some examples of 'last bastions' of male domination in sports organisations, e.g. golf clubs. Why do you think they are like this?

Other initiatives have tried to tackle key issues such as young women dropping out of sport.

In 1998 a second world-wide conference held in Windhoek, Namibia set the agenda for the twenty-first century – more positive action to address inequalities, and continuing sports development for women's activities. The following tables show participation rates at that time. They are from the General Household Survey 1996 of sport and physical activities.

In the four weeks before the survey the top five activities were:

Activity	Men – %	Women – %
Walking	49	41
Swimming	13	16
Keep fit/yoga	7	17
Cycling	15	8
Jogging	7	2

All adults using different types of facility (most significant only):

Location	Men – %	Women – %
Indoor sports hall	26	23
Other indoor facilities	15	19
Outdoor areas	18	5

Further information on women's participation is available on the website of the Women's Sports Foundation (see page 339 for the address) and in the foundation's strategic plan.

Theory into practice

Research current participation rates for women. What trends can you determine?

Young people

The need for sports development for the age group 13-24 has long been identified, because for most people this is a crucial stage of the lifecycle. There is huge variation in economic, social and personal circumstances across the country. Usually high levels of participation are to be found with this target group, and most sports organisations are keen to tap into it and sustain it into adulthood. In the 1990s the school curriculum expanded giving more choice, which helped maintain activity in the immediate post-school years, but the falling away in participation frequency and total numbers is quite marked in subsequent years. Despite having high aspirations to continue sport after school, other leisure pursuits seem to have gained ground, such a sports spectating, and home-based leisure activities such as using computers.

Sport England has taken on the challenge of encouraging young people to become and stay actively involved with sport. The current development strategy is based on three key elements – Active Schools, Active Communities and Active Sports (see page 303). The premise is that young people should be actively encouraged to become involved in sport, to make the most of their skills and develop a passion for sport that will be sustained into adulthood, even as far as a lifelong involvement.

Sport England have implemented this development strategy by:

- supporting the role of PE in the national curriculum
- assisting local education authorities to stage sports projects

- working with the Youth Sport Trust to implement its TOP programmes (see page 327) for 4-9-year-olds and 7–11-year-olds, by providing bags of kit and activity cards for schools (by 2000 nearly 2 million pupils had been reached this way). New TOPS areas are planned in outdoor sports and dance. Schools which are particularly effective can achieve a Sportsmark Award (almost 1000 schools had attained this standard by 2000) or an Activemark Award.

Sport England has worked closely with government and other sports and health bodies in its development work with young people, notably the Department for Culture, Media and Sport; the Department for Education and Skills; PE teachers; and sports coach UK.

Obviously if this continuum of provision is to work, the next stage – Active Communities – needs to be ready to receive young people and continue to develop them. To achieve this a number of schemes were set up:

- Challenge Funding was used to fund small schemes of development
- junior club development courses were offered to clubs
- sporting 'ambassadors' such as Tanni Grey-Thompson were asked to go into clubs to inspire young players.

The Active Communities programme is aimed at the young, continuing the ideals of encouragement, advocacy and funding for this target group, with awards, youth sport schemes for coaches, and smaller initiatives with youth services. The Active Communities programme has a much wider remit than just youth, as we will see later in this section.

Over 50s

This group is often known as the 'baby boomers'; they were born after the Second World War into a period of relative prosperity. Although in theory the range of suitable sports diminishes for this age group, a number of factors keep people interested in remaining active:

- an awareness of the need to stay fit and healthy
- a tendency to live longer
- larger amounts of leisure time
- freedom from family responsibilities
- good levels of earned income or retirement income.

It is hardly surprising that some of the most rapid increases in participation have come from this group, with men's indoor and outdoor participation rates going up and women's indoor rates exceeding expectations. It is often said that people in this 'grey market' don't act like older people at all; many have a spirit of adventure which encourages them to try new activities or to keep older ones going longer – including marathon running, swimming and racquet sports. By 2000 this age group was in the majority in the UK.

For the over 50s the social element is an important factor to be incorporated in any development programme – it may in fact be more important than the activity itself. Many early initiatives focused on this aspect.

Sports development for this group has typically been provided by small local projects or collaborative regional ones including local authorities, Age Concern and other bodies such as social services departments. Schemes were driven by Sports Council campaigns such as '50+ – All to Play For' or 'Look After Yourself'. More recently Active Communities has taken over the projects.

Reading Sport and Leisure Services, for example, offers a range of activities:

- 50+ Health and Fun Club (mixed activities including swimming, squash, badminton,

Many over 50s keep active

bowls, short tennis, table tennis, weights and keep fit sessions)

- 50+ workouts
- 50+ yoga and swim
- 50+ Steamers (sauna, steam room and spa sessions).

Theory into practice

Visit two local sports venues which offer programmes for the over 50s. Compare the range with those listed above for Reading. Why might they be different?

Disabled people

The 'disabled' are not a homogeneous group, but a mixture of people with a range of disabilities including deafness, sight impairment, amputation, paraplegia, cerebral palsy and learning difficulties. Not until the beginning of the 1990s did a concerted effort emerge to encourage these people to achieve their sports aspirations. The English Federation of Disability Sport (EFDS) is the national umbrella organisation for disability sport in England and brings together a number of established national and regional agencies with complementary roles. The national agencies are the seven National Disability Sports Organisations (NDSOs) recognised by Sport England, which include the British Wheelchair Sports Foundation and Cerebral Palsy Sport. The EFDS has nine regional offices with regional federations for disability sport who support the delivery of the EFDS key objectives of:

- mainstreaming disability sport with national governing bodies of sport, local authorities and other providers
- empowering disabled people.

Further details on EFDS and its programmes are available at the EFDS website www.efds.co.uk.

English Federation of Disability Sport

Ethnic groups

In the early days of sports development, ethnic participation rates were not really known. Today most sports agencies agree that now Britain is a multicultural society, ethnic minorities represent a major potential market. Individual studies and initiatives have found that cultural barriers to participation still exist, that full data has not yet been gathered and that there is a great deal of misunderstanding among providers even today.

Development projects in Coventry, Liverpool and London in the 1990s helped to point the way forward, but did not produce a concerted strategy. Sport England and other development bodies still strive to improve sporting opportunities for black, Asian and other ethnic communities, but there are still racial tensions in some areas, which make programmes controversial or difficult to deliver.

The Commission for Racial Equality has been a welcome partner for Sport England and sports governing bodies, working under the banner of 'Sporting Equals' to deliver initiatives. The fundamental starting point in all the initiatives is to establish a racial equality statement. This has been done successfully with cricket, basketball, rugby, athletics and swimming.

Theory into practice

Contact your local authority and/or two governing bodies to assess the types of programmes in your area (or nationally) which aim to help boost ethnic community involvement in sports.

Inclusiveness

Social inclusion has become part of the government's agenda and it has swept up sports development issues along with others. Inclusion is thought of as 'positive engagement with a community's daily affairs', and is meant to be synonymous with 'good citizenship'. Social inclusion through sports participation is a major feature in the government document 'A Sporting

Future for All', which clearly sets out the agenda for inclusion through sport.

Case study

'A Sporting Future for All' states that if sport is to play its part in promoting the social well being of communities, more inter-agency work is needed between partner organisations such as local authorities, social services and other neighbourhood stakeholders. Local Strategic Partnerships were set up from 2001, as part of regional plans which the Department for Culture, Media and Sport pulled together into a national strategic forum, the Community Sport Alliance. This not only gave a lead which sports development programmes could follow, but provided valuable research data to guide programme and project plans.

1   Using recent Sport England annual reports, assess how successful this strategy has been.

2   In the document 'A Sporting Future for All', an emotive quotation from Nelson Mandela was used to set the scene:

> *'Sport has the power to unite people in a way that little else can. Sport can create hope where there was once only despair. It breaks down racial barriers. It laughs in the face of all kinds of discrimination. Sport speaks to people in a language they can understand.'*

What is your reaction to this statement?

In 1997 the government set up a Social Exclusion Unit, which reflects the importance it places on this agenda. Sports development professionals need to have a high level of awareness of other social agendas at work, which they might access in order to share resources, and achieve economies of scale. Examples can be found in the following areas:

- community development
- lifelong learning
- active healthy lifestyles
- social and economic regeneration
- crime prevention
- equal opportunities.

Think it over

As a group, consider what resources and objectives might be shared between the programmes listed in the bullet points above and sports development projects.

Health

The benefits of good health in the population are far better understood and established now than in the 1980s, especially in relation to preventing coronary heart disease and osteoporosis, for example. There has been substantial growth – some would say a revolution – in health and fitness provision, and it has become a major lifestyle influence. A combination of factors fuelled this trend, such as:

- a resurgence in women's participation in aerobics, keep fit and other exercise classes
- the popularity of jogging, which sparked the provision of fun runs and other road races
- initiatives by employers to improve the health and fitness of staff
- greater use of exercise as a preventative medicine, and frequent campaigns by health authorities and other bodies to promote exercise, such as the 'Look After Your Heart' programme in Liverpool and 'Staying Well' in Wigan.

There is still inequality, however, as there is greater awareness and activity among middle-class people than lower income groups. Much of current health development is aimed at the latter, such as the healthy living centres established in many communities. It is important to remember that health is an all-embracing concept encompassing physical, social and psychological well being.

The Allied Dunbar National Fitness Survey published in 1992 highlighted how unhealthy the population was and the need for organisations to network better in order to tackle problems and attitudes. Development campaigns from health-orientated agencies were prompted by the government paper 'The Health of the Nation', published in 1992. It focused on:

- poor diet
- smoking
- lack of exercise.

Lack of exercise and a poor diet can lead to health problems

This gave sports development professionals, PE teachers, health promoters and medical practices a joint agenda. A Physical Activity Task Force was formed in 1993. Out of a great deal of concerted work came a development strategy called 'Active for Life', aimed at creating high levels of awareness and encouragement to participate in sport for health reasons. The project, which lasted until 1999, systematically targeted problem areas and groups. This development effort created a legacy of better attitudes to diet and lifelong exercise for many health-conscious people.

Performance and excellence

Promoting excellence is a huge task. Most sports development agencies focus on:

- promotion work to attract sponsorship, for example
- facility provision – state of the art facilities
- grant aiding talented individuals, for example

- financial support, for example for coaching, scientific support or training
- setting up junior networks or grass-roots schemes.

Improving performance involves many other people who must be managed, such as ambitious parents, teachers and coaches.

Historically the development of excellence has been dogged by a number of deficiencies, and this was shown in the 1980s and 1990s by the UK's failure to succeed (except in a few cases) at the highest levels of international sport. The problems included:

- lack of co-ordination among the sports bodies involved
- lack of facilities of international standard for either training or playing
- lack of coaches and educational staff, and a career pathway for them
- lack of sports science support, e.g. injury clinics, assessment and evaluation centres.

Recent developments have begun to address some of the problems identified, such as establishment of the National Coaching Foundation (now re-branded as sports coach UK), and a network of university sports science centres in Manchester, Loughborough, Leeds, Newcastle, Sheffield and London. Centres of excellence have also been established around the country under the new organisation UK Sport, to foster development of elite performers – cycling in Manchester, rowing near Nottingham, and cricket at Loughborough, mirroring the distribution of the sports science centres.

In the late 1990s an assessment of the needs of elite performers, under the banner 'More Medals', was one of three key elements of the new Sport England's strategy. A development strategy led to new participants taking up the sport and motivation for existing competitors to aspire to higher achievement. The outcome was that 37 sports were identified as being in the 'World Class' category, in terms of their national profile, international significance and chances of medal success.

Case study

The World-Class Programme is made up of three distinct elements, which are supported by lottery funding:

- World-Class Start – assisting governing bodies of sport to find and nurture performers with potential for international success
- World-Class Potential – to develop talented performers with the potential to win international competitions within ten years

Jonathan Edwards was one of too few success stories for UK athletics

- World-Class Performance – for activities at the highest level, which will produce victories within six years.

The World-Class Programme also supports the bidding for and hosting of international events, such as the successful Commonwealth Games in Manchester in 2002, the European Indoor Athletics in Birmingham in 2003, and the Olympic bid for London in 2012.

1 List some potential advantages, for performers and coaches, of the World-Class Programme (WCP).

2 Recent WCP budgets have been spent on acclimatisation, education programmes, preparation, support teams and subsistence funding. Research an issue and find out what the funding involved.

The formation of the United Kingdom Sports Institute (UKSI) has brought another dimension to development at the top level, providing further networks of facilities and support for elite players and athletes around the UK.

Case study

Speaking about the new English Institute of Sport (EIS), the Director Wilma Shakespear comments that there is a need to change sports structures and the mindsets of many British people about sport, from the amateur/volunteer ethos to an altogether more professional approach. The EIS will benchmark itself against best practice around the globe and choose new systems and processes to use in the UK.

Launching and establishing the nine centres for excellence around the country will be a daunting task, with their management and networking being key issues. There is a plan to develop the

centres gradually, with performance-level athletes first, followed by potential-level athletes.

Other areas such as sports medicine and conditioning will come onstream, followed by sports science and psychology. A really strong education programme is needed, which will enable staff to be trained and return to the regions to spread knowledge and skills. Multi-sports sites will allow for cross-fertilisation and exchange of coaching ideas. Good, clear leadership is needed to take the institutes forwards. The former runner Steve Cram, who chairs UKSI, seems to have that quality.

1 Investigate the current issues for UKSI, and prepare a short report.

2 Elite sport is expensive, for success doesn't come cheaply, but it does have great rewards – what are the benefits to the country of major sporting success?

Barriers to participation

Inequalities create barriers to participation. They can be persistent (consistently there) or transitory (possible to overcome with prescriptive action). Both types of barriers can come from a range of sources.

Key concept

Promoting inclusion and taking action against exclusion have a common starting point for sports developers, that of 'identifying inequalities'.

- **Cultural barriers** can result from direct conflict with a range of cultural factors such as codes of behaviour (e.g. about physical contact or displays of emotion); customs, such as spitting on the pitch or consuming large amounts of alcohol after a game; conventions, such as the type of clothing worn or the changing arrangements; and values inherent in the activity, such as masculinity or winning at all costs.

- **Social barriers** may relate to the image of the sport among one's peer group, such as not being 'cool' or having a low perceived status; they may also stem from a lack of motivation. Lack of consultation over sessions or programmes can create further barriers.

- **Economic barriers** can stem from lack of funds to spend on sport, high prices, poor value for money, and competing financial priorities.

- **Historical barriers** include a lack of tradition in a particular sport (such as football for Asian players) or no tradition of competitive sports. Not having played the sport as a youngster at school can be a barrier to later take-up.

- **Educational barriers** can arise from a poor relationship with a PE teacher (or a poor teacher), limited facilities or choice at school, or lack of knowledge about sports or the opportunities to participate in them.

- **Physical barriers** include problems to do with a person's size, weight, agility, dexterity, spatial awareness, and vision.

- **Access barriers** include transport, mobility, opportunity, suitable facilities, available time slots, and distance to travel.

- **Gender barriers** are usually strongly associated with inequality and discrimination. A number of sources of inequality have been identified as causing barriers for women, such as responsibilities for child care, shortage of free time, lack of personal transport and money, and low self-esteem and confidence. Gender inequalities stem from society, through networks of power and control and the marginalisation or exploitation of women in the media.

- **Disability** can be a barrier, and the integration of disabled participants is an ongoing challenge for sport. Recent legislation has forced organisations to look at physical barriers and build or rebuild suitable access. Barriers are mainly physical ones, but others include lack of

Disabled athletes often have to work doubly hard to participate

opportunity, and lack of suitable programmes or qualified coaches. Adaptations of equipment, and administrative and support mechanisms, are all needed. Perceptual barriers may exist in the minds of the disabled (who may feel they cannot take part) and in the able bodied, who do not really understand the needs of disabled people and may even regard them as unwelcome problems. Disabled people are less likely to have a high disposable income, more likely to be dependent on carers, and may have less time or energy for sport.

- **Opportunity barriers** differ from person to person and include availability of time, facilities, courses, coaches, transport, and colleagues to play with. Some barriers arise from conflicting demands on time, such as clashes of events.

- **Health and fitness barriers** include attitudes as well as physical issues. There may be an assumption that some sports have a high incidence of injury; that playing sport (badly) can be humiliating; that taking off your everyday clothes and changing into sports gear in front of others can be embarrassing; or that competition is unhealthy. Physical barriers might stem from a medical condition, or lack of co-ordination.

Think it over

In groups, identify additional barriers to participation, in terms of physical, access and gender issues.

Provision and enabling

There is great debate in the public sector between the two roles of providing and enabling; that is, whether a local authority should be providing buildings and facilities for participation in sport and leisure (using tax payers' money) or just enabling sport and leisure to happen by facilitating games, activities and programmes (at a much lower cost). Sport and leisure is a non-statutory provision in England, which means that it does not have to be provided by law. As it is an optional service for local authorities, the question is how much they should provide.

Think it over

What opinion does your class hold on this issue? Hold a discussion.

Direct provision

This is a more prescriptive approach, where provision is decided by a professional, perhaps in line with his or her training (professional knowledge), a strategic plan, or best practice in similar situations. This type of provision does not usually involve a great deal of consultation. It may be a traditional package which professionals know works well, or a short sports development programme offered while funding lasts. This type of programme is called 'supply-side delivery' and people have to take or leave what is supplied. Examples of this might be an annual tournament run by the local authority aimed at young boys in deprived areas, or a junior girls recruitment drive by a hockey club.

Enabling

Enabling is more complex as it involves responding to participants' needs. It is a 'demand-related' approach perhaps responding to needs expressed by a community group in an inner city or under-resourced rural area.

Target groups are often identified through research or consultation, and a programme can be tailored specifically for them. For example, Asian women may be invited to play some badminton or take some exercise classes in private.

Individuals often need some sports development help to get them started. A programme might be aimed at higher level performers who need a boost to get them up to the next level. This could be in the form of supplying facilities, transport or guidance. Some local authorities offer grants to performers for these purposes.

Empowerment schemes help groups to benefit from initial support – perhaps in the form of funding, facilities or a coach – which effectively 'kick starts' a scheme. The participants are expected to take over the running of the scheme soon after a structure and sustainable processes are put in place. Sports development staff can move on to the next scheme and spread their skills and expertise to other areas.

Partnerships are one of the most common ways of funding and staging a sports development scheme. A number of partners support the process, which should meet the needs of the target group, local authority and sponsor. In its simplest form, a partnership can look like one of the triangles below.

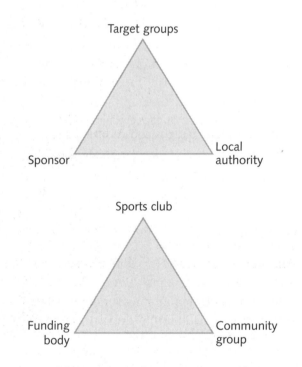

In order to meet social, political and educational needs, sport has to work in unison with other agencies – what the government calls 'joined-up thinking', a kind of synergy (joint energy) to achieve mutually held goals. The range of alliances is very broad today, and with greater professionalism and larger sums of money involved, partnership schemes have to be well managed. They bring together voluntary, private and public sector organisations; perhaps the largest one we have seen

in action was the partnership to bring the Commonwealth Games to Manchester.

Think it over

Discuss with your group the benefits of large sports development partnerships. The case study on pages 320 to 321 may help you.

The key components of a partnership scheme in sports development are like those for project management of any kind:

- a clear aim
- a management team
- SMART objectives (specific, measurable, achievable, relevant and timed)
- a launch event
- a definite time scale
- shared resources
- an implementation plan
- contingency plans
- funding
- evaluation processes.

Some common problems of partnership schemes are described below.

- Although there may be a shared vision, priorities may differ between agencies.
- Political agendas often cut across what professionals wish to do, and a compromise solution has to be chosen.
- Information on sources of help may not always be known or may take a while to secure.
- Organisational cultures may differ greatly, such as management styles, methods of working and values.
- Even with an agreed plan, implementation issues can occur – such as the delegation of tasks, sharing of responsibilities, unauthorised changes, and problems with communication.
- Workloads can be too high for key individuals, structures can fail to hold together and ad hoc arrangements may creep in.

Think it over

As a group, reflect on the above list of problems with partnerships and add at least five other possible ones.

Key stakeholders in any sports development scheme will have an important role to play, and these can range from the local community group to national bodies such as Sport England. Local authority alliances will normally place the community groups involved at the heart of the scheme. Those which involve a sports club, sponsor and maybe a funding body will put players at the heart of their scheme. Where facilities are needed, members, owners, sponsors and local authorities might collaborate to create new facilities to host sports.

Stakeholders exist at all levels of the sports development continuum – international, national, regional and local – and sport and social objectives are usually pursued hand in hand.

Theory into practice

Identify and describe the work of three organisations at each level – international, national, regional and local – which you know work as a 'key stakeholder' in sports development.

Methods aimed at foundation level

The original sports development continuum (see page 286) has 'foundation' as its basic level.

Foundation level is aimed mainly at school-age children. Aims include the acquisition of basic skills, which could involve:

- body literacy
- hand-eye co-ordination
- spatial awareness.

Award schemes

Governing bodies of sports normally have their own award schemes, and at this level they are primarily aimed at rewarding, motivating and approving basic skills among participants. The British Gymnastics website describes its award schemes as shown in the following case study.

Case study

The British Gymnastics Award Schemes have been designed to provide a nationwide personal incentive scheme for all student gymnasts. The schemes are all progressive in structure and easy to administer. All of the schemes are based on the concept of completing a number of moves from each level before progressing to the next one.

Every scheme consists of different levels of varying ability. Each level has a badge and certificate designated to it. On completion of each level the participant will become eligible to purchase the badge and certificate Awards from British Gymnastics. The badges and certificates are awarded to the gymnast for their participation and achievement.

Gymnastics is on nearly every school curriculum for both boys and girls and many of our young gymnasts started on their way to perfection by working through the Awards. The aim of the Awards is to encourage the natural ability that all children (and adults) possess to some degree, so improving the general standard of gymnastics at local, county and national levels. The Awards also aim to promote good posture and locomotor skills while allowing children to develop at their own rate through participation and enjoyment.

Gym clubs

The Award Schemes are suitable for use as a developmental tool with both recreational and competitive gymnasts.

Schools

These schemes are ideal for meeting National Curriculum requirements. The schemes provide teachers with a structured approach to gymnastics lessons while building confidence for the teachers using the vast range of resources available. The

Proficiency Scheme provides the basis for all British Schools Gymnastics Association organised competitions, thus providing an opportunity for all gymnasts to receive the awards but also allowing the school to enter gymnastic competitions.

Leisure centres

Using these schemes will allow you to make use of facilities that may be unused for periods during the week or holidays; the Pre-School Scheme is a particular favourite with leisure centres during the daytime period. The schemes can generate resources for the centre by charging participants for the sessions in which the skills of the Award Schemes are practised. They also create the opportunity for extra income generation through the reselling of badges, certificates and medals to successful participants.

1   Describe the relevance of the British Gymnastics awards to foundation level sports development.

2   Find two other examples of award schemes for a sports governing body. Compare the three examples, finding common features and unique points.

Leadership training

Organisations and individuals who normally deliver at the foundation level tend to be:

- parents (with their own children or working as assistants)
- play schemes run in holiday periods or at nurseries
- primary schools
- secondary schools
- local authority leisure services.

Leadership of foundation level work is often provided by volunteers, unless qualified coaches are required. Students may be tempted to take some form of qualification in order to work with children as an activity leader, such as the Community Sports Leader award offered by the British Sports Trust. The aims and levels of this award scheme can be seen on page 49 of *BTEC*

National Diploma in Sport core book or on the BST website at www.bst.org.uk/awards.html

In 2003 the British Sports Trust announced a new scheme to attract sports volunteers:

Case study

Step into Sport is an exciting new initiative which encourages more young people to become involved in sport in their local communities. Funded by the Department for Culture, Media and Sport and the Home Office Active Communities Unit, it brings together the British Sports Trust, the Youth Sport Trust and Sport England to provide a structured path to attract people into rewarding sports volunteering and to deploy their experience and talents to enrich local community and school sport.

Over 48,000 young people aged 14-19 will be enrolled each year over the next two years through a network of schools partnerships, which will mainly be based around the government's Sport and Education Action Zones. Training and support will be given to young people to develop their leadership skills through sport and to volunteer in their local communities.

At least 6,000 older volunteers will train with and act as mentors to these young people. The Step into Sport programme will also assist national governing bodies to devise and implement action plans to provide longer term volunteering opportunities.

Through the scheme the British Sports Trust will be providing free training to organisations and individuals who wish to run Sports Leader Awards.

Through Step into Sport, volunteers will gain nationally recognised awards culminating in the prestigious Step into Sport gold award for those who achieve the landmark of 200 hours sports volunteering.

1   Find out about any Step into Sport initiatives in your local area.

2   How will this kind of initiative help sports development?

Promotion

Promotion of sports to help their development at foundation level can take many forms. The chart below illustrates some common methods employed by all organisations.

Promotional activities are part of what is called the 'marketing mix', which consists of a number of other 'Ps'. In the case of a sports development programme, the following might be components of the package:

- Product – e.g. the sports development programme
- Price – e.g. the fee for joining
- Place – e.g. the venue for the activity
- People – e.g. spectators, players, coaches
- Process – e.g. the elements/logistics of the programme
- Physical evidence – e.g. the equipment to be used or forms to sign.

Promotional activities should be guided by research and consultation. In the case of a sports development programme, research is needed into the target group; their preferences or needs; the attractiveness of the programme; the level of interest; the price people are willing to pay, and so on. The benefits and contents of the programme should be clear to everyone. Without this type of research and preparation, later evaluations may turn out to be disappointing.

Some examples of promotional material are shown on the next page.

Supporting local development

Another key area for sports development is supporting development at local levels. Local authorities may well produce a generic 'leisure plan' which will have some aims that can be co-opted. Local clubs will undoubtedly have a junior recruitment plan, while regional sports bodies or governing bodies of sport such as the Lawn Tennis Association will have strategic development plans. The Federation of Yorkshire Sport, for example, is a body that offers membership benefits to a range

Promotional techniques in sports development		
Mode	**Purpose**	**Media**
Advertising	To create awareness, interest and a desire to participate; also to give information on price, location and times	<ul><li>Local press and radio</li><li>Magazines and newspapers</li><li>Leaflets and posters</li><li>Websites</li></ul>
Direct marketing	To target the promotional material directly at the most likely person, based on research and the target groups desired	<ul><li>Mailshots</li><li>Call centres (telemarketing)</li><li>Mail-drops through letterboxes</li><li>Direct response from media ads, e.g. freepost returns</li></ul>
Public relations	To try to create a relationship with the likely participants so that there is good will between providers and the target group	<ul><li>Media inclusion, e.g. a story on local TV</li><li>Press releases</li><li>Community relations exercises (perhaps via a local sports star)</li><li>Lobbying (by dedicated fans/groups)</li><li>Corporate literature – glossy brochures with organisational logos</li></ul>
Sponsorship	To complement the programme and give the sponsor a number of benefits in return for the patronage	<ul><li>Facilities given free</li><li>Kit bought for team</li><li>Cash given for running costs</li><li>Prizes/trophies given for winners</li></ul>

An example of promotional material

EASTER & SUMMER (SPALDING) BASKETBALL CAMPS

HUDDERSFIELD   KEIGHLEY   LEEDS   HARROGATE

nbc
SPALDING®

LAKERS
8

SPALDING®
FILA
Champion
U.S.A.
Mueller
Sports Medicine Products

SCARBOROUGH   WHITBY   DEWSBURY   LIVERPOOL   FORMBY

www.nbcbasketball.co.uk
Log on today and book your place

Association (ASA) is a good example, as the following case study shows.

Case study

The Sheffield Swimming Development Team are accredited providers of a programme based at Ponds Forge in Sheffield. This guarantees participants the highest quality and standards of courses. Some of the courses on offer include:

- ASA Club Coach Award
- ASA Teacher Certificate (swimming)
- ASA Assistant Teacher (swimming)
- ASA Assistant Teacher (diving)
- Royal Life Saving Society Pool Lifeguard Award.

1 Visit your local leisure centre or pool and find the coaching courses advertised or run there.

2 Choose a sport with which you are unfamiliar and carry out some research online to find out about its coach education programmes. Visit the sports coach UK website and view the coach education programmes offered across the country.

of clubs and organisations to help them develop. Members such as the Yorkshire Orienteering Association and the Yorkshire Volleyball Association have the benefit of:

- a network of sporting bodies
- access to administration, printing and database support
- local conferences
- opportunities to apply for funding support
- guidance on fair play charters.

Coach development

Coach development is an important method of bringing more expertise to a sport. Many organisations offer coach development schemes, for example local authorities, national organisations (such as sports coach UK), and sports governing bodies. The Amateur Swimming

Introductory sports

Many PE teachers will devise their own introductory versions of sports to suit the children in their school and the facilities they have. School initiatives are a great way to initiate pupils into basic level skills. Some examples include:

- mini rugby or touch rugby
- kwik cricket
- mini-basketball
- short tennis
- unihock
- obstacle races as a precursor to athletics.

Think it over

Carry out a survey in your class to assess how many students were introduced to a sport through a scaled-down version run at school.

Methods aimed at participation level

The second level in the sports development continuum is 'participation'. This target for development has long been an aim for sports bodies. The Sports Council, now Sport England, in its annual reports always has categories of participants it wishes to encourage, such as young people, the elderly, ethnic minorities, and women. Schemes to increase participation are therefore quite mature.

Using the sports development continuum model we can view participation as having several dimensions and therefore needing varied approaches. Action Sport is probably one of the best-known schemes, which in turn brought the Active programmes which drive Sport England's current strategy.

Sports development aimed at increasing participation can mean focusing on introducing or re-introducing people to sport, both competitive and recreational. It may mean targeting beginning performers to bring them up to performance levels. It may mean trying to prolong the playing of sport by older people – encouraging lifelong participation. Providers are diverse, but include:

- parents helping their children and other children through voluntary work or coaching
- PE teachers and lecturers in schools, colleges and universities
- local authority sports development officers
- local clubs
- youth groups and leaders
- private sector facilities such as gyms and pools
- regional sports councils and federations
- Active Community programme leaders.

People have varied motivations for taking up a sport – for enjoyment, fitness, social contact, or skill development – so development programmes must meet these needs. For many, a plateau of ability is reached or a conscious decision is made to play only at a certain level or to retire early. Participants may return after a period of caring for young children. Participation objectives have to be specific for each category, to ensure motivation is maintained or rekindled.

Sport England have a range of major sports development programmes aimed at participation – Active Schools, Active Communities and Active Sports. This is illustrated by the diagram below.

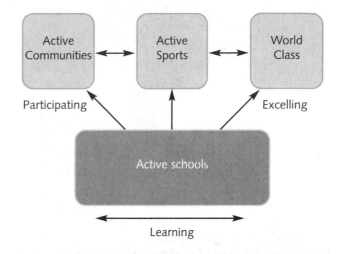

Sport England's overall development strategy

The campaign phrase 'Sport for All', coined in the 1970s, still holds good today and is a continuing theme for Sport England, with participation at its core.

Two key elements have been crucial in recent years in working towards the aim of increasing participation: lottery funding and new partnership schemes.

Lottery funding

Financial support is often given more readily to larger organisations, so a more recent strategy to help smaller clubs develop has been the lottery-funded 'Awards for All' – a minor grants initiative which has proved very successful for community schemes, often aimed at disadvantaged areas. When set criteria are met, grants in the range £500–£5,000 are given. The following case study, from the Sport England website, sums up how communities can access funding to help with local participation.

Case study

The Active Communities Development Fund (ACDF) is a new revenue programme which will increase sports participation among the following four priority groups:

- ethnic communities
- people with disabilities
- women and girls
- people on low incomes.

We will be investing at least half of the total fund in projects that tackle rural and urban deprivation; among the priority groups are the following objectives:

- a community-led approach
- partnership working
- effective links with other programmes and funding streams
- setting of projects within strategic frameworks
- long-term sustainability.

Around £7.5 million was invested in 2001/2002, rising to £9 million in 2002/2003 and £15 million in subsequent years. This is a very flexible fund. Projects could fall into one or more of the following categories:

An award to fund a community sports worker (capacity builder) to increase sports participation among one or more priority groups. The award could be for a full- or part-time worker's salary, ongoing costs and a limited budget to cover their personal equipment. The post holder may work across a broad area, using a range of sports and community facilities and resources, or may be linked to one specific facility.

An award to provide a development fund. This would normally be attached to an outreach worker but in exceptional circumstances may stand alone. The development fund **must** be directly related to increasing participation in sport but could be used for such things as child care, awareness raising, facility hire, equipment or transport hire.

An award to provide expert advice. This could involve buying in specific expertise for a fixed period of time to enable a priority group to access additional resources.

An award to provide education and training opportunities. This could provide groups with the opportunity to increase skills and become more self-sufficient in providing sporting opportunities. Localised mentoring schemes could be appropriate, as could access to accredited training opportunities.

Examples of projects receiving awards

- £80,000 awarded to an organisation in the East Midlands to employ a community development worker for 3 years to assist in the development of sporting opportunities for people on low incomes
- £63,000 awarded to an organisation in London to employ a football development officer for 3 years to work with local black and ethnic minority clubs to enable access to facilities and funding opportunities
- £15,000 awarded to an organisation in the North-East SAZ region to provide basketball coaching opportunities for a period of 3 years to increase participations amongst girls
- £125,000 awarded to an organisation in the North-West to employ a community liaison officer for 5 years to work out of a facility funded by a Sport England capital grant to encourage and develop sporting opportunities for disabled people through capacity building
- £99,000 awarded to an organisation in Yorkshire to train and employ young Asians to act as peer educators and role models who will develop and run sports, health and sustainable regeneration programmes.

1 As this book goes to press, the Active Communities Development Fund is being frozen following a review of lottery commitments. Research the current situation and whether there are any ACDF initiatives in your local area. *2004   June*

2 Do you think it is important for Sport England to keep a check on what is built where? If so, why? If not, why not?

Partnerships

As noted above, the underlying agendas often attached to community schemes are aimed not only at participation but at other social goals too. Clearly, state funding has been used for many of these schemes (either directly or indirectly, via other organisations), so the government expects to solve social problems as well as sporting ones. These are sometimes called 'interventions' – a single solution to a variety of issues. They offer what Coalter, in *Rationale for Public Sector Investment in Leisure* (1986), calls 'economies of remedies', delivering:

- control of behaviour
- welfare to meet deprivation needs
- a right to share in leisure for everyone in the community
- sport opportunities for all.

Think it over

Do members of your group feel that the government tries to solve too many problems with a single initiative? Or is the 'economy of remedies' effective? Hold a class discussion.

The input from the private sector to a partnership scheme delivering sport has very different dimensions from those of the government. Consider some of the following.

- The private sector may provide financial support with outright sponsorship, often with marketing or sales targets in mind for its own products.
- The private sector may provide logistical support with funding, allocation of staff or resources for a project, with good publicity in mind.
- The private sector may agree to build a new facility (in partnership with a local authority) and lease it for sports use to the local authority (see page 310).
- Local and regional development agencies may connect potential private sector inputs with the aspirations of local clubs and associations, with a view to developing harmonious sports provision in line with local authority plans.

Theory into practice

Contact your local authority's sport and leisure department and ask for examples of partnership schemes they are or have been involved in. Assess the aims of the project(s) in the light of the government objectives described previously.

Voluntary, governing body or sports association inputs to partnerships can be very diverse – they supply people, expertise and resources for a shared goal in conjunction with other organisations. Some examples are listed below.

- The English Table Tennis Association has in the past formed an alliance with sports goods suppliers, with sports coach UK for coach development, and with Leeds Metropolitan University for scientific support to boost playing abilities.
- Middlesbrough Council's sports development team joined with Tees & District Health Promotion to develop a GP referral scheme, 'Get Active on Prescription'.
- Wheelchair basketball benefited from support by Sport England through lottery funding, the support of local authority sports development officers, and the English Basketball Association to create a long-term scheme to attract youngsters and women to the game.
- A funding package which included inputs from Sport England's lottery fund, the Black Country Development Corporation and Baron Davenport's Charitable Trust enabled Darlaston Community Association to build a multi-use synthetic sports pitch. The community association gained a long lease from Walsall Council, also an important player in the partnership scheme.
- The Humber Sports Partnership consists of a variety of voluntary and professional organisations with two main aims:
  - to raise the quality, quantity and profile of coaches and coaching
  - to provide support and development opportunities for volunteer sports administrators and officials.

The partnership tackles these aims by offering training programmes to support volunteer work and supplying sports education programmes for administrators, plus the VIP volunteer investment programme run by Sport England. The Active Sports officers for the authorities co-ordinate these efforts.

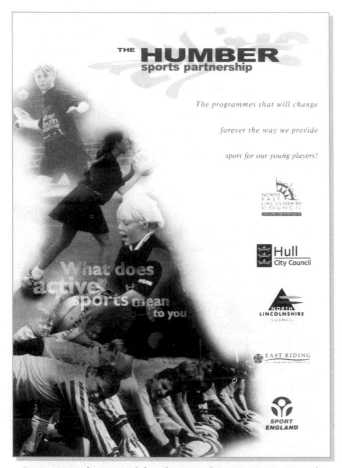

Promotional material for the Humber Sports Partnership

Key concept

Partnerships require a plan which facilitates working together on a shared agenda, with effective co-ordination of a project to ensure that all needs are respected and met.

Methods aimed at excellence

The highest level in the sports development continuum is that of excellence – achievement at the highest level. Processes at this level need to be aimed at those with the motivation and ability (but not always the opportunity) to achieve world-class standards of excellence. Traditionally, performance improvement was left to the governing bodies, to be achieved at a regional level in the main (through county standards), but performance tended to focus on good players becoming better, rather than the best performers becoming excellent. With continued disappointing international performance from the UK's sportspeople, underlying issues had to be tackled and a more effective strategy for 'excellence' was needed for the new century.

Historically, performance and excellence had been bundled together. The sports development continuum showed that a bridging plan was needed, from high performance to excellent performance. To achieve this a number of issues had to be overcome, according to the Sports Council, including:

- conflicts between governing bodies and UK or Great Britain sports bodies such as the Sports Council, CCPR, or British Olympic Association
- poorly implemented structures, co-ordination of activities and duplication of resources.

A number of approaches have been developed, and these are described in the following pages.

Advanced elite coach training

This came to fruition through the establishment of the National Coaching Foundation in 1983, which is now using the brand name sports coach UK and is responsible for education, instruction, and training for professional coaches. This organisation has set up a network of centres in universities to help achieve its aims, networked with other international coaching centres. There is still much to do to professionalise, co-ordinate, structure and finance the work of coaches. Some of sports coach UK's activities are shown in the following chart.

Work closely with governing bodies, and closely evaluate achievements	Develop partnerships with interested organisations	Develop criteria for more selective use of resources towards excellence
Work closely with the Sports Aid Foundation to assist talented athletes	Back up plans with sports medicine and science inputs	Develop policies for the funding and running of centres of excellence

Sports coach UK currently offers a range of programmes for coaches, such as those on offer in Yorkshire in 2003:

- Analysing your Coaching, at Doncaster College
- Coaching and the Law, at Hambleton Leisure Centre
- Coaching Children and Young People, at Pindar Leisure Centre in Scarborough
- Field Based Fitness Testing, at Don Valley Stadium in Sheffield.

Theory into practice

Look at the sports coach UK website to find out what they currently offer in your area. Assess the themes being developed.

Courses run at the national training centres around the UK provide a focus for top coaches, teams and trainers. A snapshot of what Crystal Palace offered in the summer of 2003 shows:

- Heathrow Youth Games in early June
- ASA Club Water Polo Championships in mid-June
- Kent Judo Association Championships in late June
- Active sports camps in July
- World Youth Games basketball and volleyball in August.

Development of 'excellence' facilities

In the late 1990s, Sport England had a triple focus as its strategy:

> More People, More Places, More Medals

This meant that the underlying drive was for more participants, more facilities and better results on the world stage. The previous section discussed 'more participation', an evergreen theme for all sports and organising bodies, but the 'more places' and 'more medals' aims gave the underlying strategy a focus on excellence as well as grass-roots sport.

This initiative was aimed at creating facilities of national or international standard for popular sports, such as cycling, skating, indoor athletics, and bowls, which did not have national centres. The starting point was to assess where there were gaps in provision and where new facilities should be built.

Sport England developed a sports facilities planning model designed to assess locations, needs and the cost effectiveness of proposals to build new facilities. Aligned with this was a drive to have every local authority and sports governing body develop their own facilities planning views, which could be incorporated into a UK-wide approach. By 1999 many had completed that task, along with inputs from organisations looking after natural sports venues such as rivers, lakes and the countryside. The emphasis was placed on quality, so that newly built facilities would be to the highest standards affordable.

Perhaps the best example of this approach coming to fruition was the building work for the 2002 Commonwealth Games in Manchester. A new stadium (to be used by Manchester City Football Club after the games), a swimming complex, and squash and indoor tennis facilities were built.

With any large scheme nowadays, lottery funding is inevitably involved, and in order to qualify for it a 'strategic fit' has to be shown.

Theory into practice

Carry out some research either on the Internet, by reading current magazines or by using the literature provided by Sport England or a sports governing body, to find out about new facilities built in the past six months. Assess the rationale behind the building – did it encompass excellence, community and development criteria?

New facilities also need good management in order to ensure they remain viable and up to standard, and to help achieve this Sport England developed an accreditation scheme to advise and set standards for facility managers. This is called Quest. Quest is discussed in more detail later in this unit (page 315).

Theory into practice

Obtain a copy of the facility manager's guide to achieving the standards that Quest sets out. Evaluate these.

The UK is slowly building a network of top-class facilities designed to help support excellence in players and athletes:

- Ponds Forge Pool, Sheffield
- indoor athletics track, Birmingham
- velodrome, Manchester
- yacht racing, Cowes

- equestrianism, Hickstead
- the new Wembley Stadium, London
- the Millennium Dome, London.

The development of new facilities has not been problem-free. Many local authorities have complex problems to solve, besides finding ways to build sports facilities for their area in partnership with a governing body and possibly a sponsor. The introduction by the government of Compulsory Competitive Tendering followed by Best Value and now Competitive Performance Assessments, combined with an economic downturn, difficult financial markets and falling budgets for a discretionary service, have left local authorities in a weak position. They are often competing with the private sector for the same clients. Lottery funding is being stretched, too, with not enough to go round for bigger schemes. The establishment of the English Institute for Sport, with its regional network, is seen as the best way forward, to take sports provision for the elite athlete on to the next

The Millennium Dome is to become a sports and leisure venue

level in combination with UKSI and the World Class Programme (mentioned on pages 294 and 295).

High performance sport in the future is addressed in the long-awaited government strategy document 'Game Plan', produced by the Department for Culture, Media and Sport and the government strategy unit in 2003. This focuses on the need to rationalise work in order to produce a more coherent approach, with funding rewarding success, less bureaucracy and more emphasis on the participant – devolving development more equitably. Does this sound more like a government agenda than a sports one?

Think it over

How well has the government handled the management of new facilities for 'mega–events', such as the Millennium Dome and the new stadium for Wembley?

Performance plans

The drive to create a strategic fit between facility building and performance development plans helped prompt many governing bodies to devise modern sports development strategies in the late 1990s. Sports such as the following now have mature performance-related plans:

- football
- basketball
- rugby
- swimming
- tennis.

Other are currently under review, such as:

- athletics – for the five years 2003–2007, clarifying roles and responsibilities
- netball – revising its governance, structure and membership
- National Ice Skating Association – nearing completion of a governance and strategic plan review
- Royal Yachting Association – completed in 2002 a review of structure, priorities, and commercial visibility

- British Equestrian Federation – organisational review, decision making and equine passport and database support.

Theory into practice

Obtain a copy of one governing body's performance plan and analyse the key features. Compare it with ones obtained by your classmates. Here are some suggestions for sports to try: gymnastics, triathlon, volleyball, judo, orienteering.

Performance and development plans are also devised for individual performers via the English Institute for Sports. The following people are among those who have been helped:

- Nicola Gautier in bobsleigh and athletics
- Giles Hancock in modern pentathlon
- Kate Howey in judo
- Mick Gault in shooting.

UK Sports Institute

The UKSI (see page 295) works towards developing excellence by helping to provide our top sportspeople with the facilities and support they need. It aims to support:

- winning athletes – it has £25 million to spend in this area
- world-class events – supporting the bidding for large events
- ethically fair and drug-free sports – supporting a national anti–doping campaign.

As well as the national centres at Lillieshall, Bisham Abbey, Crystal Palace and Holme Pierrepont, there are bases in:

- Sheffield – World Student Games venues
- Manchester – Commonwealth Games sites
- Gateshead – track
- Bath – University sites
- Loughborough – University sites
- Southampton – water activities bases.

UNIT 16 SPORTS DEVELOPMENT

Theory into practice

Using your library or the Internet, find out what sports are served at each of the facilities listed above.

In addition to the network of facilities, a central team in London offers:

- an athletes' medical scheme
- research activities and findings
- information on technical developments
- sports science knowledge
- performance planning and guidance
- IT facilities.

Sports medicine

Sports medicine is important for elite performers, and facilities offering training for these athletes need to offer this type of support. The sports medicine programme for the UKSI provides for:

- recovery from injury (rehabilitation)
- injury prevention
- massage and physiotherapy
- dietary and nutritional advice.

The UKSI funds programmes to help sports medicine specialists learn from experts and each other, creates scholarships for talented specialists, provides mentoring for new sports medicine specialists, organises integration days bringing coaches and sports medicine specialists together to prepare athletes for top-class events, and designs tailored packages for athletes and players.

Developing partnerships

This has been an emerging theme for a number of reasons, mainly financial. Central government, the various sports councils and local authorities, even with lottery funding, cannot fund everything we want for our sportspeople. Sports developers have to find additional funding from the private sector for their schemes.

For example, to build and develop facilities, public–private partnerships can be created. In

2003 the Department for Culture, Media and Sport had a budget of £90 million to support such initiatives, and in conjunction with local authorities and private developers several schemes were devised to produce new facilities.

Case study

In 2003 Wandsworth Borough Council in London needed to upgrade many of its centres. After reviewing its options, it decided to create a partnership with a private company. DC Leisure agreed to invest £1.1 million and the council spent £9.2 million on upgrading seven leisure centres. A six-year management plan was agreed with DC Leisure, with improvements the responsibility of the management company and interest repayments the responsibility of the council. Similar schemes are now found on Merseyside with Sefton, and in London with Bexley Borough Council.

1. What safeguards do you think would have to be built into the contracts very carefully and clearly?
2. What are the benefits for the parties involved?

To develop sports or sports events, a similar type of arrangement can often be created, with the private sector providing sponsorship, the local authority the facilities or location, and the not-for-profit sector the volunteers and of course participants.

Theory into practice

Find an example of this combination in your local area and evaluate who provided what. Discuss their motives for doing so.

The World-Class Programme

This is a cornerstone of the strategy to meet elite athletes' needs (see the case study on page 294). Look at the UK Sport website for an update. For top-class players or competitors, a sophisticated service is required covering a range of their needs

310

such as training, coaching, diet, medicine and nutritional support.

Youth academies

Probably the best examples of youth academies are the football academies which have sprung up around the country. They are specialist sports development centres for talented young players. Going through an academy means more than just improving skills; it encompasses personal development, coaching, education and medical care when needed. There are over 5,000 players in 40 football academies. Some football clubs offer centres of excellence, too, which have a 'charter for quality' to ensure they maintain high standards. Students enrolled at these types of facilities enjoy coaching ratios of 1:10, physiotherapy services and extensive match programmes, though this has a 60-match ceiling. Acceptance is by invitation only after trials.

Theory into practice

Identify a centre of excellence (there are 52 in the UK) or football academy and determine what education and personal development students are offered at each age range.

Specialist sports schools and colleges

Achieving specialist status for an educational institution can mean a great deal of effort (perhaps as long as two years), but also a great deal of benefit for sports at that institution. Schools and colleges have to network with key sporting bodies in their area, such as the Youth Sport Trust, Sport England, sports governing bodies and the local authority sports development team, to provide above-average opportunities for children in a sports context. This might mean having a talented athletes programme, using PE to promote social inclusion, building confidence and self-esteem through sports activities, perhaps going out into the community to create more sports opportunities. In a sense the institution becomes a 'hot spot' for sport in the area, and can access further funding to develop.

Theory into practice

Carry out some online research to find three examples of schools and colleges which have achieved this status. Evaluate what they have in common, how they achieved the status and the benefits it brought.

Assessment activity 16.1

Describe a range of key concepts and methods used in sports development, using examples from each level of the sports development continuum.

The role of local authorities in sports development

Sports development can have many underlying motives. The following section will explore a few of these.

Reasons for sports development

The range is quite extensive, but can broadly be described as being based on the individual, on benefits to the community, for educational and health purposes, or around quality issues. We shall consider a selection of these.

Health objectives

These types of objectives are usually set in response to a campaign or an action programme for an area or a set of people who are at risk of ill health. Examples are the objectives set by the British Heart Foundation, a local GP practice or an area health authority. Facilities may offer a range of services for people at different stages:

- taking up exercise for the first time, perhaps in conjunction with a new diet
- continuing healthy exercise
- improving fitness after an operation or illness
- promoting all-round health and exercise.

These programmes can be set out for different age groups or target groups, which would mean specific, relevant objectives can be set. The programmes might run for a limited period (while funding is available) then be reviewed with new objectives being set.

Educational objectives

There are several main areas where educational objectives can be applied to a sports development programme, including the following.

- Where a facility is also a community centre (joint provision), there is likely to be a close liaison to support school activities, with clubs and members drawn from the local community. The main objectives for sports development leaders here are to provide continuity of activities and progression of skills.

- Facilities may provide out-of-school activities for children at holiday time. The main objectives for the sports development team might be to have maximum participation and fun, combined with the learning of a new skill.

- Adult education programmes are often run in leisure facilities. These might range from arts and craft work to fitness sessions. Objectives for sports development workers will be set for

each programme in line with the syllabus, the activity, the target group or any awards that are being taken.

Social objectives

If a leisure facility or sports development team belongs to either a local authority or voluntary organisation and is located in an urban, deprived area it will almost certainly have social objectives. These might be based on a social inclusion programme or targeted at groups who do not normally take part in much sport or who have problems with access, such as low-income groups. Many Action Sport and other sports development programmes have this as an underlying aim. Overall social objectives will be targeted at meeting the needs of individuals such as disaffected teenagers; community groups such as disadvantaged or disabled children; or improving the quality of life for poorer families.

Evaluation of these types of programme objectives might be carried out by assessing:

- numbers of participants
- impact on crime levels
- feedback from parents and organisers.

Local clubs provide out-of-school activities

Case study

A project called Sportslinx was created by the City of Liverpool Leisure Services Directorate, in partnership with other agencies – education, health, and social services. Sports development staff ran the project with the aim of identifying young, talented performers to be offered support by existing programmes. After a pilot which proved successful, a multi-faceted approach was created to deliver coaching, coach education, teacher training, fast-tracking of good performers, and medical support. Sportslinx was accessible to all 9-10-years-olds in the City (about 7,000 children) and had the following objectives:

- to increase children's participation at grass-roots level
- to create a database detailing children's capabilities/potential
- to provide a talent-spotting system
- to supplement national curriculum PE.

Aptitude tests were used to assess children and a questionnaire collected other data on interests, eating and activity levels, which was analysed by John Moores University Sports Scientists. Many local clubs benefited, especially by having new access to potential players and athletes. The project was firmly based in science and brought together many children, agencies, clubs and schools. 130 schools enrolled, over 5,000 children were tested and at least 70 after-school clubs were set up.

1 What elements of the project made it such a success?

2 Are there any comparable efforts at social inclusion in your local area? Research any relevant projects.

Private sector facilities are less likely to be involved in extensive social programmes, but may do so from time to time. By way of supporting their local community, they may sponsor or host an event. Their motives may be more to do with their own image than social aims.

Developmental objectives

The overall focus of these types of objectives is to promote personal or community development. In this context you might find development objectives such as:

- a sports development programme to help boost less popular activities or boost the self-esteem of young people
- a taster day to help raise awareness of a facility's new activities for disaffected youngsters
- an improvement programme to develop assistant coaches into full coaches
- leadership and team development courses run by outdoor adventure facilities aiming to help young people learn better social skills.

Community or quality of life

These types of objectives tend to be specific and tailored. Examples might include:

- a facility serving a small catchment area, with a strategy to focus on one target group at a time
- an adventure centre course adapted specifically for disabled pupils
- an outreach programme for a rural area.

These facilities will focus closely on their users or target groups, so success will be measured by the extent to which needs identified at the outset have been met, such as injuries healed, numbers of disabled people achieving an abseil, or preservation work completed.

Case study

In 1999 Small Heath School, situated in a deprived area in the West Midlands, put together a sports development scheme to provide sports opportunities for children 12 hours a day. A close partnership was formed with the local authority and lottery money was accessed to improve the quality of existing local facilities, such as running tracks and netball courts. Subsequently, Birmingham City Council sports development team helped to set up programmes to encourage use of the refurbished facilities and new all-weather playing surface and cricket nets, from foundation to excellence levels. The scheme was targeted at women and boys in the mainly Asian local community.

1 Find examples of programmes with community objectives in your local area.

2 What are the advantages in having tightly focused objectives for such a programme?

Equal opportunities

These types of programmes are most likely to be written into the constitution of a voluntary organisation or be part of the philosophy of a public sector organisation. For example, a group set up to work with disadvantaged youngsters will have an open access policy to encourage as many of the target group to come along as possible. A leisure centre built in an area with few amenities will want to ensure that everyone from that area can have an equal opportunity to use the facility. As a consequence, programmes aimed at achieving equal opportunities will want to ensure that:

● no one is excluded on the basis of colour, religion, gender or race

● few barriers to participation exist, such as cost, transport or previous experience

● publicity reaches everyone in the target group or area

● the programme can be enjoyed over a period of time (is sustainable)

● the facility is properly staffed and resourced

● participants can progress to a higher level or gain an award.

Evaluation of the effectiveness of these types of programme will need to be done directly against objectives set at the beginning. These might have been set up only as forecasts or expectations initially, but must be translated into measurable objectives, such as reduction in youth crime rates or improved take-up of sport. More indirect evaluation could include levels of satisfaction, and feedback on whether the programme should be run again.

Regeneration strategies

These can often be at the heart of a sports development scheme. For example, when an area of a town is revived through re-building, quite often a sport and leisure function will be included, such as the Don Valley scheme in Sheffield which included a stadium. Sports development teams need to follow up the regeneration work to attract newcomers to the facility, designing exciting programmes to 'kick start' the use of the facility or to introduce a new sport to that part of town.

Best Value and Competitive Performance Assessment

The principles of Best Value (now CPA – Competitive Performance Assessment) are meant to guide all activities that local authorities undertake, including sports development. They should aim to fulfil wider community needs while avoiding duplication or overspending – in other words, they should deliver the best value possible for the taxpayer.

Most organisations will have either a vision statement or a mission statement, giving a summary of their purposes, why a facility is there, and what it is trying to achieve. These statements will vary depending on a number of factors – the size, nature, location and ownership of the facility and whether it is in the public (local authority), private (commercial) or voluntary (not-for-profit) sector. Local authority sports development teams will be governed by the objectives set out for the authority within the Best Value parameters. These may underpin the objectives for certain programmes. The basis of service development for local authorities has been called the four Cs: challenge, consult, compare and compete.

A facility's aims are usually laid out in its publicity literature, and they are used to flesh out the mission statement and show the overall direction for different parts of the facility. Under local authority Best Value criteria, aims could be:

● to provide a high quality service

● to promote a safe and healthy experience

● to respond to local demands.

Theory into practice

Through research and discussion with your classmates, assess the implications of the four Cs (challenge, consult, compare and compete) for local authority sports development officers.

Investors in People

IIP is a national quality standard which sets a level of good practice for an organisation's performance vis à vis its staff.

Investors in People UK was established in 1993 and is responsible for promotion, quality assurance and development of standards. Since 1991 tens of thousands of UK employers, employing millions of people, have become involved with the scheme and know the benefits of being an Investor in People. For sports development participants and workers, this could mean their organisations:

- show a commitment to develop staff
- encourage staff to develop themselves
- recognise staff contributions
- provide equal opportunities
- have a clear plan, known to all
- provide support from senior managers
- evaluate actions.

Quest

Quest is another quality award scheme. Sports centres can gain the award by showing:

- that a facility has achieved continuous improvement
- excellence in quality of sports delivery.

Theory into practice

How could a sports development programme based at a facility contribute towards achieving this award?

Charter marks

Many organisations package their mission statement, aims and objectives into what is called a 'customer charter', which clearly lays out what users can expect from the organisation. An independent body can be invited to inspect facilities to judge whether they deserve a 'charter mark' awarded for a customer-focused approach and good practice.

Local authority sports facilities may well aspire to achieve a charter mark to show that they have high standards. A sports development team and its programmes would come under scrutiny, and could certainly contribute to achieving the criteria for this award:

- set standards and perform well
- actively engage with customers
- be fair and accessible, and promote choice
- continuously develop and improve
- use resources effectively and imaginatively
- contribute to improving opportunities and quality for the community.

Theory into practice

Visit your local sports centre and assess whether they have achieved or are working towards IIP, Quest or charter mark awards. Assess what problems they may be having in achieving an award. If they are not trying for an award – why not?

Key concept

Local authorities are key deliverers of sports development programmes with a range of objectives. This means they must be innovative in the methods they use to achieve standards and targets.

Sports development methods

As there is a range of objectives for sports development programmes run by local authorities, there must also be a range of methods to achieve the goals set. The following section describes some of these.

Supporting local organisations

This is a common theme for sports development.

Some examples of current methods include:

- helping schools develop after-school clubs or a supplement to their normal PE programme, e.g. the 'Freddy Fit' campaign in the Scarborough area

- helping local sports councils (most towns will have one, mainly staffed by volunteers, to give smaller clubs a voice and support network) develop a range of sports in their area, perhaps by supporting youth games, an annual tournament or regular league fixtures

- helping small groups of clubs or larger ones in the voluntary sector strengthen their recruitment by supporting taster sessions.

Enabling

Enabling means helping, but not necessarily funding or staffing; a local authority may supply facilities such as a pitch or hall. Enabling is also sometimes called 'facilitation' and it is a direction that many people feel local authorities will end up taking as budgets get tighter (see page 297). Various methods can be used:

- **Enabling groups** Teams or clubs may be newly formed or hoping to form, but lack the know-how, structure or location – such as a martial arts group needing premises. Typically the local authority would find them a time slot at the local sports centre and perhaps offer the services of a sports development staff member to help them launch their club and set up a structure for running it effectively.

- **Enabling individuals** Talented performers may need a little help with their training. A swimmer, for example, may need access to a training pool, and the sports development team or local authority may help with this by giving access at an off-peak time, e.g. 6 am to 8 am before other customers arrive.

- **Responding to demand** Enthusiasts for a sports may put in a request for time at a sports location, or a local community may request a

Local authorities enable many small clubs to operate

particular sport for its children which is not currently on offer. The local authority's sports development section can enable this by finding time, giving resources or finding a coach or leader to run sessions until a scheme is established and running on its own.

- **Empowerment** Demand may create a club, group or team to play a sport, but after the inputs from the local authority or its sports development team the aim will be to ensure that the club or session is self-supporting, that is 'empowered' to do things for itself. This will perhaps mean having a committee to run the club, with people responsible for funding, arranging fixtures and administration. If a good membership base is created for the club or group, it becomes self-sustaining and in a sense the sports development work has been a success – enabling and empowering the participants to achieve control.

Theory into practice
Why are the concepts of 'enabling' and 'empowering' so important for our grass-roots sports development in this country?

Helping with funding applications

All the funding bodies for sports have an application procedure which sets out conditions and criteria. Not everyone is good at filling in these forms using the right data and costings, and setting out the objectives clearly. This can be a key role for a sports development person who is familiar with the requirements of funding bodies, which can include social objectives as well as sporting ones.

Bids for lottery funding must develop the case for the proposal and meet the priorities set out by Sport England. The following gives you an idea of the objectives projects often have to address. You will see why the broad skills and knowledge of a local authority sports development officer would be very useful in preparing a bid.

- The money must be used to promote the public good (not private gain).

- The bid must take into account the scope for reducing economic and social deprivation.
- Equal access must be guaranteed, especially for the young.
- The project must be sensitive to the needs of the environment.
- The project must be financially viable.
- The bid must show where partnership funding is being sourced.
- The bid must identify the other partners.

Theory into practice
Carry out some online research on another sports funding body (there are at least 15) and compare their criteria to those of lottery bids.

Facility development projects

- **Existing facilities** Sports development teams will often have a rolling programme of activities which move around different facilities, or they may be involved with launching a new sport at a particular facility or attracting a new target group to a facility. These development projects are structured to achieve different objectives, will have different resource levels and should be based on good local research to ensure their success.

  Rather like the product lifecycle in marketing, when a service or product needs a boost, a strategy for intervention is devised to revive its fortunes. These types of sports interventions are usually reviewed on an annual basis.

Theory into practice
Identify a facility-based sports development programme in your area.

- **New build** These are probably the most complex projects for sports development officers. In the main they are lengthy, need to be integrated with many social objectives, and frequently are subject to political interventions and building issues. Few good facilities, if they are to meet quality standards, can be built for much less than £1 million today, and most cost much more. Research may well identify the need for a new facility or a refurbishment, but a long trail has to be pursued until completion. A number of variables will have to be worked out by the team overseeing the project, which will usually include a sports development specialist. Tasks will include those shown below:

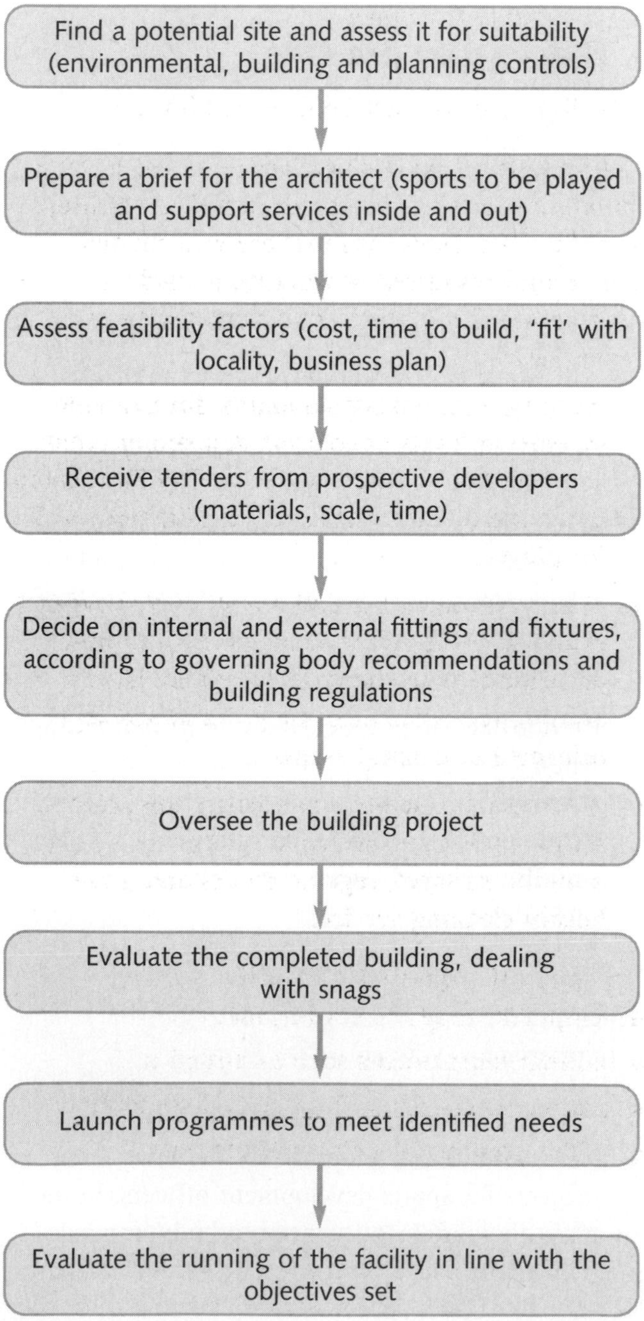

Find a potential site and assess it for suitability (environmental, building and planning controls)

↓

Prepare a brief for the architect (sports to be played and support services inside and out)

↓

Assess feasibility factors (cost, time to build, 'fit' with locality, business plan)

↓

Receive tenders from prospective developers (materials, scale, time)

↓

Decide on internal and external fittings and fixtures, according to governing body recommendations and building regulations

↓

Oversee the building project

↓

Evaluate the completed building, dealing with snags

↓

Launch programmes to meet identified needs

↓

Evaluate the running of the facility in line with the objectives set

Theory into practice

Identify a sports facility which has recently been built in your area, and carry out some research to assess how complex the funding and building process was. If possible, find out the role or inputs of the local sports development team in the process.

Leadership and coach training

The importance of this role has been emphasised in previous sections on the work of sports coach UK and other national bodies. It is vital for both grass-roots coaches and top-flight ones. If we cannot 'grow' our own coaches and leaders then a key part of sports development is not in place.

One aspect which is often forgotten is the need to train officials for sports as well – the much-maligned referees, umpires, score-keepers and administrators who support sport at all levels, often as volunteers, but increasingly as paid professionals. They need to be given the skills to run their sports fairly, with equality and using good management practice.

Theory into practice

Contact three sports governing bodies with which you are familiar and assess the development activities they organise for their officials. Make comparisons to assess who you feel does the best job.

Developing partnerships

As mentioned previously, partnerships are an important way forward for the local authority sector. Establishing and developing contacts is a central pillar of a sports development officer's management skills. Four words beginning with C spring to mind under this role: comprehension, co-operation, co-ordination and communication.

It is very important that staff in any sports development unit understand the different roles and views which potential partners can take. Through effective co-ordination and communication, potential support can be unlocked to release resources for the benefit of the community. The sports development officer is often a catalyst bringing different parties together to co-operate on a scheme, creating an operating structure and keeping everyone in touch with developments.

The key issue is the sharing of objectives to create what might be called a win-win situation for all partners – everyone achieving their objectives in a mutually agreeable way. Types of partners might include:

- schools and colleges
- health authorities
- sports councils/clubs
- welfare agencies
- neighbourhood groups
- charities
- limited companies.

The benefits of a partnership scheme include:

- pooling resources to bring economies
- avoiding duplication of effort
- maximising staffing
- sharing expertise
- applying pressure as a group (lobbying)
- spreading networks wider.

See the case study on the next page.

Think it over

Discuss the following questions in your group.

1 Different groups in a partnership scheme may have very different agendas and some may try to dominate others to achieve their own agenda. Can you identify who the strongest and weakest partners might be? How can sports development schemes ensure a powerful partner does not dominate others in an unhelpful way?

2 Is an element of 'social control' creeping into some sports development schemes, which are supposed to provide sporting freedom? Which institutions might be guilty of this?

Organisational methods

Some general objectives can be identified that all organisations would aspire to incorporate in their development programmes or facility provision:

- provide a safe leisure and recreation experience
- give value for money
- meet customer needs
- deliver the contract on time and budget.

Ability to fulfil these objectives will depend on a number of factors – resources, funding, staffing and skills. Organisations that are well funded, staffed and resourced or working towards a quality award might set higher organisational targets, such as:

- meeting high quality standards, for example increasing levels of comfort at a sports event by giving more space, better quality food, a top hotel and a comfortable air-conditioned coach for players
- giving customer care full attention by covering every detail of customer needs, for example ensuring new members to a club are shown around, receive a welcome gift and are kept informed of coming events
- giving health, safety and security top priority, for example offering swipe card entry, CCTV, non-slip surfaces, regular checks and a two-hourly cleaning service.

Examples of organisationally driven sports development programmes include:

- annual tournaments such as athletics
- team events such as a basketball competition
- taster sessions targeting newcomers.

Case study

In 1999 Hull City Council, after a review of sport and the role it plays in the city, decided to create a sports development plan which would co-ordinate with other plans for the city and produce the first 'joined-up' cultural strategy.

The idea was to blend sport into community planning, using it to combat social problems as well as provide enjoyable participation, over the period 1999 to 2003.

Four major community policy areas were to use sport as a medium:

1   Improving learning and creating a lifelong learning culture in the city: to be achieved by developing coaching opportunities, new social and physical skills, and using sport to access further and higher education.

2   Community safety: to be achieved by providing constructive activities for young people, particularly out of school.

3   Economic development: to be achieved by attracting inward investment to help regeneration and the creation of sports-related jobs in the city.

4   Protecting the vulnerable: focusing on the young, disabled and unemployed and giving them opportunities through sport for personal achievement, increasing self esteem, healthier lifestyles and social inclusion.

Hull sports development section integrated the national strategy of Sport England, 'more people, more medals, more places', in adopting four key criteria:

- focusing on defined objectives
- flexibility in the use of resources
- finding partners with shared objectives
- finishing with a result.

The plan to deliver all of these objectives was developed in the following way. An audit was carried out of sport in Hull, which found that there was a widespread participation base and a solid facility structure. This led to a decision that certain areas needed focus in order to raise them to the standards of others. For example, there was not a great deal of maritime sport, and some areas were quite deprived and needed regeneration.

Social research showed that many city wards would be eligible for lottery priority funding. Car ownership was low, and the city council were not able to allocate significant amounts to the sports development scheme.

Demographic research found that the proportion of young people in the city is higher than average (45% of residents are younger than 29, and 21% are younger than 15). Health statistics revealed that Hull is below the national average in health terms. Access for the disabled and those with special sporting needs was limited.

After further discussions and research, a number of strategic objectives were created, and within each some priorities were set:

- target groups – such as sedentary lifestylers, children, disabled, poorer people
- target sports – aimed at the above groups, based in facilities which were strong
- develop excellence – through partnerships
- build up events – stage national, regional and city-wide events in school breaks
- use education and training – to develop coaches and vocational training, use TOPS schemes
- work with children and young people – use TOPS, create role models, seek out funds
- work with people with special sporting needs – create an advisory group and clubs
- identify and work with geographical priority areas – create local action zones in deprived areas, working with new partners
- ensure equity in sport – focusing on the socially disadvantaged and excellence levels
- focus on people with sedentary lifestyles
- develop better programming and marketing of facilities – to improve income
- improve facility provision – with more general-purpose local facilities citywide
- plan the use and provision of pitches and outdoor sports areas – refurbish and provide new junior pitches.

Overall this was an ambitious programme, with some clear priorities, though less clear financial sources.

The service delivery plan for 2003–2004 shows much of this work continuing, and sport in Hull having a very high profile. Funding for capital and revenue programmes is being sought all the time. Five major priorities make up the agenda:

1 Sports facilities – objectives to build a sports hall within 15 minutes' walk of all city residents have nearly been achieved.

2 School sport – this has been steered by a strategy group from schools and has produced a strong network, giving three institutions special sports status.

3 Neighbourhood renewal – EU funding and bids for other funding have meant that several areas around the city are now the hubs for community programmes.

4 Sports policy – much of the Sport England's early work has been devolved into a local version driven by a Yorkshire Sports Board.

5 Writing a new five-year plan – focusing on continuing issues and pitch provision.

School sport is a target area for development

1 What are the implications of the findings of Hull's social and demographic research?

2 How could you evaluate success in achieving the five priorities?

Promotional events

Promotional events hosted by an organisation may have a slightly different focus – they may have a marketing agenda aiming to raise awareness and interest, in the hope that new customers will wish to take part. Examples include launching a new product or game, promoting new facilities or attracting new participants (see page 301).

A new gym may offer free taster sessions on a set of exercise bikes for a week as a promotion; a golf driving range may offer 'free swing lessons' to new members. Promotional activities sometimes involve a celebrity in order to attract more publicity, such as a famous footballer opening a new children's kick-about area or a well-known athlete taking part in a fun run.

Events or seminars for coaches

These are often hosted by facilities, particularly local authority ones. The idea is to attract coaches from the region to pass on new knowledge or know-how. Examples of themes for these development programmes might be:

● child protection
● prevention of injury
● running a club
● setting up an award scheme
● targeting non-participants
● sports promotion.

Theory into practice

Visit your local sports centre and compare what is advertised there for coaches with the list above – how does it differ?

Recent Sport England schemes have included:

● the Volunteer Investment programme
● Sports Train, aimed at youth workers

- Regional Energisers, to promote regional courses
- Managing Diversity, for Sport England staff
- Equity in Coaching
- Running Sports Workshops.

Targeting

A long-established theme for sports development programmes has often been addressed under the umbrella aim of Sports England, to reach 'more people'.

The issue is equality of access, and strategies to target those who do not have this are often implemented as part of sports development schemes.

Tackling exclusion

Probably the best way to explore this topic in terms of sports development practice is to investigate barriers to participation – to find out what creates inequality and illustrate how sports development programmes can help address some of these issues. Sports professionals in many contexts are tackling exclusion. Issues stem from inequality in:

- social factors such as income, levels of education, gender and ability
- cultural influences such as ethnicity, customs, values and image
- political agendas such as feelings of alienation and inability to influence decisions
- economic factors such as deprivation, low disposable income, and affordability
- physical barriers such as location and means of access
- personal barriers such as lack of self-esteem, poor image, or lack of motivation.

Those working in sports development who aim to target a group need to carry out research to evaluate the barriers that exist and use this to design a programme that will meet the target group's needs.

Sport has been very successful in remedying inequalities and overcoming barriers to participation. Each year in its annual reports Sport England features success stories of this nature. Sports development officers are generally very good at networking with welfare agencies to create partnerships, and they use sport very effectively as a social inclusion tool. The following case studies illustrate this.

Case study

In 2000 a partnership scheme was developed in the Manningham area of Bradford, between West Yorkshire Police, the local authority recreation services, the local community and a youth sport development team. This was an area of high ethnic population and deprivation, which meant that a range of benefits could be achieved, such as meeting the needs of disaffected or excluded youngsters and the wider community by improving access and lifestyles. The ultimate aim was to make the project self-sustaining. Similar schemes can be found in Leeds and Avon.

Sport England ran a 'Positive Futures' programme in the late 1990s, under the Active Communities umbrella, where 25 projects were carried out jointly, targeting young people considered to be at risk. Partners in the scheme were the Youth Justice Board and the Anti-Drugs Co-ordination Unit. Other projects focused on encouraging mothers with young children, disability groups and ethnic minorities to take up sport, three of the longest-standing target groups.

Another success story is the Greenbank project in Liverpool, which focuses on raising standards of and access to physical education for disabled people. A sports hall houses programmes for wheelchair basketball, badminton, weights and therapy rooms. The provision is complemented by accommodation and cycling facilities. It is now owned and run by the disabled people themselves.

1 Undertake some research to identify a sports development programme near you which has successfully reached a target group of previously excluded people.

2 What elements of the programme were the key to its success? How could it have improved on its results?

The over 50s

People who are over 50 are now likely to be far more conscious of health and fitness issues than was the case in the past. The increase in this sector of the population, sometimes called the 'baby boomers' or the 'grey market', has shifted the emphasis of sports development towards meeting their needs too.

The over 50s often have more time to indulge in sports activities, but not always the skills or confidence to get started. Much of the focus of programmes aimed at them has been to get people started, keep them going and provide a social element. Many over 50s may be single people and enjoy exercise, chat and company more than competition.

Most local sports centres will have an ongoing over 50s scheme on a year-round basis. These schemes may also be found in leisure centres, community premises, or an outreach scheme may be based in a village hall.

Theory into practice

Find local examples of over 50s programmes and assess their content and aims.

Many factors may prevent older people from starting these programmes, such as infirmity, lack of transport, insufficient volunteers, unsuitable premises or access. These are the barriers that development workers can focus on overcoming.

Health-related targeting

In 1998 the government made it clear that an improvement in health was a key priority. Leisure and recreation activities and programmes offer an obvious pathway to achieving the aim of a healthier nation. One example of this in action is GP referral schemes.

Under these schemes, GP practices and leisure centres with suitable facilities agree to collaborate in helping people back to health.

Centres can register for the scheme only after they have thoroughly familiarised staff with the scheme guidelines.

A doctor will provide background information on each patient referred, dealing with the member of staff designated to co-ordinate the scheme on behalf of the facility. This member of staff will then work through a number of options on the type of programme suitable for the patient. The process is likely to culminate in a fitness assessment for the patient. At the end of the induction process, clients can sign up for a programme which will suit their health needs.

The member of staff from the leisure centre will monitor the patient's activities, perhaps adjusting the programme as progress is made.

The patient will be referred back to the doctor at the end of the programme for a medical evaluation.

There are a number of benefits in this type of scheme:

- tailored health plans can be devised for individuals
- patients on the scheme may become new members or regular attendees at leisure centres
- fitness is improved
- confidence and a positive attitude to exercise are built up.

Competition and performance-based targeting

These types of development programmes are designed to meet the needs of players who wish to be in a league or tournament. They may be very good players or just enthusiastic amateurs, but they want a structured, regular opportunity to play others. Their motivation might be to test or improve their skills against others. Examples could include:

- a five-a-side indoor football competition during the winter months
- a tennis tournament in the summer

The role of organisations involved in sports development

For the purposes of this section of study we will focus on bodies which function on a national basis as much of sports development work is initiated by them. Some have been discussed already, such as the UK Sports Institute and Sport England. The emphasis here will be on the role they play in current sports development projects.

Organisations

Sport England

Sport England is probably the best-known national organisation, and developing sports is its primary remit. Most schemes are taken up in partnership with other national organisations, and they network to deliver their joint aims. Schemes include:

- Active Schools, Communities, Sports – underpinned by education and training
- Sportsmark and Activemark – benchmarking awards
- TOP play, Sport, and Dance – providing sports kit in conjunction with the Youth and Sport Trust
- coach, teacher and leader education schemes and awards
- helping to create a framework for national governing body development plans
- supporting games, events, matches and projects
- working with government departments, e.g. the Social Exclusion Unit
- creating sports action zones – 12 around the country
- helping to train volunteers, club managers and leaders
- carrying out research to disseminate information to coaches, clubs and other governing bodies
- helping to distribute lottery funding.

Offering a ladder competition is a targeted approach to promoting squash

- a weekly table tennis league
- an under-15 basketball league
- a martial arts competition
- a ten-pin bowling match
- a squash ladder
- a swimming gala
- a triathlon.

Assessment activity 16.2

Evaluate the achievements or success of a local authority sports development unit or department, and provide some recommendations for future efforts.

Sport England also guides the building of new facilities, helping to improve the management and quality of facilities, and supporting and part-funding new centres. It works constantly to increase participation, and sets up elite athlete schemes and world-class training facilities.

Other organisations have their own strategic aims and development plans, which should feed into the bigger picture that Sport England oversees.

Think it over

In the past, British sport has consistently under-performed in the international arena. Discuss with your group why you think this might have been the case.

The National Association for Sports Development

The National Association for Sports Development (NASD) was formed in April 2000. Its aim is to provide support, advocacy and professional development for those involved in the development of sport, and the following objectives have been set:

- to raise the profile of sports development and the people who work in sports development

- to identify and disseminate good practice in sports development at all levels (international, national, regional and local), encouraging recognised professional standards

- to provide a nationally recognised professional development programme that offers quality-assured training opportunities, as part of a qualification framework for those involved in sports development

- to represent the views of those involved in sports development to relevant external agencies

- to provide a sports development information service

- to work closely with regional and local sports development networks and to encourage, and

help in, their creation where appropriate and when invited.

The NASD plans to merge with the Institute for Sport and Recreation Management, which will give both bodies a stronger voice and network to deliver sports development.

National governing bodies

England Basketball is a good example of a national sports governing body carrying out work to develop its sport.

Basketball is one of ten sports involved in the Active Sports programme, designed by Sport England and delivered through 45 sports partnerships. Each partnership involves local authorities, national governing bodies and education services. Active Sports basketball involves boys and girls aged 12–14 who already enjoy the sport in school, and community programmes. Individual school programmes enable a significant number of young people to experience basketball, who for social or economic reasons may not have otherwise had the opportunity. It aims to meet the demand that already exists by taking young people who play the game into a locally based club and competitive environment.

Theory into practice
Select two other sports governing bodies and visit their websites to assess how they are tackling development in their sport.

Sports coach UK

Following a review of coach education programmes, sports coach UK (formerly the National Coaching Foundation) has developed two new themes – 'athlete-centred delivery' and 'lifelong learning'. The workshop sessions focus on helping coaches to:

- identify their long- and short-term goals as a coach

- profile the attributes of a good development coach
- be able to reflect on their own performance
- benchmark their own knowledge, skills and qualities
- identify their own self-development and a mentor
- action plan their development as a coach.

Coaches should of course feed this into the coaching of youngsters and be a model for their activities and achievements.

Football in the community

A whole range of sports development objectives can be found in 'football in the community' schemes. One of the earliest was Crystal Palace Football Club's scheme, set up in 1988 to work closely with Croydon's Recreation Services, providing a valuable link between the club and the local community.

Thousands of youngsters, including children with disabilities, have attended a host of footballing activities organised by Crystal Palace. Strong links have been forged with the club's youth development programme, with the hope that some particularly talented youngsters might be discovered.

An underlying purpose of the scheme is to help the club to become more fully integrated into the town.

In addition to children's sessions, Palace has launched activities for the over 50s, and has welcomed short-mat bowls clubs to Selhurst Park. It has organised school visits; after-school clubs; in-service training for staff; school teams; and

Young footballers need support if they are to progress

coaching tied in with the key stages of the National Curriculum.

The scheme has also organised mini-soccer sessions and business leagues. It wants to share facilities with the community, even among those who might not be regular football followers. Women and people with disabilities are particularly encouraged. The scheme aims to promote participation at all ability levels.

As well as Croydon Council, neighbouring Bromley Council and the Croydon Advertiser Group back the scheme.

Wrexham AFC's football in the community scheme was set up at the Racecourse Ground in 1990. It aimed to develop positive links between the football club and the local community.

Today it provides a service for every social group, regardless of age, sex, or background, and its aim is to involve as many people as possible. It arranges soccer schools, Saturday clubs, birthday treats, ground tours and has the Junior Reds Club for less energetic young supporters.

The scheme is a registered charity and all money generated is put back into the scheme to provide as many activities as possible free of charge.

Youth Sport Trust

Youth Sport Trust has developed a series of schemes called TOP programmes for young people aged 18 months to 18 years. TOP Link was adopted by the Department for Education and Skills as part of the education programme of the Manchester 2002 Commonwealth Games Spirit of Friendship Festival. The programme used the Commonwealth Games as a focus for the development of citizenship in young people, through PE and sport, with secondary students organising and leading mini-Commonwealth Games events for their feeder primary schools.

The TOP community programme now involves over 300 local authorities, facilitating sport with over 13,000 sports bags given away and 39,000 deliverers trained to work with around 380,000 children aged 7–11.

Central Council for Physical Recreation

CCPR is one of the oldest sports organisations in the UK, going back to the 1930s, so it has a long pedigree of achievements in sports development. It is mainly aimed at the playing, running and management of sports.

Some recent examples of success which have benefited sports development at the grass-roots level include the following.

- Pressure applied to the government to end charging of VAT on sports club subscriptions and to make sports funding available from the New Opportunities Fund. CCPR's research found that UK funding for sport was less than in many of our EU neighbours.

- Ensuring an equitable distribution of lottery money to sports.

- Forging better links between sport and educational institutions.

- Giving guidance to the government on issues such as delegated powers of spending for some sports governing bodies, TV rights distributions for sports, retention of playing fields, priorities for facilities across the country, and priorities for the World-Class Programme.

English Federation of Disability Sport

This national body is responsible for developing sport for disabled people in England. It works closely with a number of disability sports organisations, including:

- British Amputees
- British Blind Sport
- British Wheelchair Sport
- Cerebral Palsy Sport.

Its head office is at Manchester Metropolitan University, in Alsager near Crewe. The organisation has a network of nine regions, which support national priorities and develop sports programmes to respond to local needs.

EFDS projects seek to ensure the following before a project goes ahead:

- Empowerment of disabled people is a priority
- Funding partners are in place
- Delivery partners have been identified
- Strategic partners have agreed the project.

A good working structure and strategy is in place to support sports development for disabled athletes.

> ### Theory into practice
> Visit the British Sports Trust website to assess how it contributes to sports development compared to other national organisations.

Summary of roles

As we have seen, a great deal of sports development work is being undertaken in the UK, at local level by volunteers and sports development officers, at regional levels by county-wide initiatives, and at national level by governing bodies and national associations. The diversity of objectives is broad, and the target groups vary greatly from area to area, but some consistent themes can be identified.

- Almost every organisation seeks to increase participation at all levels of the sports development continuum.
- Social inclusion is a key theme, and is frequently tackled on a partnership basis.
- Health issues are always considered, in every scheme that is proposed or run.
- Improving performance and excellence are given high priority, as well as beginners and improvers.

> ### Theory into practice
> Identify and summarise other key themes for sports development schemes or national bodies.

> ### Assessment activity 16.3
> Examine and evaluate the role of at least two organisations involved with sports development. Compare and contrast their schemes and approaches wherever possible.

Assessing the effectiveness of organisations

When large amounts of money, effort and time are invested in a sports development project, this has to be accounted for; it is important to show how effective and efficient the programme has been. A sports development scheme also needs to evaluate its outcomes against the objectives set at the outset. The staff and clients who took part in the sessions will need to assess its value also.

These are not easy tasks, for many aspects of sports participation are intangible. Not everyone knows how to gather evaluation data effectively, then analyse the facts and figures. Clearly criteria need to be set at the beginning, and measures must be taken to gather evaluative material and feedback so that an informed judgement about success can be made.

Criteria for assessment

First, it is important to be clear about the difference between aims and objectives, so that when you are judging criteria for assessment you can have a better understanding.

An **aim** is like a vision for the project, an overview, and it is by nature broad in scope. For example, 'to promote sport in the town' is a very broad aim, and there is no indication as to how this would be done or how it could be measured.

An **objective** is much more concrete and measurable. For example, 'to attract 50 children to a basketball summer camp' is a measurable objective. This type of criterion is more easily used for assessment.

Value for money

This is an easy phrase to say but much more difficult to pin down. The starting point is obviously how much money is spent on the scheme, but to judge how much 'value' you receive from that investment is tougher. For example, the cost of taking part may be an important criterion for participants in a scheme. Organisers might judge how well the scheme met the needs of the participants in terms of their personal development or the improvement in their skills. The facility hosting the event may judge it by how many new members it gained in return for the time and effort put in by staff. The funding body may also evaluate success against costs. A value analysis, therefore, needs to be a broad assessment from many angles.

Aims and objectives

Whether in the public, private or voluntary sector, the aims of a scheme are likely to be:

- to provide a good quality service
- to promote a safe and healthy experience
- to respond to local demands.

However, a private sector gym, for example, will also have business-related aims such as to maximise its profits. A larger chain of gyms might wish to increase its market share or maximise its returns to shareholders.

A large local authority facility with limited financial aims (because it is subsidised) might aim for equitable access, or to serve the local population well.

Voluntary sector facilities such as a large YMCA will aim to support community groups, or disadvantaged groups, at low cost.

The different types of aims will influence the programmes and services offered, how the facility operates, and the use of resources for sports development.

Objectives are usually set out in measurable terms and describe the targets to be met. They will normally be a mixture of organisational, social and educational targets:

- social objectives: reaching target groups
- financial objectives: budgets and costs
- customer-related objectives: access, safety, health
- environmental objectives: using sustainable approaches
- staff-related objectives: training
- resource-usage objectives: best value for resource use

- developmental objectives: responding to trends.

The easiest way to remember how to set and evaluate objectives is to remember to make them SMART:

- Specific (precise)
- Measurable (quantifiable)
- Achievable (with the budget, resources and team you have)
- Relevant (to your overall aims)
- Timed (scheduled and with deadlines).

Examples of SMART objectives in a sports development context might include:

- to attract 20 ethnic minority children to a programme during the summer term
- to deliver a netball taster programme for under £50 this season
- to build a league of six hockey teams by the end of the year.

Achieving targets

There are ways of helping to ensure that targets are met.

- Set some intermediate check points to assess progress (for example a monthly meeting).
- As soon as a problem arises, tackle it, then reassess whether the targets are still SMART.
- Encourage early feedback from others about progress.

Challenge purpose

This is an idea taken from Best Value. You may need to take a critical approach to what is going on already in terms of sports development, and rather than continue with the traditional approach, to challenge it with a new one. Remember, the new approach has to be SMART.

Consultation

Again, this is included in Best Value. Too many schemes in the past have suffered from a lack of consultation with the target group, as professionals decide what is best or most appropriate for them. Clearly if you are to run a sports development scheme you need to consult with the likely participants and others such as coaches, parents, facility managers, sponsors, other experts, and so on. This type of 'triangulation' (gathering information from diverse sources) should give you a better chance of making your targets SMART.

Methods used to consult could be:

- a survey of the local community
- a survey of the likely target group
- a sample of opinion taken from local sports coaches or teachers
- pilot courses to assess the best way to proceed
- reports from other sports development schemes.

Local conditions also need to be assessed – this might include assessing:

- quality of provision
- levels of access
- transport factors, e.g. bus services, pedestrian access or parking
- location
- socio-economic groups and factors
- schemes available to fund the development (EU funding, sponsorship, local authority funds).

It is clear that a great deal of preparatory work has to go into a sports development programme. Much is expected of some schemes and they often come under the closest scrutiny, but if the sports development team have done their homework, the research will go a long way towards ensuring the success of the project.

The key points are to monitor and evaluate all the time. Monitoring can go on at different levels:

- observation of the process – regularly or on an ad hoc basis
- tracking a particular aspect in detail
- double-checking – going back over key aspects
- co-ordinating – being active to ensure everything flows and fits together.

Evaluating needs hard data on performance measured against objectives. Cash flow, use of resources, and the meeting of intermediate key objectives (critical path analysis) should all be considered. Long-term gains need to be part of this equation, and many cross-functional objectives need to be evaluated too, such as social and cultural ones.

Most professional sports development people aim to match effort with outcomes, meet the strategic plan for the area, sport or facility, and ensure equity of access. At the end of the project, successful or not, they should ensure that recommendations are made to help others in future doing similar work.

Theory into practice

A group of unruly 12-14-year-olds have been terrorising a local neighbourhood for months. This fact is well known to the police, the community and staff at the local sports centre. The local authority has offered to fund a scheme for this group for a period of three months.

Work out an aim, a set of objectives, and an outline proposal for a sports development scheme for this scenario, then decide on evaluation criteria. Compare your solution with those of your classmates.

Sports development schemes can turn youngsters away from vandalism and anti-social behaviour

Areas of work

Sports development can focus on different approaches by:

- selecting a specific target group
- working from or for a specific location or facility
- being sports specific or using a specific theme.

Specific target groups

A great deal of research over the years has identified target groups. Traditional examples include:

- young people
- disabled people
- ethnic minorities
- mothers with young children
- over 50s.

These groups are usually underrepresented in participation figures. Many campaigns have been aimed at getting them more involved with sport, such as Sport for All, Commit to Get Fit and the current 'Active' programmes at all levels of the community and in schools.

The modern approach is to consult the target group and the local agencies who could help to create a partnership to resource, fund, and run a successful project. Quite often these agencies are a mix of local, regional and national bodies collaborating together. For example, in Darlaston in the West Midlands, a football-based scheme was needed for a local deprived area. The community association approached the local authority, which provided an area for a pitch and some coaches. Sport England, the Foundation for Sport and the Arts, the Black Country Development Corporation and a local charitable trust all funded the project. The community association organised training courses.

Theory into practice

Identify and investigate a similar scheme for one of the target groups, and summarise your findings. Does it fit the 'partnership' model?

Working for a specific location or facility

In rural areas, sports provision is inevitably not as good as in urban ones. Around the country, councils work hard through their sports development teams to provide a reasonable service. The East and North Ridings of Yorkshire are typical examples – with vast areas of farmland and a few small villages scattered around, provision is costly and difficult. The Action Sports outreach scheme has been successful here in facilitating sessions for local people with a view to making them self-sufficient once skills are embedded. Good use has to made of local halls where sports centres are lacking.

East Riding's coach education courses have included those shown in the following table.

Course	Hours	Venue
Netball level 1/level 2 bridging course	4	Wolfreton Upper School Sports Hall
Baseball level 1	5	Sydney Smith Secondary School, Anlaby
Sports Acrobatics – Assistant Club Coach Award	18	Wolds Gymnastics Club, Driffield
General gymnastics workshop – floor and beam	4	Goole Gymnastic Centre
SRA Assistant Squash Award	12	Haltemprice Leisure Centre
Introducing tennis to key stage 3/4 children – workshop	2	Kingston Park Tennis Centre, Hull
Netball 7 to 11	4	Wolfreton Upper School
ASA teacher's course	80	South Holderness Sports Centre

Transport to venues is always a problem in rural areas, so some sort of car-sharing scheme is a good idea. Mobile resources are needed too, until groups or clubs can buy their own. As with all schemes, social and cultural objectives are relevant, as well as health and fitness ones.

Urban sports development needs an entirely different approach – facilities are already in place and need promoting. New-build projects, especially, have to work hard to develop their clubs, members and activities base. They may not have their own development team, but will certainly do some outreach work with the community. They may also work with the local sports development department to help promote individual sports or facilities within the complex, such as the pool, fitness suite, sports hall, outside courts and aerobic rooms.

Case study

In an interview with Matt Hewison, Community Sports Development Officer for Scarborough, we put a range of questions as follows:

Can you outline the schemes currently being run in your area?

Throughout the year we run several schemes that are linked into as many of the council's corporate objectives as possible (health, reducing crime, etc.). Our main projects are as follows:

- The Community Action Sport project, which provides as many opportunities for the community as possible. This proves difficult sometimes as we have the barrier of limited staff resources, but we provide sport and leisure to over 14,000 people in the Scarborough district each year.

- The North Yorkshire Area Youth Games, run in partnership with North Yorkshire Sport, is usually held in May and involves children from the county, representing their respective authorities. This is a great sports development tool as we can establish developmental squads, and hopefully provide some clear player pathways in sport.

- Community TOPS football aims to give junior clubs the appropriate equipment and resources.

- The Active Sport programme, a national programme in conjunction with the national governing bodies, is currently running basketball, girls' rugby, hockey and cricket, with netball and girls' football coming onstream soon.

Can you describe a range of funding sources you use?

The Sports Development Unit (SDU) is funded directly from the council's budget, but the budget is reduced each year due to cutbacks. We do access other funding for certain schemes, such as Active Sports for activities, Awards for All for publications, directories, and Sport England lottery fund for facility building, that is the Whitby Leisure Centre.

Do you have any partners in the schemes?

Partnerships are important to the SDU, as with our limited amount of resources we have to work with others to achieve anything. In a recent exercise within the leisure side of our department we produced a list of 50 partnerships that we work with. The SDU made up over 50% of these partnerships. They include schools, colleges, North Yorkshire Sport, other local authorities, national governing bodies, sports clubs, the police, etc.

Which groups are targeted?

We try to be as socially inclusive as possible, but we do try and focus our work on target groups, namely women and girls, the 50-plus age group, disabled performers and people on low incomes. It is difficult to tackle the race issue, which does exist here to a certain extent.

What aims and objectives are generally incorporated in the programmes?

Our main aim is to provide a safe and effective environment for the development of sport and to provide for as many sectors of the community as possible.

How do you measure success?

Success is usually measured by meeting performance indicators set by the chief officers. I also look at them in a more simplistic way by saying that if we provide a positive sports development aspect for even one person who enjoys the sport, carries it on and progresses, that is a success for me. Not too much pressure is put on us to meet income targets, as would be the case for a leisure facility.

1 Identify development activities that go on in your local sports or leisure centre.

2 Compare their funding, target groups and aims with those in the case study above.

Urban provision can be much more specific than rural as there is a greater density of population to use it. A more segmented approach may be needed to identify specific target groups such as by age, gender or geographical area. In a rural context, these might be less important factors, so that

sessions might be made up of, for example, eight badminton players of mixed age and ability.

Sports- or theme-specific work

The following case study shows how an organisation tackles sports development for a specific sport.

Case study

In 1999 the FA decided to use Sport England's Active Sports programme to develop grass-roots girls' football. The theme chosen was 'So they can be the best they can be'.

The aim was to create a scheme that would help to recruit and encourage young female players. The Active Sports model was chosen because it is based on current good practice, has a five-year lifespan and is co-ordinated nationally, but delivered locally. The scheme was based on a partnership, involving local authorities, education services and schools. Specific areas were selected around the country where it was felt best access could be achieved to the target group.

Each area selected under the scheme had an area manager and an action group to co-ordinate the work. Supporting them was the FA's Women's Football Director. Once the logistics had been worked out with the delivery team, a lottery application was put together to fund the programme. Specific programmes were devised, which were tailored to local needs, but these were based on a framework which covered all the schemes. This led to four stages being used for the sports development scheme, as follows:

Stage 1 Local schemes are designed to attract youngsters (divided into age groups) with basic skills and knowledge of the game, who want to

progress. To serve their needs new inter-school competitions are run to suit local needs and demands. Running in tandem are eight-week coaching sessions linked to local clubs.

Stage 2 Club development is designed to provide regular coaching, competitions and social programmes, to help progression. Quality standards are set using the Action Sports programme and the FA charter, to ensure safety and equality of opportunity.

Stage 3 Technical practices and small-sided games are used to assess the girls' abilities, and those who wish to take their interest further will be recommended to go to FA coaching centres or centres of excellence.

Stage 4 Squad development is the final stage for those identified as having the ability and talent to go on. Additional coaching, in age groups, over a 20-week period continues at the centres of excellence.

Some of the benefits of the scheme are felt to be:

- more coaching opportunities for girls
- better access to football for girls.

1 In discussion with your classmates, think of at least two other benefits of this scheme.

2 Find the nearest area to you where this scheme has been put in place, and assess its success.

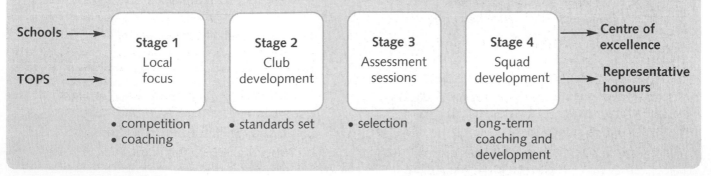

Work of other organisations

Many examples have been given of sports development work done by a range of organisations, such as the FA (a national governing body), Sport England, local authority schemes across the country, and special sports schools and colleges. This final section will look at other examples and also focus on the skills a sports development person needs to work in all these types of organisations. The section will include some profiles of current work being done by sports development people.

Work in all sports development organisations may well be refocused as the government's new strategic plan, 'Game Plan', comes onstream.

Case study

Leisure Opportunities magazine reports:

Leisure Connections is the largest operator of local authority leisure centres in the UK, and in conjunction with the Connexions card initiative (a scheme to encourage 16-19-year-olds to stay in education) have devised a point reward system for young people who get involved with health and fitness. Points can then be exchanged for goods and services, reduced access prices, free swimming, or a gym induction at more than 70 Leisure Connections sites. This is a very unusual approach to sports development aimed at getting levels of enthusiasm for sport and activity up among young people who may not have a very high commitment.

© cybertrek 2003 tel +44 (0)1462 431385 www.leisuremedia.com

1 Do some further research on Leisure Connections and summarise your findings.

2 Do you think this is a sustainable approach to sports development which could be copied elsewhere?

Case study

Dave Boddy, Development Officer for the Lawn Tennis Association in Northumberland in the north east of England, describes his work for a governing body of sport.

'All our development is through Club Vision, where we as a governing body give grants to those clubs that are forward thinking and trying to create as many tennis-playing opportunities as possible. Clubs are the sustainable element to our programme and it's through each one's management model that we can look at facility developments – fast track loans and priority projects. The main brief here is more floodlit, covered and performance courts. Partners for this are various, but usually involve local authorities and Sport England. All the usual groups are targeted, and through our City Tennis initiative we are taking tennis to those non-traditional areas successfully.'

The LTA has in effect set out on a journey which involves development in seven stages, which are:

LTA Vision – to make Britain a great tennis nation

↓

LTA Mission – more players, better players

↓

Strategies for delivery – individual club vision and a performance plan

↓

A focus on clubs, juniors, performance

↓

Key performance indicators – to measure performance en route

↓

Values – professional, progressive, expert, personal, inclusive, dynamic and fun

↓

Equity – following the Racial Equity Charter

All this comes under the slogan 'More Players Better Players', and is measured by key performance indicators (KPIs). The so-called 'headline' KPIs: are

- more affiliated club members
- more regular juniors
- more players in the international top 100.

The KPI vision also sets targets in a number of other contexts:

- more floodlit and indoor courts
- new membership targets
- new coaches
- more competitive players
- schools, juniors and mini tennis schemes and links.

1 What are the challenges that Dave Boddy faces as a sports development professional?

2 Investigate any LTA initiatives in your area.

Skills of sports development professionals

Your assessment for this unit requires you to appraise the work of two organisations for effectiveness and success. Their success may well depend to a large extent on the skills and abilities of the staff delivering the programme. The following section will help you formulate some questions aimed at assessing how they work.

The skills required to manage a sports development programme are diverse, but there is a certain pattern to the use of these skills to ensure effective working practices, and a core set of skills (some managerial, others personal) which always apply. See the chart below.

The overarching skills can be classified as 'change management skills', while the underpinning abilities are likely to be creativity, flexibility and innovation. Necessary skills include:

- research skills – both primary and secondary
- cultural understanding – encompassing urban, rural and ethnic differences
- organisational skills – related to finance, people and resources
- communication skills – verbal and written communication, and also marketing materials
- leadership skills – for projects and their stakeholders
- 'finisher'-type skills, to see the project through and evaluate outcomes.

Change management skills

Personal
- time management
- empathy
- negotiating skills
- team worker
- ability to be reflective
- political awareness
- persistence

Operational
- research
- marketing
- leadership
- administration
- applying value statements and standards

Creativity Flexibility Innovation

'Game Plan'

The government strategy report 'Game Plan' has implications for work in sports development organisations.

Four main areas are covered: 'Grass-Roots Participation', 'High Performance', 'Mega-Events', and 'Delivery'. From these headings you should be able to see it covers at least three areas of the sports development continuum.

Grass-roots participation

It is accepted that we in the UK do not participate as much as many of our European neighbours. Consequently, more sports development work is needed to target:

- older people
- women
- lower socio-economic groups
- disabled people
- ethnic minorities
- the obese and unhealthy.

The target set is 70% of people taking moderate exercise by 2020 – the figure is 30% at present. This will represent a huge cultural shift in our lifestyles and is quite a challenge for sports development. A great deal of work in many organisations will have to be done.

Theory into practice

What are the implications in terms of the following for such proposals?

a) equality issues
b) access
c) sports development approaches
d) capital investment and revenue flows.

High performance sport

The main criticism of UK high performance sport stems from the fact that we have such a fragmented tapestry of provision, and as a result management for high performance needs to be given a greater

focus. We have five sports councils, over 400 governing bodies and 100 sports in the UK system, so inevitably duplication occurs, competition for resources takes place and a lack of shared goals is evident. This makes restructuring likely, to streamline funding flows and modernise the management of governing bodies.

Think it over

This is likely to mean there will be more changes for sports development agencies and staff to contend with. Discuss with your group what you think these changes might be.

Delivery

Overall spending on sport has increased over the past few years from government and lottery funding and sponsorship, but for local authorities it has stayed static. There has always been a problem rolling out a clear national strategy for many aspects of sport, because the relationships between sports organisations in the UK are more like a spider's web than a clear structure. The report asserts that there are too few well-trained sports development officers, administrators, managers and volunteers. It is also critical of some local education authorities for not applying rigorous quality systems, performance indicators and benchmarking, and not doing more for working relationships between schools and communities.

Theory into practice

What are the problems in trying convince hard-pressed sports development professionals to re-structure and become more accountable?

Commentary by some executives of sports governing bodies (such as the Youth Sport Trust and the LTA) indicate that the plan is welcomed for its potential to streamline bureaucracy, provide more funding and give more cohesiveness. More sceptical academics see it as a useful vehicle for open debate, but criticise it as too economically driven and for setting participation targets that are desirable but may be unachievable, because of the massive change in attitudes that would need to accompany them.

The government's strategy must be moulded by opinion and the expertise of sports development professionals in order to convince the population, media and decision-makers to work towards its objectives.

Think it over

Download the 'Game Plan' report from www.strategy.gov.uk and discuss with your tutor and classmates the other implications that might be drawn for sports development workers and organisations.

Assessment activity 16.4

Compare and contrast the effectiveness of two sports development organisations and analyse how effective they have been in delivering recent programmes, and planning and devising future schemes.

Check your knowledge

1   List the four stages of the sports development continuum and describe key concepts that are used to deliver sports development within each of them. Provide examples to support your description.

2   A number of 'target groups' have been traditionally identified as needing sports development schemes to encourage them to participate. Identify four of these groups and give examples of schemes which have been run to meet their needs.

3   Discuss a range of barriers which commonly prevent participation, and show how sports development schemes can help to overcome these.

4   Describe the methods used to focus on introductory and recreational sports development.

5   Describe the methods used to develop excellence in sport.

6   Local authority organisations have long been the main providers of sports development schemes. Discuss the motives and agendas that have been at the core of their programmes, besides those to develop sport.

7   Evaluate the methods which have been employed by local authorities in sport to try to achieve their aims and objectives, in both a sports and a social context.

8   Many other organisations have been active in sports development since the early 1990s. Identify two at national level and describe their sports development schemes and targets.

9   How do the agendas and roles of these types of bodies differ from those of a local authority?

10 How can sports development organisers evaluate the success of their schemes?

Assessment guidance

This unit is internally assessed and you are required to produce evidence which demonstrates coverage of four main areas:

- key concepts used in sports development
- the work of sports development staff in local authorities
- the role of a range of sports organisations in sports development
- methods of assessing the effectiveness of sports development schemes and bodies.

When you are setting out to tackle the assignments for this unit it is important to understand that each grade – pass, merit and distinction – has certain requirements. You can use the following checklist and notes to set your targets and to help you achieve the best grade you can.

Pass

To gain a pass you must show in general, and perhaps with some tutor support, a basic understanding, thorough research and some application of knowledge in sports development contexts. More specifically your responses must show that you are able to:

✔ identify key concepts that are used in sports development, providing relevant examples

✔ explain the function of local authority sports development units, including their methods and achievements in increasing sports activities and participation for a range of different target groups

✔ describe the role of two organisations involved with sports development schemes

✔ produce criteria to measure the effectiveness of two contrasting sports development organisations, with teacher support

✔ use the criteria and describe the effectiveness and success of two contrasting sports organisations.

Merit

To gain a merit you must work more independently and show a good understanding, presenting your research in a clear and logical manner. Key concepts will be integrated, such as the work of organisations. Depth and breadth of knowledge will be shown, with good evaluation, assessment and comparison made in a range of areas. More specifically your responses must show that you are able to:

✔ describe the effectiveness and achievements of local authority sports development units in increasing sports activities and compare the success and participation of different target groups

✔ compare organisations involved with sports development schemes, commenting on their different roles

✔ independently produce criteria to measure the effectiveness of two contrasting sports development organisations

✔ use the criteria and compare the effectiveness and success of two contrasting sports development organisations.

Distinction

To gain a distinction you must work totally independently, showing excellent understanding and fluent use of terminology. Key concepts will be applied effectively, and critical analysis will be apparent, for example in local authority or other evaluations. Recommendations on improvements or other ideas will be given with supporting rationales and analysis. More specifically your responses must show that you are able to:

✔ critically analyse the achievements and effectiveness of local authority sports development units, providing recommendations and a rationale for future activities

✔ critically evaluate the impact of organisations involved with sports development schemes, drawing valid conclusions and further recommendations for future and further activities

✔ critically analyse the criteria used to measure the effectiveness of two contrasting sports development organisations, providing recommendations for changes as appropriate

✔ critically analyse the effectiveness of two sports development organisations, highlighting successes and achievements with proposals for future activities.

The overall quality of evidence will consistently be high and a range of assessment formats will be used, such as projects, reports, essays, log books and presentations.

Resources

Texts

Collins, M: *Sports Development Locally and Regionally*, 1995, ILAM report

Collins & Kay: *Sport and Social Exclusion*, 2003, Routledge

Eady, J: *Practical Sports Development*, 1993, Pitman

Gooding, A: *101 Ways to Succeed at Sports Development*, 1999, ILAM

Gratton & Henry, eds: *Sport in the City*, 2001, Routledge

Houlihan, B: *The Politics of Sports Development*, 2002, Routledge

Hylsen, K: *Sports Development: Policy, Process and Practice*, 2001, Routledge

Lawn Tennis Association, *City Tennis*, 2003, LTA

Sport England Annual Reports 1998/99, 1999/2000, 2000/1

Journals

Leisure Management

Sports Management

Websites

Sport England (www.sportengland.org)

Central Council for Physical Recreation (www.ccpr.org.uk)

British Sports Trust (www.bst.org.uk)

The Football Association (www.thefa.com)

English Federation of Disability Sport (www.efds.net)

Women's Sports Foundation (www.womenssportsfoundation.org)

Index

Page numbers in italics refer to illustrations or diagrams.

as managers 184-5
and organisational skills 197-8
and professional conduct 191-2
as role models 186
and sport-specific skills 198-9
as trainers 184
coaching
aims of 219
delivery phase of 221-2
errors 223
evaluation phase of 222-3
health and safety in 190-1, 220
lesson plans 220-1
planning phase of 219-21
process 218-19, *219*
as a profession 234
professional conduct in 191-2
progression 207-8
resources 220
responsibilities 189-90
session construction 189-90
skills 204-6, *204*, 208-9, *210*, 211, *211*
communication skills 196-7
competition
nutrition 47-8, 50-1
targeting 323-4
Competitive Performance Assessment (CPA) 314
confidentiality, in fitness testing 111, 113
consent, in fitness testing 112
cool-down programmes 162
Cooper 12-minute run 115-16
copper 19
coronary heart disease (CHD) 9, 10, 39, *39*, 40
cricket, fitness for 92-3

dance, fitness for 90
dehydration 24, 45-6, 60
demographic segmentation 247
diabetes 38-9
diet
assessment of 30-4
balanced 3
for children 28, 59-60
and coronary heart disease 9, 10, 40
and diabetes 38
healthy 27-9
intakes 26-7
and National Food Guide 28-9
over 50s 60
vegans 61-2, *61*
vegetarians 61-2, *61*
dietary reference values 26

dietary thermogenesis 25
dieting 27
dangers of 55-7, 174
and exercise 57-8
safe 57-8
dietitians 41-2
disabled people 291, 296-7, 327-8
disaccharides 4, *5*
discrimination
legislation 266-7
in participation 313-14
disease prevention, and exercise 79
drugs in sport 193
dynamometers
back 118-19, *118*
grip 118-19, *118*
isokinetic 119-20, *119*
dyspnea 104

ectomorphs 52-3, *53*
elite athletes
coaching of 306-7
facilities for 307-9
funding for 137
peaking of 161, *161*
promotion of 293-5
sports medicine for 310
employees 260-1, 265
employers, duties of 264-5
employment contracts 265-6
employment legislation 265-7
employment tribunals 267
endomorphs 52-3, *53*
endurance
aerobic 73-4, 143-4, 175-6
muscular 72-3, 146-7, 176
endurance athletes 44-6
energy 42-3
balance 24-6
from carbohydrates 4, 36, 43
from fats 10, 36, 43
from proteins 11, 36, 43
English Federation of Disability Sport (EFDS) 291, 327-8
estimated average requirements (EAR) 26
ethnic groups 291
evaluation 280, 281, 330
excellence, promotion of 293-5
exercise
see also training
benefits of 174-5, 176
and cholesterol 105

S 999 SLT A

Are you taking the Sports Massage option as part of your BTEC National Sport award?

Sports Massage

◆ Provides all the knowledge needed to pass the VTCT Certificate in Sports Massage.

◆ Contains specially-commissioned photos to illustrate massage techniques and excellent coverage of anatomy and physiology.

◆ Clear layout, full colour and accessible language ensure that **Sports Massage** makes your learning easier.

Why not have a look at Sports Massage on 60 days' free inspection?

Sports Massage   0 435 45652 0

Simply contact our Customer Services Department for more details:

(t) 01865 888068   (f) 01865 314029   (e) orders@heinemann.co.uk   (w) www.heinemann.co.uk

Heinemann

Inspiring generations

G981